palgrave macmillan law masters

criminal law

palgrave macmillan law masters

Series editor: Marise Cremona

Business Law   Stephen Judge
Company Law   Janet Dine and Marios Koutsias
Constitutional and Administrative Law   John Alder
Contract Law   Ewan McKendrick
Criminal Law   Jonathan Herring
Economic and Social Law of the European Union   Jo Shaw, Jo Hunt and Chloe Wallace
Employment Law   Deborah J. Lockton
Evidence   Raymond Emson
Family Law   Kate Standley
Intellectual Property Law   Tina Hart, Linda Fazzani and Simon Clark
Land Law   Joe Cursley and Mark Davys
Landlord and Tenant Law   Margaret Wilkie, Peter Luxton, Jill Morgan and Godfrey Cole
Legal Method   Ian McLeod
Legal Theory   Ian McLeod
Medical Law   Jo Samanta and Ash Samanta
Sports Law   Mark James
Torts   Alastair Mullis and Ken Oliphant
Trusts Law   Charlie Webb and Tim Akkouh

If you would like to comment on this book, or on the series generally, please write to lawfeedback@palgrave.com.

palgrave macmillan law masters

criminal law

jonathan herring

Fellow in Law, Exeter College, Oxford

Seventh edition

This edition first published 2011 by PALGRAVE MACMILLAN

Palgrave Macmillan in the UK is an imprint of Macmillan Publishers Limited, registered in England, company number 785998, of Houndmills, Basingstoke, Hampshire RG21 6XS.

Palgrave Macmillan in the US is a division of St Martin's Press LLC, 175 Fifth Avenue, New York, NY 10010.

Palgrave Macmillan is the global academic imprint of the above companies and has companies and representatives throughout the world.

Palgrave® and Macmillan® are registered trademarks in the United States, the United Kingdom, Europe and other countries.

ISBN-13: 978–0–230–28572–9   paperback

This book is printed on paper suitable for recycling and made from fully managed and sustained forest sources. Logging, pulping and manufacturing processes are expected to conform to the environmental regulations of the country of origin.

A catalogue record for this book is available from the British Library.

10 9 8 7 6 5 4 3 2 1
20 19 18 17 16 15 14 13 12 11

Printed and bound in the UK by Thomson Litho, East Kilbride.

Contents

Preface

This book is intended as an introduction to the basic principles of criminal liability and some of the most important criminal offences. The offences have been chosen (from amongst the vast range of criminal offences) to illustrate clearly the principles underlying the criminal law; they also feature in most courses on substantive criminal law. There is a fundamental need for the law (and especially the criminal law) to be clear, and its content easily understood by the lay person, but first-time students of the subject often find its key concepts difficult to grasp and the major textbooks somewhat formidable. This book provides a comprehensible account of major areas of the law and an introduction to the controversy and debate that are inseparable from any serious study of the law.

This textbook was commissioned by the late Lady Oliver who was a firm believer in the need for accessible student texts as an adjunct to large-scale scholarly and reference works. Its first author was Marise Cremona who is now Series Editor for the whole of the Palgrave Macmillan Law Masters series. I took on the authorship for the third edition and have endeavoured to continue with the accessible style and the reader-friendly features from the early editions. These include a Case Notes section at the end of each chapter which gives, in respect of the key cases mentioned in the text, a short account of the facts and decision. Cases that are noted in this way are marked with an asterisk (*) when they are first mentioned in the text. There are additionally Further Reading lists to offer a starting point for deeper exploration of the subject, Hot Topics which highlight high-profile and controversial topics of recent years, and Key Terms which introduce the key Terms and definitions about to be explored in each chapter.

The seventh edition of this book has required some extensive updating to take account of a number of developments, in particular changes introduced by the Coroners and Justice Act 2009 and developments in the law on accessorial liability. I am grateful for the support of the team at Palgrave, especially Rob Gibson.

I am grateful for the support and help of many colleagues and friends during the writing of this book including Alan Bogg, Shazia Choudhry, Sandy Fredman and Charles Foster. Laurel, Joanna and Darcy have been a consistent source of amusement and help. My wife, Kirsten Johnson, has, as ever, been wonderful.

Jonathan Herring
Oxford, 2010

Table of cases

As in the previous editions, cases marked with an asterisk* when they are first mentioned in the chapter are discussed in greater detail in the Case Notes at the end of the relevant chapter.

A page number in bold type indicates a Case Note giving a short account of the facts and decision in respect of the case concerned.

Table of legislation

List of Latin terms

Actus non facit reum, nisi mens si rea:	An act does not make a person guilty of a crime unless the mind is also guilty.
Actus reus:	The part of the definition of a criminal offence which does not relate to the defendant's state of mind.
Bona fide:	Good faith.
Causa sine qua non:	An event without which a result would not have occurred.
De minimis:	Minimal.
Doli incapax:	Being unaware of the difference between right and wrong and so not being liable to a criminal conviction.
Intercourse per anum:	Anal intercourse.
Intercourse per vaginam:	Vaginal intercourse.
Mala in se:	A 'true' crime (in contrast to a regulatory offence).
Mala prohibita:	A regulatory offence (in contrast to a 'true' crime).
Mens rea:	The part of the definition of a criminal offence which relates to the defendant's state of mind.
Nolens volens:	Not caring.
Novus actus interveniens:	An act which breaks the chain of causation.
Obiter dictum:	A comment made by a judge in a case which is not binding on other courts.
Per se:	In and of itself.
Prima facie:	At first glance.
Regina:	The Queen.
Rex:	The King.

Part I

Basic principles of criminal liability

Chapter 1

Introduction to criminal law

Key Terms

- ▶ **Culpability** – the blameworthiness of the defendant.
- ▶ **Harm** – the wrong done to the victim of a crime.
- ▶ **Objectivism** – a view which states the defendant should be judged by his or her conduct.
- ▶ **Subjectivism** – a view that the defendant should be judged on the basis of his or her beliefs, intents and knowledge.

1.1 The scope of this book

It is very likely that you have committed a criminal offence at some time in your life. Probably quite a few of them! So it is worth reading this book carefully.

This book is about the basic principles of criminal liability. These principles are the tools for understanding and applying the criminal law, and so can be used when you are faced by an unfamiliar or new offence. However, the common law, which is the foundation of criminal law, does not develop principles in the abstract, but in the context of concrete cases and specific crimes. Central offences against persons and property provide the basis upon which the judges have built the criminal law, and all students of criminal law need to understand them. Murder, for example, although a comparatively rare crime, has played this role because it is one of the most serious offences and so provides a testing ground for fundamental notions of culpability. The offences which are discussed in this book are chosen as examples of offences against persons and property. They either have (like murder) performed a key role in developing important legal principles, or (like theft) are common offences arising every day in the courts.

Although criminal law used to be thought a straightforward subject, it can be extremely complex and is often controversial. The aim of this book is to ensure that the basic principles are centrally presented, so that the wood does not disappear among the trees. Some of the underlying theoretical themes and conflicts are also introduced, as these are an inescapable part of current criminal law, which is undoubtedly alive and provocative. Tension between competing principles is inherent in the law; for example, in criminal law the interests of the accused can compete with the interests of the victim (see Chapter 8).

1.2 What is criminal law?

This is a question which is surprisingly difficult to answer. Most people would imagine the criminal law to be about murders, assaults and thefts, which, of course, it is; but the scope of criminal law is wider than this. It also includes pollution offences, crimes against public morals and traffic offences. It is the values and culture of a particular society which determine what conduct is regarded as being criminal. It should be noted that conduct which is contrary to criminal law at one point in time may not be seen as criminal at another time or in another country. For example, before 1967 sexual acts between two men were contrary to the criminal law, but following the Sexual Offences Act 1967 the legal prohibition on private sexual acts between two men over 21 was removed (the age limit was subsequently reduced to 18, and in 2001 it was reduced to 16). This was in part a result of a change in the general public's attitudes towards same-sex relationships. However, there are some crimes, such as murder, which have always been crimes and always will be. But even in the case of murder there are disagreements over whether euthanasia, abortion or capital punishment should be lawful.

But how can criminal law be distinguished from other parts of the law? Probably the best answer was given by Professor Glanville Williams, one of the great criminal law scholars, who argued that criminal law is best defined by the procedures it uses (see Chapter 2). He suggested that a crime is 'an act that is capable of being followed by criminal proceedings having one of the types of outcome (punishment etc.) known to follow these proceedings'. Although this may be the best definition, it is not especially useful, as it tends to be a circular one – What is criminal law? It is that part of the law which uses criminal procedures. What are criminal procedures? Those which apply to criminal law.

1.3 The role of criminal law

The criminal law plays a distinctive role in society, including the following functions: to deter people from doing acts that harm others or society; to set out the conditions under which people who have performed such acts will be punished; and to provide some guidance on the kinds of behaviour which are seen by society as acceptable. Of course, it is not only the criminal law which has a role in these areas. For example, deterrence from crime may occur as a result of pressure from families, friends and communities. But the criminal law is different from these other influences. It is the established state response to crime. This is reflected in the fact that prosecutions under the criminal law are brought on behalf of the state in the name of the Crown (see Section 2.1). Further, the breaking of the criminal law is seen as different from the breaking of other kinds of law, in that a breach of the criminal law involves a degree of official moral censure. To be ordered by a court to pay damages following a breach of contract (which is not a criminal offence) does not carry with it the same kind of moral message or stigma that it would if you had been found guilty of a criminal act and then ordered to pay a fine. As Professor Ashworth has written, 'criminal liability is the strongest formal condemnation that society can inflict'.

1.4 What conduct is criminal?

There are two aspects to the definition of most serious crimes. The first, and more important, is that the defendant has done an act which has caused a prohibited kind of harm. The second is that the defendant is culpable, worthy of censure, for having caused that harm. We will now consider these aspects separately.

1.4.1 Causing harm

The criminal law is not only concerned with the causing of direct harm to other people: it also outlaws harm to the state, public morals and the environment, for example. The criminal law goes further and punishes conduct which may not cause harm on a given occasion but endangers others (for example, dangerous driving), attempted crimes and acts which help other people commit crimes. There are also a few criminal laws which are designed mainly to protect people from their own folly. An obvious example is the law requiring the wearing of seat belts in cars.

It is often argued that the criminal law should seek to punish only conduct which causes harm to others. Such an argument is in line with the well-known 'harm principle' articulated by J. S. Mill, who stated: 'the only purpose for which power can be rightfully exercised over any member of a civilized community, against his will, is to prevent harm to others'. Some conduct may be immoral, but if it does not harm others or harms only the actor it is seen as unsuitable for punishment under the criminal law. The prohibition of non-harmful conduct is seen as too great an infringement on individuals' liberty. Although this principle has been widely accepted, there has been much dispute over what the term 'harm' means. For example, does it cover feelings of outrage some may feel at the conduct of their fellow citizens or damage to 'the moral fabric of society'?

The 'harm principle' has received support not just from academics, but also from the judiciary. For example, Lord Hobhouse in the House of Lords case of *Hinks** [2000] 3 WLR 1590 stated:

> An essential function of the criminal law is to define the boundary between what conduct is criminal and what merely immoral. Both are the subject of the disapprobation of ordinary right-thinking citizens and the distinction is liable to be arbitrary or at least strongly influenced by considerations subjective to the individual members of the tribunal. To treat otherwise lawful conduct as criminal merely because it is open to such disapprobation would be contrary to principle and open to the objection that it fails to achieve the objective and transparent certainty required of the criminal law by the principles basic to human rights.

It may be necessary to calculate the severity of the harm an act has caused. This can be important for two reasons. It is used, first, to determine whether certain conduct is sufficiently harmful for it to be criminalised and, second, to decide the hierarchy of offences. Generally the more harmful the conduct, the more serious the crime, and the higher the sentence is expected to be. But how to grade harm is controversial and difficult. From one perspective it is an impossible task as the victim's circumstances and perceptions vary from crime to crime. For example, some victims seem able to shrug off a burglary with little difficulty, while others find it a deeply traumatic and invasive experience. One could try to ignore the effect on a particular victim and instead look at the effect on an average victim, but then victims may feel that they are being pigeonholed and their individual responses are not being taken seriously. The harm to society caused by any particular act is similarly difficult to gauge.

1.4.2 Culpability

Criminal law should be distinguished from civil law, which includes breaches of contract or claims for damages for negligent conduct. Civil law is concerned more with who should compensate the victim for a loss than with determining blame. Given that the defendant has damaged the victim's property, the question in civil law is 'who should pay for that damage?' If the victim is wholly innocent and the defendant even only a little to blame, then the defendant should shoulder the liability. However, in criminal law, as explained above, the censuring function plays a crucial role. Defendants should be found guilty of a crime only when they truly deserve the stigma of a criminal conviction, and so normally a higher level of blame needs to be shown in criminal law than in civil law, at least for serious offences. For less serious offences it is common for there to be a requirement of only a low level of culpability, partly because there is a correspondingly low level of censure attached to such crimes (see, for example, Chapter 6). Despite these points some commentators have pointed out that the line between civil law and criminal law is being increasingly blurred. For example, anti-social behaviour orders are civil under the Crime and Disorder Act 1998, but breach of them amounts to a criminal offence (see *Clingham v RB Kensington and Chelsea* [2002] UKHL 39).

In deciding whether a defendant is to be blamed for her conduct, the criminal law generally presumes that a defendant is responsible for both her actions and the consequences of her actions. The criminal law does not accept that a person's conduct is simply a result of her environment and/or socio-economic background. Cases would become far too complex if each time it had carefully to be determined to what extent the defendant was responsible for her personality and the causing of the harm. Instead the law assumes that every person is a free autonomous agent who is responsible for what she does. Although generally the defendant's deprived background itself does not provide the defendant with a defence to a crime, the law does not ignore it entirely. For example, a defendant's social and financial circumstances may be taken into account at the sentencing stage of the criminal process.

There are four main ways that the law has of recognising that a defendant may not be to blame, or not fully to blame, for the harmful results of her actions, and so is not guilty of an offence:

1. *Exemption from liability.* The law accepts that there are some people who are properly exempt from criminal prosecution, that is those who have not had the opportunity to develop fully moral characters and so are insufficiently responsible for their actions to justify the censure attached to a criminal conviction. Children below the age of criminal responsibility and persons classified as insane by the law are good examples. Such people may be subject to forms of restraint under the civil law if they harm others, for example detention in a hospital under the Mental Health Act 1983.

2. *Lack of capacity.* The law may accept that the defendant (although not insane) was at the relevant time not responsible for her 'actions'. For example, if the defendant was pushed over and fell into a window breaking it, then the 'act' of falling into the window is not properly seen as the defendant's act. She was not acting in a 'human' way, as the result of conduct that was (or could have been) planned and thought about, but fell in the same way that a chair would have done had it been knocked over. It may well be, however, that the person who pushed the defendant would be criminally responsible for the broken window (see Section 17.2). Another example of this may be where the act was that of the defendant but was done under such circumstances that he was unable to exercise control over his actions, as when acting under hypnosis, for example. Here again it was not an act which he could have controlled. If the defendant could have controlled his actions but it was difficult for him to do so then this is not properly described as 'lack of capacity', but the defendant may be able to rely on a special defence (see point (4) below).

3. *Lack of required mental state.* Here the defendant was capable of exercising rational thought and considering her actions but lacked the necessary intention or foresight

required for the particular offence. Often in such a case the defendant will still be guilty of a less serious crime. For example, as we will see later, in order to convict a defendant of murder it is necessary to show that she intended to kill or cause grievous bodily harm. If she lacks that intention, she may still be guilty of manslaughter.

4. *Special defence.* Although the defendant had the required mental state, she may claim that nevertheless she is not to be blamed because she had a particular defence. These defences arise when the circumstances of the offence lessen or remove any blame that the defendant would otherwise face. For example, she was acting in self-defence, or had been threatened with death or serious injury if she did not commit the crime.

Although we have discussed harm and culpability separately, they are in fact closely linked. A victim is likely to feel only slightly aggrieved if someone accidentally knocks into him causing him to fall over, but much more aggrieved if someone deliberately pushes him over. In other words, intentionally inflicted injury is seen by victims as a different kind of harm from accidentally caused injury. Similarly the degree of culpability is perceived by most people, however illogically, to be different according to whether the harm caused is great or not. A person who drives dangerously and kills a pedestrian is seen as more blameworthy than someone who drives in an equally dangerous manner but injures no one.

1.4.3 Theories of culpability

As you can imagine, there are many different theories on how to assess culpability, and some of them have been developed to a high degree of sophistication. They have been expressed in many different ways and can be discussed here only in very bare outline. It is not possible to say that one of them is the 'right' theory or that the law clearly follows only one of these approaches. Each has been influential in the law's developments and in the writings on criminal law. Indeed many commentators take the view that trying to find a single theory of culpability which will underpin criminal law is a futile task. The three most popular theories will now be briefly discussed.

1. *The choice theory.* The argument here is that the defendant should be responsible only for the consequences of his actions which he has chosen to bring about, be that by deliberately acting in order to bring the consequence about or acting while aware that he may bring that consequence about. In *Lynch* Lord Simon stated, 'the general basis of criminal responsibility is the power of choice included in the freedom of the human will'. The theory accepts that a defendant is not liable where he chose to act but that choice was not one for which he should be morally responsible. Where the defendant acts under duress (for example, where a person is kidnapped and told he must commit a crime or he will be killed) his choice was not one for which he should be responsible.

   The choice theory has been highly influential in the development of the criminal law, but there are two particular problems with it. The first is that there are some offences which do not require proof that the defendant intended, foresaw or knew anything (for example, negligence and strict liability offences: see Chapter 6). These offences play an important part in our criminal law, but cannot be explained by the choice theory. A variant of the choice theory can deal with negligence-based offences by asking whether the defendant had a 'fair opportunity' to choose to act otherwise. Thus H. Hart has suggested, 'a moral licence to punish is needed by society and unless a man has the capacity and fair opportunity or chance to adjust his behaviour to the law, its penalties ought not to be applied to him'. This variant asks not whether the defendant did choose to bring about the consequence, but whether he could have avoided causing the harm. A second objection to the choice theory is that in making a moral judgement on the defendant's actions, choice is arguably only one criterion to consider; the defendant's attitudes and motives may also be thought to be relevant. These are excluded by this theory, which focuses on choice alone.

2. *The character theory*. This approach suggests that if the defendant's actions indicate a character trait which is unacceptable according to the standards expected by the criminal law, then the defendant deserves punishment, whereas if the defendant's actions do not reveal bad character then there is no point in punishing him. This argument needs to be treated with care. The criminal law is not interested in discovering whether the defendant is generally 'a bad person' and so will only consider inferences of bad character from conduct prohibited by the criminal law. So the criminal law can infer bad character from the fact that the defendant assaulted someone, but not from evidence that he is a gossip. Assaulting is prohibited by the criminal law; gossiping is not. The strength of the theory is its ability to explain the defences that the criminal law provides. For example, the defence of duress can be explained because if the defendant commits a theft after he has been threatened with death, the theft does not lead us to conclude that he has a bad character. One difficulty with the theory is in explaining why, when considering the defendant's bad character, consideration is limited to criminal conduct alone. Another is that the law does not generally accept a defence of 'I was acting out of character'. A bank clerk who has worked at a bank for 20 years and never before taken money has no defence to a charge of theft from the bank that, looking at her life as a whole, she is an honest person.

3. *The objective theory*. This theory in its pure form focuses on what the defendant did, rather than what was going on inside the defendant's head. It argues that it is necessary to have minimum standards of conduct that have to be met by every citizen. These standards should not be varied because of the defendant's individual characteristics. That would produce an unequal standard for different groups of people. The theory is capable of explaining those offences where the defendant is guilty if his conduct falls below the required standard, regardless of his state of mind (see, for example, Chapter 6). The objective theory is proposed by some for practical reasons. This may be because they feel the courts lack the evidence and capacity to make full moral judgements on the defendant. The court can declare certain conduct as harmful, but only an omnipotent God could decide the extent to which a defendant is morally blameworthy. Others argue a court is capable of deciding the moral blameworthiness of a defendant, but that it would take too long and be too cumbersome to carry out an individual moral investigation in each case. This argument is particularly strong in respect of minor offences. Opponents of the objective theory argue that it can produce unfair results, especially with those who lack the ability to meet the required standard (for example, because of a disability), although supporters argue that these difficulties can be dealt with at the sentencing stage. Opponents also point out that, as mentioned above, a criminal conviction carries with it a degree of censure, and this is appropriate only if the defendant is in

some sense to blame for what has happened. We can know that, they argue, only by looking at the defendant's state of mind.

1.4.4   The objective/subjective dispute

The disputes between these different theories of culpability and how to achieve a balance between them in practical terms come down to a debate over whether the law should take an objective or subjective approach to criminal liability. A pure subjectivist argues that a defendant should be responsible for only the foreseen or intended consequences of her actions. The actual consequences of a defendant's acts are to a large degree a matter of chance and beyond her control. She should be judged by those consequences with which she clearly associated herself, that is those she intended or foresaw. An example can be given of a defendant who throws a punch at a victim intending to give him a black eye. A pure subjectivist would argue that such a defendant should be punished in the same way for that act regardless of whether she does indeed cause a black eye; or the victim jumps out of the way at the last minute and so the punch misses completely; or the victim is knocked over by the punch, bangs his head and dies. The argument is that, the punch having been thrown, which of the different consequences occurs is beyond the control of the defendant, and so the level of blame attached to the defendant should be the same whichever consequence occurs.

A pure objectivist focuses not on what the defendant believed would happen but on what actually happened; not on what the defendant foresaw but what a reasonable person would have foreseen. In other words, while blame is the key concept for subjectivists, it is conduct which causes harm that objectivists see as fundamental. Objectivists argue that to say consequences are a matter of luck is unreal. For example, if a defendant dropped a pottery mug from the top of a high-rise building, it is surely not 'luck' that it breaks when it hits the ground, or at least not luck in the sense that it should affect our moral judgement of the defendant. Objectivists also often argue that it is better to have a clear conduct-based standard so that people know what conduct is or is not contrary to the law and that there should be the same standards for everyone. It is also claimed that generally we do see people as responsible for the consequences of their actions – be they good or bad consequences. What otherwise is the point of rewarding a student for doing well in an examination?

In an important decision of the House of Lords, *B v DPP** [2000] 2 AC 428, Lord Nicholls suggested that there is an important common law presumption that criminal offences require proof of a subjective state of mind. He explained:

> By definition the mental element in a crime is concerned with a subjective state of mind, such as intent or belief. To the extent that an overriding objective limit ('on reasonable grounds') is introduced, the subjective element is displaced. To that extent a person who lacks the necessary intent or belief may nevertheless commit the offence. When that occurs the defendant's 'fault' lies exclusively in falling short of an objective standard. His crime lies in his negligence. A statute may so provide expressly or by necessary implication. But this can have no place in a common law principle, of general application, which is concerned with the need for a mental element as an essential ingredient of a criminal offence.

Here, Lord Nicholls argues that the common law supports the subjectivist school of thought, although Parliament can pass a statute which creates an offence which is objectivist. In another important recent House of Lords decision (*R v G* [2008] UKHL 37)

Lord Steyn, in preferring a subjective to an objective understanding of the word 'reckless' in the Criminal Damage Act 1971, stated:

> This interpretation of section 1 of the 1971 Act would fit in with the general tendency in modern times of our criminal law. The shift is towards adopting a subjective approach. It is generally necessary to look at the matter in the light of how it would have appeared to the defendant.

The signs are therefore that over the past few years the House of Lords has been preferring a subjective to an objective approach to criminal liability.

In fact, overall the law, and indeed most commentators, reject either of the extreme forms of objectivism and subjectivism as outlined above. What is needed is a middle course to be taken between the two views. However, there is little agreement where exactly the course should be. Two areas where the dispute has been particularly fierce will now be mentioned briefly by way of example, but we will discuss the law's approach to these topics in more detail later.

1. *Liability for indifference.* The question here is how to deal with a defendant who fails to foresee that his action will cause harm. Take the example of a person who lights a match next to a haystack, which catches fire. The pure objectivist would argue that as a reasonable person would realise that such an act might lead to the burning of the haystack, the defendant should be liable for arson. However, this pure objectivist position would be clearly unfair where the defendant was, for example, suffering from a mental illness which meant that he was not able to foresee such a risk (see *Stephenson* [1979] QB 695). To say to such a person, 'you should have foreseen that' is fair only if the defendant could have foreseen that. The pure subjectivist would say the person who lights the match should be liable only if he foresaw that it might set the haystack ablaze. This might produce a fair result if the defendant were suffering from a mental illness, but it would not produce a satisfactory result if the defendant did not foresee the harm because he was indifferent to the welfare of others and simply did not care about other people's property. As this example shows, neither the pure subjective nor the pure objective theory deals satisfactorily with indifference and a middle approach; maybe focusing on the defendant's attitudes and reasons for failure to foresee a risk needs to be adopted. Indeed it is interesting to note that in the *B v DPP* case, where Lord Nicholls stressed the allegiance of the common law to subjectivism, the House of Lords would in fact have convicted a defendant who was indifferent to the age of the victim.
2. *Use of the term 'reasonable person' in defences.* If a defendant is threatened with death or grievous bodily harm unless he commits a crime and he does commit that crime, then the defence of duress may be available. The law states that he can do so only if a 'reasonable person' would have reacted as he did. This looks like an objectivist test, as a subjectivist test would probably only be interested in whether the defendant actually acted under duress. However, the strict objectivist test may be harsh when dealing with, say, a defendant suffering a mental disorder. In such a case the courts have said that it may be appropriate to ask how a reasonable defendant with that mental disorder would have reacted. Here we see an attempt to forge a middle path between the objectivist and subjectivist positions. The defendant must behave in accordance with an objective standard, but one which is tailored to his own capabilities.

In practice there may be less difference between the subjectivist and objectivist positions than there appears to be at first sight. Subjectivists have to accept that it is impossible for the jury to discover what was going on inside the defendant's head while she was committing the crime. The jury must inevitably ask what would a 'reasonable person' have foreseen, and then assume that the defendant would have foreseen what any reasonable person would have foreseen. The difference in approach is only really apparent where the jury are persuaded that the defendant is in some way different from the reasonable person.

1.5   Other influences on criminal law

Other factors apart from simply the harm caused by the act and the culpability of the defendant are relevant in the formulation of criminal law, and we will consider these now.

1.5.1   Certainty

You could, in theory, have a very short criminal law. It might read something like this: 'It is an offence wrongfully to harm someone in a blameworthy way'. However, there would be two main objections to such a law. The first is that a citizen should be able, if she wishes, to arrange her life so that she does not breach the law. This is particularly true of the criminal law, given the gravity of the consequence of breaching it. Therefore the law needs to be predictable, fairly certain and capable of being obeyed. In *Rimmington and Goldstein* [2005] UKHL 63 Lord Bingham stated:

> no one should be punished under a law unless it is sufficiently clear and certain to enable him to know what conduct is forbidden before he does it; and no one should be punished for any act which was not clearly and ascertainably punishable when the act was done.

These requirements are often called 'the rule of law'. In our imaginary very short criminal law mentioned above it would be very hard to predict how the phrase 'wrongfully to harm someone in a blameworthy way' would be interpreted. It would be difficult therefore to live your life making sure that such a law was not breached. It might also have the disadvantage of giving the police wide powers to decide whether or not to arrest or prosecute someone. Lord Bingham in *R v K** [2002] 1 AC 642 recognised this when he stated:

> The rule of law is not well served if a crime is defined in terms wide enough to cover conduct which is not regarded as criminal and it is then left to the prosecuting authorities to exercise a blanket discretion not to prosecute to avoid injustice.

Indeed Article 7 of the European Convention on Human Rights requires criminal offences to be defined with sufficient certainty.

The second objection to the very short criminal law is that if the criminal law is to impose censure on those who do wrong, then that censure needs to be fairly apportioned. It would be inappropriate to censure someone who parks his car illegally with the same level of blame as a deliberate killer. Thus the law has a 'fair labelling function', as some commentators have put it (Williams, 1983; Chalmers and Leverick, 2008). That is to say the offences should be so defined that one can know what level of blame is attached to which offence. On the other hand, if offences are too tightly defined, the way is left open for a defendant to attempt to use technical arguments that he was not charged with exactly the right offence and so escape a conviction.

1.5.2 Autonomy

Imagine a woman ends a relationship with her boyfriend. The boyfriend may feel deeply upset and pained, indeed much more so than if she had hit him. Although the physical assault would fall within the ambit of the criminal law, the breaking off of the relationship would not. The reason seems to be that the law gives protection to people's individual liberty or autonomy. Broadly speaking, freedom or autonomy means that we should be able to live our lives as we wish, in as far as that permits others to do with their lives as they wish. In the above example, although the harm caused to the boyfriend through breaking off the relationship is great, forcing the woman to remain in a relationship with him against her will by threat of a criminal sanction would be an even greater and an unacceptable infringement of her freedom of autonomy. Hence her conduct is not criminalised. Forbidding her to hit her boyfriend is much less of a restraint on her liberty than forbidding her to end the relationship, as she is still left with many other ways of expressing her anger towards him.

1.5.3 Political expediency

The law is, of course, influenced not just by the high-sounding principles of autonomy and the rule of law but also by political expediency. Even if it could be shown that the taking of soft drugs caused little harm to the user or to society, it would be unlikely that a government would legalise such drugs, at least in the present political climate, given the outcry which would follow such a change in the law. Similarly, even though the consumption of alcohol is connected with a large number of crimes and other harms to society, it is unlikely that a government would make the consumption of alcohol illegal, at least if it wished ever to win an election!

1.5.4 Power relationships

Ideally the criminal law should impact people equally so that every member of society has an equal opportunity to obey the law. However, some argue that the definitions of crimes reflect power structures within society: that the criminal law is designed to protect the interests of the rich and powerful, not the poor and weak. It is certainly true that among convicted criminals there is an over-representation of those in lower socio-economic groupings and those in ethnic minorities (Hood, 1992). The criminal law's failure to protect women effectively from sexual assault has been seen as reinforcing the exercise of power by men over women. It has also been suggested that crimes in which politically weaker sections of society are likely to engage and which are seen as dangerous by the 'middle classes' (for example, drug possession) are defined in such a way as to be easy for the police to prosecute (see Section 14.6). By contrast, 'middle-class' crimes, for instance white-collar fraud, are notoriously difficult to prosecute successfully. It is easy in a discussion of criminal behaviour to adopt an 'us and them' attitude. But it should not be overlooked that 33 per cent of men born in 1953 had been convicted of a standard list offence before the age of 46. Criminal behaviour is hardly the preserve of a tiny minority.

1.5.5 Practicality

The law is also governed by practicality. There is no point in making an activity illegal if it would be almost impossible for the police to catch people doing it, or if the only way to do so would be to give police unacceptably wide powers. This may be one reason why adultery is not illegal. Linked to this is administrative efficiency. This is particularly important in the present political climate of seeking to cut public expenditure. The definition of criminal offences should aim to be as clear and readily comprehensible as possible to ensure the swift, but fair, conviction of those deserving of punishment. The more complex the legal definition of a crime, the longer the trial is likely to take and the higher the costs. Further, if criminal procedures became too complex and so ineffective it might well be that private vengeance would start to take their place.

1.6 The reality of criminal behaviour

It would be easy to believe from reading some books that a picture of crime and criminal law is to be gleaned from the cases recorded in the law reports. However, considering only reported cases would be most misleading if you wanted to learn about day-to-day criminal activity. Many crimes, even quite serious ones, are not disclosed to the police because victims distrust the police, fear reprisals or cannot be bothered. The British Crime Survey estimates that for the years 2009/10 there were 9.6 million crimes but only 4.3 million of these were reported to the police. Further, the police are not able to catch every criminal, especially given the volume of crime with which they have to deal. Thus the perpetrators of less serious crimes are often not caught. If a criminal is apprehended the police have the discretion whether to charge, caution (give a formal police warning) or take no action. Even if the police do charge, the Crown Prosecution Service still has the discretion to decide not to prosecute, for example on the ground that there is insufficient evidence or that it is not in the public interest to do so. So, even if the perpetrator of a crime is found by the police there may well not be a court hearing. Indeed the Home Office has estimated that only 2 per cent of crimes end with the criminal being convicted. Of those which are prosecuted only a small number of cases reach the higher courts, and even fewer are reported. Notably it is exceptional for cases where the defendant has been found not guilty, or has pleaded guilty, to reach the law reports, as there are very limited grounds of appeal in such cases. Thus the cases which appear in the law reports give a distorted picture of the criminal law. What they do provide is a picture of those topics where the law is in doubt and where important principles clash, and that is one of the things in which academic lawyers (and examiners!) are particularly interested.

1.7 The Human Rights Act 1998

1.7.1 How the Human Rights Act protects rights

The Human Rights Act 1998 is designed to ensure the protection of individuals' rights under the European Convention on Human Rights. It does this in two ways:

1. *The interpretation of legislation.* The Human Rights Act requires judges to interpret legislation in line with the European Convention on Human Rights. Section 3(1) states:

   > So far as it is possible to do so, primary legislation and subordinate legislation must be read and given effect in a way which is compatible with the Convention rights.

   This makes it clear that if a statute is ambiguous and could be read in a way which is compatible with the Convention rights or could be read in a way which is not, then the statute should be read so as to be compatible. The key phrase is 'so far as it is possible'. What is unclear is how far this will be taken. Will the judges be willing to strain the natural meaning of words or even read words into statutes in order to ensure compatibility? Time will tell, and it may well be that some judges will be more willing to strive to ensure compatibility than others. The clearest guidance we have to date on how section 3 will be used is that it can be used to interpret legislation, but not amend it (*Re S, Re W* [2002] 1 FCR 577). If the judge decides that it is not possible to read a statute in line with the Convention rights then the court should issue a declaration of incompatibility which should (in brief) require Parliament to consider reform of the statute (see *Bellinger v Bellinger* [2003] UKHL 21 for a case where this was done).

2. *Duties on public authorities*. Section 6 deals with the duties on a public authority. For our purposes it should be noted that both the courts (s (3)(a)) and the Crown Prosecution Service (CPS) are public authorities. Section 6 states:

   1. It is unlawful for a public authority to act in a way which is incompatible with a Convention Right.
   2. Subsection 1 does not apply to an act if –
      a. as the result of one or more provisions of primary legislation, the authority could not have acted differently; or
      b. in the case of one or more provisions of, or made under, primary legislation which cannot be read or given effect in a way which is compatible with the Convention rights, the authority was acting so as to give effect to or enforce these provisions.

This means that unless required to do so by statute, the court and the CPS (or any other public authority) should not infringe anyone's Convention rights. The significance of these provisions on substantive criminal law is unclear. Here are three possible points of significance:

   i. If the defendant is charged with a common law offence which infringes his Convention rights it is arguable that the court should interpret the common law to be in line with the Convention under s 6. It should be noted that s 3 only deals with the situation when a court is interpreting a statute which may or may not be incompatible with a Convention right; it does not apply when the court is considering the common law. However, s 6 still requires a court when interpreting the common law to act in a way which is consistent with the Convention. As there is no statute which compels a particular interpretation of the common law, s 6 may require the court to interpret the common law to be in line with the Convention rights. But do not think that the court will consider only a defendant's rights when interpreting the law; the victim's rights may be relevant too. In *R v H** [2001] 2 FLR 431 the Court of Appeal restricted the defence of reasonable chastisement following the Human Rights Act in order properly to protect the rights of children.

   It should be added that this interpretation of the effect of s 6 is controversial. Did Parliament intend the courts to alter long and clearly established principles of common law if they conflict with the rights? Some (Buxton LJ, for example) argue that this cannot be so; others (Ashworth, for example) argue that that is what the Act says. The Court of Appeal in *R v H* assumed that s 6 would lead to an alteration of an aspect of the common law which infringed the Convention, subject to an argument that an unforeseeable change in the law might infringe a defendant's rights under Articles 6 and 7. In the context of that case it was held that it could not be said to be unforeseeable at the time of the offence that the common law would develop to adopt the stricter limits on what amounted to reasonable chastisement of children as required by the Convention.

ii. If the CPS is considering whether or not to bring a prosecution, it is bound by s 6 because it is a public body. It should therefore not bring a prosecution if that would involve an infringement of the defendant's Convention rights. This would mean that if it is clear that a particular criminal law was incompatible with an individual's Convention rights then the CPS should not bring the case. Indeed it is arguable that if it does bring a prosecution which infringes the defendant's Convention rights this could amount to an abuse of process, meaning that the court cannot hear the case.

iii. It is also submitted that s 6 applies to the court at the sentencing stage. Imagine that the defendant has been convicted of a statutory offence which cannot be interpreted in line with the Convention, and so a declaration of incompatibility has been issued by the court. In such a case, does s 6 mean that the court must impose a nominal sentence (unless the offence is one of the rare ones for which there is a statutorily imposed minimum sentence)? To impose a substantial sentence would infringe the individual's Convention rights, which a court is not permitted to do under s 6 unless compelled to do so by a statute.

1.7.2   What rights are protected by the Act?

Before looking at these rights, it is important to appreciate that the rights protected by the Act can be relevant in the criminal law in two different ways:

1. A defendant may argue that to convict him of a particular offence infringes his rights.
2. A victim (or potential victim) may argue that the state has infringed his rights by not protecting him under the criminal law. For example, in *X and Y v Netherlands* (1985) 7 EHRR 235 a girl with learning difficulties was sexually abused. Her abuser could not be prosecuted under Dutch law because she could not sign the relevant paperwork. The fact that her abuser could not be punished led the European Court of Human Rights to hold that the Netherlands had infringed her rights under Article 8 (see also *A v UK** (1999) 28 EHRR 603).

Now we will very briefly summarise the main rights in the Convention which are likely to be relevant in criminal cases. We will then consider some of the specific areas of the criminal law which might be under challenge following the Human Rights Act 1998.

1.7.2(a) Article 2

1. Everyone's right to life shall be protected by law. No one shall be deprived of his life intentionally save in the execution of a sentence of a court following his conviction of a crime for which this penalty is provided by law.
2. Deprivation of life shall not be regarded as inflicted in contravention of this article when it results from the use of force which is no more than absolutely necessary:
   a. in defence of any person from unlawful violence;
   b. in order to effect a lawful arrest or to prevent the escape of a person lawfully detained; or
   c. in action lawfully taken for the purpose of quelling a riot or insurrection.

This Article requires the protection of an individual's right to life. As we shall see, this will be relevant in discussions involving the defence of self-defence and protection of others; euthanasia and the defence of necessity to a charge of murder.

1.7.2(b) Article 3

No one shall be subjected to torture or inhuman or degrading treatment or punishment.

Under this Article, potential victims can claim protection from violence which constitutes torture or inhuman or degrading treatment.

1.7.2(c) Article 6

1. In the determination of his civil rights and obligations and of any criminal charge against him, everyone is entitled to a fair and public hearing within a reasonable time by an independent and impartial tribunal established by law. Judgment shall be pronounced but the press and public may be excluded from all or part of the trial in the interests of morals, public order, or national security, where the interest of juveniles or the private life of the parties so require, or to the extent strictly necessary in the opinion of the court in special circumstances where publicity would prejudice the interests of justice.
2. Everyone charged with a criminal offence shall be presumed innocent until proved guilty according to the law.
3. Everyone charged with a criminal offence has the following minimum rights:
   a. to be informed promptly, in a language which he understands and in detail, of the nature and cause of the accusation against him;
   b. to have adequate time and facilities for the preparation of his defence;
   c. to defend himself in person or through legal assistance of his own choosing or, if he had not sufficient means to pay for legal assistance, to be given it free if the interests of justice so require;
   d. to examine or have examined witnesses against him and to obtain the attendance and examination of witnesses on his behalf under the same conditions as witnesses against him;
   e. to have the free assistance of an interpreter if he cannot understand or speak the language used in the court.

This Article has important consequences for the law on criminal procedure and evidence, which cannot be discussed in detail in this book. However, it also has significance for the law on burdens of proof and strict liability offences. The European Court of Human Rights has taken the view that Article 6 cannot be used to claim that the substantive law itself is unfair (*Z v UK* (2002) 34 EHRR 379).

1.7.2(d) Article 7

1. No one shall be held guilty of any criminal offence on account of any act or omission which did not constitute a criminal offence under national or international law at the time when it was committed. Nor shall a heavier penalty be imposed than the one that was applicable at the time the criminal offence was committed.
2. This article shall not prejudice the trial and punishment of any person for any act or omission, which, at the time when it was committed, was criminal according to the general principles of law recognized by civilized nations.

This Article prevents states passing retrospective criminal statutes. These are statutes which now make conduct criminal which was not at the time it was done. This was already a well-established common law principle. However, the Article, as we shall see, may be relevant if the courts wish to change well-established common law rules.

1.7.2(e) Article 8

1. Everyone has the right to respect for his private and family life, his home and his correspondence.
2. There shall be no interference by a public authority with the exercise of this right except as is in accordance with the law and is necessary in a democratic society in the interests of national security, public safety or the economic well-being of the country, for the prevention of disorder or crime, for the protection of health or morals, or for the protection of the rights and freedoms of others.

This Article protects the right to respect for private and family life. It is clearly of significance in criminal law when discussing offences of a sexual nature.

1.7.2(f) Article 10

1. Everyone has the right to freedom of expression. This right shall include freedom to hold opinions and to receive and impart information and ideas without interference by public authority and regardless of frontiers. This article shall not prevent States from requiring the licensing of broadcasting, television or cinema enterprises.
2. The exercise of these freedoms, since it carries with it duties and responsibilities may be subject to such formalities, conditions, restrictions or penalties as are prescribed by law and are necessary in a democratic society, in the interests of national security, territorial integrity or public safety, for the protection of the reputation or rights of others, for preventing the disclosure of information received in confidence, or for maintaining the authority and impartiality of the judiciary.

This Article protects the right to freedom of expression. It will be relevant in cases where the defendant's words are said to be the basis of a criminal charge. But crimes prohibiting racist or offensive speech can be justified under Article 10 (*DPP v Collins* [2006] UKHL 40).

1.7.2(g) Article 14

The enjoyment of the rights and freedoms set forth in this Convention shall be secured without discrimination on any ground such as sex, race, colour, language, religion, political opinion, national or social origin, association with a national minority, property, birth, or other status.

Significantly, this Article calls into question any offence which treats men and women differently. It should be noted that in *Da Silva Mouta v Portugal* [2001] 1 FCR 653 the European Court of Human Rights explained that discrimination on the basis of sexual orientation is also prohibited under Article 14. It must be emphasised that the Article applies only once it is shown that there is an interference with one of the applicant's other rights under the Convention (or at least conduct which came within the 'ambit' of one of the other rights) (*Mendoza v Ghaidan* [2004] UKHL 30). It is not possible to rely on Article 14 if you are claiming that you have only in general been discriminated against on the grounds of sex. It would be necessary to demonstrate, for example, that your right to respect for private life was infringed in a way that discriminated against you on the grounds of your sex.

At various points during the book we will consider how the Human Rights Act might impact on particular topics, but now some of the general issues raised by the Act will be discussed here. If what has been said so far has led the reader to expect that English and Welsh criminal law will be transformed by the Human Rights Act, you are likely to be disappointed. Some argue that there will be almost no change as a result of the Act, and even those who do see legitimate challenges list a relatively small number of possible changes. However, what may legitimately be expected is a change in language when discussing the interpretation of the criminal law. The Convention rights will appear as a way of justifying or supporting the criminal law, if not causing radical change to it. So here are some of the main general areas in which the Human Rights Act could have some relevance.

1.7.3 The standard of proof

The European Court of Human Rights has implied into Article 6 a requirement that in a criminal trial the charge must be proved against a defendant beyond all reasonable doubt (*Barbera, Messegue and Jabardo v Spain* (1988) 17 EHRR 360). However, the European Commission has held that this does not mean that the prosecution has the burden of disproving a defence that the defendant may wish to raise. The impact of the Human Rights Act on circumstances in which a statute may place a burden of proof on a defendant is discussed in Section 2.4.2.

1.7.4 Uncertainty

It can be argued that if the definition of a criminal offence is too uncertain, this may infringe the Convention. First, there is Article 7, which requires any offence to be a criminal offence at the time it was committed. Second is Articles 8, 9 and 10, which protect various freedoms (for example, the right to respect for private life). These freedoms can be infringed under certain conditions, including where the infringement was prescribed by or is in accordance with the law. At first sight it is not apparent why these requirements require the criminal law to be certain, but they do so because, as the European Court of Human Rights in *Silver v UK* (1983) 5 EHRR 347 explained:

> a norm cannot be regarded as 'a law' unless it is formulated with sufficient precision to enable the citizen to regulate his conduct: he must be able – if need be with appropriate advice – to foresee, to a degree that is reasonable in the circumstances, the consequences which a given action may entail.

This suggests that to amount to 'a law' which complies with Article 7, or to justify interference with the rights protected in Articles 8, 9 and 10, the offence must be drafted with sufficient precision. In *Hashman v UK** [2000] Crim LR 800 the European Court held that the power under English law to bind the defendant to keep the peace on the basis that his conduct was *contra bonos mores* (contrary to the public good) was so imprecise that it did not amount to a law. It therefore could not justify the infringement of the defendant's right to freedom of expression under Article 10.

However, it seems that the European Court of Human Rights will not be too strict in its requirements of precision. In *Steel v UK*, 23 September 1998, RJD VII the English offence of breach of the peace (defined as 'when an individual causes harm, or appears likely to cause harm, to persons or property or acts in a manner the natural consequence of which would be to provoke others to violence') was held to be sufficiently precise to amount to law and to justify an infringement of the applicant's rights of freedom of expression under Article 10(2). The court explained:

> given the importance of personal liberty, it is essential that the applicable national law meets the standard of 'lawfulness' set by the Convention, which requires that all law, whether written or unwritten, be sufficiently precise to allow the citizen – if need be, with appropriate advice – to foresee, to a degree that is reasonable in the circumstances, the consequences which a given action may entail.

So, only the most imprecise offences are likely to be successfully challenged under the Human Rights Act (*Cotter* [2002] Crim LR 824). Those offences which could possibly be challenged include conspiracy to defraud, conspiracy to corrupt public morals and the definition of dishonesty. However, it would be a brave judge who would find these offences too vague to amount to law (see *Rimmington and Goldstein* [2005] UKHL 63, where the House of Lords refused to find the offence of causing a public nuisance too vague).

1.7.5   Retrospectivity

Article 7 specifically prevents retrospective criminal law. That means the state cannot punish a person for an offence which was not a crime at the time when the act was performed. Buxton LJ (writing extrajudicially) has argued that this principle is already accepted in the common law. The main difficulty in English law is where the criminal law is interpreted in a novel way as a result of which a defendant is convicted. Could this be said to be retrospective law? The issue arose in relation to the marital exemption in rape. In *R v R* [1992] 1 AC 599 the House of Lords confirmed that the marital exemption was now outdated and no longer existed. The defendant (who was married to the victim) could therefore be convicted of rape. The defendant applied to the European Court of Human Rights on the basis that at the time of the sexual intercourse the marital exemption was regarded as part of the law. Had he sought legal advice at the time he would have been told that he had a defence to a charge of rape. The decision of the House of Lords, removing the exemption and therefore enabling him to be convicted of rape, was in effect, he argued, retrospective criminal law-making. To the surprise of many commentators, the European Court of Human Rights in *SW v UK** (1996) 21 EHRR 363 dismissed his application. Key to its reasoning was the following statement:

> Article 7 ... cannot be read as outlawing the gradual clarification of the rules of criminal liability through judicial interpretation from case to case, provided that the resultant development is consistent with the essence of the offence and could be reasonably foreseen.

This decision indicates that decisions by the courts, even ones which appear to change the law, are very unlikely to infringe Article 7. Although, as *SW v UK* indicates, if the court were to interpret an offence in an unforeseeable way this could infringe Article 7.

Hot Topic –   Should drinking alcohol be illegal?

Few people seriously suggest that drinking alcohol should be illegal. But why not? A further investigation of the issue reveals some of the questions which need to be addressed when considering what conduct generally should be made illegal. The aim of this discussion is not to reach a conclusion on this controversial issue, but to demonstrate how the discussion on criminalisation above applies to a particular topic.

The issues which are raised by those on either side of the argument include the following:

1. Does drinking alcohol cause harm to others? It might be thought not difficult to make a case that it does. Consider the following:
   a. There are strong links between drinking alcohol and committing a crime. In 2003 nearly two-thirds of sentenced male prisoners

and four-fifths of female prisoners admitted heavy drinking before committing their crime. Forty-seven per cent of victims of violent crime reported their assailants to be under the influence of alcohol.

b. Forty-four per cent of domestic violence incidents were said to involve a drunk abuser.

c. In 2004 over 17,000 people were killed or injured in drink-drive incidents.

d. The Department of Health states that 40,000 deaths per year are related to alcohol.

e. The cost to the NHS of alcohol related admissions exceeds £3 billion.

(These are taken from www.alcoholconcern.org.uk, where further statistics can be found).

2. Despite these figures it might be argued that drinking a single drink does not cause these harms. Most people drink alcohol without causing these harms. There are many activities which can be dangerous. We cannot make them illegal simply because they may possibly cause a harm. If we did that then there would be very few lawful activities.

3. It might be argued that the harms mentioned in point 1 need to be balanced against the social benefits. These might include the income generated through tax on alcohol or the broader social benefits in encouraging communal activities linked to alcohol.

4. An alternative argument is to refer to the rights that individuals have. To many people drinking alcohol is an important part of social lives, and not being permitted to drink alcohol would be a major interference in how they like to live. Such an intervention requires very strong justification, and although the figures in 1 above may demonstrate some harm there is not enough to justify such a major infringement of people's rights.

5. Supporters of rendering the drinking of alcohol illegal might respond that some of the argument made above could be used to support all other drugs. Indeed in a recent survey of the dangerousness of illegal drugs alcohol was ranked the fifth highest, above several Class A drugs (those illegal drugs currently categorised as the most serious).

Perhaps all of this debate is academic. No government would ever seriously propose rendering the drinking of alcohol illegal. Alcohol plays such a major role in our society and has gained such social acceptability that it will not, whatever scientists may tell us, be regarded as analogous to a Class A drug. This shows that what is made criminal can be as much a matter of social norms and pressures as of science or logic.

Summary

1.1 This book is designed to provide the tools necessary to analyse the criminal law. It also seeks to discuss the tensions between the principles that underlie the law.

1.2 It is difficult to define what constitutes criminal law. Probably the best definition is to consider whether the alleged crime involves using the procedures that attend criminal law. Which conduct is classified criminal can change from society to society and generation to generation.

1.3 The criminal law seeks to deter people from conduct that causes sufficient harm to society and sets out the circumstances in which people may face punishment. A breach of criminal law is different from a breach of other kinds of law, for example contract law, as it contains an element of formal moral censure from society.

1.4 Most criminal offences involve two aspects: harmful conduct and culpability. The harm need not be the injury of another person but includes harm to the environment or society in general. The fact that conduct is simply immoral or harms only the accused is usually insufficient to justify a criminal conviction. The defendant may escape culpability by claiming to be exempt from the criminal law (for example, because of age or insanity); or lacking the capacity to commit a crime; or lacking the mental state required for the offence or having a special defence to the crime. There are several theories which seek to provide a theory of culpability that underpins criminal law, including the choice theory, the character theory and the objective theory. The different theories of culpability link into a dispute over whether the law should take an objective or subjective approach. A subjectivist holds a defendant liable for

Summary cont'd

the consequences of his actions that he has chosen to bring about. An objectivist will hold the defendant responsible for all of the reasonably foreseeable consequences that the defendant's act has caused.

1.5 The criminal law is also influenced by other factors, such as the need for certainty in the law in order that people can arrange their lives so as to ensure that they do not breach the criminal law. It also needs to be efficient in its operation. However, the law inevitably reflects society's attitudes and inequalities.

1.6 The vast majority of crimes do not reach the courts. Many are not reported or, if they are, the police are unable to find who committed the crime or decide not to prosecute the perpetrator. Thus the picture of crime as it appears in the law reports does not necessarily reflect that which occurs on the streets.

1.7 The Human Rights Act requires the courts to interpret statutes in a way which is compatible with individuals' rights under the European Convention on Human Rights if at all possible. The Act also requires public authorities (including courts and the Crown Prosecution Service) to act in a way that is consistent with those rights, unless required to act otherwise by a statute. It protects a number of rights, including the right to life, the right not to be tortured and the right to respect for one's private and family life. English and Welsh criminal law is largely compatible with the Act.

Further Reading

Williams (1955) discusses the definition of a criminal offence and von Hirsch explains the censuring function played by the criminal law. For the leading works on what conduct should be criminalised read Ashworth (2000), Devlin, Lamond, Fineberg, Hart, Husak, Tadros and Mill. For a discussion of the benefits of the character and choice theories of responsibility see Bayles, Duff and Horder. The arguments for and against a subjective or objective approach to criminal liability are to be found in Ashworth (1993), Duff, and Tur. Duff and Garland provide an excellent set of writings on the justifications for punishment. Fair labelling theory is discussed in Chalmers and Leverick. Norrie reveals the different political pressures that influence criminal law. Wells discusses the contribution of feminist thought to criminal law scholarship. Ashworth (2000 and 2001), Buxton and the Centre for Public Law discuss the impact of the Human Rights Act on Criminal Law.

Ashworth, 'Taking the Consequences', in Shute, Gardner and Horder (eds), *Action and Value in Criminal Law* (Oxford University Press 1993).

Ashworth, 'The Human Rights Act and the Substantive Criminal Law: A Non-Minimalist View' [2000] Crim LR 564.

Ashworth, 'Is Criminal Law a Lost Cause' (2000) 116 LQR 225.

Ashworth, 'Criminal Proceedings After the Human Rights Act' [2001] Crim LR 855.

Bayles, 'Character, Purpose and Criminal Responsibility' (1982) 1 Law Philos 5.

Buxton, 'The Human Rights Act and the Substantive Criminal Law' [2000] Crim LR 311.

Centre for Public Law at the University of Cambridge, *The Human Rights Act and the Criminal Justice and Regulatory Process* (Hart 1999).

Chalmers and Leverick, 'Fair Labelling in the Criminal Law' (2008) 71 MLR 217.

Devlin, *The Enforcement of Morals* (Oxford University Press 1968).

Duff, 'Choice, Character and Criminal Responsibility' (1993) 12 Law Philos 345.

Duff, *Answering for Crime* (Hart 2007).

Further Reading cont'd

Duff and Garland (eds), *A Reader on Punishment* (Oxford University Press 1994).

Fineberg, *Harm to Self, Harm to Others; Harmless Wrongdoing; Offense to Others* (Oxford University Press 1984, 1986, 1988).

Hart, *Law, Liberty and Morality* (Oxford University Press 1963).

Horder, 'Criminal Culpability: The Possibility of a General Theory' (1993) 12 Law Philos 193.

Husak, 'Limitations on Criminalization and the General Part of the Criminal Law', in Shute and Simester (eds), *Criminal Law Theory* (Oxford University Press 2002).

Lamond, 'What Is a Crime?' (2007) 27 OJLS 609.

Mill, *On Liberty* (first published 1859, Longman 2007).

Norrie, *Crime, Reason and History* (Weidenfeld & Nicolson 2001).

Tadros, *Criminal Responsibility* (Oxford University Press 2005).

Tadros, 'Crimes and Security' (2008) 71 MLR 940.

Tur, 'Subjectivism and Objectivism: Towards Synthesis', in Shute, Gardner and Horder (eds), *Action and Value in Criminal Law* (Oxford University Press 1993).

von Hirsch, *Censure and Sanctions* (Oxford University Press 1993).

Wells, 'The Impact of Feminist Thinking on Criminal Law and Justice' [2004] Crim LR 503.

Williams, 'The Definition of Crime' (1955) 8 CLP 107.

Williams, 'Convictions and Fair Labelling' (1983) 42 CLJ 85.

Case Notes

▶ *A v UK* **(1999) 28 EHRR 603. European Court of Human Rights**

The applicant was hit by his stepfather with a cane, causing severe bruising. The stepfather was acquitted of assaulting the applicant on the basis that he was using reasonable force in chastising him. The European Court of Human Rights found that the acquittal of the stepfather indicated that the applicant's rights under Article 3 were not adequately protected by the state. It rejected the UK's argument that Article 3 applied only where the state was torturing or imposing inhuman or degrading treatment on the citizen. It was explained that the state had a duty to protect a citizen's rights under Article 3 from infringement by another.

▶ *B v DPP* **[2000] Crim LR 403. House of Lords**

See Chapter 6 Case notes.

▶ *R v H* **[2001] 2 FLR 431. Court of Appeal**

The defendant hit his son with a leather belt on a date before the Human Rights Act came into force. The prosecution appealed against the judge's proposed direction to the jury.

The prosecution argued that the direction should be in line with the European Convention on Human Rights. The defence argued that the judge should direct the jury in line with the common law at the time that the offence was committed, without regard to the Convention. The Court of Appeal was persuaded by the prosecution's arguments and stated that in considering whether chastisement was reasonable it was necessary to consider the nature and context of the defendant's behaviour, its duration, its physical and mental consequences in relation to the child, the age and personal characteristics of the child and the reasons the punishment was administered.

▶ *Hashman v UK* **[2000] Crim LR 185. European Court of Human Rights**

The applicants were protesting against a hunt. They blew horns and shouted in an attempt to disturb the hounds. The Crown Court found that they had behaved *contra bonos mores* ('behaviour which was wrong rather than right in the judgment of the majority of contemporary fellow citizens') and should be bound over to be of good behaviour for a year. The European Court found that the applicants' freedom of expression under Article 10 had been infringed. The *contra bonos mores* offence did not give the applicants sufficiently clear guidance as to how they should behave in future. Therefore it lacked the quality of law and so could not justify the infringement of the Article 10 rights in Article 10(2).

▶ *Hinks* [2000] 3 WLR 1590. House of Lords

See Chapter 11 Case notes.

▶ *R v K* [2002] 1 AC 462. House of Lords

See Chapter 6 Case notes.

▶ *SW v UK* (1996) 21 EHRR 363. European Court of Human Rights

The defendant was convicted of rape following a decision of the House of Lords that the marital exemption to rape was no longer part of the law. He argued before the European Court of Human Rights that in effect this was retrospective criminal law creation and therefore infringed Article 7. The European Court rejected this argument on the basis that legal systems were permitted gradually to clarify the definition of offences on a case-by-case basis.

Chapter 2

Procedures and structures of criminal law

Key Terms

▶ **Burden of proof** – who must prove a particular fact.
▶ **The Crown** – the Crown refers to the Queen, who represents the state.

2.1 The role of the state in criminal proceedings

Civil and criminal law are both concerned with liability for wrongful conduct. The same act (such as an assault) may amount both to a civil wrong (a tort) and to a crime. So, if Sam hits Millie there are consequences in both civil law and criminal law. Millie can sue Sam for damages for her injuries under the law of tort. The police may also decide to charge Sam with a criminal offence, as a result of which Sam may receive a punishment. These civil and criminal law consequences are quite different. In the case of a tort, liability is owed to the injured party and damages may be paid to the injured party to compensate for any losses. In the case of a crime, liability is owed to the state and the state supervises any punishment. Liability is owed to the state even where the crime has no human victim, because a crime is regarded as a breach of public order. One of the ways in which England was united under the Crown in the thirteenth and fourteenth centuries was by the enforcement of order (the King's peace) by the King's officials and judges. Serious infringements of order (called felonies) were offences against the Crown, and prosecutions were brought in the name of the King. This is still the case: serious offences are tried on indictment in the Crown Court, and the prosecution is in the name of the Crown. The prosecuting authority is called the Crown Prosecution Service, and the official title of the case will be, for example, *The Queen versus Smith*, abbreviated to *R v Smith*, or even *Smith*.

2.2 The role of the judge in criminal proceedings

The criminal law is still largely common law, that is judge-made law. Of course, there are important statutes, mainly dating from the last 150 years, but these have tended to adjust the underlying common law, rather than radically change it. For example, the Homicide Act 1957 alters the law of murder without defining 'murder', and the definition of murder is still a matter of case law. Exceptions are the Theft Acts of 1968 and 1978, which completely reworked the law of theft, but even these have since been overlaid with a body of case law interpreting the various statutory provisions. Now it would not be possible to understand the law of theft by simply looking at the Acts; the cases applying the Acts must be read as well.

A clear view of the importance of the judicial role is found in the judgment of Viscount Simonds in *Shaw v DPP* [1962] AC 220, in which he denied that the courts have the power to create new crimes but asserted that in exercising their duty as:

> servants and guardians of the common law…there remains in the courts of law a residual power to enforce the supreme and fundamental purpose of the law, to conserve not only the safety and order but also the moral welfare of the State, and that it is their duty to guard it against attacks which may be the more insidious because they are novel and unprepared for.

In this case, the protection of public order justified the extension of the offence of conspiracy to cover conduct, which was not itself criminal but which, in the view of the House of Lords, was a threat to public morals (see Section 18.3). Lord Millet, in *R v K* [2002] 1 AC 642, was willing to reinterpret the law because he felt that Parliament had failed to ensure that the law accorded with current standards of morality. The case concerned (in effect) the age at which teenagers could consent to sexual activities:

> But the age of consent has long since ceased to reflect ordinary life, and in this respect Parliament has signally failed to discharge its responsibility for keeping the criminal law in touch with the needs of society. I am persuaded that the piecemeal introduction of the various elements of Section 14 [Sexual Offences Act 1956], coupled with the persistent failure of Parliament to rationalise this branch of the law even to the extent of removing absurdities which the Courts have identified, means that we ought not to strain after internal coherence even in a single offence. Injustice is too high a price to pay for consistency.

However, it is also easy to find strong statements against judge-made law. Lord Bingham in *Rimmington and Goldstein* [2005] UKHL 63 stated:

> In his famous polemic *Truth versus Ashurst*, written in 1792 and published in 1823, Jeremy Bentham made a searing criticism of judge-made criminal law, which he called 'dog-law'.
>
> > 'It is the judges (as we have seen) that make the common law. Do you know how they make it? Just as a man makes laws for his dog. When your dog does anything you want to break him of, you wait till he does it, and then beat him for it. This is the way you make laws for your dog: and this is the way the judges make law for you and me. They won't tell a man beforehand what it is he *should not do* – they won't so much as allow of his being told: they lie by till he has done something which they say he should not *have done*, and then they hang him for it.'
>
> The domestic law of England and Wales has set its face firmly against 'dog-law'.

Despite the pre-eminence of judge-made law, it is only recently that the higher courts, the Court of Appeal and the House of Lords, have paid much attention to the development of the criminal law. Criminal practice used to be regarded as hackwork, with little intellectual interest, and this coloured the ideas of judges. In the last 50 years this has changed completely: the criminal law has attracted academic attention, the Court of Appeal has developed a strong tradition, and the number of criminal cases going to the House of Lords has increased. Indeed when the House of Lords in *R v G** [2004] Crim LR 369 overruled *Caldwell** [1982] AC 341, it gave as one of the reasons for doing so the intense academic criticism the decision had attracted. In the last few years it has become increasingly common for judges, particularly in the House of Lords, to analyse academic writings carefully in criminal cases, leading sometimes to longer and more carefully reasoned judgments. This has not, of course, meant that academics have stopped criticising some of their decisions – especially when it is felt that judges have read some, but not all, of the books or articles written!

2.3 Judge and jury

Some criminal trials are carried out in front of a judge and jury (this is called trial on indictment, and takes place in the Crown Court), but most are tried summarily by magistrates. The difference between summary and indictable offences is explained below in Section 2.5. Magistrates, when they hear a case, combine the functions of both judge and jury: they decide any questions of law which arise (with the help of their clerk, who is a lawyer), they decide the facts, and they apply the law to the facts to reach a verdict. It is easier to explain these different functions in the context of a trial on indictment, but the same principles apply to a summary trial.

If the defendant pleads guilty to the offence with which he is charged then the jury have no role to play and a conviction will be entered. A defendant who pleads guilty may be influenced by the fact that a guilty plea may well lead to a lesser sentence. It may also be that if a defendant pleads guilty to a lesser crime then the prosecution will not pursue a more serious charge; this is commonly known as 'plea bargaining'. If the defendant pleads not guilty then there is a clear division of roles between the judge and the jury.

The judge has a duty to ensure that the trial is conducted according to the rules of procedure and evidence, a large subject in itself. The judge's function is to explain the law to the jury: this is a very important part of the judge's summing-up, in which she addresses the jury before they retire to consider their verdict. If any questions of law are raised during the trial, by the prosecution, by the defence or by the judge herself, it is the judge who must give a ruling on the point. The jury are bound to take the law from the judge. It may be possible for the defendant to challenge the judge's ruling on the law by appealing to a higher court after the verdict. Decisions on the law by magistrates can always be challenged in a higher court, either the Crown Court or the High Court.

It is the function of the jury to decide questions of fact and to apply the law to the facts so as to arrive at a verdict on the charge facing the defendant. The charge will be stated on a formal document, known as an indictment, which will specify, in brief, the nature of the allegation facing the defendant, including particularly the offence with which he is charged. It may well be that there are some aspects of the case on which the prosecution and defence agree. For example, the defendant may admit that he was at the scene of the crime, but deny that he hit the victim. In such a case, obviously the jury will focus on those factual issues that are in dispute.

The jury are only to consider whether the defendant committed the offence with which he is charged. For example, if the defendant is charged with stabbing the victim and during his evidence the defendant admits stealing from the victim but denies stabbing him, the jury cannot return a verdict of guilty of theft, as they are allowed to consider only the offence with which the defendant was charged. That said, sometimes the jury can return a verdict of guilty to a lesser crime if the defendant is charged with a serious offence the elements of which include the lesser offence. For example, if the defendant is charged with murder, the jury could convict him of manslaughter if the jury decided that it had not been shown that he intended to kill or cause serious injury. The judge will inform a jury if this is possible. It is not true to say that the jury are not concerned with the law at all: if that were so, then the 'verdict' would merely be a series of statements of fact about what the jury thought had happened. A verdict is the law applied to the facts, which results in a conclusion of guilt or innocence.

An important aspect of the jury's function is to decide what happened: whether a particular witness is telling the truth, for example, or whether an identification that has been denied is reliable. 'What happened' includes not only actions (what the accused did) but also the state of mind of those who were involved, including particularly the accused. For example, in a rape case the jury have to decide whether sexual intercourse took place, whether the victim was consenting at the time (her state of mind), as well as, if she was not consenting, whether the accused knew that she was not consenting (his state of mind). Questions about states of mind are often called subjective questions (see Section 1.4). Of course, the jury cannot read minds, and even if they could, they are concerned with the state of mind at the time of the alleged offence, not at the time of the trial. So they have to rely on external evidence, which includes what was done and what was said, as well as the surrounding circumstances. Sometimes the inference from the facts is overwhelming: if the accused has pointed a gun point-blank at the victim and fired, the jury will readily infer that the accused intended at least some injury. But this inference may be displaced by other evidence (see *Lamb** [1967] 2 QB 981 for an example), and it is important to remember that the jury are ultimately concerned with the actual state of mind of the accused, not with what jury members themselves would have thought.

The jury not only deal with the facts of what happened; they are also asked to decide questions such as 'what would a reasonable person have done in this situation?' or 'would a reasonable person call this book obscene?' When the criminal law poses questions such as these, it is setting an objective standard, and the jury act as representatives of reasonable people in assessing and applying that standard. The jury measure the conduct of the accused person against their view of what a reasonable person would have done or thought.

Yet another aspect to the jury's function is to determine the meaning of words used by statutes. Sometimes these words are defined, either in the statute itself or by the judges. In such cases the definition is a matter of law, and the jury are bound to apply it: the jury cannot say that they disagree with the definition given and apply a different one (if they were to do this and convict the accused, the verdict might be overturned on appeal). An example is the definition of the word 'property' found in the Theft Act 1968, which is given a particular technical definition in the statute (see Chapter 11). Sometimes, however, words are not defined either by statute or by the courts, and the jury must apply the words as they understand them. There has been a tendency in modern statutes to use supposedly simple, non-technical language, and judges increasingly avoid giving exhaustive definitions of words used in this way. They say that these are ordinary, everyday words which the jury can be expected to understand and apply without definition. An example, also from the Theft Act 1968, is the word 'dishonesty'. This use of simple words is not confined to words used in statutes: the meaning of 'intention' in a common law crime such as murder is another example. The judges are willing to explain how the jury may infer intention from the evidence, but not to define it.

2.4 The burden of proof

The burden of proof is one of the areas where the Human Rights Act 1998 has had a significant impact. The basic approach of the law will be explained and then we will look at the effect of the Act.

2.4.1 Who has the burden of proof?

It is fundamental to a criminal trial that the prosecution must prove its case: a person, however clear the evidence seems to be, is innocent until proved guilty (*Woolmington** [1935] AC 462). The prosecution has to prove its case beyond reasonable doubt, and the judge must direct the jury that they are not to convict unless they are convinced that all the elements of the offence were present. The phrase 'beyond reasonable doubt' is the conventional way of expressing the idea that the jury must feel sure of the accused's guilt. It is stronger than the standard of proof in a civil case, such as an action for negligence, which only requires 'proof on the balance of probabilities': a conclusion that the plaintiff's version of events is more probable than not. It is therefore quite possible for the jury in a criminal case to believe that a defendant probably committed the crime but still acquit her if they have some doubts over her guilt. In such a case the accused may be not guilty of a criminal offence, but be liable to pay damages in a civil case.

The judge cannot direct a conviction, because only the jury can find the facts and apply the law to those facts. However, it may be appropriate for the judge to say, 'If you find the facts to be this then you should acquit, but if you find the facts to be that you should convict'. The judge can direct an acquittal: it is sometimes the judge's duty to tell the jury that there is not, as a matter of law, enough evidence to justify a conviction, even if the jury were to believe every word of the prosecution evidence. This is sometimes explained by saying that the prosecution has both an evidential burden – to produce enough evidence to justify leaving the case to the jury – and a burden of proof – to prove the case beyond reasonable doubt. The evidential burden is to satisfy the judge; the burden of proof is to satisfy the jury.

Do these two burdens always rest on the prosecution, or do they sometimes rest on the defence? It is very important to remember the principle already stated: at the end of the trial, the prosecution must prove all the elements of the offence in order to obtain a conviction. However, this does not mean that the prosecution has to disprove every single defence on which an accused may possibly rely, such as lack of intention or knowledge, self-defence, loss of control, drunkenness, duress and so on. If such a defence is raised on the facts as presented by the prosecution, the judge will direct the jury on the law relating to the defence in question. If the defence is not revealed by the prosecution's evidence, the accused has a burden of producing sufficient evidence of the defence to justify leaving it to the jury, and if he does not the judge will refuse to let the jury consider it. This is an evidential burden only: the accused does not have to prove the defence. What amounts to sufficient evidence will depend on the nature of the defence. If the accused denies the knowledge or intention required for the offence, his own evidence will be enough to put to the jury. But in the case of automatism, for example, where the accused claims that he was not in control of his actions, the courts have looked for medical evidence to back up the accused's own testimony (see Section 3.5). If he fails to produce any evidence in his defence, he puts himself at risk of conviction by making the prosecution's burden of proof easier to discharge. If the judge puts the defence to the jury, the prosecution then has the burden of disproving that defence in order to obtain a conviction. Exceptionally a statute requires the defendant to prove the existence of a defence. We will discuss shortly how when a statute does so it can be challenged as incompatible with the accused's human rights. In all cases where there is a burden of proof on the accused, the standard of proof required is lower than that required for the prosecution: it is proof on the balance of probabilities, rather than beyond reasonable doubt.

Let us apply these principles to an example. Jack is charged with the murder of Jill and pleads not guilty. The prosecution has to prove the elements of murder: that Jack caused the death of Jill, and that he either intended to kill her or at least intended to cause her serious injury. The prosecution produces evidence that Jack shot Jill with a revolver at a range of four yards. This may include evidence of witnesses who saw the incident, and forensic evidence, such as that the bullet found in Jill's body carries markings consistent with having been fired from the revolver owned by Jack. The prosecution also needs evidence that the shot caused the death of Jill, and this will be medical evidence from the post-mortem.

Then the prosecution needs evidence of Jack's state of mind: that Jack intended to kill or seriously injure Jill. The prosecution may rely on Jack's conduct (it is alleged that he shot Jill at close range, and so the jury may be invited to infer that the only believable explanation for his conduct was that he intended to kill her) or his words at the time. There may be other circumstantial evidence, such as evidence of motive (for example, Jack was due to receive a large inheritance from Jill).

At the close of the prosecution case, the accused can submit that there is 'no case to answer', which is a claim that the prosecution has not satisfied the evidential burden. The judge must decide whether all this evidence amounts to a case against Jack, in other words whether there are sufficient grounds for a conviction if the evidence is believed and not denied. If the case is tenable, then the judge will let it continue: she will not direct an acquittal, as the prosecution will have satisfied the evidential burden. Faced with a 'case to answer', Jack has a choice. He can refuse to defend himself at all, and not produce any alternative explanation of the prosecution's evidence. This is possible, but it is scarcely consistent with a plea of not guilty, and it is likely to mean a conviction because the jury have no reason to doubt the prosecution evidence. A conviction is not inevitable, because the jury are not under an obligation to believe an unchallenged prosecution case and may think that there is still a reasonable doubt over Jack's guilt.

Jack can challenge the prosecution evidence that he shot Jill, or that the shot caused the death, or that he intended Jill any harm (or all of these). Or Jack may accept all these facts, and rely on a defence: a claim that his act was justified because he was acting in self-defence, or that it was excusable because Jill had provoked him so that he lost his self-control. He will have to produce evidence, including his own testimony, to support his assertions. This is his evidential burden, and if he does not produce any evidence (and no such evidence is raised on the agreed facts) the judge will not put that defence to the jury. If the defence goes to the jury, the prosecution, in addition to proving the elements of murder already stated, must disprove the defence (for example, that Jack was acting in self-defence). If Jack pleads either insanity or diminished responsibility, he will have to prove it, according to the legal definition of the defence.

At the end of the defence case, the judge will sum up to the jury, telling them the elements of the offence which the prosecution must prove, and summarising the evidence. The judge will point the jury towards the issues in the case, the areas of dispute between the prosecution and the accused, and explain the burden of proof. The jury will then determine the facts (what happened?), apply the law to them (is this murder?) and reach a verdict.

As indicated earlier, in those exceptional circumstances in which a defendant is under a burden of proof in relation to a defence there may be a claim that that infringes his human rights. We must now consider this argument in more detail.

2.4.2 The Human Rights Act and the burden of proof in criminal trials

Is it permissible under the European Convention to place the burden of establishing a defence on the defendant (*Lingens and Leitgens v Austria* (1986) 8 EHRR 407)? There is an argument that 'reverse onus of proof clauses' which place a burden on a defendant to establish his innocence infringe Article 6(2) of the European Convention, which appears to state that the presumption of innocence is an absolute right. In *Salabiaku v France* (1988) 13 EHRR 379 the European Court of Human Rights considered presumptions of fact, where the burden lay on a defendant to rebut a presumption. It explained:

> Article 6(2) does not therefore regard presumptions of fact or of law provided for in the criminal law with indifference. It requires States to confine them within reasonable limits which take into account the importance of what is at stake and maintain the rights of the defence.

In other words the European Court suggested that placing a burden of proof on the defendant may be permissible, but the state would need to demonstrate that to do so is necessary given the gravity of the issues involved.

A leading case is *R v DPP, ex p Kebilene** [2000] 2 AC 326, which concerned s 16A Prevention of Terrorism (Temporary Provisions) Act 1989. The House of Lords stressed that it was important to distinguish between evidential burdens (where the defendant must raise a reasonable doubt by putting a point in issue and the prosecution must disprove the defence) and legal (or persuasive) burdens (where the defendant must prove the existence of the defence on the balance of probabilities). The House of Lords suggested that an evidential burden will not infringe the Human Rights Act, while a legal burden might. Lord Hope suggested that in considering whether a persuasive burden infringed the Convention the court should consider three questions:

1. What does the prosecution have to prove in order to transfer the onus?
2. What is the burden on the accused – does it relate to something which is likely to be difficult for him to prove or does it relate to something which is readily in his knowledge or to which he readily has access?
3. What is the nature of the threat faced by society which the provision is designed to combat?

After considering these three issues, the court can decide whether the presumption is within 'reasonable limits'. This indicates that legal burdens will infringe the Convention unless they can be justified on the grounds that they are necessary for the protection of the public and/or that they will be very easy for the defendant to meet. In *Lambert** [2001] 3 WLR 206 Lord Steyn explained that when considering whether a statute imposed a legal burden on the defendant:

> The principle of proportionality requires the House to consider whether there was a pressing necessity to impose a legal rather than evidential burden on the accused.

So, the state must demonstrate that the pressing social need will not be met by placing an evidential burden and requires a legal burden of proof (see *L v DPP** [2002] Crim LR 320 for an example of a pressing social need). The more serious the offence, the harder it will be to justify imposing a legal burden of proof.

To justify a legal burden of proof it must be shown that it is reasonable and proportionate (*Sheldrake** [2005] 1 AC 246). Lord Bingham in *Sheldrake* stated that in deciding whether it meets these criteria the court should consider:

> the opportunity given to the defendant to rebut the presumption, retention by the court of a power to assess the evidence, the importance of what is at stake and the difficulty which a prosecutor may face in the absence of a presumption.

Lord Nicholls in *Johnstone** emphasised the relevance of the ease for the defendant of rebutting the presumption. If the defendant has a prohibited article and is claiming he has a licence or lawful permission to do so, then to require him to produce his licence or justify his lawful permission is far easier for him than it is for the prosecution to show he does not have a licence or permission (*L v DPP, DPP v Barker* [2006] Crim LR 140). The courts have also emphasised that it is unlikely to be permissible to place a burden of proof on the defendant in relation to what is an essential element of the offence. It is more likely to be acceptable where the burden relates to what is in essence a defence or a peripheral aspect of the *actus reus* (*Johnstone*). In *A-G's Ref (No 4 of 2002)* [2001] Crim LR 578 (which was heard along with *Sheldrake*) the defendant was charged with belonging to a proscribed terrorist organisation. He had a defence if he could prove that he had joined the organisation before it became proscribed and had not been actively involved in it since it had become proscribed. The majority of their Lordships took the view that it was essential to the wrong which was at the heart of the offence that the defendant had known that the organisation was proscribed when he joined it or was actively involved in it. It was possible that an innocent person could fall within the definition of the offence and would need to prove his or her innocence. Placing the legal burden on the defendant was therefore impermissible.

2.5 Classification of offences

The basic distinction when classifying criminal offences is among those which are tried on indictment, those which are tried summarily and those which can be tried either way. In the first group are the more serious offences, such as murder, manslaughter and rape. They are tried before a judge and jury in a Crown Court. Relatively minor offences, such as many motoring offences, are in the second group, and these are tried before magistrates, who have limited sentencing powers. In the third group are those offences, such as theft, which may vary considerably in their seriousness according to circumstances. They may be tried either way, and the choice is made in the magistrates' court. Either the magistrates or the accused may insist on trial on indictment; only if both agree will the case be tried summarily. For the magistrates, the choice will depend on the seriousness of the charge, as indicated by the prosecution statements, and whether the case seems likely to raise a difficult question of law which a judge would be better able to decide than lay magistrates. For the accused, the choice will depend on many factors: summary trial is faster and cheaper (this may be important if the accused is ordered to make a contribution to legal aid); the Crown Court can impose heavier sentences, although the magistrates can, if they convict, decide to commit the offender for sentence to the Crown Court; and magistrates have a reputation of being more likely to convict, especially if the defence relies on challenging police evidence. The rules of procedure applicable to the two forms of trial are different, the sentencing powers differ, as do the rights of appeal, but the definition of the offence (with which this book is concerned) does not change according to whether the accused is tried in the Crown Court or the magistrates' court.

2.6 Punishment

Theories of punishment are more relevant in discussing sentencing than in discussing the definition of criminal offences, and we are not going to discuss sentencing in any detail in this book. However, the definition of an offence and its punishment are linked. There would be little point in finding defendants guilty who were thought unsuitable for punishment. The main theories of why the state should punish criminals are well known and discussed in detail in many books on criminology and sentencing, but they can be summarised briefly. One theory is reformation – that the goal of punishment should be to reform the criminal so that he will not commit a crime again. Another is deterrence – that the criminal himself and other potential criminals will be discouraged from committing a crime through fear of punishment. A further theory is incapacitation – that the criminal should be prevented from committing a crime, typically by imprisonment. The dominant theory at present appears to be 'just deserts', or retribution. This theory is that defendants should be punished in proportion to their blameworthiness. At different times in penal history one or other of these theories has held sway, and no doubt all four are factors weighing on a sentencer's mind, even though they are to some extent conflicting.

2.7 The proposals for a Criminal Code

Some countries have a Code of Criminal Law, that is a single statute which sets out the definitions of each offence and defence. Increasingly there have been calls for England and Wales to have such a Code. The Law Commission has been working on a Criminal Code for over two decades. It produced its first draft Code in 1985 and recently started to produce short draft bills to deal with specific topics. As yet none of these Law Commission draft bills have been enacted. In 2008 the Law Commission announced that it had abandoned the project of producing a Criminal Code. Perhaps it had become clear that Parliament did not have the time or inclination to undertake a complete overhaul of the criminal law.

If the Law Commission's proposals for a Code were ever enacted they would signify a radical change in the nature of our criminal law. It would lead to a movement away from the primarily case law-based system to a statute-based system. The Code would be a single statute which would aim to set out the entire criminal law.

Supporters of a Code claim it would promote accessibility, comprehensibility, consistency and certainty. One aim of the Code is to summarise the law in a single document written in simple language. The law would therefore be easier to ascertain, not only for citizens but also for lawyers and the judiciary.

Critics of a Code are concerned that a Code may become obsessed with guiding principles and internal consistency and overlook the fact that apparent contradictions within the criminal law may reflect the complexity of the many political, ethical and practical issues involved. Sometimes seemingly 'logically contradictory' rules may in fact reflect the best compromise between these competing values in particular circumstances. Another argument is that it is easy to overstress the benefits of a Code and that any advantages will be minimal. Inevitably the Code will need to be interpreted by the judiciary, and it is suggested by some that a whole new body of case law would soon build up around the Criminal Code and so defeat the Code's aims of accessibility and comprehensiveness. Also, one might think that members of the public will not be quick to purchase and read copies of any new Code, and so perhaps making the Code comprehensible to a lay person should not be high on the list of priorities. That said, there is still a strong argument that if a citizen does decide to try to find out what the criminal law is, the task should not be made unduly difficult.

Hot Topic – Judges, juries and 'rape myths'

There is widespread concern at the low conviction rates in rape trials. In only 6.5 per cent of rape cases is there a conviction. There are no doubt many reasons for this. One explanation is that the jury are too prone to believe so-called rape myths (Ellison and Munro). These myths are said to include the following:

- If a woman is wearing a short skirt she is keen to have sex.
- A genuine victim will report rape quickly.
- False allegations of rape are common.
- A real rape victim will put up a struggle.
- A woman who gets drunk has only herself to blame for rape.

A survey by Amnesty International found that 30 per cent of people believed that if a woman had behaved flirtatiously she was partly or completely responsible for a rape and 26 per cent thought the same if she wore revealing clothing or had been drunk. Astonishingly, 6 per cent thought a woman wearing revealing clothing was totally responsible if she was raped, and 8 per cent that a woman who was known to have had several sexual partners was again totally responsible. If these are widely held perceptions and they are incorrect should a judge warn a jury against them? Indeed directions from the Judicial Studies Board now direct the judge to address popular misconceptions if they are relevant to the trial.

But it might be argued that there is a difficulty here in balancing the roles of the judge and jury. If the jury are meant to be representatives of the general public and the general public have certain prejudices or misconceptions then should they not be reflected in the way the law operates? Or do we not, in fact, want the jury to represent the public, but rather 'a section of the public with good values'?

In response it can be said that we cannot accept a legal system where judgments are made on demonstrably false assumptions of facts. The judge needs to ensure that the jury rely on facts not myths, and this, in some cases, requires the judge to correct popular misconceptions. That seems convincing in this case, but how far should this be taken? Should the jury be told not to make assumptions about the defendant based on his accent, mode of dress or appearance? Juries often have to make decisions about whether a person is lying or not; that is probably often done on assumptions which may not have much basis in science.

Opponents of judicial guidance on these matters are concerned that juries may attach too much weight to the judge's statements. For example, if the judge were to tell the jury that it is very rare that women make false allegations of rape, this would be true, but would it sway the trial against the defendant? The difficulty is that it would make the trial unfair for the victim if this is not said and the jury made their decisions based on the myth that women often falsely allege rape.

One solution might be for experts (perhaps psychologists or doctors) to give evidence about the experience of rape. But would that be any fairer? It might at least avoid the appearance of the judge swaying the decision of the jury.

As this discussion shows, the exact balance of power between the jury and judge raises some very important issues.

Summary

2.1 Crimes, besides often having human victims, are wrongs against the state – infringements rendering the offender liable to be punished. Proceedings against the accused are brought in the name of the Crown, on behalf of the state.

2.2 Much criminal law is still common law, although there are also important statutes. Some academic writers have been very critical of the way in which the courts have developed aspects of the criminal law, including their interpretation of statutes.

2.3 In a criminal trial the judge decides questions of law and directs the jury on the law. The jury decide questions of fact, and apply the law to the facts. In a magistrates' court, the magistrates perform both functions. Some questions of fact are subjective and some are

Summary cont'd

objective. Judges frequently leave words and concepts which have not already been defined in a statute or case law to the jury to interpret as to their ordinary meaning.

2.4 The burden of proof is on the prosecution, which has to satisfy the jury beyond reasonable doubt of all the elements of an offence. The prosecution has to produce sufficient evidence for the judge to leave the case to the jury; if the prosecution does not do this, the judge will direct an acquittal. The accused does not have to prove his innocence, but does have to produce evidence of a defence on which he wishes to rely. Where a statute imposes a legal burden of proof on an accused this may be contrary to the European Convention on Human Rights unless the state can demonstrate a compelling reason for doing so.

2.5 Offences may be tried on indictment before a judge and jury, tried summarily before magistrates or tried either way. There is also a distinction between arrestable and non-arrestable offences, which affects the powers of arrest given to police officers and ordinary citizens.

2.6 There are various theories of punishment, including deterrence, reformation, incapacitation and 'just deserts'. 'Just deserts' is the dominant theory at present but the others often influence a sentencer.

2.7 A Criminal Code has been drafted, which would describe in one document all the criminal offences. However, the government has indicated it will not make it law.

Further Reading

Ashworth (2005) provides an excellent discussion of the law on criminal procedure. The role played by a judge is described by Ashworth (1991). Ashworth and Blake, Dennis, Ellison and Munro, and Roberts discuss burdens of proof and the presumption of innocence. The Criminal Code is examined in de Búrca and Gardner, and Glazebrook.

Ashworth, 'Interpreting Criminal Statutes: A Case of Legality' (1991) 107 LQR 419.
Ashworth, *The Criminal Process* (Oxford University Press 2005).
Ashworth and Blake, 'The Presumption of Innocence in English Criminal Law' [1997] Crim LR 306.
de Búrca and Gardner, 'The Codification of the Criminal Law' (1990) 10 OJLS 559.
Dennis, 'Reverse Onuses and the Presumption of Innocence: In Search of Principle' [2005] Crim LR 901.
Ellison and Munro, 'Reacting to Rape: Exploring Mock Jurors' Assessments of Complainant Credibility' (2009) 18 *Brit J Criminol* 291.
Glazebrook, 'Structuring the Criminal Code', in Simester and Smith (eds), *Harm and Culpability* (Oxford University Press 1996).
Roberts, 'Taking the Burden of Proof Seriously' [1995] Crim LR 783.

Case Notes

▶ *Caldwell* [1982] AC 341. House of Lords

See Chapter 5 Case notes.

▶ *R v G* [2004] Crim LR 369. House of Lords

See Chapter 5 Case notes.

▶ *Johnstone* [2004] Crim LR 244. House of Lords

The respondent was charged with a variety of offences under s 92 Trade Marks Act 1994, including applying to goods or their packaging a sign identical to, or likely to be mistaken for, a registered trade mark with a view to gain and without the consent of the proprietor. He sought to rely on a defence under s 11(2)(b) that the registered trade marks were not infringed because the use of the performer's name on the discs was an indication of the performer, not of trade origin. The Court of Appeal and House of Lords agreed that this defence should have been left to the jury. Their Lordships also discussed s 92(5), which provided a defence where the defendant did not believe that his or her use infringed the trade mark or was unaware of the trade mark. However, there was a legal burden of proof on the defendant to establish such a belief. The House of Lords held (*obiter*) that this burden of proof was not incompatible with Article 6 of the European Convention on Human Rights. In the light of the public interest in combating piracy and the ease with which the defendant can raise an issue about honesty there was a compelling reason to justify the burden being placed on the defendant.

▶ *L v DPP* [2002] Crim LR 320. Divisional Court

The defendant was seen by a police officer throwing a lock-knife behind a wall and was charged with having a lock-knife contrary to s 139 Criminal Justice Act 1988. Sub-section (4) of that section provided a defence to a person who could prove that he had good reason or lawful authority for having the article with him. The district judge held that this legal burden of proof on the defendant was not contrary to Article 6 of the European Convention on Human Rights. The Divisional Court agreed. Applying *Lambert* it was confirmed that the burden lay on the state to provide a compelling reason to justify putting such a legal burden of proof on the defendant. Such reasons existed here because there was a strong public interest in preventing people carrying bladed instruments in public, and what he was required to prove (the good reason or lawful authority) was within his knowledge.

▶ *Lamb* [1967] 2 QB 981. Court of Appeal

See Chapter 10 Case notes.

▶ *Lambert* [2001] 3 WLR 206. House of Lords

The appellant was charged with possession of a controlled drug with intent to supply contrary to s 5(3) Misuse of Drugs Act 1971. The appellant accepted that he was in possession of a bag which contained a controlled drug. However, at trial he relied on the defence under s 28 of the Act that he had neither known nor had reason to suspect the nature of the contents of the bag. He appealed against his conviction on the basis that having to establish his defence on the grounds of the balance of probability, rather than just being required to introduce evidence of his belief, contravened the presumption of innocence guaranteed by Article 6(2) of the European Convention. The House of Lords held that the Human Rights Act could be used to quash a conviction made before the Act came into effect, which was the case here. Nevertheless their Lordships went on to hold that the correct interpretation (bearing in mind the Human Rights Act) of s 28 was that it required the defendant to produce evidence only of his belief; it did not require him to establish it beyond reasonable doubt. Still, his conviction was upheld on the basis that even if the jury had been correctly directed, they would inevitably have convicted him.

▶ *Majewski* [1977] AC 443. House of Lords

See Chapter 15 Case notes.

▶ *R v DPP ex p Kebilene* [2000] 2 AC 326

The applicants were arrested for the offence of possession of items for the purposes of committing terrorism abroad, contrary to s 16A Prevention of Terrorism (Temporary Provisions) Act 1989. They sought to challenge the decision of the Director of Public Prosecutions to allow proceedings to be brought against them. Their argument was that the prosecution infringed their rights under the Human Rights Act as it breached their rights under Article 6 of the European Convention. Their Lordships held that except in cases of bad faith or illegality, it would not be possible to challenge the decision of the DPP to prosecute. *Obiter*, Lord Hope acknowledged that 'persuasive burdens' could fall foul of Article 6 unless required for the protection of the public.

▶ *Sheldrake v DPP* [2004] UKHL 43

Two cases were heard before the House of Lords. The first concerned Sheldrake, who was convicted of being in charge of a car while over the blood-alcohol limit contrary to s 5(1) Road Traffic Act 1998. Section 5(2) provided him with a defence if he could prove on the balance of probabilities that there was no likelihood of him driving. He sought to raise the defence but failed to prove it, and so he was convicted. He appealed on the basis that s 5(2) created an improper reverse onus of proof. The House of Lords found that although it imposed a legal burden of proof on the defendant it was reasonable in doing so. There was a legitimate aim: to prevent death or injury caused by unfit drivers. Further, the issue of whether he planned to drive was within his own knowledge and it would have been very difficult for the prosecutor to prove that he did intend to drive.

In the second case the defendant (D) was convicted of an offence under s 11 Terrorism Act 2000 of being a member of a proscribed terrorist organisation. He sought to rely on the defence in s 11(2) that at the time he became a member, the organisation was not proscribed, and that he had not taken part in the organisation's activities since it had been proscribed. The House of Lords accepted that s 11(2) did impose a legal burden on the defendant but held that the burden was not proportionate or justifiable. Key to their Lordships' reasoning was the fact that what the prosecution had to prove (that he had at some time joined an organisation) was not necessarily criminal when he did the act. In

other words the defendant was being asked to prove a matter which was an essential element of the offence.

▶ *Woolmington* [1935] AC 462. House of Lords

The appellant was convicted of murder, having shot his wife. His wife had left him a short time after their marriage, and he went to see her, taking a shotgun with him. He claimed that he had intended to tell her that he would shoot himself if she would not return, and the gun went off accidentally, killing her. At the trial, the judge directed the jury that once it was proved by the prosecution that the accused had killed his wife, the shooting was presumed to be murder unless the accused could satisfy the jury that the killing was accidental, or justified, or should be manslaughter rather than murder. His appeal was dismissed by the Court of Appeal, but allowed by the House of Lords. Viscount Sankey, the Lord Chancellor, said that the trial judge's direction had been based on a book by Foster, written in 1762, and not on any earlier case law authority. If the judge were able to rule that the burden of proof in a case had shifted to the accused to prove that he was not guilty, that would be making the judge decide the case and not the jury. The accused is entitled to the benefit of any doubt: 'while the prosecution must prove the guilt of the prisoner, there is no such burden laid on the prisoner to prove his innocence, and it is sufficient for him to raise a doubt as to his guilt; he is not bound to satisfy the jury of his innocence. Throughout the web of the English criminal law one golden thread is always to be seen – that it is the duty of the prosecution to prove the prisoner's guilt subject to what I have already said as to the defence of insanity and subject also to any statutory exception.'

Chapter 3

The external elements

Key Terms

▶ **Actus reus** – those parts of the definition of an offence which do not relate to the defendant's state of mind.
▶ **Omission** – the absence of an act.
▶ **Voluntariness** – the ability of the defendant to control his or her actions.

3.1 The elements of a criminal offence

We must now examine some of the basic building blocks which make up the hundreds of different criminal offences. A criminal lawyer often approaches the analysis of an offence by separating its component parts into the 'external elements' (for example, the acts of the accused), called the *actus reus*, and the 'mental elements' (for example, the defendant's intention), called the *mens rea*. These Latin phrases, taken from a sentence in Coke's Institutes (written in the seventeenth century), can be misleading, as we shall see, and have been criticised by academic writers and judges. Lord Diplock stated that he preferred to speak of 'the conduct of the accused and his state of mind at the time of that conduct', rather than use the Latin terminology (*Miller** [1983] 2 AC 161). However, these phrases are still so widely used by the courts and in writing on the criminal law that they make a sensible starting point.

Coke in his Institutes said that *actus non facit reum, nisi mens sit rea* (an act does not make a person guilty of a crime unless the mind is also guilty). The principle embodied in this phrase can be traced back to the laws of Henry I in the twelfth century. As a general rule in English law, for a person to be liable for a criminal offence he must have brought about a certain prohibited state of affairs by his conduct, and this must be accompanied by a certain state of mind. This general rule has to be qualified: some crimes do not require any particular state of mind. These are crimes of strict liability and we will consider them further in Chapter 6. In other crimes, a particular state of mind (or *mens rea*) is required in respect of some elements of the *actus reus*, but not for others. In other cases, the conduct of the accused may extend over a considerable period of time, and it may not be necessary to prove that the accused had the specified *mens rea* throughout that period (see Section 5.7).

These are all qualifications to the general rule that the external elements (the *actus reus*) of the offence must be accompanied by a particular state of mind. What about the need for the external elements themselves? Are they essential? The position taken by English law is that an evil state of mind is not by itself criminal: it must have manifested itself in some conduct in order to attract liability. However wicked the defendant's thoughts, unless she acts to put them into effect she will not have committed a crime. Professor Glanville Williams has said that 'the law governs conduct, not purity of intention'. Even in crimes where no direct harm is caused, for example an attempted crime, some conduct is required. Lord Hailsham said in *Haughton v Smith* [1975] AC 476 that there is a 'distinction between the intention to commit a crime and an attempt to commit it.

In addition to the intention, or *mens rea*, there must be an overt act.' There are a few exceptional cases where this principle appears to be absent (for example, *Larsonneur** (1933) 97 JP 206), but it remains a general rule of English criminal law.

3.2 Different aspects of the *actus reus*

The *actus reus*, or external elements, will very often involve activity on the part of the accused, such as an assault, an act of appropriation of property (in theft) or entry into a building (in burglary). However, the *actus reus* of an offence is not solely a question of conduct by the accused. It can include a state of affairs, consequences caused by the act of the defendant or circumstances in which the defendant acts. This requires further explanation.

The term *actus reus* can include a state of affairs for which the accused is responsible, such as having an offensive weapon in a public place (s 1 Prevention of Crime Act 1953) or being in possession of a controlled drug (s 5 Misuse of Drugs Act 1971), permitting the smoking of cannabis on premises of which the accused is the occupier (s 8 of the same statute) or even being in the neighbourhood of a prohibited place in certain circumstances (s 1 Official Secrets Act 1911). In some cases the *actus reus* can also include a failure to act or an omission by the accused (see Section 3.3).

In some crimes something more than conduct or a state of affairs is required: the accused must have produced a particular prohibited result or consequence. In murder, the death of the victim must result from the defendant's acts; in the case of criminal damage, property must be destroyed or damaged; in s 18 Offences Against the Person Act 1861 the accused must either wound or cause grievous bodily harm to the victim. The result is just as much part of the *actus reus* as the conduct of the accused, and in its absence the *actus reus* will be incomplete (though the defendant may well be guilty of an attempt to commit the crime).

Yet another aspect of the *actus reus* is found in relevant circumstances attached to the prohibited conduct or result. Sexual intercourse is rape only if performed without the consent of the victim. The appropriation of property is theft only if the property belongs to another.

Although for simplicity we have been referring to the *actus reus* or *mens rea* (or the 'external elements' and the 'mental elements' within an offence), it is often difficult to separate them in this simple way. The *actus reus* itself may contain a mental element: that of the victim. In rape, for example, the victim's lack of consent is part of the *actus reus* as a required circumstance. We can take this further: in some cases it is impossible to distinguish the purely physical or external from the state of mind of the accused himself. For example, a person commits aggravated burglary if he commits a burglary while having with him any weapon of offence (s 10 Theft Act 1968); the term 'weapon of offence' is then defined to include any article intended by the person having it with him to cause injury to another person. Here, the definition of a term within the *actus reus* ('a weapon') depends on the state of mind of the accused (what the defendant intended to do with the item). Indeed, as we have already seen, the *actus reus* may consist of being in possession of something, such as a controlled drug. In such cases, the very notion of being in possession has been held to involve a mental element: the accused must know of the existence of a thing in order for it to be in his possession, although he need not know of its qualities (*Warner v MPC** [1969] 2 AC 256). Thus the defendant's mental state can turn what would otherwise be an innocent act into the *actus reus* of a crime. These examples reveal that a sharp distinction between the *actus reus* and *mens rea* of each offence cannot always be made. Despite this, the distinction is still a popular way of analysing offences.

3.3 Liability for omissions

As a general rule criminal liability does not attach to omissions. So if you see a blind man about to walk over the edge of a cliff but do not shout a warning you will not have committed a crime if he falls over the cliff. This is so even if it would have been easy for you to shout out and even if you deliberately refrained from issuing a warning in the hope that he might fall over the edge. However, this general rule is subject to an important exception. You can be guilty of omission if you are under a legal duty to act. The circumstances in which you have a legal duty to intervene will now be considered.

3.3.1 When there is a duty to act

There are four particular circumstances in which the duty will arise, although it appears open to the courts to find novel situations in which to impose a duty to act.

1. *Statutory duties.* Some of these are express: the statute explicitly imposes liability for a failure to act. For example, under s 7(4) Road Traffic Act 1972, it is a criminal offence to fail to supply a specimen of breath when required to do so in certain specified circumstances by a constable in uniform. Parliament recently created an offence under s 5 Domestic Violence, Crimes and Victims Act 2004 of failing to protect a child or vulnerable adult from a risk of death at the hands of a person living with them (*Khan* [2009] EWCA Crim 2). In other cases, the courts have interpreted particular words in the definition of an offence in such a way that they may be applied to a failure to act, for example 'assisting in the retention' of stolen goods in s 22(1) Theft Act 1968 (*Pitchley** (1972) 57 Cr App Rep 30).
2. *Contractual duties.* A duty to act may arise as the result of a contractual obligation. One example is *Pittwood* (1902) 19 TLR 37, where a railway-crossing keeper's failure to close the crossing gate in breach of his contract of employment led to a conviction for manslaughter after a person was killed when a train hit a hay cart. So, in the hypothetical situation posed at the start of this section, if you were employed as the nurse of the blind man to look after him, you would be under a contractual duty to care for him and so could be convicted of an offence for failing to warn him of the danger.
3. *Assumption of responsibility.* A duty to act arises in cases where the defendant has assumed responsibility for the wellbeing of the victim. This may be inferred from a blood relationship (parent and child, for example (*Evans** [2009] EWCA Crim 650)), but may also be inferred where the accused has undertaken to care for another person. In *Instan*, the accused lived with her infirm and elderly aunt; it was found that her neglect of her aunt had accelerated the latter's death and she was liable for manslaughter. In *Stone and Dobinson** [1977] 1 QB 354, the victim came to live with her brother (Stone) and Dobinson (Stone's cohabitee). According to the Court of Appeal, the jury were entitled to conclude that both defendants

had assumed a duty to care for the victim on the ground that she was living in their house, and that they had made inadequate efforts to care for her. The fact that the victim was 'helplessly infirm' was also relevant: the jury 'were entitled to conclude that once [the victim] became helplessly infirm, as she had by 19 July, the appellants were, in the circumstances, obliged either to summon help or else to care for [her] themselves'. The two were convicted of manslaughter and the Court of Appeal dismissed their appeals against the verdict. The decision in *Stone and Dobinson* has been heavily criticised and was described by the House of Lords in *Airedale National Health Service Trust v Bland* [1993] AC 789 as 'troubling'. This was because the defendants were themselves suffering from learning difficulties and indeed had enough difficulties looking after themselves, let alone anyone else.

4. *Creation of danger.* A fourth circumstance in which the court has found a duty to act is where the defendant has created a dangerous situation and then failed to prevent a harm occurring as a result. The case of *Miller* [1983] 2 AC 161 illustrates this. The accused was sleeping as a vagrant in an unoccupied house. He fell asleep on a mattress while smoking a cigarette, and the cigarette set light to the mattress. He woke up to find the mattress alight, but did nothing to put out the fire, merely moving into another room of the house. As a consequence, the house itself caught fire and considerable damage was caused. Miller was charged with arson, contrary to s 1(1) and (3) Criminal Damage Act 1971. The trial judge ruled that, even though he started the fire unintentionally, Miller came under a duty to take some action to put it out once he became aware of its existence. Lord Diplock, in the House of Lords, agreed that in these circumstances a duty to act could be implied. The duty arises out of the creation (albeit unintentional) of a dangerous situation, that is a situation likely to cause damage. Lord Diplock stated that the *actus reus* of criminal damage might legitimately include 'conduct which consists of failing to take measures that lie within one's power to counteract a danger that one has oneself created'. Another example of this principle in practice is *DPP v Santana-Bermudez* [2004] Crim CR 471, where the defendant put hypodermic needles in his pockets. A police officer later approached him, said she was going to conduct a search and asked whether he had any sharp objects. When he said 'no' she searched him and was injured by a needle. The Divisional Court upheld his conviction of an assault occasioning actual bodily harm, even though he had done no act which directly caused an injury, because he had exposed the police officer to a risk and had failed to warn her of it.

   In *Evans* the defendant gave her younger 16-year-old sister heroin. The sister took it and collapsed. The defendant failed to summon help for her and this was said to breach the duty of care that arose from creating a dangerous situation. Notably in this case the actual danger came as a result of the victim's decision to inject herself. The duty of care arose because the defendant contributed to the danger, even though she was not the sole cause of it.

5. *Other cases. Miller* indicates that the courts may be willing to find novel situations in which there is a duty to act. Another example is *Speck* (1977) 65 Cr App R 151, where a girl put her hand on a man's trousers. He allowed her to leave her hand there and was convicted of indecent assault (an offence which has since been abolished). In effect the law found that he was under a duty to remove her hand and that his failure to do so could be classified as an assault.

3.3.2 The consequences of being under a duty to act

Once it is found that the defendant is under a duty to act then he must act in a reasonable way. The jury will simply ask themselves 'is how the defendant acted a way in which a reasonable person in her position might have acted?' If not, the defendant will have breached her duty. Acting as a reasonable person may involve rescuing the victim or summoning help (*Khan* (2009)). If the defendant owes a duty to act because of his contract of employment he must act in accordance with that contractual duty. That may involve performing acts which would not be expected of a reasonable person. For example if Bob decides to swim across the English Channel and hires Ken to be his lifeguard in a boat following his adventure and Bob gets into trouble, Ken will be required to rescue him, even if the dangerous seas mean that an ordinary passer-by would not be expected to do so.

3.3.3 Distinguishing omissions and acts

In other cases the law has not relied on the concept of duty, but interprets a situation which appears to concern an omission in fact to involve an act. Indeed Lord Diplock, in *Miller*, took the view that much of the apparent difficulty of fitting liability for omissions into the traditional analysis of the *actus reus* would disappear if a less rigid phrase, such as 'course of conduct', were used instead:

> it is the use of the expression 'actus reus' that is liable to mislead, since it suggests that some positive act on the part of the accused is needed to make him guilty of a crime and that a failure or omission to act is insufficient to give rise to criminal liability ... the habit of lawyers to talk of 'actus reus', suggestive as it is of action rather than inaction, is responsible for any erroneous notion that failure to act cannot give rise to criminal liability in English law.

In *Fagan** [1969] 1 QB 439 the accused, having accidentally driven a wheel of his car onto a policeman's foot, for some time refused to move the car when asked to do so. He was convicted of assaulting a police constable in the execution of his duty, and his conviction was upheld by the Divisional Court on the ground that there was a continuing act of assault being committed throughout the time the car was on the victim's foot. In fact May LJ in the Court of Appeal in *Miller* thought that *Miller* itself could be explained on this ground. He held that the whole of the accused's conduct, from the moment he lay on the mattress with the lighted cigarette until the time he left it smouldering, should be regarded as one act, forming part of the *actus reus* of criminal damage. As he had the *mens rea* at one point during the *actus reus* (when he woke up) he could be convicted. The House of Lords, while not rejecting the reasoning of the Court of Appeal, preferred the duty approach described above. Lord Diplock did not say why, except to say that he thought it easier to explain to juries.

3.4 The voluntary nature of the *actus reus*

We have already seen that occasionally the *actus reus* does not require proof of an act; for example, a state of affairs may be sufficient. However, if the *actus reus* does require action or conduct it is seen as a fundamental principle that such action must be willed or voluntary. This does not mean that the prosecution must show that the defendant has deliberately chosen to act in a particular way. Indeed a defendant rarely decides 'I will now move my right finger'; rather she thinks in terms of the consequences of her acts, for example 'I will now fire a gun'. So what the voluntariness requirement means is that the defendant can be guilty only if she was able to prevent herself from acting in the way she did. In other words, the defendant was capable of controlling her behaviour when she acted. It is for this reason that there is no criminal liability for 'accidental' behaviour, such as breaking property after tripping over or injuring someone after jumping when startled. Clearly in such cases there is no *mens rea*, but the law goes further and says that in such cases there is no *actus reus* either. The defendant is not just saying, 'I did not mean to do that' (a claim of having no *mens rea*) but 'I did not do that'. That is because such accidental or instinctive acts are not properly described as the defendant's acts: they are not done by the defendant but happen to her. In some cases it is important for a defendant to show that she did not commit the *actus reus* rather than simply showing when she did not have *mens rea*. For example, if she is charged with an offence of strict liability she has a defence if she can show she has not committed the *actus reus*, but not if she can show only that she had no *mens rea* (see Chapter 6). It is for these reasons that the case of *Larsonneur* (1933) 97 JP 206 is often criticised, on the ground that Ms Larsonneur was not acting voluntarily, and should not have been held to have been 'acting' at all.

More difficult cases of involuntary behaviour occur when the compulsion comes not from outside the accused, but from some internal physical or mental disturbance. For example, concussion can cause involuntary behaviour, as can an imbalance in insulin and blood-sugar levels in diabetics. Such involuntary behaviour has been labelled 'automatism' and will be discussed next.

3.5 Automatism

3.5.1 The definition of 'automatism'

'Automatism' was defined by Lord Denning in *Bratty v A-G for Northern Ireland** [1963] AC 386 as 'an act which is done by the muscles without any control by the mind such as a spasm, a reflex action, or a convulsion; or an act done by a person who is not conscious of what he is doing such as an act done whilst suffering from concussion or whilst sleepwalking'. The defence can be said to involve three elements:

1. There was a total destruction of voluntary control.
2. The condition was caused by an external factor.
3. The defendant was not responsible for his condition.

These elements will now be considered separately:

1. *Total destruction of voluntary control.* It is necessary to demonstrate 'a total destruction of voluntary control'. It is not sufficient to show that the accused had only impaired control over his acts (*A-G's Ref (No 2 of 1992)** [1994] QB 91). Nor is it enough simply to show that the accused did not control his actions or did not know what he was doing if he could have controlled his actions. What must be shown is that the defendant lost the ability to control his actions.
2. *The condition must be caused by an external factor.* There is a great difficulty in drawing the boundary between automatism and insanity. The essential distinction between them depends on whether the state of mind is caused by an external or an internal factor. If it is caused by the external factor (for example, a brick falling onto the defendant's head) then the defendant is an automaton; if an internal factor (for

example, an epileptic fit) then the defence will be insanity. The difficulty is due to the very outdated and inadequate concept of insanity still found in English criminal law (see Section 15.2.2).

So how can we distinguish between external and internal factors? It has been accepted that a diabetic who harms someone involuntarily as a result of hypoglycaemia caused by an excess of insulin injected as part of medical treatment for diabetes is not insane, but may be entitled to an acquittal on the ground of automatism. In *Quick** [1973] 1 QB 910 this was said to be because the excess of insulin was an 'external factor', comparable to concussion, rather than an internal factor. If, however, the diabetic fails to take insulin and suffers excess blood sugar (hyperglycaemia) this will be due to an internal factor and only insanity will be available (*Bingham* [1991] Crim LR 433). This demonstrates that the distinction requires some very fine lines to be drawn. Indeed although Lord Denning in *Bratty* mentioned sleepwalking as a form of automatism it has since been held that this was wrong, and that sleepwalking is in fact a form of insanity (*Burgess** [1991] 2 QB 92).

The distinction can produce some bizarre results. The distinction between external and internal factors was relied upon by the House of Lords in *Sullivan** [1984] 1 AC 156, a case involving epilepsy. Epilepsy was held to fall on the insanity side of the boundary because it was not a 'temporary impairment' resulting from 'some external physical factor', such as a blow on the head or the administration of a drug, but an internal malfunctioning. Of course no doctor would ever describe an epileptic as insane.

In a Canadian case (*Rabey* (1977) 79 DLR (3d) 414) a man killed his former girlfriend after she had left him. He tried to claim he was an automaton, arguing that he killed her in an unconscious state caused by an external factor, namely the break-up of the relationship. However, the court argued that 'the ordinary stresses and disappointments of life which are the common lot of mankind do not constitute an external cause'. The case could be explained on the ground that many people suffer the ending of a close relationship without acting in the way Rabey did, and so the cause of his involuntariness must be peculiar to him (an internal factor) rather than the break-up. *Rabey* has been said to reflect the law in England in *Hennessy* [1989] 1 WLR 287, where it was stated that 'stress anxiety and depression can no doubt be the result of the operation of external factors, but they are not...in themselves separately or together external factors of the kind capable in law of causing or contributing to a state of automatism. They constitute a state of mind, which is prone to reoccur.'

3. *The defendant is not responsible for his state of mind.* If the automatism is self-induced it will not excuse a person from criminal liability. This was the view of the Court of Appeal in *Quick* and again confirmed by the House of Lords in *Sullivan*. This is in line with the courts' attitude towards drink and drugs (see Section 15.4.2). So a diabetic who could be shown to have known the effect of taking too much insulin may be liable for any harmful consequences (see, for example, *Bailey** [1983] 1 WLR 760, where such knowledge was said to be capable of amounting to recklessness, and thus of supplying the *mens rea* of an assault). It is not clear whether the test to be used here is subjective or objective. For example, if a diabetic takes too much insulin and so has a fit and causes harm, is the question whether the defendant foresaw the consequences of taking the insulin or whether he should have foreseen the consequences? In one case the test was said to be subjective (*Bailey*), and in another

objective (*Quick*). Until we have a further case we will not know the answer. The general tendency in the criminal law in recent years has been to prefer subjective tests, and so it may be *Bailey* that is followed. However, it is clear that a state of automatism produced by illegal drugs or alcohol provides no defence, even if the accused was unaware of the effects that the drugs or alcohol would have (see Section 15.4.2).

3.5.2   The consequences of a finding of automatism

What, then, are the possible consequences for an accused who argues in her defence that her conduct was involuntary as the result of automatism? If there is evidence that the automatism was self-induced, then it will provide no defence, and the accused may well be convicted if she possesses the necessary *mens rea*. If the automatism is proved to be the result of legal insanity, then it will lead to the 'special verdict' of 'not guilty by reason of insanity' and detention in a mental hospital or whatever order the judge thinks appropriate (Criminal Procedure (Insanity and Unfitness to Plead) Act 1991). If the automatism is the result of external factors, then it will lead to a complete acquittal. With the uncertainty surrounding the boundary between insanity and automatism it is not surprising that automatism is not a common defence, and an accused may well prefer to change her plea to guilty and risk a prison sentence, rather than risk the stigma of insanity and possible detention in a mental hospital. This is what happened in the case of *Sullivan*, after a ruling by the trial judge that Sullivan's defence based on epilepsy amounted to a plea of insanity.

3.6   Accessorial liability

The criminal law punishes not only the person who completes the *actus reus* of an offence but also those who assist her. This topic will be discussed further in Chapter 17. But it is important to appreciate that those who aid, abet, counsel or procure a person who goes on to commit an offence are guilty of a crime.

Hot Topic –   Criminal liability for omissions

When Princess Diana was killed in a car crash in Paris there were allegations that some journalists coming across the accident had taken photographs, rather than summoned help. In France there is a law which requires you to provide or summon assistance for someone in peril, and investigations were undertaken to see whether the journalists could be prosecuted under that law. As already noted, in England and Wales we do not have such an 'easy rescue' or 'Good Samaritan' statute because of the principle that you are not normally criminally liable for omissions. But should the law change? Should we punish those who fail to provide help to those who are in peril?

The current law's approach to omissions is a compromise between various important competing values. On the one hand there is the need to preserve freedom of autonomy (see Section 1.5.2). A law which punishes an omission is a greater infringement of liberty than a law which punishes an act. This is because punishing an omission means that in the given circumstances the only way a defendant can avoid criminal liability is by performing the required act, whereas punishing an act means that a defendant can avoid liability by performing any act except the prohibited one. On the other hand the law also seeks to protect people's lives and wellbeing. Does not the value we place on a person's life easily justify a minor infringement on others' liberty for as long as it takes to perform a rescue or summon help? Professor Ashworth has argued that 'a level of social co-operation and social responsibility is both good and necessary for the realisation of individual autonomy. ... Each member of society is valued intrinsically, and the value of one citizen's life is generally greater than the value of another citizen's temporary freedom.'

The present law balances these competing principles. Where an individual has assumed responsibility for another then the restriction on his liberty by punishing omissions is less problematic than if the duty to act is imposed on a passer-by. This balance is essentially a policy choice; other countries have 'easy rescue' statutes which punish those who fail to rescue a victim when it would be easy for them to do so.

There are also some more technical difficulties in punishing omissions. There are three particular problems here:

1. *Causation*. There are difficulties in explaining how an omission can cause a particular result. Applying the 'but for' rule of causation (see Chapter 4) seems to imply that omissions cannot in law cause a result. 'But for' an omission it is by definition true that the result would still have happened in exactly the same way. One response is to redefine the question and suggest that 'but for' the failure of the defendant to act, the harm would not have occurred.
2. *The number of defendants*. A second difficulty is the number of potential defendants. In the Princess Diana case there were a large number of photographers present at the scene of the crash. In other car crashes maybe thousands of people will pass by without summoning help. Is it realistic to punish them all? It may be that the simple answer is that it would be justifiable to hold many people responsible if it could be shown that if any one of them had stopped the victim's life would have been saved.
3. Mens rea *problems*. The jury normally has to decide whether the accused had the *mens rea* when he committed the *actus reus*. The problem with omissions is that there is no precise moment in time when the *actus reus* takes place and at which to consider whether the defendant had the relevant *mens rea*.

One of the difficulties for supporters of the approach in English law is the difficulty in distinguishing an act from an omission. This distinction was criticised in *Airedale National Health Service Trust v Bland* by Lord Mustill, who said that the distinction between acts and omissions in this kind of case is a 'morally and intellectually dubious distinction'. An oft-quoted example is where a doctor has a patient on a life-support machine – is there a distinction of any moral importance between a doctor who switches off a life-support machine and a doctor who fails to switch on a life-support machine which automatically turns itself off every 24 hours? Surely in such cases doctors should not be able to escape the real legal and moral difficulties involved in the care of the seriously ill by claiming they were omitting to switch the machines back on.

The House of Lords in *Bland* authorised doctors to withhold essential supplies of food and drink to a patient in a persistent vegetative state. This was classified as an omission, the 'withholding of treatment', and so the doctors were not liable to be charged with murder. Lord Mustill argued that a doctor should provide treatment only where this was in the patient's best interests, and it was not in the interests of a patient in a persistent vegetative state to carry on receiving the nourishment. It might not be against his interests either, but it was not positively in his interests. It is important to stress that the doctors were not liable as they had no legal duty to feed the patient and they acted in accordance with a body of medical opinion, but it may well be that a relative caring for a patient could not decide that in his or her view the patient did not require food or liquid. Another argument was that, by withdrawing the food and drink, the doctors were in effect returning Tony Bland to the position he had been in when he first arrived at the hospital, and so the overall effect of the doctors' actions was nothing. This demonstrates the real problems in distinguishing acts and omissions.

None of these are insuperable problems, but they indicate that the traditional approach of the law is not easily suited to liability for omissions. It is interesting that the Draft Criminal Code recommends retaining the balance struck by the present law, with the following provision, which details the circumstances in which a defendant may be liable for failing to act:

a person causes a result which is an element of an offence when ... (b) he omits to do an act which might prevent its occurrence and which he is under a duty to do according to the law relating to the offence. (Clause 17(1)(b) Draft Criminal Code)

Summary

3.1 As a general rule, a criminal offence consists of both the *actus reus* (external elements) and a *mens rea* (state of mind). Not every offence requires a *mens rea* for every element of the *actus reus*, but the presence of an *actus reus* is essential in every offence. There is no criminal liability merely for possessing a particular state of mind.

3.2 The *actus reus* is not just action or conduct on the part of the accused. It may involve bringing about a state of affairs, or causing a certain prohibited consequence. It will also include certain relevant circumstances surrounding the conduct, state of affairs or result. One of these circumstances may be the state of mind of another person, such as the victim. It is not always easy to separate the external elements of an offence from the state of mind of the accused.

3.3 The *actus reus* may involve a failure to act by the accused. As a general rule the criminal law does not impose liability for omissions. However, it may do so if a statute so provides, either expressly or implicitly. Liability for omissions may also be imposed by the courts in cases where there is found to be a duty to act on the part of the accused. Such duties may be the result of a statutory provision, of a contract, of a special relationship of dependence between the victim and the accused, or where the accused has by his own unintentional act brought about a dangerous situation. Sometimes the combination of unintentional act plus intentional omission can also be regarded as one course of conduct forming part of the *actus reus* of the offence, without expressly relying on the existence of a duty.

3.4 The *actus reus* must be voluntary. This means that it must be willed: the accused must have been able to choose not to act in those circumstances. If the accused acts involuntarily there is no *actus reus* and therefore no offence.

3.5 Some cases of involuntary action are the result of automatism, meaning that the muscles act without conscious control by the mind. Where this is the result of an external factor, such as a falling brick, it will provide a complete defence to criminal liability unless it was self-induced. Where the automatism is the result of an internal factor which falls within the legal definition of insanity, then the result will be a special verdict of 'not guilty by reason of insanity'.

3.6 Those who assist another to commit a crime can be guilty of an offence under the principle of accessorial liability.

Further Reading

The *actus reus/mens rea* distinction is discussed in Robinson and in Smith. The debates over when omissions should be punished are revealed in Ashworth, Baker, Elliott, Herring, Simester and Williams. The 'voluntary act requirement' is discussed in Glazebrook, Horder, Husak and Simester. A detailed and complex discussion on what an act is can be found in Moore.

Ashworth, 'The Scope of Criminal Liability for Omissions' (1989) 105 LQR 424.

Baker, 'Omissions Liability for Homicide Offences: Reconciling *R v Kennedy* with *R v Evans*' (2010) 74 JCL 310.

Elliott, 'Liability for Manslaughter by Omission: Don't Let the Baby Drown!' (2010) 74 JCL 163.

Glazebrook, 'Situational Liability', in Glazebrook (ed), *Reshaping the Criminal Law* (Stevens 1978).

Herring, 'Familial Homicide, Failure to Protect and Domestic Violence: Who's the Victim?' [2007] Crim LR 923.

Horder, 'Pleading Involuntary Lack of Capacity' (1993) 52 CLJ 298.

Husak, 'Does Criminal Liability Require an Act?', in Duff (ed.), *Philosophy and the Criminal Law* (Cambridge University Press 1999).

Further Reading cont'd

Moore, *Act and Crime* (Oxford University Press 1993).

Robinson, 'Should the Criminal Law Abandon the *Actus Reus/Mens Rea* Distinction?', in Shute, Gardner and Horder (eds), *Action and Value in Criminal Law* (Oxford University Press 1993).

Simester, 'Why Omissions Are Special' (1995) 1 Leg Th 311.

Simester, 'On the So-called Requirement for Voluntary Action' (1998) 1 Buff Crim L Rev 403.

Smith, 'On *Actus Reus and Mens Rea*', in Glazebrook (ed.), *Reshaping the Criminal Law* (Stevens 1978).

Williams, 'Criminal Omissions: The Conventional View' (1991) 107 LQR 432.

Case Notes

▶ *A-G's Ref (No 2 of 1992)* [1994] QB 91. Court of Appeal

The respondent was acquitted of causing death by recklessness after claiming he was 'driving without awareness'. The Court of Appeal held that the defence of automatism is available only if the defendant suffers a 'total destruction of voluntary control', and 'impaired, reduced, or partial control' is insufficient. The evidence showed that the defendant was aware of bright flashing lights and able to steer in a straight line, and so the Court of Appeal stated that the defence of automatism should not have been left to the jury.

▶ *Bailey* [1983] 1 WLR 760. Court of Appeal

The accused was convicted of causing grievous bodily harm, contrary to s 18 Offences Against the Person Act 1861. He was a diabetic, and had taken insulin with insufficient food, giving rise to hypoglycaemia. He appealed against conviction on the ground of automatism. The appeal was dismissed as there was insufficient evidence of automatism, but it was held that if the accused had known of the risk of hypoglycaemia, and resultant uncontrollable behaviour, then such self-induced automatism would have afforded no defence.

▶ *Bratty v A-G for Northern Ireland* [1963] AC 386. House of Lords

The accused was convicted of murder. There was evidence that he was suffering from psychomotor epilepsy, and he pleaded insanity and automatism at the trial, but the trial judge refused to let automatism go to the jury. The jury rejected the insanity defence. Appeals to the Court of Appeal and then to the House of Lords were both dismissed. Lord Denning defined automatism as an involuntary act, and held that if it was the result of a disease of the mind, then it gave rise to the defence of insanity and not automatism.

▶ *Burgess* [1991] 2 QB 92. Court of Appeal

Burgess was found not guilty by reason of insanity of wounding with intent after he attacked a neighbour while sleepwalking. The court upheld the verdict and stated that sleepwalking was caused by an internal factor, namely his sleep disorder, which was a malfunctioning in the mind.

▶ *Evans* [2009] EWCA Crim 650. Court of Appeal

Gemma Evans bought her 16-year-old sister, Carly, heroin. Carly injected herself and collapsed. Gemma Evans and her mother, who were both in the house, did not call for assistance because they feared Carly would get into trouble. Carly died in the night, and Gemma Evans and the mother were convicted of gross negligence manslaughter. Gemma Evans and the mother appealed, but the Court of Appeal upheld the conviction. Gemma owed her sister a duty of care on the basis that she had created a dangerous situation and had failed to take reasonable steps to remedy it. The mother owed Carly a duty of care by virtue of being her mother and being aware that Carly's life was in danger. Interestingly the court found that the blood relationship between Gemma and Carly did not on its own generate a duty of care.

▶ *Fagan* [1969] 1 QB 439. Divisional Court

Fagan was convicted of assaulting a police officer in the execution of his duty, contrary to s 51(1) Police Act 1964. When asked to park his car by the side of the road, he inadvertently drove his car onto the constable's foot, and then when asked to remove it switched off the ignition and waited some time before reversing off the constable's foot. He appealed on the ground that at the time when he had the necessary *mens rea* for assault he did no act which could be said to amount to the *actus reus* of assault, as merely refraining from driving his car off the constable's foot was an omission and not an act. The court dismissed the appeal, holding that 'assault' in this offence included a battery, and that a battery could be inflicted through a weapon or instrument controlled by the accused. In this case, the battery was inflicted by means of the car, which was deliberately left on the policeman's foot. Although assault could not be committed by omission, in this case the *actus reus* was an act which continued during the whole time when the car was on the constable's foot. The act was not complete at the time when the *mens rea* was formed and it was not necessary for *mens rea* to be present throughout the continuing act.

▶ *Larsonneur* (1933) 97 JP 206. Court of Criminal Appeal

Larsonneur, a French national, had been ordered to leave the United Kingdom, and she went to Ireland. She was then deported from Ireland, and, in the custody of the Irish police, brought back to the United Kingdom and handed over to the police at Holyhead. She was charged with and convicted of being found in the United Kingdom having been refused permission to land, contrary to the Aliens Order 1920. The court dismissed her appeal, and held that the circumstances in which she had returned to the United

Kingdom (in police custody and against her will) were irrelevant.

▶ *Miller* [1983] 2 AC 161. House of Lords

Miller was convicted of arson, contrary to s 1(1) and (3) Criminal Damage Act 1971. He was sleeping as a vagrant in an unoccupied house and fell asleep on a mattress while holding a lighted cigarette. When he awoke to find the mattress alight he did not attempt to put out the fire, but moved into another room. The house caught fire and substantial damage was caused. Miller appealed against the conviction, and the Court of Appeal, dismissing his appeal, certified as a question of law for the House of Lords whether, having accidentally started a fire, the accused would be liable for arson if he thereafter (with the necessary *mens rea*) failed to take any steps to extinguish the fire or prevent damage being caused to property by the fire. The House of Lords dismissed the appeal and held that the *actus reus* of arson could include, as well as a positive act of setting fire to property, a failure to take measures which lie within one's power to counteract a danger that one has oneself created. The House adopted the view of the trial judge that once Miller became aware of the existence of the fire he was under a duty to take some action to put it out, although not disapproving of the alternative view of the Court of Appeal that the whole course of conduct of the accused, both actions and omissions, should be seen as part of one uninterrupted *actus reus*, during the latter part of which he had the necessary *mens rea*.

▶ *Pitchley* (1972) 57 Cr App Rep 30. Court of Appeal

The accused was convicted of assisting in the retention of stolen goods for the benefit of another, contrary to s 22 Theft Act 1968. He had been handed some money by his son to keep for him and had paid it into his post office savings account. He subsequently discovered that the money was stolen and left it in the savings bank. His appeal against conviction was dismissed, and the court held that 'retain' meant 'not lose, continue to have'. Permitting the money to remain in the bank after finding out that it was stolen was sufficient to amount to assisting in the retention of the money.

▶ *Quick* [1973] 1 QB 910. Court of Appeal

The accused was convicted of assault occasioning actual bodily harm. He was a nurse in a mental hospital and had assaulted a patient. He was diabetic and had been suffering a hypoglycaemic episode at the time. He pleaded automatism. On a ruling by the trial judge that this amounted to a plea of insanity, Quick changed his plea to guilty and then appealed against his conviction. The Court of Appeal allowed his appeal on the ground that automatism should have been left to the jury: hypoglycaemia arising from an excess of insulin was not insanity, it was the result of an external factor, comparable to the effect of other drugs or violence. Nevertheless, if the automatism were self-induced, or could reasonably have been foreseen, as where there is a failure to take medical advice, then it could not excuse someone from liability.

▶ *Stone and Dobinson* [1977] 1 QB 354. Court of Appeal

See Chapter 10 Case notes.

▶ *Sullivan* [1984] 1 AC 156. House of Lords

Sullivan was charged with causing grievous bodily harm, contrary to s 18 Offences Against the Person Act 1861. He had attacked the victim during an epileptic fit, and pleaded automatism. However, the trial judge ruled that this amounted to a plea of insanity and refused to let automatism go to the jury, whereupon the accused changed his plea to guilty of the less serious assault occasioning actual bodily harm and then appealed against conviction on the ground that the ruling of the trial judge was wrong. The court dismissed his appeal and held that epilepsy amounted to insanity in law; it did not matter that its effects were merely transitory. Epilepsy affected the mind, in the sense of the mental faculties of reason, memory and understanding, and was not the result of some external cause such as drugs, alcohol or violence.

▶ *Warner v MPC* [1969] 2 AC 256. House of Lords

See Chapter 6 Case notes.

Chapter 4

Causation

Key Terms

- **Causation** – the rules which decide whether a defendant is responsible for a harm.
- **'But for' cause** – a finding that 'but for' the defendant's actions the harm would not have occurred.
- ***Novus actus interveniens*** – the intervention of the victim, third party or natural event which means that the defendant is no longer responsible for the subsequent consequences of his or her actions.

4.1 The nature of causation

Some commentators have argued that you should be responsible for your actions, but not their consequences (see Section 1.4.3). The argument is that having acted (for example, pulling the trigger of the gun), what happens next is to some extent a matter of chance (for example, whether the victim jumps out of the way or whether the gun will work). However, this view has not been accepted by the law. The consequences of actions do play an important role in determining criminal liability. The difficulty lies in deciding for which consequences of our actions we are responsible. This is where the rules of causation come into play.

Imagine a situation in which Bob has been abused by his father in childhood and has been brought up under socially deprived circumstances. He is in a depressed state because his girlfriend has left him. He stabs a policeman with a knife given to him by a friend. An ambulance is called but arrives late on the scene because there is an ambulance strike, and by the time the policeman arrives in hospital his condition is serious. The doctor who sees him is terribly overworked and mistakenly concludes that the policeman does not need urgent treatment. The policeman dies shortly afterwards. In this situation who caused the policeman's death? Bob? His friend? His father? His girlfriend? The ambulance unions? The doctor? The hospital? The government? Society? A doctor, a sociologist, a theologian, a politician and the victim's relatives might all give different answers to this question.

It would be wrong to think that the law on causation can be reduced to a mathematical formula. The House of Lords in *Kennedy* [2007] UKHL 38 explained: 'Questions of causation frequently arise in many areas of the law, but causation is not a single, unvarying concept to be mechanically applied without regard to the context in which the question arises'.

It is often stressed that legal causation is different from factual causation. This is true because legal causation is not strictly a logical, factual or medical question, but more a moral one: is the defendant morally to blame for a consequence of her actions? In *McKechnie* (1992) 94 Cr App R 51 the defendant attacked the victim with a television set, causing him head injuries. On his being taken to hospital it was discovered that the victim had a duodenal ulcer. It was not possible to operate on the ulcer because of the head injuries caused by the defendant, and the victim died from the ulcer shortly afterwards. The defendant was held to have caused the victim's death in law. As a matter of pure factual causation this might be hard to justify, as the medical cause of death was the ulcer and not the injuries inflicted by the defendant. But as a matter of ascribing moral responsibility the decision appears correct. (It should be added that the case seems to be based on the assumption that, had he not been attacked, the victim would have sought medical help and would have had a successful operation to deal with the ulcer.)

The problem is that moral responsibility is a controversial topic. As we have seen, ascribing responsibility for a criminal injury could involve consideration of contentious political or sociological factors. The criminal law tries to avoid these by focusing on one person, the defendant, and asking whether he or she can be said to have caused the consequences, regardless of the extent to which his or her background or social circumstances may also have been responsible for the commission of the crime. So where a person carelessly driving a car at high speed kills a pedestrian, the law focuses on the driver. Whether car manufacturers who make cars which can travel at high speeds and advertise cars in a way that encourages high-speed driving are responsible is not considered in a criminal trial. That said, sometimes the law permits the rules of causation to be affected by policy considerations, and this will become evident as we consider the legal rules of causation in further detail.

It is sometimes said that questions of causation are largely matters of common sense, best left to the jury (*Finlay* [2003] EWCA 3868). However, there are legal principles that the judge can use to guide it. As one judge explained:

> generally speaking causation is a question of fact for the jury...But that does not mean that there are no principles of law relating to causation, so that no directions on law are ever to be given to a jury on the question of causation...It is for the judge to direct the jury with reference to the relevant principles of law relating to causation, and then to leave it to the jury to decide, in the light of those principles, whether or not the relevant causal link has been established. (*Pagett** (1983) 76 Cr App R 279 (Goff LJ))

4.2   The guiding rule of causation

The cornerstone of the law on causation is that the prosecution must show that the defendant's act was 'a substantial and operating cause' of the harm (*Cheshire** [1991] 3 All ER 670). The term 'substantial' makes it clear that the defendant's act need not be the sole cause, but the act must be more than a *de minimis* (minimal) cause (*Cato* [1976] 1 All ER 260), or 'a slight or trifling' contribution to the result (*Kimsey* [1996] Crim LR 35). As Goff LJ put it in *Pagett* (1983) 76 Cr App R 279, 'in law the accused's act need not be the sole cause, or even the main cause, of the victim's death, it being enough that his act contributed significantly to that result'. It is therefore quite possible for a harm to be caused by two or even more people, each of whom contributed significantly to the creation of the harm. In such a case the jury is asked simply to consider whether the actions of the particular defendant before them contributed significantly to the death. The fact that someone else may also have contributed to the death is irrelevant to the jury's enquiry (*Mellor* [1996] 2 Cr App R 245). For example, in one case (*Benge* (1865) 4 F&F 504) there was a railway accident after a foreman negligently arranged for tracks to be removed and the driver of the train failed to keep a proper lookout. The court held that the foreman could be criminally responsible for the accident even though the driver was also to blame. Similarly the fact that the victim may be seen as acting stupidly and having contributed to the harm occurring is no defence if the defendant's acts were a cause of the harm. In *Longbottom* (1849) 13 JP 270 a defendant was convicted of manslaughter after running over the victim while speeding, even though the victim had been in part to blame by walking along in the middle of the road.

If there is ever a case where it is unclear which act of a series of acts caused the harm, but all of the acts were committed by the accused, the above problem does not arise. There is no need for the prosecution to show which of the accused's acts caused the harm as long as it is clear that one of his acts did (*A-G's Ref (No 4 of 1980)** [1981] 1 All ER 617).

In order to explain further what the phrase 'operating and substantial cause' means, the law has developed a number of further rules.

4.3   'But for' causation

A starting point for the law's approach to causation is to ask whether 'but for' the defendant's act the result would have happened. This test is sometimes known by its Latin tag, *causa sine qua non*. The jury must ask themselves what would have happened had the defendant not acted in the wrongful way in which the defendant did. If the harm would still have occurred in the same way and at the same time then the act cannot be said to have caused the harm in law. For example, if Albert poisons Victoria's tea, but before she has drinks it she suffers an unrelated heart attack and dies, then Albert cannot be said to have caused Victoria's death (although he may be guilty of attempted murder). 'But for' his act Victoria would still have died in exactly the same way (see *White* [1910] 2 KB 124, which has similar facts to this example). The converse of this is that if the defendant kills someone who was in fact due to die from other causes shortly afterwards she will still be said to have caused the victim's death. It is true that 'but for' her act the victim would still have died, but at a different time and in a different way. The jury will decide what would have happened 'but for' the defendant's act using their common sense and general experience of the world and the predictability of the way things or people behave.

It is important to remember that the defendant is liable under the criminal law only if a wrongful act of his own causes the injury. For example, in *Dalloway* (1847) 2 Cox CC 273 a man who was driving a horse cart without properly controlling the reins or looking where he was going ran over a young child. The court found that even if he had been exercising all due care and control he would not have been able to avoid injuring the girl as she jumped out in front of the cart without any warning. Although 'but for' the driving of the cart the child would not have been injured, it was not true that 'but for' his negligence the child would not have been killed, and it was this which was the crucial question for the jury to decide.

The mere fact that 'but for' causation is established does not mean that the accused will be said to have caused the result in law. Otherwise every criminal's parents could be said to have caused the crime, because 'but for' their act of procreation their child's crime would not have occurred! Hence the law has further requirements. A defendant is taken to be responsible for and to have caused the consequences of his actions unless there has been a break in the chain of causation, a *novus actus interveniens* as it is known – that is an event by which someone or something else has taken over responsibility for the chain of events which follows.

4.4 Novus actus interveniens

The *novus actus interveniens* doctrine has been developed in a highly influential book by Professors Hart and Honoré. They argue that to understand the doctrine it is necessary to distinguish conditions from causes. To demonstrate this distinction they give the example of a fire. In order for the fire to start it is necessary to have a dropped match, oxygen in the air and combustible material. Only the dropped match would be seen as a cause, and the others as conditions. The distinction is that conditions are those things which are normal, such as oxygen in the air. However, the dropping of the match is abnormal; it 'made the difference' and so can be said to have caused the fire. Only abnormal causes can be *novus actus interveniens* and break the chain of causation. Conditions cannot break the chain of events. The main difficulty with this approach is how to distinguish between normal and abnormal events. Three kinds of *novus actus interveniens* will now be considered to explore this distinction.

4.4.1 Acts by third parties

If a third party engages in a 'free, voluntary and informed' act it will normally be a *novus actus interveniens*. To explore that further it is necessary to discuss the following:

1. *Free and voluntary acts of third parties*. Normally if a third party is of criminal capacity (that is, over 10 years old and sane) then she assumes responsibility for the consequences which follow from her acts if the acts are 'free, deliberate and informed' (*Pagett* (1983) 76 Cr App R 279 (Goff LJ)). Hart and Honoré explain that this is because a third party's acts are 'abnormal' (they are unpredictable) and so break the chain of causation. It can also be explained as a matter of principle – that a person is not to be blamed in law for someone else's actions, as otherwise that would be to make someone responsible for things outside his or her control. Thus if Anne puts poison into Charlotte's food, but before the poison takes effect Emily shoots and kills Charlotte, then Anne is no longer liable for her death, and Emily, by her act of shooting, assumes responsibility for the death. Anne will not have caused the death because Emily's act was a *novus actus interveniens*, breaking the chain of causation. Indeed this analysis reflects the general principle of causation because Anne's act is no longer an operating cause of Charlotte's death. Similarly in *Rafferty* [2007] EWCA Crim 1846 the defendant as part of a gang had elbowed the deceased in the course of a fight. He then ran off. The other members of the gang then drowned the victim. Their actions broke the chain of causation and the defendant could not be said to have caused the death. He could, however, be prosecuted for the injuries he caused.

2. *Lawful acts of third parties*. There are some circumstances in which the act of a third party will not assume responsibility and it is necessary to look earlier in time to find the cause. This will occur where an act is not 'free, deliberate and informed'. The following are examples of the acts of a third party that do not break the chain of causation:

   a. *Lack of capacity*. If the third party lacks criminal capacity (for example, he is insane or is below the age of criminal responsibility) his or her act will not break the chain of causation. In *Michael* (1840) 173 ER 867, for example, the accused intended to kill her baby son. She gave his nurse a bottle of laudanum, telling her that it was medicine for the baby. The nurse put the bottle on one side, but her child, aged five, took the bottle and gave a large quantity of the laudanum to the baby, who died as a result. The mother's conviction for murder was upheld on appeal. Although two other people had acted after she had, they were both 'innocent agents' (see Chapter 17) – the young child because she was below the age of criminal responsibility, and the nurse because she was completely unaware that the bottle was poisoned. Therefore their acts did not break the chain of causation and the mother could be said to have caused the death of the child.

b. *Lack of* mens rea. If the third party has no *mens rea* and is unaware of the harm he or she is causing, this will not break the chain of causation. For example, if Susan sends Anthony a poisoned chocolate cake through the post, the cake will be delivered by a post office worker. However, the postal worker will not be guilty of poisoning Anthony as he has no *mens rea*. If he were working in cahoots with Susan and were aware that the parcel was a poisoned cake then the result would be different, as he would be seen to have the *mens rea* and so could be said to have caused the death. Susan would then be his accomplice (see Chapter 17). In *Haystead v Chief Constable of Derbyshire* [2000] Crim LR 758 the defendant deliberately pushed a woman. She dropped the baby she was carrying, who hit his head on the floor. It was held that the defendant could be said to have caused the injuries to the child because the mother's act in dropping the baby was entirely accidental and was caused by the defendant. It could not be described as a free, voluntary and informed act.

c. *Defences*. If the third party is legally justified in acting as she does, this will not break the chain of causation. An example is the Court of Appeal decision in *Pagett*, where a defendant kidnapped his former girlfriend and was pursued by police officers. He fired a gun at the police officers while using the woman as a 'human shield'. The police fired back and unfortunately killed the woman. The Court of Appeal decided that the defendant could be said to have caused the death of his former girlfriend. The police officer acted in self-defence, in pursuance of his legal duty, and so did not break the chain of causation.

4.4.2 Medical treatment

There have been a number of cases where the defendant has tried to argue that the victim was killed not by the injury inflicted by the defendant, but by the bad medical treatment she later received. For example, in *Malcherek and Steel** [1981] 2 All ER 422 the victim was so badly injured by the defendant that he had to be put onto a life-support system. Some time later, following normal medical practice, the doctors decided that the life-support machine should be switched off. The defendant tried to claim that he had not caused the death of the victim, but that this had happened because of the doctors' act in switching off the life-support machine. Not surprisingly the court rejected this argument, saying that had the doctors not used the life-support machine the victim would have died quickly, and then the defendant would clearly have been guilty. A defendant cannot complain where the doctors try to save a patient but fail. The court applied the normal 'substantial and operating cause' test: the cause of the death was the wound inflicted by the defendant, not just the lack of a life-support machine. Notably, had the machine been switched off by an intruder then the intruder could be said to have caused the victim's death and broken the chain of causation (*Bland*). There are two ways of explaining this. It may be that the doctors, in switching off the life-support machine, were acting in accordance with their legal duty and so did not break the chain of causation – in the same way that the police officers in *Pagett* in shooting were said to be carrying out their legal duty. Clearly an intruder would have no legal duty to switch off the machine, and so his acts would be said to cause the death. A second possible explanation is that looking at the doctors' conduct as a whole they had first intervened to try to save the victim's life but had later taken away the assistance by switching off the life-support machine. This returned the victim to the same situation he would have been in had the doctors not intervened, and the total effect of the doctors' actions was nothing. However, the same could not be said of the intruder, who was not withdrawing help previously offered.

More difficult are cases where medical treatment provided by the hospital was inappropriate and caused death. In such cases the test is still whether the original wound was a 'substantial and operating cause (not necessarily the only or even main cause of death)' or whether the treatment 'was so independent of [the act of the accused], and in itself so potent in causing death, that [the jury] regard the contribution made by [the accused's] acts as insignificant' (*Cheshire* [1991] 3 All ER 670). So, for example, in *Jordan* (1956) 40 Cr App R 153 the patient was recovering well from a stabbing and the wound had 'mainly healed' in hospital when he was given a drug to which he was allergic, despite the hospital having known of his intolerance. The patient's reaction to the drug was such that he died. The court called his medical treatment 'palpably wrong' and said that it broke the chain of causation. So the defendant did not cause the victim's death, although he would still be guilty of wounding him. However, *Jordan* seems to be an exceptional case and was referred to in *Smith*** [1959] 2 All ER 193 as a 'very particular case depending on its exact facts'. The Court of Appeal in *Smith* went on to state, 'only if it can be said that the original wound is merely the setting in which another cause operates can it be said that death does not result from the wound. Putting it another way, only if the second cause is so overwhelming as to make the original wound merely part of the history can it be said that it does not flow from the wound.' *Jordan* can be contrasted with the more recent case of *Cheshire*, where the wound was so serious that the patient needed a tracheotomy. This was done negligently and it led to the victim's death. However, on this occasion the court decided that the defendant could still be said to have caused the death of the victim. The court argued that negligently wrong treatment is not completely abnormal (referring to Hart and Honoré's test mentioned above), and does not necessarily break the chain of causation. Accidents regularly happen even in the best-run hospitals.

To summarise, it seems that in cases where it is alleged that medical treatment has broken the chain of causation the court will look at two issues:

1. How negligent or wrongful was the treatment?
2. Was the original wound still an operating and substantial cause?

Only if the treatment is manifestly wrong and the original wound no longer an operating and substantial cause of the injury will the medical treatment break the chain of causation. If the defendant's acts are a significant cause of death then the culpability of the doctors is irrelevant and should not be considered by the jury (*Mellor* [1996] 2 Cr App R 245).

As we have seen, the courts seem very reluctant to find that medical help can break the chain of causation. There may be two reasons behind this. First, there is a feeling that it is no thanks to the defendant that the victim receives any medical help at all, and the defendant cannot really complain if it is not of the highest standard. Second, the courts are wary of turning a criminal trial into a trial of the doctors involved. The question of whether the doctors were negligent may be a suitable question in civil proceedings against the doctors, but their blameworthiness or otherwise is irrelevant when considering the criminal liability of the defendant.

4.4.3 Acts and omissions of the victim

It is important to distinguish between cases where it is argued that the victim does an act which is said to break the chain of causation and those which claim that the victim fails to do something and that the omission breaks the chain of causation.

1. *Acts of the victim.* In *Kennedy** [2007] UKHL 38 the defendant was asked by the victim for some drugs. The defendant gave the victim a heroin-filled syringe and the victim injected himself. The victim died shortly afterwards. Surprisingly the Court of Appeal held that the defendant could be said to have caused the death of the victim. However, the House of Lords overruled that finding. As the victim acted voluntarily in injecting himself, this free, voluntary, informed act broke the chain of causation. As their Lordships explained:

   > The criminal law generally assumes the existence of free will. The law recognises certain exceptions, in the case of the young, those who for any reason are not fully responsible for their actions, and the vulnerable, and it acknowledges situations of duress and necessity, as also of deception and mistake. But, generally speaking, informed adults of sound mind are treated as autonomous beings able to make their own decisions how they will act, and none of the exceptions is relied on as possibly applicable in this case. Thus D is not to be treated as causing V to act in a certain way if V makes a voluntary and informed decision to act in that way rather than another.

   However, things are rather different where the victim is not acting in a free, voluntary and informed way. Most commonly this occurs where the victim runs away from his attacker and in so doing injures himself (*DPP v Dally and McGhie* [1979] 2 WLR 239). In *Roberts* (1971)* (1971) 56 Cr App R 95 the defendant gave the victim a lift in his car but started to molest her, and she jumped out of the car, injuring herself. Stephenson LJ, in upholding the defendant's conviction, explained that if the action of the victim in trying to escape was reasonably foreseeable, then the accused may be held to have caused the resulting injuries. Here her response was reasonably foreseeable, and so the defendant could be said to have caused the victim's injuries. On the other hand:

   > if of course the victim does something so 'daft',...or so unexpected, not that this particular assailant did not actually foresee it but that no reasonable man could be expected to foresee it, then it is only in a very remote and unreal sense a consequence of his assault, it is really occasioned by a voluntary action on the part of the victim which could not reasonably be foreseen and which breaks the chain of causation between the assault and harm or injury.

   The Court of Appeal in *Williams and Davis* [1992] 1 WLR 380 slightly modified the *Roberts* test, suggesting that the jury should consider:

   > whether [the victim's act]...was within the range of responses which might be expected from a victim placed in the situation which he was. The jury should bear in mind any

particular characteristic of the victim and the fact that in the agony of the moment, he may act without thought and deliberation ...

In *Lewis* [2010] EWCA Crim 151 the Court of Appeal approved a judge's direction asking whether the victim's response in running away across a road 'might have been expected'. Rather confusingly the Court also suggested the judge could have asked the jury whether the victim's response was proportionate. That unfortunately creates confusion. In the face of sudden attack it is foreseeable that a victim might react disproportionately. So proportionality and foreseeability are not the same thing. Most of the case law focuses on foreseeability, and that seems a preferable test to use. In *Dhaliwal* [2006] EWCA Crim 1139 the Court of Appeal accepted that hypothetically if a husband seriously abused his wife so as to cause her to suffer a psychological illness and she therefore committed suicide, he could be said to have caused her death.

It should be stressed that the question is whether a reasonable person would have foreseen the way in which the victim reacted, not whether the defendant actually foresaw the way in which the victim reacted or even what a reasonable person of the defendant's age and characteristics would have foreseen (*Marjoram* [2006] EWCA Crim 1139).

Even if the victim's reaction was unforeseeable it might still be held that the defendant's actions were a substantial and operating cause of the injury. So in *Dear* [1996] Crim LR 595, where the victim made the wounds caused by the defendant worse by reopening them, the defendant was held to have caused the resulting death on the basis that the wounds inflicted by the accused were still operating and substantial.

2. *Omissions of the victim.* As we noted earlier, the criminal law is reluctant to ascribe responsibility for any act of omission. It follows that if a victim fails to seek treatment for a wound, the law will not find a break in the chain of causation. In *Holland* (1841) 2 Mood & R 351 the victim failed to seek medical treatment for a wound which became infected and led to his death. The failure did not break the chain of causation. This is also the best explanation of *Blaue** [1975] 3 All ER 466, in which the victim was stabbed and required a blood transfusion. She was a Jehovah's Witness and for religious reasons refused the blood transfusion. She in due course died. This refusal of treatment was an omission (that is, a failure to consent to the treatment) and so did not break the chain of causation. The death was due to the stabbing of the victim by the defendant, not the refusal to consent to the transfusion. The decision is clearly correct. In *Blaue*, the victim died from the stab wounds inflicted by the defendant, so it could hardly be said that the stabbing was not an 'operating and substantial cause' of the victim's death.

3. *Condition of the victim.* In some cases the accused's actions may have unexpectedly serious consequences because of some pre-existing condition of the victim. The accused will be liable (provided she has *mens rea*) even though the condition was unknown to her and could not reasonably have been foreseen. This is sometimes known as the 'thin-skull rule'. You take your victim as you find him, whether he suffers from an unusually thin skull or from haemophilia, for example. In *Hayward* [1908] 21 Cox CC 692 the victim died after being chased into the street by her husband. She was found to have been suffering from an abnormality of the thyrus gland, and her husband was found guilty of manslaughter. Ridley J directed the

jury that 'the abnormal state of the deceased's health did not affect the question, whether the prisoner knew or did not know of it, if it were proved...that the death was accelerated by the prisoner's illegal act'. In *Blaue*, the case with the Jehovah's Witness mentioned above, Lawton J argued, 'it has long been the policy of the law that those who use violence on other people must take their victims as they find them. This in our judgment means the whole man and not just the physical man.' So in *Blaue* the defendant had to take the victim as a Jehovah's Witness who would refuse a blood transfusion. The 'take your victim as you find her' argument is a little odd here as it should not really matter whether the victim became a Jehovah's Witness before or after the stabbing. Lawton J considered the argument that the appropriate test should be whether the victim acted in a reasonable way. However, he rejected this, pointing out:

> At once the question arises reasonable by whose standards? Those of Jehovah's Witnesses? Humanists? Roman Catholics/Protestants of Anglo-Saxon descent? The man on the Clapham omnibus?

The case is best supported on the basis suggested above that the omission of the victim cannot break the chain of causation.

4.4.4 Acts of God

It may be that the defendant tries to claim that a freak occurrence of nature, or 'Act of God', broke the chain of causation. In *Pegrum* [1989] Crim LR 442 it was said that an Act of God was 'an operation of natural forces so unpredictable as to excuse a defendant all liability for its consequences'. Of course, a defendant cannot claim if he dropped a vase out of a second-floor window and the vase broke that he did not cause the damage to the vase but that the law of nature (that is, gravity) did. However, if the Act of God was 'abnormal and extraordinary' (*Empress Car Co v NRA* [1998] 1 All ER 481) then the defendant might be able to claim that there was a break in the chain of causation. Thus, for example, if the defendant put a vase on a windowsill and it was struck by lightning, the argument would be more likely to succeed.

This is an area where the Hart and Honoré test of normality seems to work particularly well. However, policy factors can again be relevant. For example, a company was charged with a pollution offence (of allowing pig effluent to enter a river) and argued that it had not caused the pollution, which had been caused by unusually high rainfall that had led to its lagoon of waste overflowing. This argument was rejected by the Divisional Court (*Pegrum*). The basis of the decision seems to be that the defendant company was engaging in an activity for profit which had the potential to pollute and therefore it should have taken all possible steps to ensure pollution did not occur, including taking precautions against highly unlikely occurrences. This is an example of policy factors affecting the rules of causation.

4.5 The relevance of *mens rea* in questions of causation

It is, of course, quite possible that the person who causes a result is not to blame, for example because he was insane at the time. However, it is sometimes said that 'intended results are never too remote', subject to the 'but for' test. That is, if the defendant intentionally acts to produce a result, he cannot claim not to have caused that result unless the result would have occurred however he had acted. The idea here is that if a defendant acts hoping that the act will lead to a result then she will be said to cause that result, however peculiar the way in which the harm resulted from the defendant's act. To use an example above, if the accused put the vase on the windowsill hoping that it might be struck by lightning and amazingly it was, then he might be said to have caused that result. *Michael* (1840) 173 ER 867 is a good example from the case law of this principle at work. The mother intended that the baby be given the laudanum; the fact that it was given by the child rather than the nurse does not matter, given that her intended result occurred. It may be that here we see that moral and policy considerations can become entangled in the questions of causation. If the defendant intended to cause an injury it would be understandable if the court were unsympathetic to an argument that he was not responsible for the consequence.

4.6 Reform of causation

The Draft Criminal Code suggests that:

A person causes a result which is an element of an offence when

(a) he does an act which makes a more than negligible contribution to its occurrence; or
(b) he omits to do an act which might prevent its occurrence and which he is under a duty to do according to the law relating to the offence.

A person does not cause a result where, after he does such an act or makes such an omission, an act or event occurs

(a) which is the immediate and sufficient cause of the result;
(b) which he did not foresee, and
(c) which could not in the circumstances reasonably have been foreseen.

This clause is designed largely to replicate the present law. However, there are difficulties, in that the 'reasonable foreseeability' test is not identical to the present law on third parties, where a third party's act can break the chain of causation if it is 'free, voluntary and informed', even if unforeseeable (G. Williams, 1989).

Hot Topic – The suicidal rape victim

A hypothetical case which has been much discussed in the academic literature is that of a victim raped by the defendant who is so traumatised by the incident that she kills herself. Could the rapist be said to have caused the victim's death and be convicted of homicide? Three views could be taken:

1. One view is that the rapist must 'take his victim as he finds her'. It is well established that a defendant who injures a victim cannot argue that the resulting death was caused by the victim's medical condition or physical frailty. If the

defendant pushes over a person with a thin skull and she bangs her head, breaks her skull and dies, then the defendant will be found to have caused the death. The Court of Appeal in *Blaue* [1975] 3 All ER 466 held that this applies equally to psychological conditions and religious beliefs. The defendant there could not argue that it was the victim's religious beliefs which caused her death. He had to take the victim (the whole person) as he found her. In this hypothetical case it could be argued that the defendant had to take the victim with her propensity to commit suicide having been raped. He therefore can be said to have caused her death.

2. An alternative view is that the *Roberts* (1971) 56 Cr App R 95 'reasonable foreseeability test' should be applied. An analogy could be drawn between the woman jumping out of the car in *Roberts* and the suicide in the hypothetical case. The question for the jury would therefore be whether the victim's suicide was a reasonably foreseeable consequence of the defendant's actions. It may be thought that the inevitable answer to this question would be 'no'. Only a tiny number of rape victims respond to the trauma of rape by committing suicide. However, this will not necessarily follow. First, remember the *Williams and Davis* [1992] 1 WLR 380 modification to the *Roberts* test. Asking whether it was reasonably foreseeable that the victim (given her psychological condition) would respond to rape in this way may produce the answer 'yes'. Second, in *Roberts* it was asked whether the response was reasonably foreseeable or completely daft. Surely the suicide here could not be classified as 'daft', in which case maybe it should be regarded as reasonably foreseeable.

3. A third view is that the issue should be the extent to which the victim's acts are 'free, voluntary and informed'. There is 'but for' causation between the defendant's act and the death of the victim. So the question is whether there was a *novus actus interveniens*. In *Pagett* (1983) 76 Cr App R 279 it was confirmed that only the 'free, voluntary and informed' act of a third party could break the chain of causation. It could be said that the act of suicide was not free or voluntary as it was committed while in a state of trauma (an analogy could be drawn with *Haystead v Chief Constable of Derbyshire* [2000] Crim LR 758), in which case there was no *novus actus interveniens* and so the defendant caused the death.

It is difficult to predict which line of reasoning would be adopted by the court. Indeed there is case law which would support all three. This demonstrates the flexibility in the rules of causation which enables the courts to ensure that the rules of causation are able to achieve what is perceived to be 'the right result'. Whether or not that is desirable is, of course, a matter of much debate.

Summary

4.1 The question of causation raises complex moral and political questions about the extent to which we are responsible for our actions and the consequences of our actions. Although some cases have suggested that causation is a matter of common sense, the law has still formulated some rules to guide the jury.

4.2 The guiding rule for causation is to ask whether the defendant's act was an 'operating and substantial cause' of the consequence. If it was, then the defendant can be said to have caused the consequence. Simply because one act may also have been a 'substantial and operating cause' does not prevent any other act also being a cause.

4.3 If it can be said that, had the defendant not acted in the way he did, the consequence would have occurred in exactly the same way in which it did, then it cannot be said that the defendant caused that consequence.

4.4 An accused is assumed to be responsible for the consequences which flow from his acts unless another cause assumes responsibility and becomes a *novus actus interveniens*. A third party, an act of the victim or an act of God can be a *novus actus interveniens*.

4.5 If the defendant intends to produce a consequence then the law is likely to find that he caused the result, even if it occurred as a result of an unlikely set of events.

4.6 The Law Commission has proposed a straightforward formulation of the causation rules, but these proposals do not really resolve the difficult issues.

Further Reading

Hart and Honoré provide the leading analysis on causation. Bruder, Klimchuck and Norrie discuss some alternatives to their approach. Cherkessky, Padfield, Shute and Williams discuss ambiguities within the present law.

Bruder, 'Owning Outcomes: On Intervening Causes, Thin Skulls, and Fault-undifferentiated Crimes' (1998) 11 Can J L Juris 90.

Cherkessky, 'Kennedy and Unlawful Act Manslaughter: An Unorthodox Application of the Doctrine of Causation' [2008] J Crim L 387.

Hart and Honoré, *Causation in the Law* (2nd edn, Oxford University Press 1985).

Horder and McGowan, 'Manslaughter by Causing Another's Suicide' [2006] Crim LR 1035.

Klimchuck, 'Causation, Thin Skulls and Equality' (1998) 11 Can J L Juris 115.

Norrie, 'A Critique of Criminal Causation' (1991) 54 MLR 685.

Padfield, 'Clean Water and Muddy Causation' [1995] Crim LR 683.

Shute, 'Causation: Forseeability v. Natural Consequences' (1992) 55 MLR 584.

Williams, 'Finis for Novus Actus' (1989) 48 CLJ 391.

Case Notes

▶ *A-G's Ref (No 4 of 1980)* **[1981] 2 All ER 617. Court of Appeal**

The Attorney-General asked the Court of Appeal for its opinion (under s 36 Criminal Justice Act 1972) on the following point of law: 'whether a person who has committed a series of acts against another, culminating in the death of that other person, each act in the series being either unlawful and dangerous or an act of gross criminal negligence, is entitled to be acquitted of manslaughter on the ground that it cannot be shown which of such acts caused the death of the deceased'. The accused was charged with manslaughter following the death of his fiancée. He gave evidence of a series of actions any one of which might have been the direct cause of her death, but there was insufficient forensic evidence to prove which act had in fact caused the death. In the opinion of the court it was unnecessary to prove which act caused the death; the jury should have been directed to convict if they were satisfied that, whichever act killed the victim, each act was committed with the necessary fault element for manslaughter.

▶ *Blaue* **[1975] 3 All ER 466. Court of Appeal**

The appellant was convicted of manslaughter on grounds of diminished responsibility. He had stabbed the victim, and in hospital she was told that a blood transfusion would be necessary to save her life. She refused a transfusion as being contrary to her beliefs as a Jehovah's Witness. She died. Medical evidence at the trial indicated that if she had consented to a transfusion she would not have died. The appellant argued that causation was not established. The Court of Appeal dismissed the appeal, holding that the refusal of medical treatment on religious grounds did not break the chain of causation, as the rule that 'you take your victim as you find him' applies to the whole person and not just the physical person.

▶ *Cheshire* **[1991] 3 All ER 670. Court of Appeal**

The defendant shot the victim, who was taken to hospital. He required a tracheotomy, which the doctors performed negligently, and the patient died. The trial judge had suggested that the doctors' acts had broken the chain of causation if the jury decided that they had acted recklessly. The Court of Appeal suggested that the sole question for the jury was whether the defendant's acts were a substantial cause of death. If they were, he could be said to have caused the victim's death even though the doctors' mistreatment might also have contributed to the death.

▶ *Kennedy* [2007] UKHL 38

The appellant gave a syringe full of heroin to the victim. The victim injected himself with it. The victim died as a result. The appellant was convicted of manslaughter. He appealed on the ground that the victim has broken the chain of causation by injecting himself. The Court of Appeal dismissed his appeal, but the House of Lords upheld it. It explained that the victim had made a fully informed and voluntary choice to inject himself which broke the chain of causation, and so the defendant could not be said to have caused the death.

▶ *Malcherek and Steel* [1981] 2 All ER 422. Court of Appeal

The appellants were convicted of murder. In each case, the appellant had seriously injured a victim. The victims were both put on life-support machines, which were switched off when the victims were found to be dead according to the medically accepted tests of brain death. The appellants argued that the juries in their respective cases had been misdirected on the issues of causation. The court held that switching off the life-support machines had not broken the chain of causation between the injuries and the deaths of the victims. The court approved the dictum of Lord Parker CJ in *Smith* (see below) and was satisfied that the injuries were the operating cause of death. The court did not decide whether death occurred before or after the life-support machines were switched off, or which tests should be applied to determine death. Whichever tests were applied, the victims had died, and the medical treatment was 'normal and conventional', given bona fide by competent and careful medical practitioners. Evidence that other doctors might have acted differently did not affect the issue of causation. The appeals were dismissed.

▶ *Pagett* (1983) 76 Cr App Rep 279. Court of Appeal

The appellant was convicted of manslaughter. He shot at police officers, using the victim as a shield against her will. The victim was hit by bullets shot in return by the police officers, and died. The court held that it was usually unnecessary to direct the jury on causation, it being enough to tell them that the act of the accused must have contributed significantly to the result. In this case, the intervention by the police officers did not break the chain of causation because it was not voluntary: it was a reasonable act of self-preservation. The appeal was dismissed.

▶ *Roberts* (1971) 56 Cr App Rep 95. Court of Appeal

The appellant was convicted of an assault occasioning actual bodily harm, contrary to s 47 Offences Against the Person Act 1861. He had given the victim a lift in his car and as a result of his advances she jumped out of the car while it was moving, and was injured. The court dismissed his appeal, holding that it is not a requirement under s 47 for the accused to have foreseen the actions of the victim which resulted in the actual bodily harm. The test was whether it was something that could reasonably have been foreseen, the 'natural consequence' of what the accused said and did. If the victim does something so unexpected that no reasonable person could be expected to foresee it, then the injury is caused by a voluntary act on the part of the victim which breaks the chain of causation between the assault and the injury. The appeal was dismissed.

▶ *Smith* [1959] 2 All ER 193. Courts Martial Appeal Court

The appellant was convicted of murder. He had injured the victim in a fight in a barracks. The victim was dropped twice by a third man on the way to the medical station. On arrival, the seriousness of one of his wounds was not diagnosed and inappropriate treatment was given. He died. There was evidence that if the victim had received immediate and different treatment he might not have died. The court dismissed the appeal, distinguishing *Jordan*.

Chapter 5

The mental element

Key Terms

- ▶ **Intention** – the aim or purpose of the defendant.
- ▶ **Negligence** – the defendant's failure to act according to the standard of the reasonable person.
- ▶ **Recklessness** – the unreasonable taking of a risk by the defendant.

5.1 Mental element in a criminal offence

The majority of serious criminal offences require, in addition to the *actus reus*, a specific state of mind on the part of the accused, usually referred to as the *mens rea*. Many less serious crimes require no *mens rea*, but simply proof that the defendant caused the prohibited harm. These are known as strict liability crimes and will be discussed separately in Chapter 6. They tend to be crimes which carry lower sentences, and the focus is on discouraging a particular harm rather than imposing moral blame. Most serious crimes require proof of some blameworthy state of mind, for example that the defendant intended or foresaw a particular result. The requirement of *mens rea* can be justified on several grounds. If the criminal law is to act as a deterrent it is only sensible to punish people who deliberately break the law. Likewise if a criminal conviction is to carry an element of censure (see Section 1.3) then the law should require a guilty state of mind. Of course, just because the defendant has the *mens rea* it does not follow that she is necessarily guilty, because she may have a defence. For example, a defendant may kill another intentionally but still be not guilty of murder if the killing was carried out in self-defence. So the *mens rea* requirement is part of, but not the whole of, the law's assessment of whether the defendant deserves criminal blame.

As the *actus reus* of an offence may contain a number of different elements, there may be a different *mens rea* required for each of these elements, so the *mens rea* of an offence may consist of several components. The offence of handling stolen goods requires that the act of handling be dishonest, as well as the knowledge or belief that the goods were stolen. The offence of burglary, under s 9(1)(a) Theft Act 1968, requires entry of a building as a trespasser (the *actus reus*) with an intent to commit one of a range of offences, such as an intent to steal, and in addition that the accused knows that he is entering a building as a trespasser, or realises that he may be.

It should be noted that although the phrase *mens rea* literally means 'guilty mind', a defendant may have a *mens rea* even though he is blameless. For example in *Yip Chiu-Cheung** [1995] 1 AC 111 the Privy Council considered the *mens rea* of the defendant, who was an undercover anti-drug officer who had joined with a drug smuggler in arranging the importation of drugs in an effort to uncover a drug-smuggling gang. The court decided that he could be said to have an intention to conspire to arrange the importation of drugs. The fact that he was acting from the best of motives did not affect the question whether the *mens rea* existed.

5.2 Different types of *mens rea*

Although, as we have stressed, each offence has its own *mens rea*, there are a number of *mens rea* words which occur frequently in the definitions of offences and which need to be examined. It might appear logical and desirable for the criminal law to possess a 'library' of concepts, with clear definitions, which could then be used for a variety of offences: it would make the drafting, interpretation and application of the criminal law easier and more consistent. However, there is a difficulty in drafting a definition of a word such as 'intention' which is suitable for such widely different offences as, for example, theft, murder attempts and criminal damage. As a result it has not been unknown for the same word, such as 'intention', to bear a different meaning in two different offences. Such a position cannot be seen as logical or desirable, and it certainly does not make the interpretation or application of the criminal law any easier. It is perhaps in reaction to this problem that judges have recently taken to avoiding the definition of *mens rea* words, preferring to trust the common sense of juries acting with the minimum of guidance.

We will examine three key *mens rea* concepts: intention, recklessness and negligence. They can be seen as existing on a scale, with intention being the most serious form of *mens rea*, recklessness the next most serious and negligence the least serious.

5.3 Intention

5.3.1 The meaning of 'intention'

The word 'intention' has proved difficult for the courts to define and has been given different meanings in different contexts. In fact it is rare for the courts to have to consider the precise meaning of 'intention'. This is partly because there are not many offences for which intention alone will suffice for the *mens rea*; it is much more common for the *mens rea* to be intention or recklessness. For such offences there is no need to distinguish between recklessness and intention. This means that the crucial theoretical question of the boundary between intention and recklessness is not often of practical importance. However, intention should be examined for two reasons. The first is conceptual: intention and has been described as the 'paradigm of self-determined action'; that is, to intend a consequence is to associate oneself with that consequence to a greater extent than one would be if one were being reckless or negligent. So in a sense it is the most serious form of *mens rea*. The second is more practical. Most cases on intention have arisen in the context of homicide, where the difference between intention and recklessness marks the fundamental difference between murder and manslaughter.

What, then, does it mean to say that a person intends a particular result? A consistent theme in all the cases on intention is that the term should be given its normal meaning. Therefore the core meaning of intention is that a person intends a result when he wants or desires it to happen. In *Mohan* [1976] QB 1 a case dealing with the meaning of intention in the context of the offence of attempted murder, James LJ explained that intention meant 'aim' or 'a decision to bring about a certain consequence'. He considered it was irrelevant whether the result was likely or unlikely to occur. You can intend to kill a victim by shooting at him hoping to kill him even though he is a long way away and you are unlikely to succeed.

It has also been made clear that 'intention is something quite distinct from motive or desire' (*Moloney** [1985] AC 905 (Lord Bridge)). This means that the law is not concerned with why the defendant acted. So, in a case of a 'mercy killing', for example, there is an intent to kill, even though there may be a good motive (to put an end to the victim's pain and suffering). Motive may, however, be very relevant as a means of proving the existence of intention, making it more (or less) likely that the accused possessed the necessary intention. If the defendant was due to inherit a large fortune from the victim whose cup of tea she poisoned, the jury are unlikely to believe that the poisoning was an unfortunate accident and more likely to decide that the defendant deliberately set out to kill the victim. Indeed, Lord Bridge was not questioning the suggestion that where a result is wanted or desired it is intended; he was just saying that a result may be intended, but not desired.

The core definition of intention, then, is that it was the defendant's purpose in committing an action. This is thought to coincide with the normal understanding of the word, and so Lord Bridge in *Moloney* suggested a 'golden rule' – that judges do not need to give juries detailed guidance on the meaning of intention. Juries simply use the normal meaning of the word. In most cases references to 'the chameleon-like concepts of purpose, foresight of consequence and awareness of risk' are likely only to confuse the jury (*Wright*, 5 April 2000, Unreported, CA).

However, in difficult cases (which are 'rare and exceptional' (*Gregory and Mott* [1995] Crim LR 507)) it may be necessary to give further direction. These cases arise when the defendant does an act in order to bring about one particular consequence but it is highly likely that another result will occur. In many cases it will be unbelievable that a defendant could have performed the act he or she did with any intent apart from causing death or grievous bodily harm. For example, in *Christofides* [2001] EWCA Crim 906 the Court of Appeal suggested that no special direction was needed where the defendant hit the victim repeatedly on the head with a stick. He could have had no other purpose apart from causing serious harm. However, in other cases it is possible that the defendant did an act which was very likely to produce one result, but the defendant was acting in order to produce another. An oft-quoted example (taken from a Law Commission report) is of a person who puts a bomb on an aircraft with the purpose of collecting insurance money from the goods on board which will be blown up. Although his purpose is only to blow up the goods (indeed he will be delighted if the pilot is able to escape unhurt) he is aware that the pilot's death is effectively inevitable. This kind of intent (where the result was not the defendant's purpose but was foreseen as virtually certain) is often known as 'oblique intent'. Is this 'oblique intent' sufficient to amount to intention in the eyes of the law?

The courts have struggled with this question. The House of Lords attempted answers in *Moloney* and *Hancock and Shankland** [1986] AC 455, but it is its most recent judgment in *Woollin** [1999] 1 AC 82 which represents the current law. Their Lordships adopted (with slight modification) a direction first proposed by the Court of Appeal in *Nedrick* [1986] 3 All ER 1:

> Where the charge is murder and in the rare cases where the simple direction is not enough, the jury should be directed that they are not entitled to [find] the necessary intention, unless they feel sure that death or serious injury was a virtual certainty (barring some unforeseen intervention) as a result of the defendant's actions and that the defendant appreciated that such was the case.

So, taking the example of murder, where it must be shown that the defendant intended to kill or cause serious injury, the current law on intention is as follows:

> In most cases the judge needs simply to tell the jury to give intention its ordinary meaning; that is, the defendant intended to kill or cause serious injury if that was his aim or purpose. Indeed to give the *Woollin* direction in a normal case would be inappropriate (*MD*). If the case is one where the defendant had some other aim, but death or serious injury was very likely to occur as a result of the defendant's actions then the judge should invite the jury to consider two questions:
>
> 1. Was death or serious injury virtually certain to result from the defendant's acts?
> 2. Did the defendant appreciate that death or serious injury was virtually certain to result from his or her acts?

Only if the answers to both these questions are 'yes' is the jury entitled to find intention.

A number of points should be stressed about the present law:

1. If it is not the defendant's purpose to kill or cause serious injury and if death or serious injury was not virtually certain or appreciated to be so by the defendant, the jury is not permitted to find intention, even if it feels the evidence indicates intention. Consider this example. A terrorist plants a bomb in a city centre and telephones a warning in plenty of time to evacuate the city, but the bomb goes off when it is touched by a passer-by, killing her. The jury may decide that the terrorist's purpose was to gain publicity and cause disruption, but not to kill or cause serious injury. If so, it cannot convict of murder because it cannot be said that it was virtually certain that the bomb would kill or injure anyone.

2. To satisfy the *Woollin* test it must be shown both that death or serious injury was virtually certain and that the defendant realised that this was so. This means that if the defendant believed death or serious injury to be certain, but in fact they were not, the jury is not entitled to find intention. This seems surprising, given that intent is seen as a subjective concept, looking at the defendant's state of mind. Consider the example of a defendant firing a gun at a person who, unknown to the defendant, has a bullet-proof vest on, but whom the defendant still kills. Although it would not be virtually certain that the victim would die, is it sensible that the existence of the vest affects our assessment of the defendant's state of mind?

3. The courts have stressed that foresight of virtual certainty is not intent, but it is evidence from which the jury may find intent. Intent is a subjective concept. The fact that a reasonable person in the defendant's shoes may have foreseen or intended the consequence is only evidence of the defendant's state of mind. This is stressed by s 8 Criminal Justice Act 1967, which states:

> A court or jury, in deciding whether a person has committed an offence,
>
> (a) should not be bound in law to infer that he intended or foresaw a result of his actions by reason only of it being a natural and probable consequence of those actions; but
> (b) shall decide whether he did intend or foresee that result by reference to all the evidence, drawing such inferences from the evidence as appears proper in the circumstances.

4. The direction approved in *Woollin* states that the jury are entitled to find intention. The word 'entitled' suggests that the jury may find intention, but they do not have to (*Matthews** [2003] 2 Cr App R 30). In other words if death or serious injury was not the defendant's aim or purpose, the jury are permitted to decide that even though death

or serious injury was virtually certain and the defendant realised this, the defendant did not intend death or serious injury. An example of where it may be appropriate not to find intention is given by William Wilson (1999). A father is holding his baby at the top of a burning building. As the flames get very close he throws the baby to the ground, aware that this is virtually certain to kill or seriously injure the baby, but believing that it is the only way of saving the baby from burning. Even though he realised it was virtually certain that the baby would die, to say that the father intended to kill or seriously injure the baby seems wrong. In fact he was acting with the intention of saving the baby from death. Saying that the jury are entitled to find intention leaves the jury with 'moral elbow room' (to use Horder's phrase) to decide in cases such as the father's that there is no intention. It may be that, although not wanting to say so openly, the courts are saying that for these cases which are at the borderline of intention, motive can be taken into account by the jury.

5. Lord Steyn in *Woollin* modified the direction in *Nedrick* to replace the word 'infer' with 'find'. Unfortunately he did not explain why he thought this was a better word to use, and commentators have discussed the question at some length. Here are some of the possible explanations:

   a. There is no significance in the change. Lord Steyn simply thought that 'finding' would be an easier word for juries to understand than 'inferring'.
   b. Lord Steyn was indicating that sometimes foresight of virtual certainty is not just evidence from which intention can be found; rather, foresight of virtual certainty can actually itself be intention. However, in *Matthews*, Rix LJ was clear that *Woollin* was not seeking to provide a definition of intention and such a view makes this view of the change in the *Nedrick* test unlikely.
   c. It may be that 'finding' intention was seen as setting a lower hurdle than 'inferring' intent, and therefore the change was designed to encourage juries to find intent.

5.3.2 Intoxication and intent

If the defendant was drunk or drugged at the time of the crime and is charged with an intent-based offence then the intoxication (be it voluntary or involuntary intoxication) can be taken into account alongside all the other evidence in deciding whether the defendant intended to cause the harm. If the defendant, although intoxicated, intended to cause the harm he will be guilty because 'a drunken intent is still an intent' (*Majewski** [1977] AC 443). However, if in a murder case, in the defendant's drunken state he did not mean to kill the victim and did not foresee the victim's death as virtually certain he will not be guilty of murder. He may, however, be guilty of manslaughter. Indeed wherever the defendant's drunkenness is used as an argument that the defendant did not intend a result he may be convicted of a recklessness-based crime. In short there are no special rules about intoxication when intent is in issue. Intoxication is simply one of the pieces of evidence taken into account when deciding whether the defendant intended the result.

5.4 Recklessness

The cases we have just been considering in relation to intention have focused on the distinction between intent and foresight of consequences. This is, in fact, the distinction between intention and recklessness. The cases on recklessness which we will now examine tend to focus on the distinction between recklessness and negligence.

Fortunately the House of Lords has reconsidered the law on recklessness and greatly simplified it. In the past there were two different kinds of recklessness. These are usually known by the names of the House of Lords cases which defined them – *Cunningham** (*Cunningham* [1957] 2 QB 396) recklessness and *Caldwell** (*Caldwell* [1982] AC 341) recklessness. However in *R v G** [2003] UKHL 50 the House of Lords abolished *Caldwell* recklessness, and so now there is only one kind of recklessness to consider. We will, however, later briefly look at *Caldwell* recklessness so that you can understand why it was abolished.

5.4.1 The definition of 'recklessness'

Lord Bingham in the House of Lords' decision in *R v G* approved of the following definition of recklessness:

> A person acts recklessly ... with respect to –
>
> (i) a circumstance when he is aware of a risk that it exists or will exist;
> (ii) a result when he is aware of a risk that it will occur;
>
> and it is, in the circumstances known to him, unreasonable to take the risk.

Recklessness therefore requires that the defendant 'has foreseen that the particular kind of harm might be done and yet has gone on to take the risk of it' (*Cunningham*). It does not need to be shown that the risk was a large one – just that the defendant was aware that there was a risk (*Brady* [2006] EWCA Crim 2413). The risk must be one which it was unreasonable for the accused to take. In considering whether the risk is one which it was unreasonable to take, the law will take into account the risk of the harm and the nature of the act. So, if a defendant is driving his car when a child runs into the road and in order to avoid the child he swerves, realising that he is likely to crash into and damage a parked car, the jury may well decide that the taking of this risk of damage to property is reasonable and so is not reckless.

In order to prove recklessness it is necessary to show that the defendant is subjectively aware of the risk that her act will cause harm. If the defendant is found not to have foreseen the risk of harm that her conduct creates then she is not reckless, even if it is a blindingly obvious risk. For the purposes of recklessness it does not matter whether a reasonable person would have foreseen the harm, but only what the defendant herself actually foresaw. So, in *Stephenson* [1979] QB 695 a schizophrenic man lit a fire inside a haystack, burning it down. He did not foresee the risk of damage to the haystack and therefore he was not reckless. The fact that most people would have foreseen the risk or that it was an obvious risk was beside the point. Of course, the jury is still permitted to infer that because a reasonable person would have foreseen the risk the defendant must have foreseen it, and so in effect the burden may be on the defendant to explain to a jury why she failed to foresee an obvious risk.

A trickier issue for the law of recklessness is a defendant who was aware of the risk 'in the back of his mind'. In *Parker* [1977] 1 WLR 600 a man in a rage slammed down a public telephone and broke its receiver. He claimed he was not reckless because at the time he was so angry that he did not foresee he might damage the telephone. No doubt this was true, because at the time he slammed down the telephone he was not consciously thinking of the risk of damage to it but rather thinking angry thoughts. The Court of Appeal held that if a defendant was aware of a risk but put it to the back of his mind he would still be found to be *Cunningham* reckless, and it decided that this must have been true of Mr Parker. This decision seems to have stretched *Cunningham* recklessness to its limit in accepting that having a risk in the back of one's mind is being aware of the risk. It is understandable that the Court of Appeal felt that a defendant like Mr Parker had to be found reckless, because many people when committing a crime will not be consciously thinking of the risk at the time they commit the act. There is perhaps a degree of fiction in including within the notion of recklessness those whose foresight of the risk was in the back of their mind.

There is one very important addition to the definition of recklessness. If a defendant is voluntarily intoxicated, for example through taking alcoholic drink or drugs, she is not allowed to rely on her intoxication as evidence that she did not foresee a risk. In effect she will be deemed to be reckless if the risk was one which she would have seen had she been sober, even if, in fact, in her intoxicated state she was not aware of the risk (see Chapter 15 for further discussion of intoxication).

So, to summarise, the law now is simple: if the defendant foresees a risk of harm and unreasonably takes that risk, she is reckless as to that harm. But we cannot be that quick. There are three issues which slightly muddy the waters. The first is that, as Lord Bingham made clear, if the defendant who is voluntarily intoxicated fails to foresee a risk she will still be reckless. In a way this makes sense; if someone does not see the possible harm to another because he has made himself intoxicated he deserves to be punished. But why is intoxication singled out as a blameworthy reason for failing to see a risk. Is not a person who is angry or arrogant or inconsiderate and so does not see a risk just as blameworthy as the person who is intoxicated and fails to see the risk? Are those who are careless or indifferent to other people's welfare not properly called reckless? Lord Bingham offers no explanation for singling out voluntary intoxication as the only 'unforgivable reason' for failing to see an obvious risk. Further, it should not be forgotten that many offenders are drunk when they commit crimes. For example, 88 per cent of criminal damage cases involve a drunken defendant. So the 'intoxication exception' is hardly an exception in criminal damage cases; it is rather the rule. Second, there is the category of cases similar to *Parker* where the defendant is aware of the risk because it is in the back of his mind. Third, there is the question of whether the law is realistic. In cases of minor crimes do juries or magistrates really try to discover what was in the defendant's mind at the time of the crime or do they simply reason, 'The reasonable person would have foreseen the risk and so we presume you did'? If that is what they are doing would it be more honest to admit that the law says that if the risk was an obvious one the defendant will be convicted unless he or she has a good reason for not seeing the risk.

5.4.2　The abolition of *Caldwell* recklessness

As already mentioned, *Caldwell* recklessness has been abolished by the House of Lords in *R v G*. The House of Lords in *Caldwell* defined reckless as:

1. The defendant performed an act that created a serious risk of harm.
2. Either

   a. he recognised that there was some risk of that harm occurring, but nevertheless went on to take it; or
   b. he did not even address his mind to the possibility of there being any such risk and the risk was in fact obvious.

'Serious risk' in (1) means a risk that a reasonable person would not dismiss as negligible and that the harm would amount to the *actus reus* of a criminal offence. The requirement in (2)(a) is the same as *Cunningham* recklessness. If you foresee a risk of harm (it does not need to be a serious risk) then you will be *Caldwell* reckless. This means that anyone who is *Cunningham* reckless would also be *Caldwell* reckless. However, (2)(b) states that if the defendant failed to consider the obvious risk she is *Caldwell* reckless (although she is not *Cunningham* reckless). *Caldwell* recklessness was strongly criticised by commentators.

In *R v G* the House of Lords felt the time had come to abolish *Caldwell* recklessness. Four main reasons can be found for the abolition in their Lordships' speeches. First, Lord Bingham stated that *Caldwell* recklessness infringed the important principle that a person was guilty of a serious crime only if they had a guilty mind. He stated:

> it is not clearly blameworthy to do something involving a risk of injury to another if (for reasons other than self-induced intoxication ...) one genuinely does not perceive the risk. Such a person may fairly be accused of stupidity or lack of imagination, but neither of those failings should expose him to conviction of serious crime or the risk of punishment.

This reflected a criticism often levelled at *Caldwell*, namely that by not requiring proof of foresight it blurred recklessness and negligence.

Second, Lord Bingham in *R v G* also thought *Caldwell* recklessness capable of producing unfair results. He argued:

> It is neither moral nor just to convict a defendant (least of all a child) on the strength of what someone else would have apprehended if the defendant himself had no such apprehension.

Lord Steyn picked up on unfairness to child defendants, referring to the United Nations Convention on the Rights of the Child. The unfairness arose because in deciding whether the risk was obvious, the jury had to consider whether it was obvious to a reasonable person and not whether it should have been obvious to the defendant. The injustice of this was shown in the case of *Elliot v C** [1983] 2 All ER 1005, in which a 14-year-old with learning difficulties was out late at night and lit a fire in a shed, burning it down. It was said that the lighting of the fire created an obvious risk of damage to the shed, and she was convicted, even though the risk might not have been obvious to a person of her age and in her circumstances. It is one thing to punish a defendant for failing to foresee a risk that he should have foreseen, but to do so is only fair in cases where a defendant could have foreseen the risk.

A third reason for abolishing *Caldwell* recklessness was that the decision had received fierce criticism from leading scholars (notably Professors John Smith and Glanville Williams) and judges. Unfortunately no mention was made of the voluminous writing supporting *Caldwell* recklessness or variants of it.

Finally, Lord Bingham held that the House of Lords in *Caldwell* had simply misinterpreted the word 'recklessly' in the Criminal Damage Act 1971.

5.5 Negligence

Negligence compares the actions of the accused with those of a hypothetical 'reasonable person'. A negligent act is one which falls below the standards expected of a reasonable ordinary prudent person. The state of mind of the defendant, what she intended or foresaw, is irrelevant. The jury simply ask whether the defendant acted in a way in which a reasonable person would not. In fact, although negligence is of very great importance in the civil law of tort, it does not feature in many serious criminal offences. However, there are many statutory crimes which are negligence-based, particularly in areas of professional regulation. Many believe that negligence should not play a role in criminal law, that criminal liability should require that the accused actually possess a specific state of mind and does not merely fall short of some required standard of conduct. Lord Diplock himself expressed a similar view in *Caldwell* [1982] AC 341 when he said that '*mens rea* is by definition a state of mind of the accused himself at the time he did the physical act that constitutes the *actus reus* of the offence; it cannot be the mental state of some non-existent, hypothetical person'. In *Sheppard* [1981] AC 394 Lord Diplock also expressed doubts about the place of negligence in the criminal law:

> The concept of the reasonable man as providing the standard by which the liability of real persons for their conduct is to be determined is a concept of civil law, particularly in relation to the tort of negligence; the obtrusion into criminal law of conformity with the notional conduct of the reasonable man as relevant to criminal liability, though not unknown (e.g. in relation to provocation sufficient to reduce murder to manslaughter), is exceptional, and should not lightly be extended.

The most serious offence in which negligence has formed part of the *mens rea* or fault element is common law manslaughter. In this case the negligence required has to be very great, or 'gross' (see Section 10.3).

Some argue that negligence should not be regarded as a form of *mens rea*, as that concept is concerned with states of mind and negligence is essentially a description of conduct. To include negligence within *mens rea* broadens the concept to include wider ideas of fault, blameworthiness or culpability.

There are several other words commonly found in criminal offences which import an element of *mens rea*, but these are best considered in the context of the specific offences in which they appear. For example, 'knowledge or belief' is found in the offence of handling stolen goods, and 'dishonesty' is commonly found in the offences against property discussed in Part III.

5.6 Transferred *mens rea*

A general principle, well established in the case law, though sometimes criticised by academics, is the doctrine of transferred *mens rea* (sometimes called 'transferred malice'). This is a rule which is connected to the rules of causation in the criminal law (see Chapter 4). If Jennifer shoots at Mark intending to kill him, but in fact kills Jim, she will be held liable for the murder of Jim. The law says that Jennifer's *mens rea* (intention to kill Mark) is transferred to the actual victim and so Jennifer can be convicted of Jim's murder. By contrast, in *Pembliton* (1874) LR 2 CCR 119 the defendant threw a brick at a person but missed and damaged a window. He was not guilty of maliciously damaging a window as he had no *mens rea*. Transferring the intention to injure a person did not enable the conviction to stand because the *mens rea* transferred has to be the correct *mens rea* for the offence. Intention to injure a person plus damage to property does not create an offence. Had the defendant thrown the brick at a door and missed and hit the window then he would have been guilty, as that *mens rea* (maliciously damaging property – the door) was the *mens rea* needed for the offence with which he was charged.

In *A-G's Ref (No 3 of 1994)** [1997] 3 WLR 421 the defendant stabbed his pregnant girlfriend. The stab wound injured the unborn child, who was born prematurely and died from the stab wound 121 days after birth. It was argued by the prosecution that it was possible to convict the man of murder on the basis of transferred malice: he intended to kill or cause grievous bodily harm to the mother and this could be transferred to the child. The House of Lords rejected this on the basis that at the time of the stabbing the foetus was not a person in the eyes of the law. This meant that to convict the defendant there had to be a double transfer of malice: from the mother to the foetus, then from the foetus to the person she would become. This they felt was to stretch the doctrine of transferred malice too far, especially as the prosecution was relying on an intention to cause serious injury as the *mens rea* for murder, which Lord Steyn said was anomalous, even though it was well established in the case law. As we shall see in Section 10.2, the defendant could have been properly convicted of manslaughter. The House of Lords' decision has been criticised. The defendant caused the death of the child and intended to cause grievous bodily harm to someone. Is his argument 'I did not intend to injure the child, I intended to injure the mother' any more attractive in this case than in the standard case of transferred malice in a murder case?

Some commentators argue that the doctrine of transferred *mens rea* is too wide: one should not be liable for unintended and unforeseeable consequences. The correct charge, they argue, is attempt against the intended victim. However, it is understandable that the law is unsympathetic to a defendant who seeks by way of excuse that the wrong victim died (see Horder, 2006).

5.7 Coincidence of *actus reus* and *mens rea*

In order for a criminal offence to be complete, the *actus reus* and *mens rea* must coincide in time. As James J said in *Fagan** [1969] 1 QB 439, 'the subsequent inception of mens rea cannot convert an act which has been completed into an assault'. The rule is of relevance in two different situations:

1. If the *mens rea* occurs after the *actus reus*. For example, if Brian was driving carefully and within the speed limits when Josh jumped out in front of his car and despite his best attempts Brian ran Josh over and killed him, there would be no offence. If Brian jumped out of his car and saw it was Josh and shot him not realising that Josh was already dead, this intent to kill could not turn the original accidental killing into a criminal offence. Of course, there would be an offence if Brian saw Josh and deliberately drove into him.
2. If the *mens rea* occurs before the *actus reus*. If the *mens rea* exists before the *actus reus* but is not present at the time the *actus reus* is performed there is no offence. If Glen, in a fit of rage, says to his enemy Vladimir, 'I want to kill you', and several days later is involved in a car accident where, quite without fault on his part, he happens to run over Vladimir, he is not guilty of murder. That is because, although at one point in time he had an intention to kill Vladimir (the *mens rea* for murder) and at another point in time he killed him (the *actus reus* of murder), the two did not coincide. He did not intend to kill when performing the act which killed the victim.

The requirement of coincidence of *actus reus* and *mens rea* seems a sensible limitation on the width of criminal law without which we would get dangerously close to punishing people just for their bad thoughts. However, there are situations in which there is an apparent separation in time between the *mens rea* and *actus reus* but the law still convicts the defendant:

1. There could be an *actus reus* with no *mens rea*, followed later in time by the *mens rea*. Fred takes Penelope's umbrella from a stand, thinking it is his own, and later he realises his error but decides to keep it. The law may allow a conviction in this situation. First, the law may see the first act as a continuing act. It could be held that Fred is continuing to appropriate Penelope's umbrella and therefore is continuing to commit the *actus reus* of theft at the time when the *mens rea* arises. An example of this is *Fagan*, where the defendant's act of parking a car on a policeman's foot was seen as an ongoing *actus reus*, and once the *mens rea* arrived (he realised that the car was on the foot) the offence was complete. A second way in which the law can deal with this is by looking at the later occasion when there is a *mens rea* and considering whether there may be liability for an omission. *Miller** [1983] 2 AC 161 can be analysed in this way (see Section 3.3). When he fell asleep there was an *actus reus* but no *mens rea*. However, when he awoke and saw the fire there was a *mens rea*. By stating that his failure to deal with the fire was an *actus reus*, the House of Lords was able to circumvent the problem of the apparent separation of the *actus reus* and the *mens rea*. In Fred's case it could be said that the moment he was aware the umbrella was not his he was under a duty to return it. His failure to do so was an omission, but because he was under a duty to act this constituted the *actus reus*.

2. Sometimes it is possible to convict a defendant even though there is *mens rea* but no *actus reus*, later followed by the *actus reus*. An example is *Church** [1966] 1 QB 59, in which the defendant attacked a woman, with the *mens rea* for murder. He thought that he had killed her but in fact he had only injured her. He put the 'corpse' into a river and the victim died while in the river. Again, the law has used two devices to deal with this problem. The first is the development of a special doctrine. The Court of Appeal in *Church* held that the defendant was guilty if 'the jury regarded the appellant's behaviour from the moment he first struck her to the moment when he threw her into a river as a series of acts designed to cause death or grievous bodily harm'. The difficulty in applying this test has been in deciding exactly what constitutes a 'series of acts'. It is clear that if there is a plan and the defendants are mistaken as to when during their plan they have killed the victim, they are still guilty (*Thabo Meli* [1954] 1 All ER 373). However, the doctrine also applies where there is no preconceived plan, as *Church* itself shows.

    In *Le Brun** [1992] QB 61 the defendant and his wife had an argument in a street. He wanted her to come home with him and she did not want to go. He hit her and she fell over. He then tried to pick up her body in order to carry her inside the house. It appears that the defendant dropped his wife and she banged her head on the side of a pavement. This killed her. Although it was an accident when he dropped his wife, he had *mens rea* when he hit her. The Court of Appeal argued that, although they were not part of a preconceived plan, these acts formed a 'single transaction', and he was therefore guilty of manslaughter. It seems that their reasoning was that his act of picking his wife up was done in order to take her into the house, perhaps to cover up his crime. It is generally thought that the result would have been different had he picked her up to take her to hospital, as then he would have been seen to be trying to undo the earlier harm rather than exacerbate it. If this had been the case the *actus reus* and the act with *mens rea* could not have been linked and he would not have been guilty of manslaughter.

An alternative argument used by the Court of Appeal in *Le Brun* was to try to apply the rules of causation to this situation. It can be said that the defendant's initial act of hitting his wife caused him to pick her up, which caused her death. His act of picking her up would not then be seen as a break in the chain of causation (see Chapter 4).

5.8   'The correspondence principle'

It might be thought that there should be a correspondence between the *actus reus* and the *mens rea*; that is, the *mens rea* should be a state of mind relating to the *actus reus*. For example, the *mens rea* for murder would be an intent to kill; for an offence of causing grievous bodily harm it would be that the defendant intended or foresaw grievous bodily harm. However, such a principle is not part of the law and the *mens rea* can relate to a lower level of harm than that which forms part of the *actus reus*. For example, the *mens rea* for murder includes an intent to cause grievous bodily harm. Also, there are some other offences which require an 'ulterior intent', that is performing an act with an intention to cause some harm in the future. For example, as we have seen, burglary involves entering a building as a trespasser with intent to commit one of various crimes. The *mens rea* therefore does not necessarily correspond to the *actus reus*, although it often will do so. Intention or foresight of a lesser harm than that involved in the *actus reus* may be sufficient in some cases; intention or foresight of a greater harm than the *actus reus* is required in others.

Some commentators argue that 'the correspondence principle' (that the *mens rea* should correspond to the *actus reus*) is one to which the law should aspire as an ideal. Others disagree, and argue that if a defendant does an act foreseeing that it will cause some harm, then she should be responsible for any harm resulting from her acts; the consequence is not 'bad luck', as she has 'made her own bad luck'. She should be responsible for the consequences of her actions. She has lost any sympathy for 'bad luck' by acting in a way which she knows may harm another. Horder has proposed a 'proportionality' principle. This is that a defendant can be responsible for more harm than she intended or foresaw as long as it was proportionate to the harm she foresaw.

Hot Topic –   Euthanasia and mercy killing

If a person is suffering from a terminal illness and asks a doctor to help her die, what can the doctor lawfully do? If the doctor hastens the death of the patient, can she be convicted of murder? Two key questions are involved. First, did the doctor cause the death of the victim? Second, did the doctor intend to kill or seriously injure the victim?

1. The law draws a sharp distinction in this context between acts and omissions. These will be dealt with separately:

   a. If the doctor does an act (for example, gives a lethal injection) the *actus reus* of murder will be established if the act is a substantial and operating cause of death (*Cheshire* [1991] 3

All ER 670; *Moor*, 11 May 1999, Unreported). This must, of course, be demonstrated beyond reasonable doubt. In one trial of a doctor for murder, the trial judge withdrew the murder charge from the jury on the ground that there was insufficient evidence that the accused had caused the death (rather than that the death resulted from the patient's illness). A charge of attempted murder went to the jury and the doctor was acquitted (*Arthur* (1981) 12 BMLR 1).

Devlin J in *Adams* [1957] Crim LR 365 stressed that if an act of a doctor shortened the life expectancy of a terminally ill patient, the doctor would still be held to have caused the death of the patient even though the patient would have died a few weeks afterwards anyway. However, he went on:

> But that does not mean that a doctor aiding the sick or dying has to calculate in minutes or hours, or perhaps in days or weeks, the effect on a patient's life of the medicines which he administers. If the first purpose of medicine – the restoration of health – can no longer be achieved, there is still much for the doctor to do, and he is entitled to do all that is proper and necessary to relieve pain and suffering even if measures he takes may incidentally shorten life.

This suggests that a doctor who is seeking to relieve pain may not be found to have caused the death of a patient if he shortens life expectancy by only a few minutes or hours. This may be seen as an example of the law on causation being influenced by policy considerations (see Section 5.1). This might be inferred from Devlin J's direction to the jury in *Adams* to apply common sense to the case. In a more recent case on euthanasia, Hooper J preferred simply to ask the jury whether it believed that the doctor's acts were an operating and substantial cause of the death (*Moor*).

b. Now we will consider the situation where the defendant does not act; for example, she does not provide the medical treatment necessary to preserve the victim's life. Here, perhaps strangely, a distinction is drawn between doctors and members of the deceased's family.

i. Doctors are required to act in the patient's best interests. This will never permit the doctor to act in a way which causes the death of the victim (*Bland*; *Cox*, 18

September 1992, Unreported). However, the law has accepted that sometimes it is not in the patient's best interests to receive treatment, even if without it the patient will die. This will be true where either the patient's projected life will be intolerable (for example, a baby is born with terrible disabilities and a short, pain-filled life is predicted: *Re J* [1993] Fam 15) or the patient is suffering from persistent vegetative state and so is unaware of what is happening to him or her (*Bland*).

ii. Carers are expected to act as reasonable people. This means that they must follow medical advice. Therefore a carer who does not give the patient the drugs prescribed by the doctor will infringe his duty. If the patient falls seriously ill and the carer does not summon a doctor this will also infringe her duty. In both cases the defendant can be liable for murder or manslaughter. The law takes the view that it is for doctors, not carers, to decide whether it is in the patient's interests to receive further medical treatment.

2. If it is established that the doctor did cause the patient's death, the next question is whether there was an intention to kill the patient. It is possible to distinguish three states of mind:

a. If the doctor acts with the purpose of killing the patient this appears to be an example of direct intention and the *mens rea* of the murder is established. The fact that the doctor or patient may be acting with the best of motives (for example, believing that the patient has suffered enough) is irrelevant if the doctor's purpose is to kill.

b. A little more complex may be an argument that the defendant killed in order to prevent the patient suffering any more. It could be argued that the primary purpose was to end the suffering, not to kill. However, it is submitted that although this issue has not been directly addressed by the courts, this is a case where the end (ending the pain) necessarily involves the killing. The purpose is to be achieved through the killing. This should therefore be regarded as a case of directly intended death. Therefore the *mens rea* of murder could be established.

c. The most controversial case is where the doctor or carer administers a substance which is a pain reliever, while being aware that this substance will also lead to a shortening of the patient's life. This is different from (b), where it is the death that will relieve the pain; here it is the drug that will ease the pain, and the death can be regarded as an incidental consequence. This therefore is a case of 'oblique intent' and the *Woollin* [1999] 1 AC 82 direction applies. The doctor or carer will have to admit that he was aware that death or serious bodily harm was a virtually certain consequence of his action and therefore the jury are entitled to find there is intent. Some people take the view that faced with such a case, the jury would in fact be sympathetic to a doctor or carer and decline to find intention. Indeed Lord Goff in *Bland* stated as a fact that if a doctor administers pain-relieving drugs and death is caused as a side-effect of this treatment, he is not guilty of murder. Ognall J in *Cox* and Hooper J in *Moor* directed the jury that if the doctor's primary intent was to relieve pain there was no *mens rea* for murder. It may be that what these judges are saying is that a jury should not (or would not) find intent in such a case, but that appears to go against the view in *Matthews* [2003] 2 Cr App R 30 that it is up to the jury to decide whether to find intention. It may, however, be that Lord Goff was explaining that in cases involving the treatment of terminally ill patients the normal law on intention does not apply.

To complete the picture, defences need to be briefly mentioned. It is, of course, no defence simply to rely on the fact that the patient had consented to the killing. A carer may be able to rely on diminished responsibility if the pressure of the caring had caused an abnormality of mind (see Section 10.9). Provocation may be available, but *Cocker* indicates that there will be difficulties in proving that the defendant lost his or her self-control (see Section 10.8). There is no special defence of mercy killing. There are those who argue that a special defence of mercy killing should be developed for carers who kill their terminally ill relatives. There is also a case for developing a special defence available to doctors who act in accordance with established medical practice. Indeed there are a few dicta which could suggest that such a defence already exists. In *Gillick v West Norfolk and Wisbech Area Health Authority* [1986] AC 112 Lord Scarman stated that 'the bona fide exercise by a doctor of his clinical judgement

must be a complete negation of the guilty mind'. Hooper J's direction in *Moor* also suggests that a special defence is available.

The issue of euthanasia is, of course, a moral minefield. Strong views are taken on each side of the issue. The present state of the law is unlikely to satisfy either those who are keen to legalise euthanasia or those who believe it is never justifiable to take another's life. As the above discussion reveals, the present law draws some very fine distinctions between acts and omissions and different forms of intention. It is therefore easy to criticise the law because it draws artificial distinctions. However, it must be accepted that in order to set the line between lawful and unlawful killings in this context, some very fine distinctions must be made.

Before we leave this issue there is a question of whether the law will need to be re-examined in the light of the Human Rights Act. In *R (Purdy) v DPP* [2009] UKHL 45 Ms Purdy was complaining that the Director of Public Prosecutions had refused to guarantee that if her husband helped her to commit suicide he would not be prosecuted for aiding and abetting suicide. She claimed that this interfered with her right to choose how and when to die, which was protected by the right to respect for private life (Article 8 Convention). Their Lordships accepted this argument but noted that under Article 8 the state was entitled to interfere with her rights if necessary in the interests of others. They held that the state was entitled to prohibit assisted suicide in order to protect vulnerable people being 'helped on their way' without their true consent. However, if the state were to interfere in a peron's rights the law had to be clear. She ultimately won her case because the guidance offered by the DPP on when people will be prosecuted for assisting in a committed suicide was not sufficiently clear. As a result new guidance has been issued.

The fact that a doctor can withdraw treatment from a patient in a case such as *Bland* even though the patient will die without the treatment could be said to infringe a patient's right to life. However, Article 2, by referring to deprivation of a life, only protects the right not to be killed by an act and does not cover omissions (*NHS Trust A v M; NHS Trust B v H* [2001] 1 FLR 406). Indeed, in *An NHS Trust v D* [2000] 2 FLR 501 Cazalet J suggested that Article 3 could require withdrawing treatment from a patient close to death who was suffering an intolerable level of pain.

Summary

5.1 *Mens rea* is the term used to describe the mental element in an offence, the state of mind that the offender must possess at the same time as committing the *actus reus*. It may consist of several different components, and may be inferred by the courts as well as expressed in a statutory definition of the offence.

5.2 Some *mens rea* words, such as 'intention' and 'recklessness', are used in many different offences. Although it would be logical for these words to bear the same meaning wherever they occur, this does not in fact happen. As a result, words are given different interpretations by the courts and there is considerable variation in the context of the offences in which they appear.

5.3 The meaning of 'intention', according to the House of Lords, should be left to juries to define for themselves in the vast majority of cases, giving the word its normal meaning. Where further help is needed the judge can tell the jury the following: intention must be distinguished from motive; if the defendant foresaw a consequence as virtually certain and the result was virtually certain then the jury are entitled to find that the defendant intended the consequence.

5.4 A defendant is reckless if he or she unreasonably takes a risk of harm to another or another's property. If the defendant is voluntarily intoxicated at the time of the offence he or she will be found to be reckless even if he or she did not foresee the risk of harm.

5.5 Negligence is concerned with an objective standard of behaviour and often involves a failure to think rather than a state of mind. Negligence is rarely found as a component of serious criminal offences; manslaughter is an exception, and here the negligence required is 'gross'.

5.6 If the accused intends to injure one person but succeeds in injuring a different person the *mens rea* is sometimes said to be 'transferred' from the intended victim to the actual victim. In many cases this rule will not be needed because of the definition of the offence, or because it will be possible and sufficient to prove recklessness with respect to the actual victim.

5.7 *Actus reus* and *mens rea* must coincide in time for the offence to be complete. However, if the *actus reus* takes place over a period of time, or consists of a series of acts, the *mens rea* need not be present throughout – it may be superimposed on a continuing *actus reus*.

5.8 Some commentators argue that the law should uphold the correspondence principle. This requires the *mens rea* of a crime to refer to the *actus reus*. Others support a proportionality principle, that there need only be a proportion between the *actus reus* and the harm referred to in the *mens rea*.

Further Reading

Theoretical discussions of the nature of intention and recklessness are found in Alexander and Kessler Ferzan, Duff, Hart, Horder (1995, 2000), Keating, Kugler, Lacey and Norrie. The present law on intention is analysed in Norrie, Simester (1996, 1999), Pedain and Williams. Recklessness and negligence are discussed in Crosby, Gardner (1993, 1994), Horder (1997), Kimel and Tadros. Issues surrounding the legal treatment of euthanasia and similar problems are examined in Arlidge, Ashworth, Goss and Smith. Sullivan reviews the link between *mens rea* and *actus reus*. The correspondence principle is discussed in Horder (1995, 1999) and Mitchell. Transferred *mens rea* is discussed in Horder (2006) and intoxication in Law Commission.

Alexander and Kessler Ferzan, *Crime and Culpability* (Cambridge University Press 2009).
Arlidge, 'The Trial of Dr David Moor' [2000] Crim LR 31.
Ashworth, 'Criminal Liability in a Medical Context', in Simester and Smith (eds), *Harm and Culpability* (Oxford University Press 1996).

Further Reading cont'd

Crosby, 'Recklessness – The Continuing Search for a Definition' (2008) 72 J Crim L 313.

Child, 'Drink, Drugs and Law Reform' [2009] Crim LR 488.

Duff, *Intention, Agency and Criminal Liability* (Blackwell 1990).

Gardner, 'Recklessness Redefined' (1993) 109 LQR 21.

Gardner, 'The Importance of Majewski' (1994) 14 OJLS 26.

Goss, 'A Postscript to the Trial of Dr David Moor' [2000] Crim LR 568.

Hart, *Punishment and Responsibility* (Oxford University Press 1968).

Horder, 'A Critique of the Correspondence Principle' [1995] Crim LR 759.

Horder, 'Intention in the Criminal Law – A Rejoinder' (1995) 58 MLR 678.

Horder, 'Gross Negligence and Criminal Culpability' (1997) 47 U Tor LJ 495.

Horder, 'Questioning the Correspondence Principle – A Reply' [1999] Crim LR 206.

Horder, 'On the Irrelevance of Motive in Criminal Law', in Horder (ed.), *Oxford Essays in Jurisprudence* (Oxford University Press 2000).

Keating, 'Reckless Children?' [2007] Crim LR 546.

Kimel, 'Inadvertent Recklessness in the Criminal Law' (2004) 120 LQR 548.

Kugler, *Direct and Oblique Intention in the Criminal Law* (Ashgate 2002).

Lacey, 'A Clear Concept of Intention: Elusive or Illusory?' (1993) 56 MLR 621.

Lacey, 'In(de)terminable Intentions' (1995) 58 MLR 592.

Law Commission, *Intoxication and Criminal Liability* (Law Com No 314, 2009).

Mitchell, 'In Defence of the Correspondence Principle' [1999] Crim LR 195.

Norrie, 'After Woollin' [1999] Crim LR 532.

Norrie, 'Between Orthodox Subjectivism and Moral Contextualism: Intention and the Consultation Paper' [2006] Crim LR 486.

Pedain, 'Intention and the Terrorist Example' [2003] Crim LR 579.

Simester, 'Moral Certainty and the Boundaries of Intention' (1996) 16 OJLS 445.

Simester, 'Murder, Mens Rea and the House of Lords – Again' (1999) 115 LQR 17.

Simester, 'Can Negligence Be Culpable', in Horder (ed.), *Oxford Essays in Jurisprudence* (Oxford University Press 2000).

Simester, 'Intoxication Is Never a Defence' [2009] Crim LR 3.

Smith, 'A Comment on Moor's Case' [2000] Crim LR 41.

Sullivan, 'Cause and Contemporaneity of Actus Reus and Mens Rea' (1993) 52 CLJ 487.

Tadros, 'Recklessness and the Duty to Take Care', in Shute and Simester (eds), *Criminal Law Theory* (Oxford University Press 2002).

Williams, 'Oblique Intent' (1988) 47 CLJ 417.

Wilson, 'Doctrinal Rationality after Woollin' (1999) 62 MLR 448.

Case Notes

▶ *A-G's Ref (No. 3 of 1994)* **[1997] 3 WLR 421. House of Lords**

See Chapter 9 Case notes.

▶ *Caldwell* **[1982] AC 341. House of Lords**

The appellant was convicted of arson, contrary to s 1(2) and (3) Criminal Damage Act 1971. He had pleaded guilty to arson contrary to s 1(1) and (3). The appellant had set light to a hotel in which there were guests staying because he had a grudge against the proprietor. He pleaded intoxication as a defence, but the trial judge ruled that intoxication was no defence to s 1(2), which requires intention to endanger the life of another or recklessness as to whether life would be endangered. The Court of Appeal allowed his appeal on the ground that this was a misdirection. The House of Lords dismissed the appeal by the prosecutor, but held that intoxication was a defence to s 1(2) only in cases where the charge was based on an intention to endanger life. In cases where recklessness was alleged, intoxication was no defence. The majority agreed with the judgment of Lord Diplock, who redefined recklessness for the purposes of the Criminal Damage Act 1971, overruling earlier Court of Appeal decisions such as *Stephenson*. He held that recklessness was not confined to people who were aware of the risk that the harmful consequence would result. It included those who, in circumstances in which the risk was obvious, had not given any thought to the possibility of such a risk.

▶ *Church* [1966] 1 QB 59. Court of Criminal Appeal

See Chapter 10 Case notes.

▶ *Cunningham* [1957] 2 QB 396. Court of Criminal Appeal

See Chapter 7 Case notes.

▶ *Elliot v C* [1983] 2 All ER 1005. Divisional Court

The accused was acquitted of arson, contrary to s 1(1) and (3) Criminal Damage Act 1971. She was a girl of 14 who, after staying out all night, had set light to a garden shed by pouring white spirit over the floor and throwing two lighted matches onto the spirit. The magistrates accepted the defence argument that, in applying Lord Diplock's ruling in *Caldwell* as to the meaning of recklessness in this offence, they should take into account whether the risk of damage to property would have been obvious to the particular defendant if he or she had given any thought to the matter. The Divisional Court allowed the appeal by the prosecutor. The court rejected the magistrates' interpretation of Lord Diplock's judgment and held that an 'obvious risk' was one which would be obvious to a reasonably prudent person, not necessarily to the particular defendant.

▶ *Fagan* [1969] 1 QB 439. Divisional Court

See Chapter 3 Case notes.

▶ *R v G* [2003] UKHL 50. House of Lords

One night two boys, aged 11 and 12, went camping without their parents' permission. Early in the morning they set fire to some paper near a wheelie-bin they found outside a supermarket. The fire spread and burned down the supermarket and nearby buildings. They were convicted of criminal damage under the *Caldwell* test on the basis that it would have been obvious to a reasonable person that what they were doing was posing a risk to property. The House of Lords overruled *Caldwell* and defined recklessness as follows: 'A person acts recklessly ... with respect to (i) a circumstance when he is aware of a risk that it exists or will exist; (ii) a result when he is aware of a risk that it will occur; and it is, in the circumstances known to him, unreasonable to take the risk.'

▶ *Le Brun* [1992] QB 61. Court of Appeal

The defendant hit his wife and she fell to the ground. He picked her up to carry her into their house but dropped her, causing her to bang her head, which caused her death. The Court of Appeal argued that the apparent separation in time between *mens rea* and *actus reus* could be dealt with by seeing the events as 'one transaction', or on the basis of causation in that there had been no intervening causes between his hitting her and her death.

▶ *Majewski* [1977] AC 443. House of Lords

See Chapter 15 Case notes.

▶ *Matthews* [2003] 2 Cr App Rep 30. Court of Appeal

The defendants threw the victim from a bridge into a river after they had beaten him up. He had told them he could not swim, and indeed he drowned. The Court of Appeal dismissed the appeals. It confirmed that the *Woollin* direction created a rule of evidence rather than a rule of law. In other words it was setting out the circumstances in which the jury could, if they wished, find intention, and it was not a rule of law setting out when intention existed. On the facts of this case Rix LJ suggested that the finding of intention was 'irresistible'.

▶ *Miller* [1983] 2 AC 161. House of Lords

See Chapter 3 Case notes.

▶ *Moloney* [1985] AC 905. House of Lords

See Chapter 9 Case notes.

▶ *Woollin* [1999] 1 AC 82. House of Lords

The appellant was charged with the murder of his baby son, who had died of head injuries. He was convicted of murder after admitting that he had caused the injuries. The House of Lords allowed his appeal. A modified form of the *Nedrick* test was approved. The jury would be entitled to find intention if death or serious injury was virtually certain and the defendant realised that this was so.

▶ *Yip Chiu-Cheung* [1995] 1 AC 111. Privy Council

See Chapter 18 Case notes.

Chapter 6

Corporate crime and strict liability

Key Terms

▶ **Corporate liability** – the circumstances in which a company can be convicted of a criminal offence.
▶ **Strict liability** – a crime in which a defendant can be convicted without proof of the defendant's state of mind.
▶ **Vicarious liability** – a crime in which the defendant can be convicted because of the acts of someone else.

6.1 The meaning of 'strict liability'

'Strict liability' is the phrase used to refer to criminal offences which do not require *mens rea* in respect of one or more elements of the *actus reus*. They are nearly all offences created by statute. Although strict liability is sometimes said to be exceptional, in fact it has been estimated that over half of the criminal offences triable in the Crown Court require no proof of *mens rea* (Ashworth and Blake, 1996). The phrase 'absolute liability' is sometimes used, but this is misleading because it implies both that an offence of strict liability possesses no fault element at all and that it is not possible to plead a defence to such crimes. Neither of these suggestions is true. Often the statute itself will provide for a defence, such as a defence of 'due diligence' (the accused will be acquitted if he can show that he was not negligent) or the 'act of third party defence' (the accused demonstrates that the prohibited conduct or result was due to the act or default of a third party; see Chapter 5). It is also possible for the accused to plead a general defence if that defence is not a mere denial of *mens rea* (see Section 15.1). Examples are self-defence or automatism, which deny either the unlawfulness of the *actus reus* or its voluntary nature, and so are not affected by the absence of *mens rea* in an offence of strict liability. That said, it was recently held that insanity is not a defence to a strict liability drink-driving offence, the argument being that insanity is a denial of *mens rea* (*Harper* [1997] 1 WLR 1406). This is hard to accept, as insanity is best seen as exemption of liability (see Section 15.1). The case may be explained by special policy reasons relating to road safety. However, strict liability offences differ from negligence-based crimes because the prosecution in a strict liability offence does not need to prove that the defendant acted reasonably. If the defendant caused the prohibited harm he can be guilty of a strict liability offence even if he acted reasonably (*Barnfather v Islington LBC* [2003] ELR 263).

6.2 The justifications for strict liability offences

At first sight it seems unjust that people can be convicted of a criminal offence even though they had no knowledge of the circumstances rendering their conduct unlawful. Indeed in some strict liability offences a person can be guilty even though she has behaved entirely reasonably. Can such offences be justified? Here are some of the possible explanations:

1. *Protection of the public.* The main justification of strict liability offences is that they protect the general public. It is significant that the nineteenth century saw a wider acceptance of strict liability by the courts alongside a considerable increase in legislation designed to protect people from dangers in the workplace and public places. In a decision of the House of Lords (*Lemon** [1979] AC 617), Lord Diplock explained:

   > The usual justification for creating by statute a criminal offence of strict liability, in which the prosecution need not prove mens rea as to one of the elements of the actus reus, is the threat that the actus reus of the offence poses to public health, public safety, public morals or public order.

   Strict liability offences are most commonly found in statutes dealing with, for example, the sale of alcohol, food and drugs; the prevention of pollution; safety at work; and public health. The argument in favour of strict liability in these areas is that it ensures that a company does everything it can to prevent there being, for example, any pollution or dangerous substances in food. The fear of a criminal conviction may encourage a company to take every step possible to ensure that it does not infringe the law. Just requiring a company to take 'reasonable steps' to prevent pollution may not be sufficient protection to the public as that might be interpreted to mean that companies only need to do the minimum that is reasonable to prevent the harm. However, this argument can be countered: how will the punishment of a person who has taken all reasonable care, and so has not been negligent, encourage others to avoid liability by taking more care? Do we want people to take unreasonable steps to try to prevent harm?

2. *Ease of proof.* Strict liability offences are easier for the prosecution to prove. There is no need to produce evidence of the defendant's state of mind. All the prosecution need do to establish a case is prove that the defendant acted in a certain way. Requiring a court to find that the defendant knew certain facts makes cases more complex for the police to prepare and for courts to hear. Imagine that it were possible to convict a motorist of a speeding offence only if it were shown that he knew that he was driving over the speed limit. Making speeding a strict liability offence and requiring proof only that the car was being driven at excess speed makes the courts' and police's job so much easier. It is also notable that in the case of many strict liability offences the defendant will be a company. As we shall see later, there can be great difficulty in finding that a corporation has *mens rea*, and strict liability offences overcome this problem.

3. *Strict liability offences are not really criminal.* Strict liability may also be justified in such cases by suggesting that strict liability offences are regulatory offences and not truly criminal. The argument is that there is no grave injustice if a person is convicted of a strict liability offence despite acting entirely reasonably because a conviction for a strict liability offence is not 'a real crime'. In *Sherras v De Rutzen* [1895] 1 QB 918 Wright J referred to strict liability offences as involving acts which 'are not criminal in any real sense, but acts which in the public interest are prohibited under a penalty'. However, there seem to be no objective criteria by which to differentiate between so-called true crimes (*mala in se*) and regulatory offences (*mala prohibita*). It is largely a matter of retrospective rationalisation once

the decision has been taken to impose strict liability: strict liability offences tend to be perceived as regulatory rather than truly criminal because they are sometimes committed without fault.

This alleged distinction between regulatory and truly criminal offences has no practical consequence relating to the procedures of trial or punishment. However, prosecution for some regulatory offences is carried out by a government agency rather than the police or Crown Prosecution Service. This can be significant, as some regulatory agencies rarely prosecute and prefer to rely on negotiation and encouragement to enforce compliance with the law.

4. *Human Rights Act*. It has been argued that Article 6 of the Convention prohibits the use of strict liability offences. However, the courts have rejected an argument that a strict liability offence infringes Article 6 rights (see *Muhammed* [2002] EWCA 1856; *Barnfather v Islington LBC* [2003] ELR 263; *Deyemi* [2007] EWCA Crim 2060). This was recently confirmed by the House of Lords in *R v G* (2008). Lord Hope explained that Article 6 'is concerned essentially with procedural guarantees to ensure that there is a fair trial, not with the substantive elements of the offence with which the person has been charged. ... It is concerned with the procedural fairness of the system for the administration of justice in the contracting states, not with the substantive content of domestic law.'

6.3 Construing statutes which appear to impose strict liability

When courts are construing a statute which creates a criminal offence but does not state what the *mens rea* requirement is, they must decide whether to imply a *mens rea* requirement or to treat the offence as one of strict liability. The law is governed by the presumption of *mens rea*, although this presumption can be rebutted.

6.3.1 The presumption of *mens rea*

Two important recent decisions of the House of Lords (*B v DPP* [2000] 2 AC 428 and *R v K* [2002] 1 AC 642) have emphasised the 'presumption of *mens rea*'. The presumption means that if there is any doubt about whether an offence requires *mens rea* it should be presumed that it does. In other words there is a presumption against an offence being one of strict liability. The general presumption of *mens rea* was explained by Lord Nicholls in *B v DPP*. In discussing cases where a statute did not explicitly state what the *mens rea* for an offence was, he stated:

> In these circumstances the starting point for a court is the established common law presumption that a mental element, traditionally labelled mens rea, is an essential ingredient unless Parliament has indicated a contrary intention either expressly or by necessary implication. The common law presumes that, unless Parliament indicated otherwise, the appropriate mental element is an unexpressed ingredient of every statutory offence.

In *R v K*, Lord Steyn appeared to go even further. He explained that the presumption does not arise only if the statute is silent or ambiguous as to any *mens rea* requirement. He stated:

> The applicability of this presumption is not dependent on finding an ambiguity in the text. It operates to supplement the text. It can only be displaced by specific language, i.e. an express provision or a necessary implication. In the present case there is no express provision displacing the presumption. The question is whether it is ruled out by a necessary implication.

As a result of these decisions, an offence will be one of strict liability only if Parliament makes it quite clear in a statute that it is to be so. That may be by clear wording of the statute or a 'compellingly clear' inference from the wording (*Kumar* [2005] Crim LR 470).

But, if a *mens rea* is presumed, exactly what *mens rea* will that be? It appears from *B v DPP* and *R v K* that the defendant will have a defence if he believed that an aspect of the *actus reus* did not exist. So in *B v DPP* the defendant was charged under s 1(1) Indecency with Children Act 1960 (an offence abolished by the Sexual Offences Act 2003) of inciting a girl under the age of 14 to commit an act of gross indecency with him. As the statute did not require any *mens rea* the House of Lords implied that the defendant would have a defence if he believed that the circumstances of the case were such that he was not committing an offence. Crucially here, the defendant would have a defence if he thought the girl in question was over 14. A fine distinction must be made. It does not have to be shown that the defendant was aware of the circumstances of the offence. What must be shown is that he did not believe that the circumstances were such that there was no offence. The distinction becomes important when one considers a defendant who does not think about the age of the victim. In such a case he would be guilty under this rule.

Most controversially, their Lordships went on to hold that the defendant had a defence if he believed she was over 14, even if this was an unreasonable belief. Lord Nicholls rejected an argument that a belief had to be honest if it was to provide a defence, explaining:

> Considered as a matter of principle, the honest belief approach must be preferable. By definition the mental element in a crime is concerned with a subjective state of mind, such as intent or belief. To the extent that an overriding objective limit ('on reasonable grounds') is introduced, the subjective element is displaced. To that extent a person who lacks the necessary intent or belief may nevertheless commit the offence. When that occurs the defendant's 'fault' lies exclusively in falling short of an objective standard. His crime lies in his negligence. A statute may so provide expressly or by necessary implication. But this can have no place in a common law principle, of general application, which is concerned with the need for a mental element as an essential ingredient of a criminal offence.

6.3.2 Rebutting the presumption of *mens rea*

The circumstances in which the presumption of *mens rea* will be rebutted are far from clear. In *B v DPP* the House of Lords indicated that the presumption of *mens rea* should be rebutted only if it is a necessary implication that Parliament intended the offence to be one of strict liability. The phrases used by their Lordships to indicate how strong the evidence had to be to rebut the presumption included 'compellingly clear' (Lord Nicholls), 'sufficiently clear' (Lord Steyn) and 'necessary' (Lord Hutton and Lord Mackay).

In deciding whether the presumption of *mens rea* is rebutted, the courts will consider the following:

1. *The wording of the statute.* As is clear from *R v K* and *B v DPP*, the wording of the statute will be important. If the presumption is to be rebutted it now appears that there must be words in the statute indicating that the offence is to be strict. If the statute makes no mention of the defendant having a defence of mistake, it is very unlikely that the presumption will be rebutted. If there is some evidence in the

statute that the offence is to be strict, the courts will consider the other factors. If some offences in the statute explicitly include a *mens rea* requirement and others do not, this will be one factor indicating that those which do not are to be offences of strict liability (*Matudi* [2003] EWCA Crim 697).

2. *The nature of the offence.* The subject matter of the statute and the nature of the particular offence will be considered (*Sweet v Parsley** [1970] AC 132). In *Alphacell Ltd v Woodward* [1972] AC 824 the purpose of the statute (to prevent the pollution of rivers) was also stressed by the House of Lords. Lord Salmon said:

> If this appeal succeeded and it were held to be the law that no conviction could be obtained under the 1951 Act [the Rivers (Prevention of Pollution) Act 1951] unless the prosecution could discharge the often impossible onus of proving that the pollution was caused intentionally or negligently, a great deal of pollution would go unpunished and undeterred to the relief of many riparian factory owners. As a result many rivers which are now filthy would become filthier still and many rivers which are now clean would lose their cleanliness. The legislature no doubt recognised that as a matter of public policy this would be most unfortunate.

The interpretation of drug offences also illustrates the importance of the subject matter of the offence. The House of Lords considered the issue of strict liability for the first time in a case involving the possession of controlled drugs (*Warner v MPC** [1969] 2 AC 256). The appellant had been convicted of possessing a controlled drug found in a box in his possession; he claimed that he did not know that the box contained the drug and that he had thought it contained perfume. Lord Reid, who was in a minority in the House of Lords, took the view that this was a 'truly criminal and disgraceful offence, so that a stigma would attach to a person convicted of it', and for this reason held that the offence should require knowledge on the part of the accused that he had prohibited drugs in his possession (not necessarily knowledge as to the precise drug). However, the majority held that this degree of *mens rea* was not required; as long as the accused knew that he possessed something, there was no need to prove that he knew he had a prohibited drug. Lord Pearce thought that the 'efficacy of the Act' would be seriously impaired if it were to be held that the accused must know the nature of the drug concerned. The House of Lords in *Lambert** [2001] 3 WLR 206 recently confirmed the *Warner* interpretation of possession.

3. *Profit-making activities.* The imposition of strict liability may be more justifiable where the defendant is engaging in a profit-making activity which creates hazards for the public than for 'the conduct of ordinary citizens in the running of their everyday life' (Lord Diplock in *Sweet v Parsley*).

4. *Seriousness of the offence.* There is some dispute over the relevance of the seriousness of the crime in deciding whether the offence is one of strict liability. Some cases suggest that the less serious the offence, the more likely the crime was intended by Parliament to be one of strict liability (*Alphacell Ltd v Woodward*). However, in other cases the seriousness of the crime is seen as a reason in favour of imposing strict liability. In *Howells* [1977] QB 614 a case concerning possession of a firearm, the court stated:

> the danger to the community resulting from the possession of lethal firearms is so obviously great that an absolute prohibition against their possession without proper authority must have been the intention of Parliament when considered in conjunction with the words of the section.

Lord Nicholls in *B v DPP* appeared to prefer the earlier view, stating:

> The more serious the offence, the greater is the weight to be attached to the presumption, because the more severe is the punishment and the graver the stigma which accompany a conviction.

The fact that imprisonment is available as a sentence does not necessarily indicate that the offence is not regulatory (*Blake* [1997] 1 All ER 963).

5. *Ensuring compliance*. The Privy Council has held that courts should consider whether the imposition of strict liability will be effective in encouraging 'greater vigilance to protect the commission of the prohibited act' (*Gammon v A-G for Hong Kong* [1985] 1 AC 1). However, it might be thought that imposing liability only if the defendant has failed to take reasonable steps (that is negligence-based liability) would fulfil this function.

6. *Justice and the public interest*. In *R v K* Lord Steyn argued that the courts could take into account the public interest in deciding whether an offence should be strict. He said it was not in the public interest that sexual acts involving anyone under 16 would automatically be a criminal offence. Lord Millet preferred to talk in terms of justice. He thought it would be unjust to convict of a sexual offence a defendant who honestly believed that the victim was over 16 and was consenting.

6.4 Alternatives to strict liability

It is clear now that if Parliament wants to create a new strict liability offence it should make this absolutely clear on the face of the statute. However, it may consider alternatives to the rigours of strict liability. Two in particular were mentioned by Lord Reid in *Sweet v Parsley* [1970] AC 132 and have attracted adherents. The first is to require *mens rea* for the offence, but to transfer the burden of proof to the accused, so that once the *actus reus* of the offence is proved, the burden of disproving *mens rea* lies on the defence. In *Sweet v Parsley*, Lord Pearce favoured this approach, referring to it as a 'sensible half-way house', although he conceded that there might be difficulty in reconciling it with the opinion of Viscount Sankey in *Woolmington** [1935] AC 462 (which puts the burden of proving every element of an offence on the prosecution; see Section 2.4).

The second possibility mentioned by Lord Reid would be to substitute negligence for 'mens rea in the full sense'. Instead of having to prove intention, or knowledge or recklessness, the prosecution would merely have to prove that the accused was negligent. A variation of this comes from *Tolson* (1889) 23 QBD 168, and is sometimes referred to as the 'defence' of a reasonable mistake of fact. Lord Diplock in *Sweet v Parsley* preferred this option, and explained that it involved:

> the implication that a necessary element in the offence is the absence of a belief, held honestly and upon reasonable grounds, in the existence of facts which, if true, would make the act innocent ... This implication stems from the principle that it is contrary to a rational and civilised criminal code, such as Parliament must be presumed to have intended, to penalise one who has performed his duty as a citizen to ascertain what acts are prohibited by law (*ignorantia iuris non excusat* [ignorance of the law is no excuse]) and has taken all proper care to inform himself of any facts which would make his conduct unlawful.

Professor Hogan (1978) has used more direct language: 'a provision which labels criminal a man who has taken all reasonable care to stay on the right side of the law is, on the face of it, just plain daft'.

6.5 Vicarious liability

Normally a person is not liable in criminal law for the acts of another. Vicarious liability is an exception to this rule and can be regarded as a form of constructive liability, as the act, and in some cases even the *mens rea*, of another person is imputed to the defendant. When vicarious liability applies, the accused's conviction does not rest on anything done or omitted by him, but on the acts and mental state of another. Vicarious liability can therefore be distinguished from accessorial liability (see Chapter 17), where the defendant is liable for helping someone else commit a crime.

English law lacks a comprehensive and coherent set of rules on vicarious liability, and the report on the Draft Criminal Code says of the cases on the subject, 'there is no principle underlying these cases. Their existence is simply the product of statutory interpretation.' In *Seaboard Offshore v Secretary of State for Transport* [1994] 2 All ER 99 the House of Lords confirmed that whether vicarious liability can be relied upon depends on the wording of the statute and whether vicarious liability is necessary to give effect to legislation. Although usually vicarious liability operates where the offence is one of strict liability, it is not limited to such crimes (for example, *Tesco v Brent* [1993] 2 All ER 718 and *Re Supply of Ready Mixed Concrete* [1995] 1 AC 500).

If the offence is found to be one where vicarious liability operates then the accused is responsible for anyone employed by her, or authorised to act on her behalf as an agent. An employer is vicariously liable only for an employee who is acting within the scope of her employment. For example, a chauffeur who uses his employer's vehicle as a getaway car for a robbery is acting outside the scope of employment.

6.6 The criminal liability of corporations

There has been increasing interest in recent years in finding companies guilty of crimes, particularly in the light of several large-scale disasters – the distressing number of railway crashes in recent years, the Zeebrugge ferry disaster, the King's Cross fire and the Piper Alpha explosion, to name but a few. In such cases awarding civil law damages (where possible) seems inadequate when gross misconduct by the company appears to warrant the censure of a criminal conviction. In some disaster cases the deaths may have occurred because of the way the company was structured and managed, and because of the company's general ethos towards safety, rather than through the fault of any particular individual. In such a case, punishing the company itself seems more appropriate than punishing one or two of its employees.

There is, however, great difficulty in treating the company as a defendant within the traditional concepts which define a crime. The law recognises that the company is a legal person, separate from its directors or shareholders, but the problem is in what way can we say that a company acts? Or has *mens rea*?

Parliament has responded to these difficulties by passing the Corporate Manslaughter and Corporate Homicide Act 2007, which creates a new offence of corporate manslaughter. The offence is defined in s 1(1):

> An organisation to which this section applies is guilty of an offence if the way in which its activities are managed or organised –
>
> (a) causes a person's death, and
> (b) amounts to a gross breach of a relevant duty of care owed by the organisation to the deceased.

In order for a company to be guilty of this offence the following must be shown:

1. There must be a duty of care owed by the organisation to the deceased. The phrase 'duty of care' is to be understood in the sense in which it is used in the law of tort. This is a complex notion, but the essential element is that it was reasonably foreseeable that the defendant might harm the victim. Sections 3 to 7 exclude activities from falling within the offence. These include decisions concerning military operations, policing and child protection.

2. There must be a breach of the duty of care which is gross. This is defined to mean that the 'conduct alleged to amount to a breach of that duty falls far below what can reasonably be expected of the organisation in the circumstances' (s 1(3)(b)). It is not enough to show that the defendant behaved below the standard expected; it must have behaved far below it. Section 8(2) and (3) provides further guidance by listing factors a jury should take into account in deciding whether the breach is gross:

    (2)... (a) how serious that failure was;
    (b) how much of a risk of death it posed.
    (3) The jury may also –
    (a) consider the extent to which the evidence shows that there were attitudes, policies, systems or accepted practices within the organisation that were likely to have encouraged any such failure as is mentioned in subsection (2), or to have produced tolerance of it;
    (b) have regard to any health and safety guidance that relates to the alleged breach.

    Note that the jury must take into account the factors in subsection (2) ; the factors in subsection (3), they may if they wish.

3. It must be shown that the gross breach of the duty caused the death. It would be possible to imagine a case where, even though there had been serious breaches of health and safety standards, the victim would have died even if they had been followed to the letter. If that was so there would no criminal liability.

4. Section 1(3) makes it clear that an organisation will be guilty only if 'the way in which its activities are managed or organised by its senior management is a substantial element in the breach'. This is important because it means that if the only breaches that occurred were due to junior employees the company cannot be guilty. The phrase 'senior management' is defined in s 1(4)(c) as:

    the persons who play significant roles in –

    (i) the making of decisions about how the whole or a substantial part of its activities are to be managed or organised, or
    (ii) the actual managing or organising of the whole or a substantial part of those activities.

    It should be emphasised that the focus here is on the role performed by the person, rather than their job title. So, if, in effect, a junior worker makes all the decisions for the company, the offence can still be made out.

 **Is the new law on corporate killing effective?**

There can be little doubt that the law on corporate killing is now clearer than it was, but it still leaves some uncertainty and some gaps. First, the Act does not apply to certain public bodies, including many government departments (e.g. the Department of Health), the armed forces and certain other public bodies. Also under s 3(1) if a public authority is making a decision of public policy this will not be covered by the Act. This will limit the potential width of the offence. The justification for the exclusion is that public bodies should not be deterred from making decisions in the public interest for fear of facing a criminal sanction. For example, a health trust choosing not to fund a cancer treatment due to lack of resources should not fear prosecution under the Act.

Second, as we have seen, the Act relies on the notion of 'duty of care' as established in the law of tort. Taylor and Ormerod (2008) claim this adds 'layers of complexity' to the defence. Indeed it would have been easier simply to ask whether when the defendant was acting it was reasonably foreseeable that he or she might cause the victim harm. Fortunately judges, rather than juries, will determine whether there is a duty of care (s 2(6)).

Third, central to the offence is the requirement that there is a gross breach by management. It should be noticed that this does not require the management to have actually directly acted in a way which endangered the victim. If the management was aware that the company's employees were acting in a way which was dangerous but failed to stop

them this could amount to a management failure. Indeed it might be a management failure even if the managers did not know that the employees were acting dangerously, but this was foreseeable. The definition of a person involved in senior management is also fairly wide, and no doubt there will be cases where it will be difficult to determine whether a person is a senior manager.

Fourth, the concept of a breach being 'gross' is somewhat ambiguous, but the list of factors to be taken into account is welcome. It will be interesting to see whether juries will be sympathetic to an argument that, although the company was behaving in a bad way, it was no worse than many other similar companies.

Finally, there is the issue of punishment. The Act states that this can be an unlimited fine. Critics argue that a significant fine is likely to lead to loss of employment and wage cuts. No doubt the actual managers would be able to ensure they did not personally suffer greatly. Other possibilities such as 'capital punishment' for the company (closing it down) or 'imprisonment' (not allowing it to operate for a period of time) could have similar harmful effects on employees.

Summary

6.1   A strict liability offence is one where it is not necessary for the prosecution to prove any *mens rea*.

6.2   Judges have justified the imposition of strict liability by referring to public policy and effective enforcement of the law. Some strict liability offences are described as regulatory or quasi-criminal.

6.3   If it is not absolutely clear from the statute that an offence is to be one of strict liability, the courts will presume a *mens rea*. This *mens rea* will be that it will be a defence for the accused to demonstrate that he believed that an element of the *actus reus* did not exist. In interpreting a statute and deciding whether the presumption of *mens rea* should be displaced and strict liability imposed, the courts will look to the words of the statute, the subject matter of the offence, whether the imposition of strict liability would make compliance with the statute more likely, and the public interest involved.

6.4   As alternatives to strict liability, Parliament could pass a statute creating a negligence-based defence or alter the burden of proof.

6.5   Vicarious liability involves holding one person liable for the acts of another. The acts of an agent or an employee, acting within the scope of his employment, may be imputed to the principal or employer. If the offence requires *mens rea*, then the employer must be shown to possess the necessary state of mind, such as knowledge. In other cases, where there has been a complete delegation of authority, both the acts and the state of mind of the employee have been imputed to the employer.

6.6   Corporations are legal persons. The Corporate Manslaughter and Corporate Homicide Act 2007 has created a new offence of corporate manslaughter.

Further Reading

The leading work on corporate liability is Wells. The controversy over corporate liability is revealed by reading Braithwaite and Fisse, Clarkson, Gobert, Gobert and Punch, Ormerod and Taylor, and Sullivan. Strict and vicarious liability is discussed in Ashworth and Blake, Duff, Gardner, Green, Honoré, Hurd, Husak, Roberts and Simester.

Ashworth and Blake, 'The Presumption of Innocence in English Criminal Law' [1996] Crim LR 306.

Duff, 'Strict Liability, Legal Presumptions, and the Presumption of Innocence', in Simester (ed.), *Appraising Strict Liability* (Oxford University Press 2005).

Gardner, 'Wrongs and Faults', in Simester (ed.), *Appraising Strict Liability* (Oxford University Press 2005).

Gobert, 'The Corporate Manslaughter and Corporate Homicide Act 2007 – Thirteen Years in the Making but Was It Worth the Wait' (2008) 71 MLR 413.

Gobert and Punch, *Rethinking Corporate Crime* (LexisNexis 2003).

Green, 'Six Senses of Strict Liability: A Plea for Formalism', in Simester (ed.), *Appraising Strict Liability* (Oxford University Press 2005).

Honoré, 'Responsibility and Luck' (1988) 104 LQR 530.

Horder, 'How Culpability Can, and Cannot Be Denied in Under-Age Sex Crimes' [2001] Crim LR 15.

Horder, 'Strict Liability, Statutory Construction and the Spirit of Liberty' (2002) 118 LQR 459.

Hurd, 'Whose Values Should Determine When Liability Is Strict', in Simester (ed.), *Appraising Strict Liability* (Oxford University Press 2005).

Husak, 'Strict Liability, Justice, and Proportionality', in Simester (ed.), *Appraising Strict Liability* (Oxford University Press 2005).

Ormerod and Taylor, 'The Corporate Manslaughter and Corporate Homicide Act 2007' [2008] Crim LR 589.

Roberts, 'Strict Liability and the Presumption of Innocence', in Simester (ed.), *Appraising Strict Liability* (Oxford University Press 2005).

Simester, 'Is Strict Liability Always Wrong?', in Simester (ed.), *Appraising Strict Liability* (Oxford University Press 2005).

Sullivan, 'The Attribution of Culpability to Limited Companies' (1996) 55 CLJ 515.

Wells, *Corporations and Criminal Responsibility* (Oxford University Press 2001).

Case Notes

▶ *B v DPP* [2000] Crim LR 403. House of Lords

The appellant was aged 15. He was convicted of inciting a girl under 14 to commit an act of gross indecency by persistently asking her to perform oral sex on him. The key issue was whether it would be a defence if the appellant believed the girl to be over the age of 14. The House of Lords noted that s 1(1) Indecency with Children Act 1960 was silent as to the *mens rea* requirement. They stated that the starting point was that unless Parliament expressly or by necessary implication had indicated that there was to be no *mens rea*, there was a presumption that the offence had a *mens rea* requirement. There was nothing in the Indecency with Children Act to rebut this presumption. This meant that it would be a defence for the appellant if he honestly believed that the girl was over 14. He did not need to show that this belief was based on reasonable grounds.

▶ *R v K* [2001] UKHL 41. House of Lords

The appellant was charged with a sexual assault on a 14-year-old girl. He was unaware that she was 14 and believed that she had consented to the sexual activities. The House of Lords held that it was a defence to a charge under s 14 Sexual Offences Act 1956 for the defendant to demonstrate that he honestly believed the victim to be over 14 and that she consented. Such a belief did not need to be reasonable.

▶ *Lambert* [2001] 3 WLR 206. House of Lords

See Chapter 2 Case notes.

▶ *Lemon* [1979] AC 617. House of Lords

The appellant was convicted of blasphemous libel. He was the editor of a magazine, *Gay News*, in which a poem had been printed which was found to be blasphemous. The trial judge directed the jury that it was necessary for the prosecution to prove that the accused had intended to publish the poem, but that it was not necessary to prove that the accused had any intention to publish blasphemous material. The appellant argued that it was necessary to prove an intention to blaspheme: to outrage and insult the religious feelings of a Christian. The Court of Appeal and House of Lords dismissed the appeal. The House of Lords approved the direction of the trial judge that an intention to blaspheme was not a necessary part of the offence, as long as there was an intent to publish material which was in fact blasphemous.

▶ *Sweet v Parsley* [1970] AC 132. House of Lords

The appellant was convicted of being concerned in the management of premises used for the purpose of smoking cannabis, contrary to s 5(b) Dangerous Drugs Act 1965. She had let rooms in a farmhouse to tenants; at first she also lived in the house, but after some time she ceased to do so. She did not know that cannabis was being smoked on the premises. Her conviction was quashed on the ground that this was not a strict liability

offence: the word 'purpose' in the definition referred to the purpose of the management of the premises. There is a presumption that offences created by statute contain an element of *mens rea*, unless it appears that it must have been the intention of Parliament to create a strict liability offence.

▶ *Warner v MPC* [1969] 2 AC 256. House of Lords

The appellant was convicted of possessing unauthorised drugs contrary to s 1 Drugs (Prevention of Misuse) Act 1964. He had been found with two cases, one of which contained a quantity of amphetamine tablets and the other bottles of scent. He claimed that he had collected them from another man at a café, and thought that both cases contained bottles of scent. The jury was directed that lack of knowledge of the contents of the cases was no defence if it was proved that the accused had control of the cases himself. The House of Lords held that the jury had been misdirected, but dismissed the appeal on the ground that no miscarriage of justice had occurred as a properly directed jury would have been bound to find the appellant guilty. It was held that the offence under s 1 did not require any specific mental element. However, it did require possession, and it was not possible for a person to possess something when he did not know of its existence. Where the drugs were in a container, it was necessary to prove that the appellant possessed not only the case but also its contents. If the appellant had been completely mistaken as to the contents of the case then he could not be in possession of those contents, although ignorance as to the precise qualities of the contents would be no excuse. However, their Lordships thought that this exception did not assist the defendant in this case.

▶ *Woolmington* [1935] AC 462. House of Lords

See Chapter 2 Case notes.

Part II

Offences against the person

Chapter 7

Assaults

Key Terms

- **Actual bodily harm** – harm which is more than trifling or transitory.
- **Assault** – the defendant intentionally or recklessly causes the victim to apprehend the application of some force.
- **Battery** – the defendant intentionally or recklessly applies force to the victim.
- **Grievous bodily harm** – really serious harm.

7.1 Common law and statutory assaults

The criminal law of assault has developed in a piecemeal manner. It is a mixture of early common law (common law assault being derived from the medieval writ of trespass), statute (mainly nineteenth century) and more recent case law. The results can often appear illogical both in content and in terminology, and many believe that the whole area needs reform. In this chapter we will examine the most important non-sexual assaults. Rape and sexual assault will be discussed in the next chapter.

The non-sexual statutory assaults are mainly to be found in the Offences Against the Person Act 1861. In the style of many nineteenth-century statutes, a large number of different offences were preserved in what was essentially a consolidating statute. The result is a collection of offences many of which are of extreme specificity and are rarely prosecuted, such as unlawfully and maliciously impeding a person in his endeavour to save himself or another from shipwreck, punishable with life imprisonment (s 17), or obstructing or assaulting a clergyman in the performance of his duties, punishable with two years' imprisonment (s 36). We will concentrate on the less colourful but more frequently used assaults.

7.2 Common assault and battery

The least serious of the assault offences are common assault and battery. In both common law and statute, the word 'assault' is used in two senses: first, as a generic name for the two common law offences of assault and battery; second, as the specific offence of assault (often called 'common assault' or 'psychic assault'). The essence of an assault, in its narrow sense, is the causing of a victim to fear some immediate use of force against him. Battery is the direct application of such force to the victim.

Both assault and battery are triable summarily (punishable with six months' imprisonment or a fine: s 39 Criminal Justice Act 1988).

7.2.1 Common assault

In order to convict the accused of an assault the following elements must be shown:

- The victim must apprehend imminent unlawful violence.
- The defendant must intentionally or recklessly cause the victim to have this apprehension.

The *actus reus* of an assault involves the creation of an expectation (not necessarily fear) of immediate unlawful violence in the mind of the victim. So an assault may be committed by shaking a fist or brandishing a knife at someone, causing him to apprehend immediate violence. It is necessary to consider some of the elements of the offence in further detail.

1. *The form of conduct*. It used to be thought that it was impossible to assault someone by words alone, but it is now clear that an assault can consist solely of a verbal threat. In *Ireland and Burstow** [1998] AC 147, a defendant was said to have committed an assault when he telephoned his victims a number of times and then remained silent. If silence alone can constitute an assault, then so can words, letters, e-mails, texts, Facebook posts and facial expressions. Indeed after *Ireland* it does not matter how the defendant has created the apprehension. Sometimes, on the other hand, words can belie the seriousness of the threat, as in the early case of *Tuberville v Savage* (1669) 1 Mod R 3, where Tuberville, in a quarrel with Savage, put his hand on his sword and said, 'If it were not assize-time, I would not take such language from you.' The words spoken so contradicted the gesture that they made it clear that the threat would not be carried out, and so the victim did not experience the necessary expectation of violence.

2. *Apprehension of violence*. There is no assault if the victim does not apprehend immediate violence. So if the victim does not see the defendant shake his fist (her back is turned, or she is asleep) or does not believe that the threat will be carried out, there is no assault. So if Simon tried to frighten Alison by making threatening gestures, but Alison just laughed at him because she thought he was being funny, there would be no assault. There can be an assault even if the defendant has no intention or means of carrying out the threat: in *Logdon* [1976] Crim LR 121, a threat with an imitation gun was held to be an assault, because the victim believed that force was about to be inflicted upon her. The accused had apparently never intended to use force, and indeed the gun was not loaded, but this was irrelevant. Common assault is not about a person being on the point of carrying out an attack; it is about creating the apprehension of immediate violence.

3. *Immediacy*. The threat must be of immediate violence or unlawful touching. A threat to injure someone in three weeks' time will not amount to an assault. Generally this requirement of immediacy will mean that for an assault, the actor and victim must be in each other's presence. However, looking in through the window of a woman's home with the intention of frightening her was held to be sufficiently direct to be an assault in *Smith v Chief Superintendent of Woking Police Station* (1983) 76 Cr App R 234, even though there was no evidence that the accused was trying to enter the room. In *Ireland*, it was held that silent telephone calls could give rise to an apprehension of immediate harm because the victims did not know what the defendant was doing and he could have been on his way to their house. Lord Steyn suggested that saying 'I will be at your door in a minute or two' is sufficient to create a fear of immediate violence and the silent telephone call could be interpreted by the victims as having a similar message. This suggests that the immediacy requirement is not to be applied very strictly. In *Constanza* [1997] Crim LR 576, the defendant sent more than 800 letters to the victim and generally harassed her. Two letters were particularly threatening and she suffered stress as a result. The court found that the defendant could be said to have committed an assault. The immediacy requirement

was satisfied because after receiving the letters she was afraid that she might be attacked at any time, including the near future. We await further guidance as to how distant in time a threat needs to be before it ceases to be imminent.

4. *Apprehension that there may be harm.* As Lord Steyn made clear in *Ireland*, it is enough if the victim fears that the defendant *may* use violence. It does not need to be shown that the victim fears that the defendant definitely will use violence. This is useful for the prosecution in a case like *Constanza*, where the victim believes that the defendant may be on the point of attacking at any time in the future.

5. *The* mens rea *of an assault.* The *mens rea* of both assault and battery is intention or recklessness as to the creation of an apprehension of unlawful force (*Venna* [1975] 3 All ER 788, *Spratt* (1990) 91 Cr App R 362 and *Parmenter** [1992] 1 AC 699).

7.2.2 Battery

The offence of battery involves:

▶ Unlawful use of force against another person.
▶ Intention or recklessness that force will be used against another.

Again we will examine some of the more controversial aspects of the offence:

1. *There does not need to be any injury.* A defendant can be guilty of a battery even if the victim does not suffer an injury. Merely touching the other person will be enough if it is done without the consent (express or implied) of the victim. Even touching a person's clothing seems to be sufficient (*Thomas* (1985) 81 Cr App R 331). Battery involves what might colloquially be known as 'invasion of personal space'.

2. *Battery through objects.* A battery can be committed with a weapon or object, as stated by James LJ in *Fagan* [1969] 1 QB 439. He explained that a battery could be committed by the laying of a hand on another, or by using a stick, or even, as in that case, by intentionally allowing the wheel of a car accidentally driven onto the victim's foot to remain where it was. This was confirmed in *DPP v K* (1990) 91 Cr App R 23, where a schoolboy put some acid in a hand-drier and another boy was splashed with the acid when he later used the drier. This was said to constitute a battery. In *Haystead v Chief Constable of Derbyshire* [2000] Crim LR 758 a man punched a woman who was holding her baby. The man was held to have committed a battery against the baby by causing the baby to hit the floor.

3. *The touching must not be an everyday touching.* The offence of battery does not include everyday touching, or 'generally acceptable standards of conduct', for example bumping into someone on a crowded tube train or tapping someone on the shoulder to point out that they have dropped something (*Collins v Wilcock* [1984] 1 WLR 1172). For this reason, holding onto a drunk woman's elbow to escort her from a pub garden was held not to be an assault (*McMillan v CPS* [2008] EWHC 1457 (Admin)). It used to be thought that such conduct was not battery as the victim impliedly consented to it. However, this has not been followed by the courts, and it is hard to imagine that someone in a crowded tube train could withdraw her implied consent by shouting out that no one was allowed to touch her. It is better explained on the ground that such conduct is simply excluded from the definition of a battery.

4. *Does the touching need to be hostile?* There is some debate over whether there is a need to show hostility, in the sense of aggression, in order to establish a battery. In *Faulkner*

v Talbot (1981) 74 Cr App R 1 a woman took a boy to her bed and touched him in an indecent manner. It was said that there was a battery, even though the touching was not aggressive but rather 'affectionate'. In *Brown** [1993] 1 AC 212, *obiter*, the House of Lords held that there was a need to show that the battery was hostile, but only in the sense that it was not consented to. So the act must be hostile in the sense of not consented to, but not hostile in the sense of aggressive.

5. *The* mens rea *for battery.* The *mens rea* for an offence is intentionally or recklessly using force against someone (*Spratt* and *Parmenter*). That means that accidentally touching someone will not be a battery.

7.3 Assault occasioning actual bodily harm

Assault occasioning actual bodily harm (s 47 Offences Against the Person Act) is an aggravated assault, that is an assault with the additional element of actual bodily harm, making it more serious than common assault. It comprises the following elements:

▶ An assault (that is, a common assault or battery)
▶ Occasioning
▶ Actual bodily harm.

The *actus reus* of s 47 requires the commission of an assault or battery, and in addition that this assault or battery caused the actual bodily harm. For example, in the case of *Roberts** (1971) 56 Cr App R 95, the accused had given the victim a lift in his car. He tried to pull off her coat and she jumped out of the car, suffering injuries. The defendant had committed an assault (in causing her to fear immediate violence) and this had caused actual bodily harm (the injuries she suffered in jumping out of the car), and so he was guilty of the offence under s 47.

The terms require a little more explanation:

7.3.1 Assault

Assault here means either an assault or a battery. Both the *actus reus* and the *mens rea* need to be shown.

7.3.2 Occasioning

Occasioning here means the same as causing. It is not enough simply to show that the defendant assaulted the victim and that the victim suffered actual bodily harm. It must be shown that it was the assault that caused the actual bodily harm. This can be particularly problematic in a case, like *Ireland* [1998] AC 147, involving unpleasant telephone calls. It must be shown that it was the fear of imminent unlawful violence that caused the psychological injuries. If the illnesses were caused by the general distress following the telephone calls or fear that the defendant might telephone again, this would not be sufficient to establish a conviction under s 47. In other words, it is not enough just to show that there has been an assault or a battery and that the victim has suffered actual bodily harm. It must be shown that the actual bodily harm resulted from the assault or battery. If the defendant has subjected the victim to a campaign of assaults as a result of which the victim has suffered actual bodily harm, it is not necessary for the jury to decide which of the many assaults caused the harm as long as it is clear that one or more of them did (*Cox* [1998] Crim LR 810).

7.3.3 Actual bodily harm

In *Donovan* [1934] 2 KB 498, before the Court of Criminal Appeal, Swift J gave the 'ordinary meaning' of 'actual bodily harm' as:

> any hurt or injury calculated to interfere with the health or comfort of the [victim]. Such hurt or injury need not be permanent, but must, no doubt, be more than merely transient and trifling.

Bruises, grazes and causing tenderness could amount to actual bodily harm. In *DPP v Smith** [1961] AC 290 it was held that cutting hair could be actual bodily harm. 'Harm', it was held, included not just injury, but also hurt or damage. There was no need to prove the victim suffered pain. In *T v DPP* (1985) 81 Cr App R 331 the victim was rendered temporarily unconscious. It was held that although the harm might be transient, it was not trifling, and it had to be both to fall outside the definition of actual bodily harm. In *Chan Fook** [1994] 2 All ER 552, it was confirmed that psychological illnesses could be included in the term 'actual bodily harm' as long as the harm was a medically defined illness and not a mere emotion, such as fear or panic. In *Ireland*, the House of Lords approved *Chan Fook*, and confirmed that medically recognised stress, for example, was capable of amounting to actual bodily harm.

7.3.4 *Mens rea*

The *mens rea* of s 47 is the *mens rea* of the assault or battery. It is not necessary for the accused to have foreseen that actual bodily harm would be caused to the victim as a result of his assault. It is necessary to prove only that the bodily harm was caused in fact and in law by the assault. This was confirmed by the House of Lords in *Parmenter* [1992] 1 AC 699. This is one of the offences which is criticised by those who support the correspondence principle, discussed in Section 5.8.

7.4 Malicious wounding

Section 20 Offences Against the Person Act is often referred to briefly as 'malicious wounding'. The offence can in fact be committed in two ways, either by wounding or by inflicting grievous bodily harm:

> Whoever shall unlawfully and maliciously wound or inflict any grievous bodily harm upon any other person, either with or without any weapon or instrument, shall be guilty...

The offence is punishable with five years' imprisonment. The offence can be broken down into the following elements:

- Unlawfully
- Maliciously
- Wound or inflict any grievous bodily harm upon any other person.

The *actus reus* here is an act which either causes a wound in the victim or inflicts grievous bodily harm upon him. The *mens rea* is 'maliciousness'. It is useful to consider the elements of the offence separately.

7.4.1 Wound

A wound is any injury which breaks the skin and is more that a mere surface scratch (*JJC v Eisenhower* [1984] QB 331). There is no need for the cut to be serious. It may seem rather odd that what may be a little cut is classified in the same offence as grievous bodily harm. The reason for this may be that in 1861, when the statute was enacted, all breaks of the skin were potentially serious without antiseptic treatment. The inclusion of wounding in this serious offence can also be seen as a deterrent against the use of knives.

7.4.2 Grievous bodily harm

The phrase 'grievous bodily harm' was defined by the House of Lords in *DPP v Smith* [1961] AC 290 as 'really serious bodily harm', and this was approved by the House in *Hyam v DPP** [1991] 1 QB 134. The Court of Appeal in *Sander* and *Junjua and Choudury* [1999] 1 Cr App R 91 held that it was not a misdirection for a trial judge to omit the word 'really' and to describe grievous bodily harm as 'serious injury'. In deciding whether the injury was serious, the jury should be instructed to look at the injuries caused by the accused in total, and so it may be that even though none of the injuries was sufficient in itself to amount to grievous bodily harm, their combined effect was (*Grundy* [1977] Crim LR 543). In deciding whether injuries are grievous the jury ask whether an ordinary person would say that they were. The jury should not take into account whether the particular victim regarded them as grievous (*Brown and Stratton* [1998] Crim LR 485). However, the jury can take into account the impact of the injuries on the victim. So in *Bollom* [2003] EWCA Crim 2846 the jury could take into account the fact the bruises were to a 17-month-old child. The same-sized bruises on an adult might not have amounted to grievous bodily harm, but they could to this victim. It has now been recognised that psychological injuries can constitute grievous bodily harm if they are really serious medically recognised conditions (*Burstow** [1997] 3 WLR 579).

7.4.3 Inflicting

There has been much debate over the correct meaning of the term 'inflict', particularly because in s 18 the word 'cause' is used. It used to be thought that the term 'inflict' required the direct application of force, while 'cause' meant to bring about grievous bodily harm in any way (*Wilson* [1984] AC 242). However, this view was rejected by the House of Lords in *Burstow*. Lord Steyn accepted that the words had the same meaning for the purpose of the 1861 Act. *Dica** [2004] EWCA Crim 1231 makes it clear that the comments in *Burstow* about the similarity in meaning between inflict and cause apply equally whether the injury is a physical one or a psychological one. So although the position is still a little confused, it seems that there is no significant difference in meaning between 'cause' and 'inflict' in ss 18 and 20 and both can be understood to mean 'cause'.

For many years it was generally accepted that s 20, like s 47, required an assault. However, the House of Lords has now decided that s 20 does not necessarily require an assault, although it will very often involve one (*Burstow* and *Wilson*).

7.4.4 Maliciously

The *mens rea* of s 20 is contained in the word 'maliciously', and its meaning is now well established. In *Parmenter* [1992] 1 AC 699 in the House of Lords it was decided that 'maliciously' in this section meant that the accused must have foreseen that some harm might occur, that is recklessness as to some harm. Lord Ackner stated, 'it is enough that he should have foreseen that some physical harm to some person, albeit of a minor character, might result'. It should be stressed that the accused does not need to have foreseen that grievous bodily harm may result from his actions, and that the accused need only foresee that some harm may occur, not that it will occur (*Rushworth* (1992) 95 Cr App R 252).

7.4.5 Unlawfulness

This requirement simply refers to the fact that the defendant will not be guilty if he can establish a defence, such as self-defence (see Chapter 15).

7.5 Wounding with intent

Wounding with intent is the most serious of the statutory assaults and is punishable with life imprisonment. It is found in s 18 Offences Against the Person Act:

> Whosoever shall unlawfully and maliciously by any means whatsoever wound or cause any grievous bodily harm to any person, with intent to do some grievous bodily harm to any person, or with intent to resist or prevent the lawful apprehension or detention of any person shall be guilty...

The *actus reus* of s 18 is similar to that required by s 20. The terms 'wound' and 'grievous bodily harm' carry the same meaning as they do for s 20, as just described. The word 'cause' is given its normal meaning (see Chapter 4). One difference in the *actus reus* of the offences in ss 18 and 20 may be of significance. Section 20 requires the injuries to be 'to any other person', whereas s 18 just states 'to any person'. This may suggest that you can be guilty of intentionally causing yourself grievous bodily harm contrary to s 18, but not inflicting grievous bodily harm upon yourself contrary to s 20.

The *mens rea* of s 18 is in two parts. First, the offence requires a specific intent, and gives three possibilities, any one of which may be used with either of the two possible forms of *actus reus*. The first possible intent is an intent to do some grievous bodily harm to any person. The wording ('any person') makes it clear that the doctrine of transferred *mens rea* will apply (see Section 5.6), so that the accused need not intend to injure the person who is in fact injured. The other two categories of specific intent are an intent to resist lawful apprehension and an intent to prevent the lawful apprehension of any other person. It is in these cases that particular attention should be paid to the additional requirement of malice (*Morrison* (1989) 89 Cr App R 17).

The second part of the *mens rea* of s 18 is, as with s 20, the word 'maliciously'. In *Mowatt* [1967] 3 All ER 47, Diplock LJ took the view that in s 18 'the word "maliciously" adds nothing', and that it is best ignored in directions to the jury on this offence. This is only partly true. Certainly, if the accused is charged with wounding or causing grievous bodily harm with intent to cause grievous bodily harm, then, as Diplock LJ said, nothing further is added by requiring that the act be malicious. However, if the charge is of wounding or causing bodily harm with intent to resist or prevent the lawful apprehension or detention of any person, then it may be crucial to the case that the prosecution also has to prove that the accused acted maliciously in respect of the *actus reus*, that he either intended to cause or was reckless as to causing at least some harm to another person.

7.6 Maliciously administering poison

If poisoning causes death it may be murder or manslaughter; if done with an intent to kill it may be attempted murder; or it may be an offence under s 18 if it causes grievous bodily harm and is done with the necessary intent. It may even constitute a battery or an offence against s 47. In addition, the Offences Against the Person Act 1861 created two specific offences to deal with poisoning. The more serious, carrying a possible sentence of 10 years' imprisonment, is in s 23:

> Whosoever shall unlawfully and maliciously administer to or cause to be administered to or taken by any other person any poison or other destructive or noxious thing, so as thereby to inflict upon such person any grievous bodily harm, shall be guilty...

Section 24, carrying a sentence of five years' imprisonment, does not require the consequence of endangering life or causing grievous bodily harm, but instead contains the additional *mens rea* element of a specific intent:

> Whosoever shall unlawfully and maliciously administer to or cause to be administered to or taken by any person any poison or other destructive or noxious thing, with intent to injure, aggrieve or annoy such person, shall be guilty...

So s 23 focuses on the effect of the poison (endangering life), while s 24 focuses on the intention of the accused.

We will now examine in more detail some of the requirements of these offences.

7.6.1 Administer

Poison may be administered in the classic manner by adding it to the victim's food or drink, but there are many other ways of achieving the same result. In *Cunningham** [1957] 2 QB 396, a gas meter was ripped off a wall by the accused, releasing coal gas which injured the victim. In *Gillard* (1998) 87 CR APP R 189, CS gas was sprayed in the victim's face. In *Cato** [1976] 1 All ER 260, the accused injected the victim with a syringe of heroin. In all of these cases there was found to be administration. The wording of both sections covers direct or indirect administration of the poison. So it can include a case where the victim administers the poison to herself, if she is not aware of the poisonous nature of the substance. In *Kennedy* [2007] UKHL 38, where a drug dealer gave the victim some drugs and the victim injected himself, it was held that the drug dealer could not be said to have administered the drugs or caused them to be administered. The victim had decided to administer the drugs to himself and so was responsible for that act.

7.6.2 Poison or other destructive or noxious thing

In the early case of Cramp, Lord Coleridge CJ held that a poison was something 'injurious to health or life'. In deciding whether a substance is a poison the court will look at the nature of the substance and the amount supplied (*Marcus* [1981] 1 WLR 774). Some substances are in their nature a poison regardless of how much is administered give a person arsenic is to poison him, even if only a tiny amount is given. Similar give a drug user heroin is to poison him, even if because of his use it has no effect Consent wellbeing (*Cato*). Other substances which are not in their nature poisonous may be so if administered in such large doses that they harm the victim.

A substance is noxious if it is hurtful, unwholesome or objectionable (*Marcus*). Therefore a waiter who spits into a customer's soup may be administering a noxious substance even if the customer is not physically harmed as a result.

7.6.3   Maliciously

In s 23 the *mens rea* is supplied by the familiar word 'maliciously'. It is clear that this means recklessly. What is not clear is what must be foreseen. It appears from *Cunningham* that what needs to be foreseen is that there will be the administration of a poison or noxious substance.

7.6.4   Intent to injure, aggrieve or annoy

Section 24, in addition to malice, requires a specific intent to injure, aggrieve or annoy the person to whom the poison is administered. It has been held by the House of Lords that an intent to injure means an intent to cause harm either by means of the substance itself or by enabling the accused to harm the victim in some other way (for example, by assaulting him while asleep: *Hill** (1986) 83 Cr App R 386). Unlike in s 23, there is no room here for the operation of transferred *mens rea* (see Section 5.6).

7.7   Consent

One of the most controversial issues on the law of offences against the person is the relevance of the law on consent. The following are the key questions.

7.7.1   Is the consent of the victim a defence or is lack of consent an aspect of the *actus reus*?

There is much dispute over whether consent should be seen as a defence to a criminal assault (the 'defence view') or whether absence of the victim's consent should be part of the definition of the *actus reus* (the '*actus reus* view'). According to the defence view, one person being violent towards another is a legal wrong, but a wrong which can in some circumstances be justified by the consent of the victim. According to the *actus reus* view, if the assault is consented to, no wrong of any kind has taken place, unless there are special reasons why the law wishes to render that conduct unlawful. The difference between the two views has important practical consequences. The evidential burden of proof will fall on the prosecution if consent is part of the definition of the offence, while it will fall on the defendant if consent is a defence. The issue was sidestepped in *Shabbir* [2009] EWHC 2754, where it was said that the prosecution did not need to prove that the victim did not consent to an attack in a street. The court did not make it clear whether this was because the burden of proving consent lay on the defence or because it could be assumed that a member of the public would not consent to being attacked by strangers!

The difference between the defence view and the *actus reus* view is not just a technical one but reflects some profound philosophical disagreements. The *actus reus* view tends to be supported by those who adopt the traditional liberal view that prizes autonomy (see Section 1.5.2). The principle of autonomy emphasises that people should be able to live their lives as they wish, and the criminal law should only prohibit conduct that causes harm to others. If a person consents to the harm it should therefore not be criminalised and no legal wrong has taken place. Supporters of the *actus reus* view point to an example of two friends walking down the street holding hands as a gesture of friendship. To say in such a case that there is a legal wrong and a battery but fortunately the consent of the friend provides a defence seems artificial. The *actus reus* view explains that there is no battery because there is no legal wrong and is more realistic.

The defence view would be supported by those who argue that it is important for our legal system to protect and uphold the moral values that underpin our society. There is an important taboo that we should not hurt each other deliberately. If that principle is not upheld by the law, society may begin to unravel. The law should therefore see one person committing violence against another as prima facie unlawful, although there may be circumstances in which the victim's consent will provide a defence. The majority of commentators who have written on this area have preferred the *actus reus* view. However, Simester and Sullivan suggest a compromise view. They suggest that some touchings are harmful only if there is no consent. For example, a handshake is only harmful if the victim does not consent. In such cases the *actus reus* view seems preferable. On the other hand some touchings, for example a punch in the face, are prima facie harmful. These are prima facie illegal, but the law may wish to provide a defence in some cases if the defendant has consented (for example, as part of a boxing match). In such cases the defence view seems preferable.

What have the courts had to say about the two views? In the House of Lords' case of *Brown* [1993] 1 AC 212, the majority (Lords Jauncey, Lowry and Templeman) saw consent as a defence to a charge of assault. They adopted the approach that violence against another is prima facie unlawful. More recently, Lord Hobhouse in *R v K** [2001] UKHL 41, discussing the offence of indecent assault, took the opposite view and referred to absence of consent as an aspect of the *actus reus*. Laws LJ in *Andrews* [2003] Crim LR 477 also thought that the better view. So no consistent approach has been adopted, but the defence view seems to have greater support from the authorities, and so consent will be referred to as a defence in the following discussion.

7.7.2 To what crimes of violence is consent a defence?

The consent of an adult provides a defence to an assault or battery (otherwise it would be unlawful for two consenting adults to kiss). However, the House of Lords in *Brown* explained that consent to an act which causes actual bodily harm or a greater level of harm does not provide a defence unless the act falls within certain categories accepted by the law or there are good public policy reasons why a new exempt category should be created. In *Wilson* [1996] 3 WLR 125, a more recent Court of Appeal case, a different approach was suggested. It stated that the question which should be asked in novel situations is 'does public policy or the public interest demand that the appellant's activity should be vested by the sanctions of the criminal law?' This seems clearly in conflict with the decision of the majority of their Lordships in *Brown*, which as a matter of precedent represents the present law.

There is no clearly stated list of the exempt categories in the case law, but there seems to be authority for the following as being situations where consent is a defence even though the victim has suffered actual bodily harm or worse:

1. *Sports and organised games*. If in the course of an organised sport or game one player injures another, consent may provide a defence. The exception covers only organised games and does not cover, for example, a punch-up in the street (*A-G's Ref (No 6 of 1980)* * [1981] 2 All ER 1057). The argument in favour of the exception is that the playing of sports and games is in the public interest: it improves the participants' health and provides enjoyment to many. These benefits justify permitting sporting activities even though, in the course of sports, injuries inevitably occur. However, if in the course of a game a player commits a breach of the rules which involves a level of force beyond that which might be expected in the game, then the fact that the victim consented to play the game appears to provide no defence to the defendant (*Barnes* * [2004] Crim LR 381). This can be explained on the basis that in playing a sport, a participant consents to only the kinds of injuries that may be expected during the sport. Those unexpected injuries caused by a player outside the rules of the game are simply not consented to and so, not surprisingly, there is no defence.

2. *Tattooing, ritual circumcision of males, ear piercing and personal adornment*. This is a self-explanatory category. The Court of Appeal included within this category a man who, at her request, burned his wife's buttocks with a hot knife to leave scars spelling out his initials (*Wilson* [1996] 3 WLR 125). Circumcision of women is prohibited by the Prohibition of Female Genital Mutilation Act 2003. It is generally presumed that the circumcision of males is lawful.

3. *Religious mortification*. This covers cases where, as part of an act of religious repentance, the penitent asks another to inflict pain on him. This category was specifically mentioned by Lord Mustill in *Brown*. In 2008 a man was convicted of child cruelty after encouraging two boys to beat themselves as part of a religious ceremony (*Zaidi, The Times*, 28 August 2008). Notably he was not prosecuted for beating himself. It seems that in this case the jury must have decided that the boys did not consent, either because they were too young or because they were acting under duress.

4. *Rough horseplay*. This seems to apply where children play rough games together (*Jones* (1986) 83 Cr App R 375). If this were not exempt there would be many hundreds of criminal offences committed in playgrounds across the country every day. However, it is important that rough horseplay and bullying are distinguished, although the courts have not yet been asked to clarify this distinction.

   This exception has rather controversially been said to apply to members of the RAF who played a drunken game, setting each other alight while wearing their fireproof suits (*Aitken* * (1992) 95 Cr App R 304). Such conduct, you might think, could legitimately be thought unacceptable and should be discouraged. Certainly had it been civilians acting in this way in a pub it is unlikely that the court would have taken the same approach. Not only have RAF officers been found analogous to children playing rough games, so too have students playing pranks on each other (*Richardson and Irwin* [1999] 1 Cr App R 392)!

5. *Surgery carried out by a medically qualified person*. There is a question mark over how far this exception could apply. Clearly it applies to ordinary medical surgery and presumably cosmetic surgery. There were allegations that a doctor cut a rugby

player's mouth to fake an injury (Callow, 'Bloodgate Doctor Admits to Cutting Tom Williams' *Guardian* (23 August 2010)). That presumably would not be covered by the exception.

6. *Dangerous exhibitions*. This covers stunt shows and circus acts, for example. The Court of Appeal in *A-G's Ref (No 6 of 1980)* established the existence of this exception.

7. *Consensual non-violent sexual relationships*. In *Dica* [2004] EWCA Crim 1231 the Court of Appeal considered the legal position where a defendant who was HIV positive had sexual intercourse with his partner, who was aware of his condition, leading to her infection. In such a case could the defendant be charged with inflicting grievous bodily harm on his partner or could her consent constitute a defence? The Court of Appeal held that the consent of the partner (if she knew of his condition) would provide the defendant with a defence. It distinguished *Brown* in the following way:

> In our judgement the impact of the authorities dealing with sexual gratification can too readily be misunderstood. It does not follow from them, and they do not suggest, that consensual acts of sexual intercourse are unlawful merely because there may be a known risk to the health of one or other participant. These participants are not intent on spreading or becoming infected with disease through sexual intercourse. They are not indulging in serious violence for the purposes of sexual gratification. They are simply prepared, knowingly, to run the risk – not the certainty – of infection, as well as all the other risks inherent in and possible consequences of sexual intercourse, such as, and despite the most careful precautions, an unintended pregnancy.

In *Brown* the majority of the House of Lords appeared to suggest that any exception had to be supported on the basis that the activity was in the public interest. However, it will be apparent that these exceptions do not all seem to be situations where there is a positive public interest in the events being carried out; horseplay is one obvious example. In *Brown* in the House of Lords it was decided that no new exception should be created for sadomasochistic acts which cause actual bodily harm or more serious injury. The majority held that it could not be said that sadomasochistic acts were positively in the public interest, and so no new exception could be created and the acts were criminal. The majority was concerned by two factors in particular: that the conduct was immoral and degrading, and that the individuals needed protection from themselves, as the level of injury was unpredictable and there were concerns that young people might become involved. It was also concerned that the activities might lead to the spreading of AIDS. The majority has been criticised for not producing proof of these concerns, but it seems to have taken the view that the burden lay on the defendants to allay these concerns. The minority emphasised the importance of protecting the right to respect to private life and argued that the acts could not be said to be against the public interest and so should be legal.

The majority's approach has been heavily criticised by commentators who have said that insufficient weight was placed on the defendant's freedom of sexual expression. Very few academics appear to support the decision. The case was taken to the European Court of Human Rights but the decision was upheld on the basis that it was arguably necessary in a democratic society to promote health (*Laskey, Jaggard and Brown v UK** (1997) 24 EHRR 39). The Court of Appeal has confirmed that the *Brown* ruling applies equally to heterosexual sadomasochistic activity (*Emmett*, 15 October 1999, Unreported).

Some academics have asked whether there really is much difference between blows delivered in a boxing match or religious mortification and beating as part of sadomasochistic sex, apart from the sexual element. Clarkson and Keating have characterised the law's approach in this way:

> Violence in the playground or barrack-room is what is expected and normal in the male world; it is a 'manly diversion'. Two men expressing their sexuality together and in private are not doing the sort of thing real men do. It is an 'evil thing' and 'unnatural' and cannot be the subject of valid consent.

In *Dica* the Court of Appeal explained that the basis of *Brown* is an objection to the intentional infliction of pain. This suggests that the courts will be particularly willing to create new exceptional categories if the activity carries the risk of causing pain, rather than being intended to cause pain (although in *Wacker** [2003] QB 1207 the consent of illegal immigrants to being transported in an ill-ventilated lorry provided no defence to a charge of manslaughter when they died). So the best way to understand the House of Lords' ruling in *Brown* is to distinguish between the infliction of pain for the very purpose of inflicting pain or the enjoyment of pain, and the infliction of pain for an ulterior motive, for example the purpose of winning a boxing match or for personal adornment (as in *Wilson*). In all of the exceptions, if there were no pain the participants would still regard the activities as a success. In *Wilson*, for example, if Mrs Wilson had felt no pain but still received the initials on her buttocks she would have been very pleased. In *Brown*, if there was no pain the enterprise would have been a flop. Inflicting pain for the purpose of causing pain, then, is what the law here is designed to prevent. This distinction also explains the existence of many of the exceptions. Two exceptions would perhaps not be explained by this justification. One is the sport of boxing, where inflicting pain appears to be the purpose of the sport. Lord Mustill in *Brown* explained that boxing, where the use of force is an inherent part of the game, was an anomalous exception which existed 'because society chooses to tolerate it'. The other is religious mortification where, without the pain, the feelings of repentance would not be induced.

7.7.3   When will belief in consent provide a defence?

So the consent of the victim will provide a defence in cases of assault or battery, but not in cases involving actual bodily harm or more serious injuries unless the activity falls into one of the exceptional categories. Even if the victim was not consenting, if the defendant believed she was and had she been that would have provided a defence, the defendant is not guilty (*R v K*). So if Tom, a short-sighted man, sees Penelope, whom he mistakes for his wife, Nicole, and gives her a kiss, this is not an assault despite the fact that Penelope does not consent. Surprisingly, it has even been held that a drunken belief that the victim consents will provide a defence (*Richardson and Irwin*). That decision sits so uneasily with the general law on drunkenness that it may well be incorrectly decided.

But what of a case where the defendant believed that he was doing something which would only involve a battery and that the victim consented to it, but which in fact involved a more serious injury? Would this belief provide a defence? Two cases have discussed this issue. Both involved vigorous sexual activity. The participants consented to the acts performed and intended only to commit batteries upon each other; however, far more serious injuries resulted from their acts. In *Boyea* [1992] Crim LR 574 it was held that if the more serious injuries were foreseeable (even if not foreseen) then the defendant could not rely on the victim's consent and could be convicted of an offence under s 47 Offences Against the Person Act 1861. However, in *Slingsby* [1995] Crim LR 570 it was said that the belief in consent would provide a defence, provided that the defendant did not actually foresee that his actions would cause more than actual bodily harm. Of these two cases *Slingsby* seems preferable as it fits in better with the general approach on assaults against the person, which require recklessness (see Section 7.2.1).

7.7.4 What is consent?

There are two issues here. The first is who can give effective consent. In the case of children, consent to medical treatment or other actions which do not clearly harm the child (such as ear piercing) can be given by those who have parental responsibility for a child. A child who is sufficiently mature to understand what is involved may be able to give consent herself (*Gillick v West Norfolk and Wisbech Area Health Authority* [1986] AC 112). Adults are able to give effective consent unless they lack capacity. There is a presumption that adults have capacity. The Mental Capacity Act states in s 2 that 'a person lacks capacity in relation to a matter if at the material time he is unable to make a decision for himself in relation to the matter because of an impairment of, or a disturbance in the functioning of, the mind or brain'. Section 3 states:

> a person is unable to make a decision for himself if he is unable –
>
> (a) to understand the information relevant to the decision,
> (b) to retain that information,
> (c) to use or weigh that information as part of the process of making the decision, or
> (d) to communicate his decision (whether by talking, using sign language or any other means).

This definition will be used in the context of consent in the criminal law too (*C* [2009] UKHL 42). The definition of consent in relation to offences against the person has largely followed the law defining consent in the context of rape. We will therefore discuss the notion of consent in greater detail in Chapter 8. There must be a positive act of consent by the victim. If the apparent consent is provided by a person who is mistaken as to the nature of the act, or as to the identity of the other individual involved, this may mean that the consent will not provide a defence. In *Richardson* (Diane) [1999] QB 444, the 'victims' had been treated by a dentist who had been suspended from practice by the General Medical Council. The Court of Appeal confirmed that the patients' consent was effective unless there was a mistake as to the nature of the act or the identity of the individual performing the act. Here there was no deception as to the nature of the act because the treatment they received was the very treatment they expected. It might have been different if the treatment had been performed in an utterly negligent way. Further, there was no deception as to identity because she was the Richardson that the patients thought she was. It was true that the patients were mistaken as to whether she was a registered dentist, but that was a mistake as to attribute rather than identity. This line of reasoning seems weak. If a person on leaving a hospital is told 'I am afraid there was a mistake. You were treated by Dr Jones, not Dr Smith as you were told' they would probably not mind; but if told 'you have been treated by an unqualified person' they would be very concerned. In cases of medical treatment, the attribute of medical qualification is of far more importance than identity. In *Tabussum* [2000] 2 Cr App R 328, the Court of Appeal held that a man who pretended to be medically qualified and so persuaded three women to let him give them a breast examination did commit an assault. This was because they were deceived as to the nature of the act: they thought the defendant was touching with medical motivations in mind, but in fact he was touching them with indecent motivations.

Consent can be inferred. As mentioned earlier (see Section 7.2.2) people are assumed to consent to everyday touching. Similarly, if a person consents to play football he will be taken to consent to a normal level of violence associated with that sport (*Barnes*). However, the Court of Appeal refused to hold that a teacher at a special needs school could be taken to have consented to minor assaults from pupils (*H v CPS* [2010] EWHC 1374).

7.7.5 Reform of consent

The Law Commission, in its Consultation Paper Number 139, suggested that consent should, subject to a few exceptions, be a defence only if the injury was less serious than a 'serious disabling injury'. It defined serious disabling injury as injuries which

1. cause serious distress, and
2. involve the loss of a bodily member or organ or permanent bodily injury or permanent functional impairment, or serious or permanent disfigurement, or severe and prolonged pain, or serious impairment of mental health, or prolonged unconsciousness.

This would greatly extend the kind of injuries to which the victim's consent would provide a defence.

7.8 Spreading infectious diseases

We will be discussing this in the Hot topic at the end of this chapter. In *Dica* [2004] EWCA Crim 1231 the Court of Appeal considered the position of a defendant who was HIV positive and had sexual relations with someone else. Could he be guilty of inflicting grievous bodily harm contrary to s 20 Offences Against the Person Act 1861 if he thereby infected his partner? The Court of Appeal thought the key issue was whether his partner knew of his condition and consented to run the risk of catching HIV. If she did then her consent could provide a defence. To obtain a conviction the prosecution would also need to show that the victim did not consent and that the defendant foresaw that there was a risk of his partner suffering some harm as a result of the sexual relations. There would be no difficulty in finding this if the defendant was aware of his medical condition. It would also be possible in cases of this kind to rely on the poisoning offences discussed above.

7.9 Chastisement of children

Under English law, a parent has a defence of reasonable chastisement to a charge of violence against his or her child if the parent has used force to punish the child. In a very important decision, the European Court of Human Rights, in *A v UK** [1998] Crim LR 892, held that the English criminal law did not adequately uphold the child's rights under Article 3 to protection from torture and inhuman or degrading treatment. As a result Parliament intervened. Section 58 Children Act 2004 makes it clear that lawful chastisement is only a defence if the punishment does not cause actual bodily harm or a more serious harm. In other words parents can commit a battery by way of corporal punishment of a child, but if they cause actual bodily harm they will be guilty of an offence. To many the law is unacceptable: it is wrong to hit people, and children are people too. However, the current coalition government has indicated that although it is willing to legislate in this area it will not outlaw smacking altogether, as some European countries have done. In part it was influenced by surveys showing that a huge majority of parents do smack their children.

7.10 Assault with intent to rob

This is an aggravated assault, provided for by s 8 Theft Act 1968 as a companion offence to robbery (see Section 12.1). Like robbery, the offence is punishable with life imprisonment. Assault here means an assault or battery. Intent to rob is not defined in the statute, but robbery involves theft, accompanied by the use of, or threat of the use of, force. The intent to rob must therefore involve an intent to steal (that is, to satisfy all of the elements of theft) and an intent to use force to assist in the robbery. The intent to rob must exist in the accused's mind at the time of the assault.

7.11 Assault with intent to resist arrest

Under s 38 Offences Against the Person Act:

> Whosoever shall assault any person with intent to resist or prevent the lawful apprehension or detention of himself or of any other person for any offence, shall be guilty...

This offence is punishable with a maximum of two years' imprisonment. It has been largely superseded by the offences of assaulting and obstructing a police constable in the execution of his duty (see below), but may, of course, be used where the person attempting to make the lawful arrest is not a police constable.

7.12 Assaulting, resisting and wilfully obstructing a police constable

Section 89 Police Act 1996 creates three offences. Of these, it is the first, in subsection (1), which necessarily involves an assault, although the other two may also be committed by assault. Section 89 provides:

> (1) Any person who assaults a constable in the execution of his duty, or a person assisting a constable in the execution of his duty, shall be guilty of an offence...
> (2) Any person who resists or wilfully obstructs a constable in the execution of his duty, or a person assisting a constable in the execution of his duty, shall be guilty of an offence...

Because of their link with assault generally, they are briefly mentioned here, but they primarily relate to the topic of police powers, which is beyond the scope of this book.

7.13 Protection from Harassment Act 1997

The Protection from Harassment Act 1997 was passed because it was felt that the criminal law failed to provide adequate protection to victims of stalking and sustained campaigns of violence. In fact the Act has been used to cover a far wider range of conduct than this: from neighbours disputing a boundary to someone writing threatening letters to a Member of Parliament. However, there are limits to the extent of the offence. The Act has been held not to apply to anti-vivisectionist protesters who campaigned outside the offices of a company which carried out experiments on animals. Eady J held that the Act was not intended to restrict the public's rights to protest reasonably about matters in the public interest (*Huntingdon Life Sciences Ltd v Curtin, The Times*, 11 November 1997). There are two key offences under the Act.

7.13.1 Harassment

Under s 1 Protection from Harassment Act 1997:

(1) A person must not pursue a course of conduct –
   (a) which amounts to harassment of another; and
   (b) which he knows or ought to know amounts to harassment.
(2) For the purposes of this section the person whose course of conduct is in question ought to know that it amounts to harassment of another if a reasonable person in possession of the same information would think the course of conduct amounted to harassment of the other.
(3) Subsection (1) does not apply to a course of conduct if the person who pursued it shows it was
   (a) pursued for the purpose of preventing or detecting crime;
   (b) that it was pursued under enactment or rule of law or to comply with any condition or requirement imposed by any person, under any enactment; or
   (c) in the particular circumstances, the pursuit of the course of conduct was reasonable.

The offence can be broken down into the following four elements:

1. *A course of conduct.* Conduct is defined widely in s 7(3) to include speech. It would therefore cover silent telephone calls of the kind which were discussed in *Ireland* [1998] AC 147. However, there must be at least two incidents to establish a course of conduct. A single incident, however unpleasant, will not constitute the offence. Sometimes it can be difficult to tell whether there have been two incidents or one. In *Wass v DPP* [2000] WL 1151391, the defendant followed the victim and tried to stop her entering a shop. He then confronted her when she left the shop a short time later. This was held capable of amounting to two separate pieces of conduct, and hence a course of conduct.

   In order to amount to a course of conduct, the two incidents must be linked. The larger the number of incidents, the easier it will be to establish a course of conduct. The fewer there are, the harder. It would be wrong to say that there must be a 'campaign' against the victim, but there must be some connection between the pieces of conduct (*Patel* [2005] Crim LR 649). In *Lau v DPP* [2000] Crim LR 586 the defendant slapped the victim, and then four months later he threatened the victim's new boyfriend with violence. This did not constitute a course of conduct because of a combination of two factors: the length of time between the two incidents and the different nature of the events. The Divisional Court stressed that there could be a course of conduct if there was a lengthy gap between the events, but in that case there needed to be a close connection between the incidents. It gave the example of the same harassing conduct being performed each year on the victim's birthday. In *Hills* [2001] Crim LR 318 the prosecution relied on two incidents of violence six months apart. Again there was no course of conduct, although much weight was placed on the fact that between the two incidents the defendant and victim had had consensual sexual relations. This meant that the two were not sufficiently linked to indicate a course of conduct. In *Curtis* [2010] EWCA Crim 123 it was held that 'spontaneous outbursts of ill-temper and bad behaviour, with aggression on both sides, interspersed with considerable periods of affectionate life, could not be described as such a course of conduct'.

In *Kelly* [2003] Crim LR 43 it was emphasised that it is not necessary to show that the victim suffered harassment twice. In that case the defendant left two telephone messages on the victim's voice mail. She listened to them at the same time and suffered harassment. The court held that as long as there were two items of conduct which caused the victim harassment at least once, the s 1 offence was made out.

2. *The course of conduct must amount to harassment.* In s 7(2) it is explained that references to harassing a person include alarming the person or causing the person distress. In *DPP v Ramsdale* [2001] EWHC 106 (Admin) it was stressed that this reference is inclusive, not exhaustive; in other words, harassment includes alarming or distressing the victim, but there could be other ways of harassing someone. A wide range of conduct can amount to harassment and the courts have been unwilling to restrict the meaning of the word. Home Office Circular 28/2001 stated that '[h]arassment in any form is anti-social behaviour, which needs to be tackled'. This is not legally binding on the courts, but it is a remarkably wide definition. A narrower definition was proposed in *Curtis*, where it was held that to be harassment 'the conduct must be unacceptable to a degree which would sustain criminal liability and also must be oppressive'. That is not a particularly helpful definition. Notably in that case they rejected an argument that conduct which caused the victim to fear violence would necessarily be harassing.

The following points have been established by the courts concerning the meaning of harassment:

a. A person can be harassed by words communicated to a third party. In *DPP v Kellett* (1994) 158 JP 1138 the defendant contacted the victim's employer, complaining that the victim was not at work when she should have been and was defrauding her employer. These allegations were in fact untrue. It was held that the complaints could amount to harassment. The key finding was that it was foreseeable that the employer would ask the employee about the allegations and this would cause the victim distress. This was so even though the defendant had specifically requested that the victim not be informed of the allegations.

b. The courts have been careful to distinguish acts where the defendant was essentially asking the victim whether she would be interested in a relationship and which do not amount to harassment, and acts which go beyond this. In *King v DPP*, 20 June 2000, Unreported, it was explained that offering a plant to the victim as a gift and writing one letter to the victim asking her whether she would be interested in a relationship would not amount to harassment. However, such conduct could play an important part as the background against which other conduct could amount to harassment. In that case, the defendant subsequently searched through the victim's dustbins and removed some underwear. This could constitute harassment. In *DPP v Hardy* [2008] EWHC 2874 telephoning a small business more than 95 times in an hour and a half amounted to harassment. This was beyond a reasonable attempt to make a complaint about a business.

c. A controversial issue is whether conduct about which the victim is unaware constitutes harassment. For example, in *King v DPP*, unknown to the victim, the defendant had been filming the victim outside her house. This was held to amount to harassment. This may be surprising because if the victim does not know about the activity she can hardly be alarmed or distressed (s 7(2)), or anything like it. It is true that if she later finds out she will suffer distress and there will then be harassment. Of course, where such a case is brought, the victim will nearly always have found out about the conduct.

   d. Conduct can amount to harassment even if the victim has chosen to enter the defendant's presence. So, in *James* [2009] EWHC 2925 the defendant committed an offence when he was abusive to his care worker, even though it was the care worker who phoned the victim.

3. *The defendant must know or ought to know that the conduct is harassing.* It should be noted that the test contains alternatives of either a subjective or objective *mens rea*. This is significant. It means that it is no defence for a defendant to claim, 'I thought I was expressing my love for the victim; I did not realise she would find this distressing' if it would be obvious to a reasonable person that the conduct was harassing. Further, if the defendant was acting in a way which he knew was harassing the victim, even if a reasonable person would not realise that the conduct was harassing, he can still be convicted of the offence.

   In *Colohan** [2001] Crim LR 845 the defendant was a schizophrenic who wrote a number of threatening letters to his Member of Parliament. He argued that when considering whether a reasonable person would think the conduct amounted to harassment, the reasonable person should be given the characteristics of the victim (that is, in this case asking what a reasonable schizophrenic person would think). He sought to draw an analogy with the law on provocation (see *Smith*, discussed in Section 10.8.2). However, the Court of Appeal rejected the argument and decided that the court should consider what a straightforward reasonable person would think.

4. *Defences to harassment.* Section 1(3) sets out the statutory defences available to the offence. The one which is likely to be relied upon the most is (c): that the conduct of the defendant is reasonable. The courts have made it clear that unlawful conduct will not be regarded as reasonable. In *Colohan*, discussed above, the defendant sought to argue that his conduct was reasonable given that he was schizophrenic. The Court of Appeal rejected the argument that his mental illness was a relevant factor.

7.13.2 Harassment designed to prevent lawful conduct

Section 1A Protection from Harassment Act 1997 creates an offence of pursing a course of conduct which is harassment and is intended to persuade a person not to do something that he is entitled to do. The offence was specifically designed to deal with animal rights protestors who tried to stop people working with scientific laboratories, but can apply to anyone.

7.13.3 Creation of fear of violence

Section 4 Protection from Harassment Act 1997 states:

   (1) A person whose course of conduct causes another to fear, on at least two occasions, that violence will be used against him is guilty of an offence if he knows or ought to know that his course of conduct will cause the other so to fear on each of those occasions.
   (2) For the purposes of this section, the person whose course of conduct is in question ought to know that it will cause another to fear that violence will be used against him on any

occasion if a reasonable person in possession of the same information would think the course of conduct would cause the other so to fear on that occasion.

To establish a conviction it is not necessary to show that the victim was harassed, but it has to be shown that the accused has undertaken a course of conduct which on at least two occasions led to the victim having cause to fear that violence would be used against her. Seriously frightening the victim is not enough; the fear must specifically be of violence if the offence is to be made out (*Henley* [2000] Crim LR 582).

7.14 Racially aggravated assaults

There has been increasing concern over racially motivated crimes. The Crime and Disorder Act 1998 responded to these concerns by creating a new category of racially aggravated assaults. There are two elements which need to be shown:

1. The defendant has committed one of the listed assaults: a common assault; an offence contrary to s 20 or s 47 Offences Against the Person Act 1861; or offences contrary to s 2 or s 4 Protection from Harassment Act 1997. For other offences against the person a racial element may increase the sentence, even if there is not a specific crime.
2. The offence must be 'racially aggravated'. This is defined in s 28 Crime and Disorder Act 1998:

   (1) An offence is racially aggravated ... if –
       (a) at the time of committing the offence, or immediately before or after doing so, the offender demonstrates towards the victim of the offence hostility based on the victim's membership (or presumed membership) of a racial group; or
       (b) the offence is racially motivated (wholly or partly) by hostility towards members of a racial group based on their membership of that group.
   (2) In subsection (1)(a) above –
       'membership' in relation to a racial group includes association with members of that group;
       'presumed' means presumed by the offender.
   (3) It is immaterial for the purpose of paragraph (a) or (b) of subsection (1) above whether or not the offender's hostility is also based to any extent, on –
       (a) the fact or presumption that any person or group of persons belongs to any religious group; or
       (b) any other factor not mentioned in that paragraph.
   (4) In this section 'racial group' means a group of persons defined by reference to race, colour, nationality (including citizenship) or ethnic origins.

The most difficult element for the prosecution for the offence may be that the defendant must have demonstrated his hostility based on the victim's race or must be shown to have been motivated by racial hostility. The demonstration of racial hostility can easily be shown where the defendant utters racial insults as he attacks the victim. In *DPP v Dykes* [2008] EWHC 2775 it was held that a single racial insult uttered during a 30-minute attack was sufficient to indicate the attack was racially aggravated. If nothing is spoken and the prosecution needs to rely on the defendant's motivation then the success of the prosecution will depend on how ready the jury will be to assume from the surrounding evidence that the attack was racially motivated. In *SH* [2010] EWCA Crim 1931 the defendant called the victim, a Nigerian national, a 'monkey'. The defendant claimed he merely intended to be vulgar and did not intend a racist slur, but the Court of Appeal held that the jury were entitled to find that the defendant had demonstrated racial hostility.

Even if the defendant is not attacking the victim because of his or her race, if during the attack racial hostility is demonstrated the offence will be made out (*DPP v Woods* [2002] EWHC 85). So, if there were an argument in a pub among a group of academic lawyers over the finer points of criminal law and an academic from one race attacked another academic of another race, and a racial insult were uttered during the attack, the offence could be established. This would be because racial hostility was demonstrated, even if the real cause of the fight was the dispute over the law. However, in *DPP v Pal* [2000] Crim LR 756 it was stressed that the mere fact that a racial insult is uttered prior to an attack does not necessarily prove that race was the motivation for the attack. In that case the court accepted that the attack on a caretaker was entirely due to the fact that he was demanding that some youths leave a community centre. Although a racial insult was made before the attack, the Divisional Court accepted that the attack was not racially motivated.

It should be noted that the offence includes 'presumed' membership of a group. So if a person attacks a victim believing that the victim belongs to a particular group, but in fact the victim does not, the offence is still made out. Also, as confirmed in *DPP v Pal*, an attack may be racially motivated even if the defendant and victim are of the same race. The court gave the example of a white man attacking another white man because he was going out with a black woman.

It is clear that the courts are not going to be sympathetic to arguments over the technical meaning of the term 'race'. In *White* (2010), an argument that the attack was motivated by the fact that the victim was African, but that African was not a race, was rejected. The court explained that the word 'race' was not to be interpreted restrictively (see also *DPP v M* [2005] Crim LR 392). Similarly, in *A-G's Ref (No 4 of 2004)* [2005] Crim LR 799 the phrase 'immigrant doctor' could be said to relate to race, despite not doing so in its literal meaning.

7.15 Reform of offences against the person

In 1998 the government proposed reform of this complex area of the law. The aim of the reforms was said to be to ensure that the archaic language was replaced, to create a law which complied with the correspondence principle (see Section 5.8) and to give the law a clearer structure. To replace the Offences Against the Person Act 1861, the draft Offences Against the Person Bill included the following key clauses:

1(1) A person is guilty of an offence if he intentionally causes serious injury to another...

2(1) A person is guilty of an offence if he recklessly causes serious injury to another...

3(1) A person is guilty of an offence if he intentionally or recklessly causes injury to another...

4(1) A person is guilty of an offence if –
  (a) he intentionally or recklessly applies force to or causes an impact on the body of another, or
  (b) he intentionally or recklessly causes the other to believe that any such force or impact is imminent.

15(1) In this Act 'injury' means –
  (a) physical injury, or
  (b) mental injury.

15(2) Physical injury does not include anything caused by disease but (subject to that) it includes pain, unconsciousness and any other impairment of a person's physical condition.

These reforms would do much to simplify and modernise the language used for these offences. However, it can also be argued that the fine moral distinctions between different forms of assault are lost in the anodyne wording of the Bill. There is no sign that the Bill will ever become law.

Hot Topic – Criminalising the spread of disease

In the Court of Appeal decision of *Dica* [2004] EWCA Crim 1231 the issue was raised whether a defendant who was HIV positive and through sexual relations passed on the virus to his partner would be guilty of causing grievous bodily harm contrary to s 20 Offences Against the Person Act 1861. The Court of Appeal had no difficulty in finding that he could be. If the victim became HIV positive then that would be grievous bodily harm (GBH). Section 20 required infliction of GBH, but that could be proved simply by showing that he had caused GBH. This left two more tricky requirements.

First, it needed to be shown that the defendant was aware that there was a risk that he would cause the victim some harm. In *Dica* itself this was unproblematic because he had been diagnosed as having the virus and was aware of the risks of having unprotected sexual intercourse. More difficult – and courts will need to address this issue in the future – will be cases where the defendant is aware that he may be infectious. How small does the defendant have to think the risk must be before not being reckless? Can any sexually active person be entirely confident that they are free from any sexually transmitted disease? And what about a defendant who is aware that he is infectious but believes that he has taken precautions (for example, used a condom) to prevent the disease spreading? Does it matter that his belief in the effectiveness of a precaution is an absurd one?

Second, the court accepted that if the victim was aware that the defendant was HIV positive and nevertheless was willing to take the risk of catching the virus this would provide a defence. However, it needed to be shown that the victim was aware of the risk and agreed to take it. As *Konzani* [2005] EWCA Crim 706 shows, this meant that not only would a defendant who lied about not being infectious when he was be potentially guilty of an offence, but so too would a defendant who failed to inform his partner of his condition. This, however, leaves some questions open. What about the victim who is not told by the defendant of his condition, but nevertheless suspects that the defendant is infectious? Will that amount

to consent? Or what of a victim who is aware of the defendant's condition but believes that the sex will be safe if precautions are taken? Has such a victim consented to run the risk of infection? And what of a victim who is aware that the defendant may pass on one disease, but in fact catches a different one?

The Court of Appeal was persuaded to allow the consent of the victim to run the risk of catching the condition by virtue of the following policy considerations:

The problems of criminalising the consensual taking of risks like these include the sheer impracticability of enforcement and the haphazard nature of its impact. The process would undermine the general understanding of the community that sexual relationships are pre-eminently private and essentially personal to the individuals involved in them. And if adults were to be liable to prosecution for the consequences of taking known risks with their health, it would seem odd that this should be confined to risks taken in the context of sexual intercourse, while they are nevertheless permitted to take the risks inherent in so many other aspects of everyday life, including, again for example, the mother or father of a child suffering a serious contagious illness, who holds the child's hand, and comforts or kisses him or her goodnight.

To some the approach taken by the Court of Appeal in these cases has been straightforward common sense. If A knows that by doing something to B he will cause B a serious injury and B does not consent to that then A should be guilty of a crime. The fact that A happens to do this through sexual intercourse is irrelevant.

However, the issue is not quite that straightforward. Some have questioned whether people should not be responsible for their sexual health (see Weait). If people do not ask their partners about any risks of sexually transmitted diseases then they can hardly complain if they are infected. Indeed, we should take those who do not ask their partners about their sexual health to have consented to running the risk of catching any disease they acquire. Everyone in society has a responsibility to ensure that sexually transmitted diseases do not spread. *Dica* unfairly puts the burden of this on those who are infected and leaves the uninfected with no responsibility.

In response it might be said that even accepting that people who do not ask their partners about their sexual health are acting foolishly, that does not mean that no crime is committed if they are infected by their partners. If I leave my front door unlocked and my house is burgled then I have been foolish, but that does not mean the burglar is not guilty of a crime. Similarly, it might be argued, if a defendant infects his partner without telling him of his condition then, although the partner may have been foolish not to ask, the defendant has still harmed his victim. Do we not want a law that encourages sexual partners to be open and honest with each other?

The issue is, however, further complicated by public policy considerations. Will people be deterred from seeking medical help for suspected sexually transmitted diseases or HIV for fear that if they are diagnosed then they will be required to inform their partners of their condition or face criminal prosecution? If they do not seek medical help they will have a defence if they can persuade a jury that they had no idea they were infectious. Further, is it fair for society to impose on HIV positive individuals an obligation to disclose their status to partners, while society fails adequately to meet the social and medical needs of the positive community?

Summary

7.1 The criminal law of non-sexual assaults is a combination of common law offences (assault and battery) and statutory assaults, mainly to be found in the Offences Against the Person Act 1861.

7.2 Common law assault consists of intentionally or recklessly causing another person to apprehend immediate and unlawful personal violence. It is now clear that words alone, or even silence, can amount to an assault. In an assault, the threat must be of immediate unlawful violence, and it must be a threat which is actually apprehended by the victim. It is immaterial that the accused may never intend to carry out the threat, as long as an apprehension is caused in the mind of the victim. A battery is the intentional or reckless direct application of unlawful personal violence. Violence includes any non-consensual touching and need not cause injury.

7.3 Assault occasioning actual bodily harm (s 47 Offences Against the Person Act) is an aggravated assault. Although the assault must be direct, the actual bodily harm may be caused indirectly, in accordance with the normal rules of causation. Bodily harm is an interference with the victim's health or comfort (including state of mind) and need not be permanent, and can include medically recognised psychological illnesses. *Mens rea* is required only in respect of the assault, and not the bodily harm caused.

7.4 Malicious wounding or inflicting grievous bodily harm (s 20 Offences Against the Person Act 1861) does not require an assault. Grievous bodily harm means serious injury, and a wound involves breaking the skin. The accused must either intend or foresee the possibility of some physical harm to another person, albeit of a minor character. An intent to frighten is not enough.

7.5 Wounding with intent (s 18 Offences Against the Person Act) is the most serious statutory assault. The *actus reus* is very similar to that for s 20. The *mens rea* includes malice, and in addition a specific intent: either the intent to cause grievous bodily harm or the intent to resist or prevent a lawful arrest.

7.6 Two offences in the Offences Against the Person Act deal with poisoning: ss 23 and 24. Both require the administration of a poison or destructive or noxious thing to another person. In deciding whether a substance is noxious, regard must be paid to the quantity and

Summary cont'd

circumstances in which it was administered. The poison may be administered directly or indirectly. In s 24, a specific intent to injure, aggrieve or annoy is required. In the case of s 23, the administration of the poison must have the result of either endangering the life of the victim or causing grievous bodily harm, and the *mens rea* is limited to malice (which probably has the same meaning as in s 20).

7.7 The consent of the victim provides a defence to a charge of assault or battery. It is a defence to charges involving a greater level of harm only if the case falls into an exceptional category. Consent must be positive consent given by a competent victim who is not suffering from a mistake as to the nature of the act or as to the identity of the defendant.

7.8 A defendant suffering from a sexually transmitted disease can be guilty of inflicting grievous bodily harm if he or she knows he or she has the condition and his or her partner does not consent to running the risk of catching the disease.

7.9 A parent can rely on a defence of reasonable chastisement if he uses a reasonable level of force against his child.

7.10 Assault with intent to rob (s 8 Theft Act 1968) involves, in addition to an assault, an intent to steal and an intent to use or threaten to use force in order to steal, all of which must exist at the time of the assault. There is some doubt about whether there is the offence of assault with intent to rob.

7.11 It is an offence to commit an assault with intent to resist arrest.

7.12 There are a variety of offences involving resisting and obstructing police officers.

7.13 The Protection from Harassment Act protects victims from courses of conduct which harass the victim or cause the victim to fear immediate violence.

7.14 Racially aggravated offences are those where the defendant was motivated to attack the victim on the ground of the victim's race, or where during the attack racial hostility was revealed.

7.15 The previous government prepared a Bill which would reform the law on assaults, but it is doubtful it will ever become law.

Further Reading

A discussion of the law on assaults and harassment is found in Finch and Madden Dempsey. Reform of the law on offences against the person is discussed in Gardner (1994) and Horder (1994, 1998). The role of consent in the criminal law and discussion of *Brown* are covered in Anderson, Bamforth, Duff, Elliott and de Than, Kell, and Shute. The criminal law and HIV transmission are discussed in Ashford's, Cherkassky's and Weait's writings.

Anderson, 'No Licence for Thuggery: Violence, Sport and the Criminal Law' [2008] Crim LR 751.
Ashford, 'Barebacking and the "Cult of Violence": Queering the Criminal Law' (2010) J Crim L 74.
Bamforth, 'Sado-Masochism and Consent' [1994] Crim LR 661.
Cherkassky, 'Being Informed: The Complexities of Knowledge, Deception and Consent When Transmitting HIV' (2010) 74 J Crim L 242.
Duff, 'Harms and Wrongs' (2001) 5 Buff Crim L Rev 13.
Elliott and de Than, 'The Case for a Rational Reconstruction of Consent in Criminal Law' (2007) 70 MLR 225.

Further Reading cont'd

Finch, 'Stalking the Perfect Stalking Law' [2002] Crim LR 703.

Gardner, 'Rationality and the Rule of Law in Offences Against the Person' (1994) 53 CLJ 502.

Geach and Haralambous, 'Regulating Harassment: Is the Law Fit for the Social Networking Age?' (2009) 73 J Crim L 241.

Horder, 'Rethinking Non-fatal Offences Against the Person' (1994) 14 OJLS 335.

Horder, 'Reconsidering Psychic Assault' [1998] Crim LR 392.

Kell, 'Social Disutility and Consent' (1994) 14 OJLS 121.

Law Commission, *Consent in the Criminal Law* (Law Com CP No 139, HMSO 1995).

Madden Dempsey, *Prosecuting Domestic Violence* (Oxford University Press 2009).

Ryan, 'Reckless Transmission of HIV: Knowledge and Culpability' [2006] Crim LR 981.

Shute, 'Something Old, Something New, Something Borrowed ...' [1996] Crim LR 684.

Weait, 'Criminal Law and the Sexual Transmission of HIV' (2005) 68 MLR 121.

Weait, 'Harm, Consent and the Limits of Privacy' (2005) 13 Fem LS 97.

Weait, 'Knowledge, Autonomy and Consent' [2005] Crim LR 763.

Weait, *Intimacy and Responsibility* (Routledge 2007).

Case Notes

▶ *A v UK* (1999) 28 EHRR 603. European Court of Human Rights

The applicant was hit by his stepfather with a cane, causing severe bruising. The stepfather was acquitted of assaulting the applicant on the basis that he was using reasonable force in chastising him. The European Court of Human Rights found that the acquittal of the stepfather indicated that the applicant's rights under Article 3 were not adequately protected by the state. It rejected the UK's argument that Article 3 applied only where the state was torturing or imposing inhuman or degrading treatment on the citizen. It was explained that the state had a duty to protect a citizen's rights under Article 3 from infringement by another.

▶ *A-G's Ref (No 6 of 1980)* [1981] 2 All ER 1057. Court of Appeal

The accused was charged with assault. He and another youth decided to settle a quarrel by fighting in the street. They fought with fists and the other youth suffered a nosebleed and bruises. The trial judge directed the jury that consent would be a defence if the accused had used 'reasonable' force, and the accused was acquitted. The Court of Appeal held that consent could not be a defence if actual bodily harm was intended or caused, as it was not in the public interest that people should try to cause each other actual bodily harm for no good reason. It is immaterial whether the act occurs in public or private.

▶ *Aitken* (1992) 95 Cr App Rep 304. Courts Martial Appeal Court

Officers in the RAF were playing drunken games and set one another alight while wearing their fireproof outfits. The victim was seized by the appellants and set alight. He suffered serious burns. Their conviction under s 20 Offences Against the Person Act 1861 was overturned on the basis that the officers' belief in the victim's consent could be a defence as this was conduct which fell into the rough horseplay exception.

▶ *Barnes* [2004] Crim LR 381. Court of Appeal

In the course of an amateur game of football the victim suffered an extremely late high tackle from the defendant. The defendant was convicted of unlawfully and maliciously inflicting grievous bodily harm. He appealed, complaining that the jury had not been adequately directed on when consent may be a defence in the context of sport. The Court of

Appeal stated that consent could be a defence in the case of a legitimate sport if the use of force by the defendant was of the kind which could be expected during the game. When considering the type of force which could be expected the jury will consider the level at which the sport was being played (amateur or professional), the nature of the act, the degree of force used, the extent of the risk of injury and the state of mind of the defendant. The court emphasised that criminal prosecutions should be reserved for only the most serious fouls and that normally a sport's disciplinary procedures were appropriate. In the heat of a game it was to be expected that breaches of the rules would be committed and these would not necessarily be criminal. A key question here was whether the tackle was so obviously late and violent that it could not be regarded as an instinctive reaction, error or misjudgement in the heat of the game.

▶ *Brown* [1993] 1 AC 212. House of Lords

A group of sadomasochists committed violent acts towards each other and were convicted of assault occasioning actual bodily harm and unlawful wounding. They argued before the House of Lords that their consent was a defence to the charges. The majority of their Lordships argued that consent to injuries greater than batteries could be a defence only if the conduct fell into one of the accepted categories of exceptions or it could be shown it was in the public interest to create a new exception. The risk of infection by AIDS, the fact that participants might withdraw their consent or not really have consented, and the fear that young people might be involved were cited as reasons why a new exception should not be created here. The minority of their Lordships focused on the accuseds' rights of privacy and argued that their consent should be an effective defence unless it could be shown that their conduct was harmful to the public interest.

▶ *Burstow* [1997] 3 WLR 534. House of Lords

The accused had a social relationship with the victim. After she broke it off he harassed her over a lengthy period. This included making abusive telephone calls and sending unpleasant letters. As a result the woman suffered a severe depressive illness. The House of Lords, which heard the case along with *Ireland* (see below), argued that this conduct could amount to inflicting grievous bodily harm, as required by s 20 Offences Against the Person Act 1861. There was no difficulty in saying that the defendant inflicted psychological grievous bodily harm. Lord Steyn stated that the words 'cause' and 'inflict' were not exactly synonymous but that there was no 'radical divergence between the meaning of the two words'. Lord Hope thought the two words were interchangeable. Lord Steyn also confirmed that assault was not an element of the offence under s 20.

▶ *Cato* [1976] 1 All ER 260. Court of Appeal

The appellant was convicted of administering a noxious thing, contrary to s 23 Offences Against the Person Act 1861, and of manslaughter. He had injected a friend with heroin. The Court of Appeal upheld his conviction on both counts, holding that heroin was a 'noxious thing' within s 23, because it was 'liable to injure in common use', even though the victim in this case had a high tolerance to heroin. The court also held that malice in s 23 did not imply any foresight on the part of the accused as to the likelihood of causing injury, where (as in this case) the injury was caused directly.

▶ *Chan Fook* [1994] 2 All ER 552. Court of Appeal

The appellant was convicted of a s 47 offence after assaulting the victim, whom he suspected of stealing a ring. The victim suffered psychiatric illnesses after being terrorised by the appellant. The Court of Appeal held that a psychiatric illness could constitute actual bodily harm if the illness was a recognised illness and more than fear, distress or panic.

▶ *Colohan* [2001] EWCA Crim 1251. Court of Appeal

The defendant was a schizophrenic who wrote a number of long letters to his Member of Parliament. The letters contained a measure of abuse and some material capable of being construed as threats of violence and/or death. The Member of Parliament gave evidence that the letters caused him to feel threatened and suffer from nightmares. The defendant was convicted under ss 1 and 2 Protection from Harassment Act. He appealed on two grounds. First, he argued that in deciding whether he had *mens rea* under s 1(2) the court should consider whether a reasonable person with his characteristics (namely schizophrenia) would have appreciated that his conduct was harassing. Second, he argued that when considering whether he had a defence on the basis that his conduct was reasonable under s 1(3)(c) the court should take into account the fact that he was a schizophrenic. Both of these arguments were rejected by the Court of Appeal, which held that the defendant's schizophrenia was irrelevant in either case.

▶ *Cunningham* [1957] 2 All ER 412. Court of Criminal Appeal

The appellant was convicted of an offence under s 23 Offences Against the Person Act 1861. He had pulled a gas meter off the wall of a house with the intention of stealing money from it. In so doing, he broke the main supply pipe and released gas into the rest of the house, poisoning an old lady he knew to be living there. The trial judge directed the jury that 'malicious' in s 23 meant 'wicked'. The Court of Criminal Appeal allowed the appeal and quashed the conviction. Byrne J adopted the meaning of 'maliciously' given by Professor Kenny: 'in any statutory definition of a crime "malice" must be taken not in the old vague sense of wickedness in general, but as requiring either (i) an actual intention to do the particular kind of harm that in fact was done, or (ii) recklessness as to whether such harm should occur or not (i.e., the accused has foreseen that the particular kind of harm might be done, and yet has gone on to take the risk of it)'. Byrne J then held that in s 23 foresight of the risk of causing injury was sufficient.

▶ *Dica* [2004] EWCA Crim 1103. Court of Appeal

The appellant was convicted of inflicting grievous bodily harm on two women with whom he had had sexual relations. He was HIV positive and had infected them with the virus. At the trial the judge ruled that whether or not the victims were aware that the defendant was HIV positive was irrelevant to the case because, even if they had consented, following *Brown* their consent was no defence. The Court of Appeal held that this ruling was incorrect. If the victims were aware of the appellant's HIV status and had consented to the risk of catching the virus then their consent provided a defence to a s 20 charge. However, if the victims were not aware of his status and had not consented to run the risk then the defendant could be convicted of the offence if he was aware that by engaging in sexual relations with the victims he was exposing them to a risk of infection. As it was shown that he knew he was HIV positive this would not prove difficult. In an *obiter* comment Judge LJ added that even if the women had not been told by the defendant of his status this could not be rape, because they had consented to sexual intercourse and they had not been deceived as to the nature of the act. This approach was subsequently followed in *B* (2006).

▶ *Fagan* [1969] 1 QB 439. Divisional Court

See Chapter 3 Case notes.

▶ *Hill* (1986) 83 Cr App Rep 386. House of Lords

The appellant was convicted of administering a noxious thing with intent to injure, contrary to s 24 Offences Against the Person Act 1861. He had given two teenage boys a number of tablets which were only available on prescription as an aid to slimming. The only issue at the trial was whether the appellant had administered the drugs with intent to injure. The Court of Appeal allowed the appeal on the basis that the trial judge had directed the jury that an intent to keep the boys awake could amount to an intent to injure. The House of Lords restored the conviction, holding that although an intent to keep the victim awake would not by itself amount to an intent to injure, the direction of the trial judge was not at fault. It had been made clear to the jury that an intent to cause physical injury was required.

▶ *Ireland* [1997] 3 WLR 534. House of Lords

The accused telephoned several women a number of times and simply remained silent. They suffered from a variety of psychiatric illnesses. Lord Steyn affirmed the interpretation of actual bodily harm in *Chan Fook* (see above). He stated that words alone and indeed silence could form the basis of an assault. He explained that the assault in this case could be said to have arisen because the victims would not have known what the accused was going to do next and they might have feared that he was about to come round to their houses and attack them.

▶ *R v K* [2001] UKHL 41. House of Lords

See Chapter 6 Case notes.

▶ *Laskey et al v UK* (1997) 24 EHRR 39. European Court of Human Rights

The applicants were convicted of assaults following sadomasochistic behaviour in private. They argued that the convictions infringed their rights under Article 8 of the European Convention. The UK argued that the criminalisation of such acts was necessary to protect public morals and the health of citizens, and so justified under Article 8(2). The European Court accepted this argument, arguing that the activities involved a risk of physical injury and undermined 'the respect which human beings should confer upon each other'.

▶ *Moloney* [1985] AC 905. House of Lords

See Chapter 9 Case notes.

▶ *Parmenter, Savage* [1992] 1 AC 699. House of Lords

Mrs Savage had intended to throw beer over Miss Beal, her husband's former girlfriend, but the glass slipped out of her hand and broke, injuring Miss Beal. Mr Parmenter had injured his child by rough handling, which he said he did not realise would harm his child significantly. These cases were brought before the House of Lords in order to determine the correct *mens rea* for ss 47 and 20. The House held that the *mens rea* for s 47 was that necessary for assault or battery. There was no need to prove a further *mens rea* as to the actual bodily harm. For s 20 the *mens rea* was foresight as to some harm, albeit not serious harm.

▶ *Roberts* (1971) 56 Cr App Rep 95. Court of Appeal

See Chapter 4 Case notes.

▶ *DPP v Smith* [1961] AC 290. Court of Appeal

The respondent cut off his ex-girlfriend's pony tail without her consent. The justices accepted his submission that the cutting of hair could not amount to actual bodily harm, and so he could not be convicted of an assault occasioning actual bodily harm under s 47 Offences Against the Person Act 1861. On an appeal by the prosecution the Divisional Court held that cutting hair could be actual bodily harm. 'Harm' included injury, hurt or damage. There was no need to prove that the victim had felt pain. The phrase 'bodily' referred to the whole body including the organs, nervous system, brain and hair.

▶ *Wacker* [2003] QB 1207. Court of Appeal

See Chapter 10 Case notes.

Chapter 8

Sexual offences

Key Terms

- **Consent** – the permission of the victim to the act of the defendant.
- **Rape** – penile penetration of the victim's vagina, anus or mouth without the consent of the victim.
- **Sexual** – acts which appear to involve or do involve a sexual motivation.

8.1 The scope of sexual offences

The scope of sexual offences is always controversial and raises the question of what purpose the criminal law serves in this area. Temkin has written, 'the overriding objective which ... the law ... should seek to pursue is the protection of sexual choice, that is to say the protection of a woman's right to choice whether, when and with whom to have sexual intercourse'. Whether it achieves this end or whether the law is so concerned about protecting the position of a potential defendant that it condones many cases of sexual violence against women is a matter of much controversy. As well as protecting or undermining sexual choice, the law can also be seen as a means of defending the sexual morality of a particular society (see Section 1.2).

There is also debate over whether it is appropriate to consider sexual offences as a separate category of offences from other violent assaults. Some argue that the seriousness of sexual offences is belittled by their being seen as 'sexual' offences, rather than as a form of violent offence, especially as violence is often an aspect of rape. Others argue that it is crucial to emphasise that, as well as the violence usually involved, sexual offences include a unique element. This unique wrong in sexual offences can be difficult to put into words. One suggestion is that in the same way that sexual contact can be used as the highest form of intimacy and the ultimate expression of love, misuse of such acts is a uniquely harmful invasion of privacy and damage to a person's identity. Also there is the infringement of the victim's sexual autonomy. Being able to choose with whom to have sexual relations is regarded by many as a fundamental freedom.

It is important to appreciate that the popular perception of rape is misleading. The traditional image of rape as a crime launched by a stranger against a woman out walking alone at night belies the fact that studies indicate that about two-thirds of victims are raped by people they know. This fact causes particular problems for prosecutors, who need to show beyond all reasonable doubt that the victim did not consent to the sexual intercourse. The difficulty over proof of the victim's consent reveals the ever-present conflict between the interests of the victim and those of the accused, and is particularly visible in the procedural difficulties raised by the proof of these offences. The debate concerning sexual offences tends to centre on issues which illustrate these conflicts of interest: the question of consent, the appropriate *mens rea* for sexual offences and whether acts committed by consenting adults in private should be penalised.

The law in this area has recently been transformed by the Sexual Offences Act 2003. The new Act replaces the old law, which the government had described as 'archaic, incoherent and discriminatory'. We have not yet had many cases interpreting the Act, so some of the cases discussed in this chapter are cases under the old law but are ones the courts may still refer to when interpreting the new Act. We start with the most serious and perhaps the most controversial sexual offence: rape.

8.2 Rape

Rape is defined in s 1 Sexual Offences Act 2003:

(1) A person (A) commits an offence if –
  (a) he intentionally penetrates the vagina, anus or mouth of another person (B) with his penis,
  (b) B does not consent to the penetration, and
  (c) A does not reasonably believe that B consents.
(2) Whether a belief is reasonable is to be determined having regard to all the circumstances, including any steps A has taken to ascertain whether B consents.

The offence can be broken down into the following elements:

1. The defendant penetrated the anus, vagina or mouth of another person with his penis.
2. The victim did not consent to the penetration.
3. The defendant intended to penetrate the victim's anus, vagina or mouth.
4. The defendant did not reasonably believe that the victim consented.

These elements will be considered separately:

8.2.1 The defendant penetrated the anus, vagina or mouth of another person with his penis

Several points emerge from this requirement. First, notice that the definition of rape is not restricted to vaginal intercourse, but includes forced penetration of the anus or mouth of the victim. The term vagina includes vulva (s 79). Second, although most victims of rape are women it is possible for a man to be a victim of rape in English law, if his anus or mouth is penetrated by a penis. Third, only men can commit rape. A woman who forces a man to have sexual intercourse with her is not committing rape. This is because the penetration must be with a penis. Such a woman could be guilty of other offences under the 2003 Sexual Offences Act such as sexual assault (s 3) or causing another person to perform a sexual act without consent (s 4). A woman can also be convicted of assisting in the commission of a rape (*DPP v R and B*, 2000, Unreported). Fourth, it should be noted that a husband can be guilty of raping his wife. This became established law following *R v R* [1992] 1 AC 599. Finally, only a penetration is required. So it is not necessary for there to be full sexual intercourse in order for the offence to arise. Section 79(2) states that '[p]enetration is a continuing act from entry to withdrawal'. The significance of this is that if the complainant consents to the defendant initially penetrating her and then asks him to withdraw but he deliberately does not and continues to remain inside her, then from the time when the victim asked the defendant to withdraw he will be committing rape.

8.2.2   The victim did not consent to the penetration

This is probably the most complex aspect of the offence of rape. It is important to appreciate that the issue of consent can be raised in two ways by the defence at a rape trial. The defendant may argue that the victim did consent or that he reasonably believed that the victim consented. The first is a claim that the *actus reus* of the offence was not present and the second is a claim that the defendant lacked the *mens rea*. Here we will be looking at the first of these arguments: that the victim consented to the penetration.

The Sexual Offences Act has attempted to clarify the law on the meaning of consent, but the law is still very complex. A victim can be found not to have consented in one of three ways:

1. The victim is conclusively presumed not to consent under s 76.
2. There is an evidential presumption that the victim did not consent under s 75 and there is no evidence to rebut the presumption.
3. The victim did not consent under the general meaning of that word.

So the defendant will want to persuade the jury that the prosecution has failed to demonstrate that the victim did not consent in any of these three ways. We need to consider them now in more detail.

1. *Conclusive presumptions under s 76.* There are two circumstances in which the 2003 Act conclusively presumes that the victim did not consent and that the defendant had the necessary *mens rea*. In these circumstances there is nothing the defendant can do to rebut the presumptions. Whatever evidence he can find cannot show that the victim did consent. He is automatically guilty of rape. The two circumstances are as follows:

   (a) 'the defendant intentionally deceived the complainant as to the nature or purpose of the relevant act' (s 76(2)(a)). The kinds of cases which the law has in mind here are cases where the defendant tells the victim that he is going to perform a medical treatment (*Flattery* (1877) 2 QB 410) or a procedure to improve the victim's singing (*Williams* [1923] 1 KB 340) and she therefore consents, but in fact he engages in sexual intercourse. In such cases although the victim consents to the act of penetration she has been misled as to the nature of the act and so does not consent. In *B* [2006] EWCA Crim 2945 the Court of Appeal held that a man who had not disclosed his HIV status before having sex with a woman had not lied to her about the 'nature of the act'. The woman had consented to sexual intercourse with him. The deception did not relate to the nature of the act. He might have committed an offence of inflicting grievous bodily harm (see Section 7.8), but that was not the offence he had been charged with.

   In *Linekar** [1995] QB 250, a case before the 2003 Act was in force, a man told a prostitute he was going to pay her for sexual intercourse, but afterwards he ran off without paying. The Court of Appeal said that this was not rape because she had not been deceived as to the nature of the act of sexual intercourse, only what would happen afterwards (whether she would be paid). It is likely the same result would be reached after the Act. However, the issue is not beyond doubt, because of the reference in s 76 to 'purpose'. From the prostitute's point of view the purpose of the sexual intercourse was to make money, so was she deceived as to that? The reference to 'purpose' may have even more dramatic repercussions: if a boyfriend suggests to his girlfriend that they have sex in order to demonstrate their great love for each other and she accepts, although in fact he has decided to end their relationship, has he deceived her as to the purpose of the act? In *Jheeta** [2007] EWCA Crim 1699, decided after the new Act was in force, it was held that the facts of *Linekar* would not fall within s 76(2)(a). It was not enough to show that the victim had been deceived about an issue that related to the sexual intercourse. The deceptions must go to the actual nature or purpose *of the penetration*. That was not so in *Linekar*, where the deception, it was said, related to what would happen after the penetration (that is, the payment). However, the position is in some doubt following the decision in *Devonald** [2008] EWCA Crim 527. That case involved the offence of causing another to perform a sexual act contrary to s 4 of the 2003 Act. However, the definition of consent in that offence is the same as that used in relation to rape. The defendant, via a computer, misled the victim into believing he was a young woman and persuaded him to engage in a sexual act on a webcam. In fact the defendant was the father of the victim's ex-girlfriend and was seeking to embarrass him by recording the incident and then broadcasting it. The court concluded that the victim had been deceived as to the purpose of the act. The victim thought the purpose of the act was to give pleasure, whereas in fact it was to create embarrassing material. This suggests it is not impossible that a man who had sex with a woman after pretending that he loved her, when in fact he was hoping to win a bet or impress his friends, was deceiving her as to the nature of the act. It will be interesting to see how the case law in this area develops.

(b) 'the defendant intentionally induced the complainant to consent to the relevant act by impersonating a person known personally to the complainant' (s 76(2)(b)). This category is designed to cover cases where the defendant impersonated the husband or boyfriend of the victim (*Elbekkay** [1995] Crim LR 163). It should be noted that the provision only applies to a person impersonating someone known 'personally' to the complainant. Therefore if the defendant impersonates a well-known pop star whom the complainant adores but does not know personally, and the complainant consents to sexual relations with the defendant, the presumption will not apply. It should also be noted that it only covers cases where the defendant intentionally induces the complainant to think he is someone else. So if the complainant drunkenly thinks a man is her boyfriend when he is not and is not pretending to be, again the presumption will not apply.

With these conclusive presumptions don't forget that simply because it is found that the facts of a case do not fall into the presumptions, that does not mean that there is consent. It may be, for example, that although a deception does not go to the nature or purpose of the act, it is sufficient to mean there is no consent under the general meaning of the term (*Jheeta*).

2. *Cases where there is an evidential presumption that the complainant did not consent (s 75).* In these cases there is an evidential presumption that the complainant did not consent to the penetration, but that presumption can be rebutted if 'sufficient evidence is adduced to raise an issue as to whether he consented'. For example, as we shall see in a moment, there is a presumption of no consent if there was a threat of violence immediately before the penetration, but this presumption could be rebutted if the defendant could introduce evidence that immediately after the threat he apologised, the complainant forgave him and they had sexual relations to reconfirm

their love for each other. If the defendant is able to introduce sufficient evidence to raise the issue that the complainant may have consented then the prosecution has to establish beyond reasonable doubt that the complainant did not consent. It is not clear how much evidence will be required to 'raise an issue' as to whether the victim consented. Would it be enough if the defendant just gave evidence that she had? That would be 'eye witness' evidence and so would appear at least to raise an issue over consent. If that is correct, as seems likely, these presumptions are of little use in practice. Indeed, using them may simply confuse the jury.

The following are the circumstances in which there will be an evidential presumption of no consent:

(a) *any person was, at the time of the relevant act or immediately before it began, using violence against the complainant or causing the complainant to fear that immediate violence would be used against him.* Note that it does not need to be shown that the defendant was threatening the victim with violence. So the section would apply if the defendant had intercourse with the complainant after his friend threatened her. It also is worth emphasising that the threat or violence must occur 'immediately' before the penetration. No doubt at some point the courts will be required to interpret the meaning of that word. Also, the threat must be of violence. This suggests that a threat to embarrass, distress or damage property will not invoke the presumption.

(b) *any person was, at the time of the relevant act or immediately before it began, causing the complainant to fear that violence was being used, or that immediate violence would be used, against another person.* This is similar to the scenario just discussed except that it involves a threat to a third person. So if A said he would injure B unless C permitted him to have sexual intercourse with her the presumption would be that C did not consent to the act.

(c) *the complainant was, and the defendant was not, unlawfully detained at the time of the relevant act.* Here the Act considers that a person being kidnapped or otherwise unlawfully detained does not consent to sexual intercourse with anyone, although the presumption does not apply if the other person was also being unlawfully detained.

(d) *the complainant was asleep or otherwise unconscious at the time of the relevant act.* The Act makes it clear that a person who is asleep during the penetration or is unconscious, for example due to drink or drugs, is presumed not to be consenting. Remember this is a rebuttable presumption. If a wife told her husband that she wanted her husband to penetrate her while she was asleep, that being a fantasy of hers, the jury may be persuaded that the presumption could be rebutted.

(e) *because of the complainant's physical disability, the complainant would not have been able at the time of the relevant act to communicate to the defendant whether the complainant consented.* It may seem obvious that where the complainant has a physical disability which prevents communication she cannot consent to penetration, but this provision means that the prosecution is relieved of the burden of proving that she did not. It will be for the defendant to introduce evidence that the person was consenting. You should note that this presumption does not apply in cases of mental disability.

(f) *any person administered to or caused to be taken by the complainant, without the complainant's consent, a substance which, having regard to when it was administered or taken, was capable of causing or enabling the complainant to be stupefied or overpowered at the time of the relevant act*. This is clearly designed to apply to a 'drug rape' case. Note that the substance does not need to have been administered by the defendant. It can have been administered by a third party, although it must have been taken without the complainant's consent. It must be shown that the drug was capable of either stupefying the complainant (for example, so that she did not really know what was going on) or enabling the defendant to overpower the complainant. But it does not need to be shown that the drug actually had that effect. This is to assist the prosecution. Once it has shown that the drug was given to the victim without her consent it does not need to prove the impact of the drug on the victim. But what would happen if the defendant gave the complainant a tablet saying it was ecstasy, whereas in fact it was a drug which facilitated sexual intercourse? Would the victim be said to have consented to the taking of the drug? It is submitted that if the drug was not of the kind the victim thought it was the court should find that she had not consented to the taking of that drug. A final point: it is odd that this does not create a conclusive presumption. In what circumstances could it be argued that the victim in such a case in fact consented?

3. *Consent: the general meaning*. If the case does not fit into any of the provisions so far discussed the jury will have to consider whether the complainant consented in the general meaning of the word. Now we must face head-on the question 'what does consent mean?' Section 74 Sexual Offences Act 2003 explains:

> a person consents if he agrees by choice, and has the freedom and capacity to make that choice.

The following points can be made about this provision and the meaning of consent:

(a) *The complainant consents only if he or she agrees*. This makes it clear that it is no defence for the defendant to complain that the victim did not object. The definition of rape does not require that the victim resist or oppose penetration, but simply that he did not object. Therefore intercourse with a woman who is asleep (*Lartner and Castleton* [1995] Crim LR 75) or so drunk that she is unaware of what is happening to her (*Malone* [1998] 2 Cr App R 447) constitutes the *actus reus* of rape. In theory it would be rape if the victim were ambivalent about whether she wanted sexual intercourse, because in such a case she would not positively consent.

(b) *The complainant must have capacity to make the choice*. This means that if the complainant is too young to be able to consent or lacks the mental capacity to do so there is no consent even if she has said the word 'yes'. In relation to age the House of Lords in *Gillick v West Norfolk and Wisbech Area Health Authority* [1986] AC 112 held that if a child (that is, a person under 16) has sufficient competence to understand what is proposed and to reach his own decision considering the alternatives, he can consent to medical treatment. It is likely the same approach will be taken in relation to capacity to consent to sexual matters. For adults the courts will probably adopt a test similar to the one in the Mental Capacity Act 2005 (quoted in Section 7.7.5). The issue of consent can be problematic if the victim is drunk. The Court of Appeal in *Bree** [2007] EWCA 804 confirmed that even if a victim is drunk she can still give consent. However, a victim may become so drunk that she loses her capacity to choose. It will be left to the jury to decide whether the victim was so drunk she was unable, effectively, to consent. That may not be easy for the jury to assess. In *R v H* [2007] EWCA Crim 2056 the Court of Appeal held that it was open to a jury to convict a defendant in a case where the 16-year-old victim had no recollection of the sexual intercourse. It was held that the jury could conclude that a 16-year-old alone at night would not have consented to sex with a complete stranger she had met minutes previously. The courts are yet to provide clear guidance on the issue. It is clear that a very drunk victim may lack the capacity to consent, while a victim who is only a little drunk may have the capacity to consent. The difficulty surrounds the fairly drunk. Should the law say that sexual autonomy is important and that only a fully competent decision should be sufficient to count as consent? Or is that unrealistic given that a lot of sex occurs when the parties are drunk?

(c) *The complainant must have the freedom to make the choice.* Clearly if the complainant consents to penetration only because the defendant has placed a gun to her head there is no real consent. But that is an easy case. What if the victim has consented only because of pressures or minor threats from the defendant? Will this mean that there has been no freedom to make the choice? It is submitted that the courts are likely to follow the approach taken by the courts under the common law.

In *Olugboja** [1982] QB 320 Dunn LJ in the Court of Appeal held that there was an important distinction to be drawn between consent and submission:

> It is not necessary for the prosecution to prove that what might otherwise appear to have been consent was in reality merely submission induced by force, fear or fraud, although one or more of these factors will no doubt be present in the majority of cases of rape ... [T]he dividing line ... between real consent on the one hand and mere submission on the other may not be easy to draw. Where it is to be drawn in a given case is for the jury to decide, applying their combined good sense, experience and knowledge of human nature and modern behaviour to all the relevant facts of that case.

Where the issue of the victim's consent is raised, the jury has to decide whether the victim has reluctantly acquiesced and so consented, or submitted and so did not consent. In *Olugboja* Dunn LJ took the view that this would be a question for the jury in each case 'applying their combined good sense, experience and knowledge of human nature and modern behaviour to all the relevant facts of that case'. Therefore the jury has to consider the effect of the threat on the particular victim in each case. The same threat that negates the consent of one victim in one case may not negate the consent of a different victim in another case. It all depends on the victim's character and the circumstances of the case. What matters is not the nature of the threat, whether it is a threat of violence, but the effect of the threat. No doubt where the threat is of death or grievous bodily harm, the jury will readily find that the victim did not truly consent. But there may be cases where threats not involving violence will negate the consent of the victim. Imagine a defendant who threatens to tell the victim's father that she has been seeing him unless the victim has sexual intercourse with him, and the victim fears that her father will react by ostracising her from her family and that she will have nowhere to live. The 'consent' in such a case could not be regarded as true consent; it is submission. In *Jheeta*, where the defendant had sent the victim messages purporting to come from the police and insisting that she have sex with the defendant or face a fine, it was held there was no consent from the victim. She was terrified by these threats.

It is sometimes suggested that a victim who agrees to sexual intercourse following a promise of a benefit will not be raped. A popular example is an actress who consents to sexual intercourse with a director after he promises her a part in his film. Consent, it is said, can only be vitiated by a threat, not by a promise of a benefit. Others argue that this is not necessarily a useful distinction. Should the actress case be seen that differently if the actress had been given a part in the film and the director threatened to sack her unless she agreed to sexual intercourse? The better view, it is suggested, is that although a jury is far more likely to find consent vitiated by a threat than by an offer of a benefit, there may be cases where the offer of the benefit could negate consent. In *Kirk* [2008] EWCA Crim 434 a 14-year-old girl ran away from home and was living as a homeless person. She went to the defendant, who had previously abused her, seeking food. He offered her £3.25 for sex, which she accepted. It was found on the facts of the case that the jury was entitled to find there was not genuine consent to sexual intercourse; rather there was submission.

An important point to emphasise about the common law on consent is that it focuses on the victim's state of mind. So if the victim appears to consent due to a fear of violence this may be regarded as no consent even if in fact the victim was not being threatened (for example, she had misinterpreted a gesture of the defendant). So it is the fear of the complainant, not the threats of the defendant, which is important to the common law understanding of consent.

(d) *Cases where the complainant consents but under a mistake.* If the complainant consents but does so while under a mistake, is this to be taken as negating consent? Section 74 does not provide a ready answer, and again the courts are likely to look back at the approach taken under the common law. Under the common law only two kinds of mistake would negate consent (*Clarence* (1888) 22 QBD 23): first, mistakes as to the nature of the act and, second, mistake as to the identity of the person. These are reflected in the presumption in s 76. However, mistakes may also negate consent under the general meaning of the word, even if they fall outside the terms of s 76 (*Jheeta*). It is too early to tell the extent to which mistakes which do not relate to the nature or purpose of the act may mean there is no consent.

The traditional approach of the common law took a strict view on mistakes as to the nature of the act. Reference has already been made to *Linekar*, where the prostitute was taken to consent to sexual intercourse. An indication that such an approach will be followed under the 2003 Act is *B* [2006] EWCA Crim 2945. As already mentioned, a man who had sexual intercourse without telling his partner that he was HIV positive would not be deceiving her as to the nature of the act. His HIV status did not change the nature of the act, and so did not fall under s 76. The court appears to have assumed that it did not affect whether there was consent in its general meaning too. This is a controversial view. To say there is no fundamental difference between an act which offers nothing but pleasure and one that is life threatening seems remarkable. The point is that the Court of Appeal was saying there was consent to sexual intercourse, but not to being infected. The correct charge was therefore inflicting grievous bodily harm (see Chapter 7), not rape.

But there are some cases indicating that a broader approach may be taken. In *Tabussum* [2000] 2 Cr App R 328 three women permitted the defendant to examine their breasts after he said (untruthfully) that he was medically qualified. The Court of Appeal explained (uncontroversially) that the law on the meaning of consent was the same in relation to indecent assault as it was in relation to rape. It was held that although the women had consented to the nature of the acts, they had not consented to their quality. The Court of Appeal did not make crystal clear precisely what was meant by this. One explanation is that the women were deceived as to the quality of the act because they were deceived as to the purpose of the defendant's examination. It was not for medical purposes but for other reasons (presumably sexual). A similar approach can be found in *Devonald*, mentioned above, where a man deceived a boy into performing a sex act by pretending on the computer to be a young woman.

Gardner (1997) has suggested that this approach, focusing on the kind of deception used, overlooks the fact that different deceptions will affect different victims in different ways. As we have seen, the Court of Appeal in the leading case of *Olugboja* stressed that the question of whether the victim's consent is invalidated by the threat or use of force is not based on the form of threat or outward appearances, but on the reality of the victim's consent. Gardner suggests that a similar approach should be taken in relation to mistakes, and whether the victim consents should not depend on the nature of the fraud but on the 'victim's perception of her own interests'. Thus to one victim a mistaken belief that she was married to the defendant may be hugely important and negate her apparent consent. But to another victim that mistake may be of little significance and have no effect on her consent. A more radical view is that there is no consent if the victim is mistaken about something and had she known the truth, she would not have consented (Herring, 2005). That would extend the scope of the law of rape far wider than many people would feel is appropriate.

(e) *Agreement and not consent*. Section 74 defines consent in terms of an agreement. Is there any difference between agreement and consent? It could be argued that there is. Consider the following hypothetical example: a girlfriend notices her boyfriend enter her bedroom. 'For fun' she decides to pretend to be asleep. To her excitement her boyfriend penetrates her. There is little doubt that she consented to the penetration, but did she agree to it? It all depends on whether you give a subjective or an objective understanding to the word 'agree'. Is agreement a state of mind or an outward manifestation of approval of the act? The courts will be required to answer that question before too long, no doubt.

(f) *The key issue on consent*. Underpinning all the issues on consent is what quality of consent is required if the sexual penetration is not to be rape. Do we require a strong consent: consent given free from pressure and with a good understanding of all the issues raised? Or a weak consent, with no overwhelming pressure and an understanding of the basics? For consent to heart surgery we would require a strong consent. For consent to a haircut, maybe only a weak consent. Where should sexual intercourse fit on this model?

8.2.3 An intent to penetrate

It will be a rare case where the defendant will be able to claim that he accidentally penetrated the complainant. It might arise if a couple had agreed to have a naked cuddle, but not to engage in penetration, but that occurred. One issue which the courts may have to address is where the defendant intended to engage in vaginal intercourse but in fact engaged in anal intercourse. It is unlikely the courts will accept that this provides any kind of a defence. The most likely interpretation is that an intent to penetrate any orifice is sufficient.

8.2.4 The defendant did not reasonably believe that the victim consented

The defendant will be guilty unless he reasonably believed that the victim consented. This means that the defendant will be guilty if he knows the victim does not consent, does not care whether the victim consents, or believes the victim consents, but does so unreasonably. There are three alternative ways in which the prosecution can prove this aspect of the *mens rea* for rape:

1. The defendant is conclusively presumed to have the *mens rea* under s 76.
2. There is an evidential presumption that the defendant had the *mens rea* under s 75.
3. Under the basic definition the *mens rea* is proved.

These need to be considered separately.

1. *Conclusive presumptions of* mens rea. Where the defendant has intentionally deceived the complainant as to the nature or purpose of the relevant act or induced the complainant to consent by impersonating a person known personally to the complainant then it will be presumed that the defendant had the *mens rea* for the offence (s 76). It will be noted that these are the same circumstances in which there will be a conclusive presumption that the complainant did not consent.
2. *Evidential presumptions of* mens rea. Where the defendant knew of the circumstances mentioned above in s 75 (for example, that there had been a threat of violence immediately before the penetration), as well as it being presumed that the complainant did not consent to the act, it will also be presumed that the defendant did not reasonably believe that the victim consented. So if the defendant knows at the time of the penetration that the victim is asleep it will be presumed that he did not reasonably believe that the victim consented, and also that the victim did not consent. However, because the presumptions in s 75 are only evidential he is able to introduce evidence that he reasonably believed that the complainant was consenting.
3. *The basic definition of the* mens rea. If the presumptions do not apply then the jury must simply consider whether it has been proved that the defendant did not reasonably believe that the victim consented. There will be two questions here for the jury. First, did the defendant believe that the victim consented? Second, if he did have that belief, was it a reasonable one?

Section 1(2) Sexual Offences Act 2003 tells us that '[w]hether a belief is reasonable is to be determined having regard to all the circumstances, including any steps A has taken to ascertain whether B consents'. This suggests that a defendant who makes no attempt to find out whether the victim consented because, for example, he believes that he is irresistible to all women is unlikely to persuade the jury he had reasonable grounds to believe she consented. On the other hand a defendant who repeatedly asks his partner whether she consents to sexual intercourse and receives a meek smile in reply may be taken to have reasonable grounds to believe in consent if in fact it turns out his partner did not consent. Notably in the Government White Paper *Protecting the Public* it was suggested: '[t]he jury would…have to take into account the actions of both parties, the circumstances in which they have placed themselves and the level of responsibility exercised by both'. This seems to suggest that, although the man must take reasonable steps to ascertain whether his partner was consenting, the jury may also consider whether the partner had taken reasonable steps to make it clear that she was objecting. There are serious concerns that with such an approach juries may be encouraged to adopt outdated thinking along the lines 'the victim was wearing a short skirt and she was therefore asking for it'.

One argument which is bound to arrive at the courts' doorstep at some point is that when considering 'all the circumstances' the defendant's mental disabilities or sexual experience should be taken into account. In other words the jury should be invited to decide that, bearing in mind the defendant's mental condition or his sexual inexperience, his belief in consent was reasonable. Some commentators argue that such factors should not be taken into account. Warning bells reminding the courts of the difficulties involved with the defence of provocation in considering the notion of a reasonable person with the defendant's characteristics may persuade them not to accept such arguments (see *Colohan* [2001] Crim LR 845, where the court refused to consider characteristics of the accused when interpreting the reasonableness test in the Protection from Harassment Act 1997).

8.3 Assault by penetration

Section 2 Sexual Offences Act 2003 states:

(1) A person (A) commits an offence if –
   (a) he intentionally penetrates the vagina or anus of another person (B) with a part of his body or anything else,
   (b) the penetration is sexual,
   (c) B does not consent to the penetration,
   (d) A does not reasonably believe that B consents.
(2) Whether a belief is reasonable is to be determined having regard to all the circumstances, including any steps A has taken to ascertain whether B consents.

This offence covers occasions where the defendant has put an object or a part of his body into the vagina or anus of the complainant. The offence can be committed by men and women. The requirement that the penetration be sexual is important; otherwise routine medical examinations could constitute an offence. The presumptions about consent and *mens rea* in ss 75 and 76 apply to this offence.

8.4 Sexual assault

Section 3 Sexual Offences Act reads:

(1) A person (A) commits an offence if –
   (a) he intentionally touches another person (B),
   (b) the touching is sexual,
   (c) B does not consent to the touching, and
   (d) A does not reasonably believe that B consents.
(2) Whether a belief is reasonable is to be determined having regard to all the circumstances, including any steps A has taken to ascertain whether B consents.

This offence deals with non-consensual sexual touching. If there is no touching there can be no sexual assault. So a man who exposes himself to someone is not committing this offence. Section 79(8) explains that touching includes 'touching with any part of the body, (b) with anything else, (c) through anything'. This makes it clear that touching the clothing of the complainant or making something touch the complainant amounts to the offence (*H** Crim LR 735). But not every touching, of course, amounts to the *actus reus* of this offence. The touching must be sexual. This term is clarified in s 78:

> penetration, touching or any other activity is sexual if a reasonable person would consider that –
> (a) whatever its circumstances or any person's purpose in relation to it, it is because of its nature sexual, or
> (b) because of its nature it may be sexual and because of its circumstances or the purpose of any person in relation to it (or both) it is sexual.

The best way to understand this definition is to distinguish three kinds of case:

1. *Those where the act is in its nature sexual.* In such a case the act is sexual regardless of the purposes of the defendant. So, if a man forced a woman to strip in public the jury may find this to be a sexual act even if the man was motivated by a desire to humiliate the woman, rather than sexual motivation.
2. *Those cases where it is ambiguous whether the act is sexual.* In such a case the jury can consider the purpose of the act and its circumstances. In *Court** [1989] AC 28 a shopkeeper was found smacking a 12-year-old girl whom he claimed to have found shoplifting. Such an act might or might not be sexual. In fact the defendant in that case admitted he was motivated by a 'buttock fetish'. Under the new Act the smacking would probably therefore be regarded as sexual.
3. *Those cases where the act is clearly not in its nature sexual.* Such acts cannot be sexual, whatever their motivation. It might be thought that *George* [1956] Crim LR 52 (a case decided before the 2003 Act) was an example of such a case. In that case a man removed a woman's shoe. He had a foot fetish and therefore was acting for sexual motivation. However, because the act was clearly not in its nature sexual it was found not to be indecent. In *Kumar* [2005] Crim LR 470 it was suggested that a doctor who carried out a breast examination by touching in the standard way, but who was sexually gratified by the examination, would not be acting in an indecent way (he was charged under the old offence of indecent assault). On the facts of that case, however, his touchings were not standard practice and so he was guilty. The same distinction between standard and non-standard may be applied under the new Act in deciding whether in such a case a doctor's touchings were sexual. However, in *H* the Court of Appeal thought that it would be for the jury to decide whether the conduct could be in its nature sexual, and that was not an issue for a judge to decide. A jury may take a rather different view from the Court of Appeal in *Kumar*.

8.5 Causing sexual activity without consent

This offence is found in s 4:

1. A person (A) commits an offence if –
   a. he intentionally causes another person (B) to engage in an activity,
   b. the activity is sexual,

c. B does not consent to engaging in the activity, and

d. A does not reasonably believe that B consents.

2. Whether a belief is reasonable is to be determined having regard to all the circumstances, including any steps A has taken to ascertain whether B consents.

This offence is designed to cover situations where the defendant forces the victim to perform a sexual act against her wishes. This might include forcing the victim to masturbate or have sex with someone else. Again, ss 75 and 76 apply to this offence.

8.6 Sexual offences protecting children from sexual abuse

One of the principal aims of the 2003 Act was to improve the legislation designed to protect children. There is now a raft of offences designed to ensure that sexual abuse of children is an offence. The offences include the following:

Section 5: Rape of a child under 13

Section 6: Assault on a child under 13 by penetration

Section 7: Sexual assault on a child under 13

Section 8: Causing or inciting a child under 13 to engage in a sexual activity

Section 9: Sexual activity with a child

Section 10: Causing or inciting a child to engage in a sexual activity

Section 11: Engaging in a sexual activity in the presence of a child

Section 12: Causing a child to watch a sexual act

Section 13: Child sex offences committed by children or young persons

Section 14: Arranging or facilitating the commission of a child sex offence

Section 15: Meeting a child following sexual grooming

There is not space to explain each of these offences in detail. But it is worth making several points. For the offences involving under-13-year-olds there is no *mens rea* requirement apart from an intention to penetrate, touch or cause the victim to engage in an activity. This means that it is no defence to show that the victim consented, that the defendant thought the victim consented, or even that the defendant did not realise the victim's age. In *R v G* UKHL 37 the House of Lords confirmed it was no defence for a defendant to show he reasonably believed that the defendant was over 13. In that case the defendant claimed that the victim had told him she was 15, even though in fact she was 12. This did not provide him with a defence. Baroness Hale was blunt:

> Every male has a choice about where he puts his penis. It may be difficult for him to restrain himself when aroused but he has a choice. There is nothing unjust or irrational about a law which says that if he chooses to put his penis inside a child who turns out to be under 13 he has committed an offence (although the state of his mind may again be relevant to sentence).

One issue which troubled the government in preparing the legislation is what to do with teenagers engaging in sexual relations with each other. Perhaps surprisingly, two 14-year-olds kissing could be guilty of the offence under s 13. The government's approach was that sexual experimentation by teenagers would not be prosecuted by the police, but it was useful to create a general offence to deal with cases where there was 'manipulation'. However, in *R v G* (2008), as we have seen, a 15-year-old was prosecuted for rape. The House of Lords rejected an argument that the rights of children under Article 8 of the European Convention on Human Rights could be infringed if an inappropriate prosecution was brought.

In addition to those listed there are a series of offences which can be committed by those who are in a position of trust in relation to a child aged under 18 (for example, teachers). There are also offences which are designed to combat child prostitution and child pornography.

8.7 Sexual offences against those with a mental disorder

Sections 30 to 41 create offences which are designed to protect those with a mental disorder from sexual exploitation (C, 2009).

8.8 Miscellaneous offences

The Act contains a range of miscellaneous offences. These include exposure (s 66), voyeurism (s 67), intercourse with an animal (s 69) and sexual penetration of a corpse (s 70).

Hot Topic – Sexual offences and sexual autonomy

Imagine that Tim and Susie have met at a party and have returned to Tim's flat because it is a long way to Susie's room. Tim suggests that they have sex, but Susie declines. Tim says she must have sex with him or leave his flat immediately. Susie becomes very worried. It is dark, very late and the weather is appalling. She is a long way from home and there are no buses. She has no money for a taxi. She reluctantly allows Tim to have sex with her. Has Tim committed rape?

The most common way to consider an issue like this would be to ask whether the pressures facing Susie were sufficient to mean that her 'consent' was not genuine consent for the purposes of the law on rape. That is how the courts would probably approach the question. It is a question on which people would disagree. After all it is not Tim's fault that Susie has no money for a taxi and he is entitled to ask her to leave the flat. On the other hand Susie can be so terrified by the threats that she is not able to think clearly. This way of approaching such cases places the focus on the victim, because the question is all about whether she consented. This can easily lead to blaming the victim for what has happened: 'why did Susie agree to go back to Tim's flat in the first place?'; 'she should not mind a bit of cold and

dark too much'; 'she had led Tim on' and so forth. Starting from the perspective that a sexual penetration requires a justification means that the focus is put on the defendant's actions and whether he had a sufficient reason for his actions.

A rather different way of looking at the issue would be to start from the basis that a sexual penetration is a *prima facie* wrong (see Madden-Dempsey and Herring, 2007). This would mean that Tim must have a good reason for sexually penetrating Susie. Viewed in this way the question looks very different. He may point out that she allowed the sex to take place, but he knew this was only because of the lack of alternatives open to her.

It is notable that the law takes a very strict approach to those who obtain property through using threats, fraud or deception. However, when it comes to sex much less is expected. It is true that there is a balance to be struck between protecting the freedom to engage in sexual relations and the right to be protected from unwanted sexual relations. But in striking the balance the right to say 'no' is far more important than the right to say 'yes'. Not being able to have sex when you want may be frustrating. Having sex forced upon you against your will is dehumanising.

Summary

8.1 The scope of sexual offences is controversial and presents special problems of proof connected with the inevitable conflict of interest between the victim and the accused.

8.2 Rape involves the penetration of the vagina, anus or mouth of the victim without her consent. The *mens rea* of the offence is that the defendant did not reasonably believe that the victim consented.

8.3 There is an offence of assault by penetration which involves penetration with objects or parts of the body other than the penis.

8.4 Sexual assault is sexual touching without the consent of the victim.

8.5 Causing a sexual activity involves making someone perform a sexual act without their consent.

8.6 There are a wide range of offences designed to protect children from sexual abuse.

8.7 There are a variety of offences which protect those with mental disorders from abuse.

8.8 The Sexual Offences Act 2003 also contains offences connected with voyeurism, incest and necrophilia.

Further Reading

For theoretical issues relating to rape see Bryden, Gardner and Shute, Gardner, McGregor, Madden Dempsey and Herring, and West. Hering, Gross, Temkin and Ashworth, Elvin, and Temkin and Krahe discuss the 2003 Act. Issues surrounding intoxication and rape are discussed in Finch and Munro and in Wallerstein. *Mens rea* issues are discussed in Huigens and in Power.

Bryden, 'Redefining Rape' (2000) 3 Buff Crim L Rev 317.

Elvin, 'The Concept of Consent under the Sexual Offences Act 2003' (2008) 72 J Crim L 519.

Finch and Munro, 'Intoxicated Consent and the Boundaries of Drug-assisted Rape' [2003] Crim LR 773.

Finch and Munro, 'Intoxicated Consent and Drug Assisted Rape' [2004] Crim LR 789.

Finch and Munro, 'Breaking Boundaries? Sexual Consent in the Jury Room' (2006) 36 LS 303.

Gardner, 'Appreciating Olugboja' (1997) 16 LS 175.

Gardner and Shute, 'The Wrongness of Rape', in Horder (ed.), *Oxford Essays in Jurisprudence* (4th series, Oxford University Press 2000).

Gross, 'Rape, Moralism and Human Rights' [2007] Crim LR 220.

Herring, 'Mistaken Sex' [2005] Crim LR 511.

Herring, 'Human Rights and Rape: A Reply to Hyman Gross' [2007] Crim LR 228.

Huigens, 'Is Strict Liability Rape Defensible?', in Duff and Green (eds), *Defining Crimes* (Oxford University Press 2005).

Mcgregor, *Is It Rape?* (Ashgate 2005).

Madden Dempsey and Herring, 'Why Sexual Penetration Requires Justification' (2007) 27 OJLS 467.

Power, 'Towards a Redefinition of the Mens Rea of Rape' (2003) 23 OJLS 379.

Tadros, 'Rape without Consent' (2006) 26 OJLS 515.

Temkin and Ashworth, 'Rape, Sexual Assaults and the Problems of Consent' [2004] Crim LR 328.

Temkin and Krahe, *Sexual Assault and the Justice Gap* (Hart 2008)

Further Reading cont'd

Wallerstein, '"A Drunken Consent Is Still Consent" – or Is It? A Critical Analysis of the Law on a Drunken Consent to Sex following *Bree*' (2009) 73 J Crim L 318.

Wertmeimer, *Consent to Sexual Relations* (Cambridge University Press 2003).

West, 'A Comment on Consent, Sex and Rape' (1996) 2 Leg Th 233.

Williams, 'Deception, Mistake and Vitiation of the Victim's Consent' (2008) 124 LQR 132.

Case Notes

▶ *Bree* [2007] EWCA Crim 804. Court of Appeal

The defendant and complainant had been drinking heavily together and then had sex. The complainant had a hazy recollection of what had happened, but was adamant she had not consented to sex. The defendant claimed that although the complainant was intoxicated she had consented. The Court of Appeal allowed the defendant's appeal against his conviction. The judge should have made clear that even though a person is intoxicated they may still have capacity to consent. However, a person may become so intoxicated that they lack the ability to consent. The court noted that there was nothing abnormal or unusual about people having sexual intercourse after having consumed a great deal of alcohol. As long as there was consent that was not an offence.

▶ *Court* [1989] AC 28. House of Lords

The appellant was convicted of indecent assault (an offence which is now abolished). He was a shop assistant who had seized a 12-year-old girl and, pulling her across his knees, had struck her across the buttocks. He admitted the assault, but denied that it was indecent, although in an interview with the police he had given 'buttock fetish' as an explanation for his conduct. The House of Lords distinguished between an act which a reasonable person would say is clearly indecent, one which is clearly not indecent and one which is ambiguously indecent. If the act is clearly indecent, then whatever the defendant's motive the act is indecent; if clearly not, then it is not; and if ambiguous, it depends on the defendant's motive.

▶ *Devonald* [2008] EWCA 527

This case concerned the offence of causing a sexual activity without consent. The complainant was a 16-year-old boy who had been in a relationship with the defendant's daughter. The defendant believed the boy had treated his daughter very badly. He assumed the persona of a young woman and started corresponding with the complainant on the Internet. He persuaded the boy to masturbate in front of a webcam, and gave the impression that the woman he was pretending to be was enjoying this. The key issue in the case was whether the complainant had consented to engage in the masturbation. That turned on s 76(2)(a) and whether it could be said that the complainant had been deceived as to the nature or purpose of the act – specifically that the boy had been deceived into thinking he was doing an act for the sexual enjoyment of a young woman, whereas in fact he was doing the act for his ex-girlfriend's father, who was seeking material to embarrass him with. The defendant was convicted and the Court of Appeal upheld the conviction on the basis that it was open to the jury to find that the complainant had been deceived as to the purpose of the sexual act. This is a surprisingly broad interpretation of 'purpose' in s 76(2)(a).

▶ *Dica* [2004] EWCA Crim 1103. Court of Appeal

See Chapter 7 Case notes.

▶ *Elbekkay* [1995] Crim LR 163. Court of Appeal

The accused had intercourse with the victim, who was sleepy and intoxicated, and she believed that he was her boyfriend. The Court of Appeal suggested that under the common law, consent based on the mistaken belief that the man was her husband 'or another' could vitiate the victim's consent. The appellant's appeal against his conviction was therefore dismissed.

▶ *R v H* [2005] Crim LR 735. Court of Appeal

The defendant approached the complainant as she crossed some fields and said, 'Do you fancy a shag?' She declined the invitation. He then grabbed her tracksuit trousers. She broke free and escaped. He was convicted of a sexual assault contrary to s 3 Sexual Offences Act 2003. He appealed on the basis that he had only touched her clothing and so had not touched her. The Court of Appeal held that touching for the purposes of s 3 included touching the clothing.

▶ *Jheeta* [2007] EWCA Crim 1699

The defendant sent various threatening text messages to the victim. Not realising who had sent them the victim consulted the defendant (who was an ex-boyfriend) for advice and he recommended that she go to the police. He then sent her messages, purporting to come from the police, encouraging her to have sex with the defendant; otherwise she would face a fine. As a result of these messages she had sex with the defendant on many occasions. His conviction was upheld by the Court of Appeal. The deceptions did not relate to the nature or purpose of the Act under s 76. However, the jury could conclude on the facts of the case that there was no consent in the general sense.

▶ *Linekar* [1995] QB 250. Court of Appeal

The accused agreed to pay £25 for sexual intercourse, but ran off without paying. The Court of Appeal held that only deceptions as to the nature of the act or the identity of the accused could vitiate consent. Here the deception concerned whether the victim would be paid for the sexual intercourse, not the nature of the act itself, and so the mistake could not vitiate the victim's consent. The appellant's conviction of rape was overturned.

▶ *Olugboja* [1982] QB 320. Court of Appeal

The victim did not struggle or resist while the accused had intercourse with her, as she was terrified following another rape by the defendant's friend. The Court of Appeal said whether the victim consented, albeit reluctantly, or whether she was submitting was a question for the jury, bearing in mind all the circumstances. The appellant's convictions were dismissed.

Chapter 9

Murder

Key Terms

▶ **Death** – the medical definition of the end of life.
▶ **Intention** – the aim or purpose of the defendant.

9.1 Homicide

There is general agreement that causing another person's death in a culpable way is the most serious of criminal offences. This reflects the high value society puts on each individual's life and the fact that to kill someone is the most permanent of injuries. As Professor Ashworth (2007) has written:

> death is final. This finality makes it proper to regard death as the most serious harm that may be inflicted on another, and to regard a person who chooses to inflict that harm without justification or excuse as the most culpable of offenders.

However, the law does not treat all killings in the same way. It is perhaps best to see manslaughter as the basic charge with respect to a homicide and murder as an aggravated crime of killing – a killing with an intent to kill or cause grievous bodily harm. Given the seriousness of the consequence (that is death), only a low level of blame is necessary for a manslaughter conviction. As Fletcher has written, 'In the law of homicide the formal point is neither the act nor the intent, but the fact of death. Fletcher, *Rethinking Criminal Law* (Oxford University Press 2000). This overpowering fact is the point at which the law deigns to draw the radius of liability.'

Murder is the most serious type of homicide, requiring an intention to kill or cause grievous bodily harm. Manslaughter includes cases of homicide where the *mens rea* of murder is lacking. However there are cases where, even though the defendant has the *mens rea* for murder, the presence of an additional factor reduces what would otherwise be murder to manslaughter. The most important of these are manslaughter by loss of control (previously known as provocation) and manslaughter by reason of diminished responsibility (a form of mental abnormality).

So, key to the distinction between murder and manslaughter is the intention of the defendant. The definitions of murder and manslaughter take no account of other factors, such as the method of killing (for example, whether or not a gun was used), or the context of the offence (was it in the course of a robbery, rape or terrorist attack, or was it a domestic killing? was it part of a series of killings by the same defendant?), or the identity of the victim (a policeman or a child, for example). These factors are considered by the court only after conviction, at the sentencing stage. In the case of murder, moreover, the extent to which they can be taken into account in sentencing is very limited, as the offence is subject to a compulsory sentence of life imprisonment and the trial judge merely has the power to recommend that the offender should serve a minimum number of years in prison before being released on licence. In sentencing for manslaughter, the judge has greater powers as the maximum sentence is life imprisonment, but the judge can impose a more lenient sentence, such as a shorter term of imprisonment or even a community-based sentence or absolute discharge.

The existence of the mandatory life sentence is capable of producing apparent injustices. For example, in *Cocker* [1989] Crim LR 74 a man had been caring for his terminally ill wife for years. She had continually pleaded with him to kill her. After many sleepless nights he placed a pillow over her head and she died. Whatever one's views on the rights and wrongs of euthanasia, to give a life sentence in such a case seems inappropriate, but the Court of Appeal stated that there was no alternative following his conviction for murder but to impose a life sentence. Cocker had an intention to kill his wife and could not rely on a defence. The Court of Appeal could not reduce his conviction to one of manslaughter simply because it was sympathetic to him or thought a life sentence inappropriate. Such cases have led many, such as Lord Kilbrandon in *Hyam v DPP* [1991] 1 QB 134, to suggest that the distinction between murder and manslaughter should be abolished, and with it the compulsory life sentence for murder.

What constitutes murder or manslaughter is a reflection of a certain set of values. Further it is also a political choice that certain killings fall outside murder and manslaughter. A notable example of this is killing by motor car, which is covered by a separate offence: causing death by dangerous driving (see Section 10.5), an offence under s 2A Road Traffic Act 1988. There is no justification for separate treatment of this kind of killing except that prosecutors have reported difficulties in persuading juries to convict in cases of car killing, even in clear cases of recklessness. Juries, it appears, are sympathetic to those who kill while driving. Similarly, killings which are 'accidents at work' tend not to result in homicide convictions, but are dealt with by regulatory bodies concerned with health and safety at work (see Chapter 6). Whether the way in which the law operates in relation to killings in car accidents and at work is consistent with the Human Rights Act is debatable. Under Article 2 of the European Convention which is given effect to by the Human Rights Act there is a duty to protect the right to life of its citizens. It might be arguable that by failing seriously to punish the killing of those on the roads or in the workplace the state is failing in its duty.

The nature and frequency of murder are often misunderstood. There were only 615 recorded homicides in the year 2009/2010, probably a similar number to the killings viewable on television dramas and in films over a weekend. It is interesting to note that most murder convictions involve people known to each other, and the most dangerous age for becoming a victim of homicide is under one year. This indicates that the popular view of murder portrayed on television and in films is not the most common kind of homicide found in the courts. It may be that much of the development on the law of murder and manslaughter has been based on an image of murder which is in fact quite exceptional. The killing of babies, partners and those in road accidents and at work is more common, but has received little attention from the courts or criminal lawyers.

This chapter will focus on the law of murder. Chapter 10 will discuss the crime of manslaughter. First it is appropriate to draw the line between murder and other criminal offences, such as child destruction and abortion. These distinctions are found in the definition of the *actus reus*.

9.2 The *actus reus* of murder

The *actus reus* of murder is unlawfully causing the death of another person. These elements require further discussion.

9.2.1   Unlawfully

As with other criminal offences, the element of 'unlawfulness' indicates the absence of a valid defence, such as self-defence or killing with lawful authority (for example, killing under orders in time of war). It should be noted, however, that the consent of the victim does not provide a defence to murder. If the victim has asked the defendant to kill him or her, it will still be murder, provided that the defendant has the necessary *mens rea*. This is discussed in greater detail in the Hot topic of Chapter 5.

9.2.2   Causing a death

It must be shown that the defendant caused the death of the victim. The normal rules of causation, discussed in Chapter 4, will be applied. There are a couple of topics which require a little more analysis. What about those cases in which a doctor decides to withdraw life-saving treatment from a very ill patient? Lord Goff in *Airedale National Health Service Trust v Bland* [1993] AC 789 has recently summarised the position:

> the law draws a crucial distinction between cases in which a doctor decides not to provide, or to continue to provide, for his patient treatment or care which could or might prolong his life, and those in which he decides, for example by administering a lethal drug, actively to bring his patient's life to an end.

This subject is discussed in detail in the Hot topic in Chapter 5.

There used to be a rule that for murder the death of the victim had to occur within a year and a day from the action of the accused. However, the Law Reform (Year and a Day Rule) Act 1996 has abolished the rule as it applies to all acts committed after 17 June 1996. If more than three years have elapsed since the act which was said to have caused the death then the consent of the Attorney-General is required for a prosecution.

9.2.3   Causing the death of a person

The victim of murder must be a human being who was alive when the accused caused his or her death. This may lead to problems of definition both of the beginning and end of life.

1. *When does life begin?* The unborn child is protected elsewhere within the criminal law, but not by the law of murder (*A-G's Ref (No 3 of 1994)** [1997] 3 WLR 421). The destruction of a foetus will be punishable as a crime unless it falls within the provisions of the Abortion Act 1967. If the foetus is 'capable of being born alive' then it is protected by the offence of child destruction, under the Infant Life (Preservation) Act 1929. If the foetus is not 'capable of being born alive' then the offence will be of procuring a miscarriage under s 58 Offences Against the Person Act 1861. It has recently been confirmed that the prescription or supply of the 'morning after pill' does not amount to an offence under s 58 (*R (On the Application of Smeaton) v Secretary of State* [2002] Crim LR 661), on the basis that the pill is widely regarded as a form of contraception rather than as causing a miscarriage.

   In order to be the victim of murder (or manslaughter) the child must be fully born (that is, completely outside his or her mother) and have an existence independent of his or her mother, if only for the briefest of moments (*Crutchley* (1837) 7 C&P 814). This is taken to mean that the child must have started breathing and have independent circulation. This rule does not mean that no account can be taken of injuries inflicted on a child while still in the womb in a case of murder or manslaughter. If the defendant injures the unborn child who is subsequently born alive but then dies from his or her injuries, this amounts to the *actus reus* of murder or manslaughter. The most likely offence would be manslaughter. If the defendant has committed a dangerous criminal act against the mother, foetus or some other person which causes the death of a child then a conviction can follow using the law of constructive manslaughter (*A-G's Ref (No 3 of 1994)*). In the unlikely event that the defendant intended that the foetus be born alive and then die as a result of his act, this would be murder.

2. *When does life end?* Discussion of the legal test of death has recently been renewed with the development of medical technology (such as life-support machines). The traditional tests of breathing, heartbeat and blood circulation are no longer adequate, but they have not yet been definitively supplanted by new tests in the courts. The medical profession has developed its own tests for 'brain death', and it is obviously important that doctors should be able to rely on the legality of these procedures when switching off life-support machines or performing transplant operations. *Re A (a minor)* [1992] 3 Med LR 303, a civil case, accepted that 'brain death' was the correct test of death. It is likely that a criminal court would accept this medical definition of death. Certainly, the Court of Appeal has refused to countenance the argument that the action of a doctor in switching off a life-support machine can break the causal link between the injuries inflicted by the accused and the death of the victim (*Malcherek and Steel** [1981] 2 All ER 422).

9.3 The *mens rea* of murder

The *mens rea* of murder is known as 'malice aforethought', but this is a misleading term in that the state of mind referred to is not 'malice' in its ordinary meaning, and there is no need for the premeditation which the word 'aforethought' implies. The *mens rea* of murder is an intention to kill or cause grievous bodily harm to the victim (*Cunningham** [1982] AC 566, *A-G's Ref (No 3 of 1994)* [1997] 3 WLR 421). If the defendant intended to kill someone other than the victim but in so doing caused the victim's death, then the doctrine of transferred *mens rea* (see Section 5.7) operates to enable the defendant's conviction for murder of the victim. If the defendant commits an act intending to kill anyone who happens to be in the area (for example, a terrorist bomber who places a bomb in a city centre) this is known as 'general malice' and is sufficient for the *mens rea* of murder (*A-G's Ref (No 3 of 1994)*). It should be remembered that the prosecution must show beyond reasonable doubt that the defendant intended to kill. In *Haigh* [2010] EWCA Crim 90 a mother, when alone with her child, smothered her. The Court of Appeal held that the jury could not be sure that the mother intended to kill her child. This shows how difficult it can be for the prosecution to prove intention, in the absence of a confession from the defendant.

It is quite clear that the *mens rea* of murder is an intent to kill or cause grievous bodily harm. But what is grievous bodily harm? It means a really serious harm (*DPP v Smith* [1961] AC 290; for further discussion see Section 7.4). Notably an injury may amount to grievous bodily harm even though it does not endanger a person's life. For example, a terrorist may shoot a victim in the knee; if unexpectedly the wound becomes infected and the victim dies, the defendant could be guilty of murder, even though it was not foreseeable that his act would lead to the victim's death. The rule that intention to commit grievous bodily harm is sufficient for the *mens rea* of murder has been recently confirmed, albeit reluctantly, by the House of Lords (*A-G's Ref (No 3 of 1994)*). Lord Mustill commented that the 'rule is an outcropping of old law from which the surrounding strata of rationalisations have weathered away'. Similar criticisms are to be found in Lord Steyn's judgment in the House of Lords' decision in *Powell and English* [1997] 3 WLR 959, where he suggested that a person convicted of murder having only an intent to cause grievous bodily harm was not 'in truth' a murderer. Despite these criticisms it is unlikely that the House of Lords will overrule the grievous bodily harm rule which is now well established. It will be up to the Parliament to change the law.

9.4 Intention in murder

In Chapter 5 we considered in detail the meaning of intention. Notably it is in the context of murder that the definition of murder has received the greatest attention. This is because if there is no intent to kill or cause grievous bodily harm, the defendant cannot be guilty of murder but may be guilty of manslaughter. Five times in recent years the issue has been addressed by the House of Lords: *Smith v DPP, Hyam v DPP* [1991] 1 QB 134, *Moloney* [1985] AC 905, *Hancock and Shankland* [1986] AC 455 and *Woollin* [1999] 1 AC 82. These concepts have been discussed in greater detail in Chapter 5, but will be summarised here. The House of Lords has declined to give a definition of intention, apart from saying that intention is a word which should be given its normal meaning. Indeed in most cases the judge should not address the jury on the meaning of intention. In the rare cases where it is necessary to direct the jury, two questions should be asked:

(i) Was the victim's death or grievous bodily harm virtually certain? and
(ii) Did the defendant realise that the victim's death or grievous bodily harm was virtually certain?

If the answer to both questions is 'yes' then the jury are entitled to find that the defendant intended death or grievous bodily harm (*Woollin*).

9.5 The relevance of the mandatory life sentence

The development and understanding of the law of murder have been strongly influenced by the mandatory life sentence for murder. As already mentioned, if a person is convicted of murder then the court has no discretion but to impose a sentence of life imprisonment. This is highly controversial. The main justification for the present position is that the sentence marks the fact that murder is the most heinous offence. However, others reject this argument, pointing to the breadth of the offence. As Lord Hailsham in *Howe* [1987] AC 417 has explained:

> Murder, as every practitioner of the law knows, though often described as one of the utmost heinousness, is not in fact necessarily so, but consists in a whole bundle of offences of vastly differing degrees of culpability, ranging from brutal, cynical and repeated offences like the so-called Moors murders (R v. Brady and Hindley, 6 May 1966, unreported) to the almost venial, if objectively immoral, 'mercy killing' of a beloved partner.

The existence of the mandatory life sentence may explain why intention can only be found from foresight of circumstances as virtually certain (see *Woollin* [1999] 1 AC 82).

The cases on the meaning of intention can be interpreted as seeking to limit the offence of murder to the most serious of circumstances, the kind in which a mandatory sentence is appropriate. On the other hand the existence of the mandatory life sentence is used by those seeking to reform the *mens rea* for murder, either by restricting further the definition of intention or by rejecting the law that an intention to cause grievous bodily harm is sufficient to amount to the *mens rea* for murder (see, for example, Lord Steyn in *Powell and English* [1997] 3 WLR 959).

The mandatory life sentence may also explain the existence of the partial defences to murder, such as loss of control or diminished responsibility. These partial defences will reduce the conviction from murder to manslaughter and thereby give the court discretion as to sentence. It is certainly possible that if there were a wide discretion as to the sentence in murder, there might be no need to have these defences.

9.6 Reform of the law on murder

The Law Commission has recently considered reform of the law of homicide. It has recommended that homicide be divided into four categories:

1. 'first degree murder' (mandatory life sentence);
2. 'second degree murder' (discretionary life sentence);
3. manslaughter (fixed term of years sentence); and
4. specific homicide offences, such as assisting suicide and infanticide (fixed term of years sentence).

We will discuss the proposals in relation to manslaughter in Chapter 10. For now we will focus on the proposals to separate out murder into two degrees. The Law Commission explained its thinking in this way:

> The law of England and Wales categorises homicide offences in a very blunt, rudimentary fashion…. murder encompasses both the 'contract' killer who commits a premeditated killing for gain and the person who, suddenly involved in an argument, instinctively picks up a knife and inflicts a wound that he or she did not intend to be, but which proves, fatal. Each is guilty of murder and subject to the mandatory life sentence. The difference in the respective culpability can only be reflected in the period that each must spend in prison before he or she can be considered for release on licence.

The aim, therefore, of the distinction between first and second degree murder is to distinguish between the worst and less bad murders. First degree murder is restricted to cases where the defendant intended to kill and 'killings with the intent to cause serious injury where the killer was aware that his or her conduct involved a serious risk of causing death'. The meaning of intention proposed by the Law Commission is discussed further in Chapter 5, but it is restricted to cases where death was the aim of the defendant, or was integral to what the defendant set out to achieve.

Second degree murder is explained by the Law Commission to include the following:

> (1) killings intended to cause serious injury; or
> (2) killings intended to causer injury or fear or risk of injury where the killer was aware that his or her conduct involved a serious risk of causing death; or
> (3) killings intended to kill or cause serious injury where the killer was aware that his or her conduct involved a risk of causing death but successfully pleads provocation, diminished responsibility or that he or she killed pursuant to a suicide pact.

The offence would accommodate those cases where the level of criminality is too high to be categorised as manslaughter but is not high enough to merit the mandatory life sentence.

Note then that the second degree murder category would include some cases which under the current law are straightforward murder, carrying the mandatory life sentence, but also some cases which are currently manslaughter. Notably second degree murder would not carry the mandatory life sentence. The Law Commission believes that those who are 'recklessly indifferent to death'; whose attitude is that it is just 'too bad' if death results from their actions, deserve the label of murder, albeit of the second degree kind.

Hot Topic – Murder of a disabled child

In September 2008 Joanne Hill was convicted of the murder of her 4-year-old daughter, Naomi, and sentenced to life imprisonment. She will not be eligible for parole for 15 years. She drowned her daughter in a bath after drinking wine. Her daughter suffered from cerebral palsy and the prosecution claimed that the mother was embarrassed by her daughter's condition. The judge stated, 'There can be no excuse for what you did.... You killed your own daughter because you could not cope with her disability. You had other pressures upon you, a disintegrating marriage, and you decided to kill your own daughter by drowning her.'

There are, however, some troubling aspects of the decision. Joanne Hill had been receiving treatment for mental health issues. She was estranged from her husband. She had asked him if Naomi could be fostered or adopted because she was struggling with her care. The father explained to the court he refused to agree because he was a 'doting father'. That may be so, but Joanne Hill was the one left with the burden of care. Social service support was virtually non-existent. This was justified on the basis

that the mother did not want it. But this seems to be in part because she was trying to ignore the existence of her daughter's disability, insisting that her legs were always covered so they could not be seen by others. Also there was evidence that she blamed herself for her daughter's condition.

Joanna Hill had been receiving treatment for serious mental health problems since the age of 17. She had attempted suicide twice in 2000 and suffered with post-natal depression following Naomi's birth. She raised diminished responsibility at her trial, but it was rejected by the jury who determined that she was sufficiently responsible to be guilty of murder.

The case is undoubtedly a sad one. It demonstrates how the focus of a criminal trial is a narrow one – as on this particular defendant. The responsibilities of others and the wider society can be lost. Mary Dejevsky, a journalist writing about this case, said that '[s]ociety's expectations of women, inadequate care services, and an adversarial court system that magnifies vice and virtue could, and should, have been in the dock, too'.

Summary

9.1 Murder is the most serious form of homicide, and carries a compulsory sentence of life imprisonment. Murder is distinguished from manslaughter by its *mens rea*, malice aforethought. It is a common law offence.

9.2 The *actus reus* of murder is the unlawful killing of the victim. It has to be proved that the accused caused the death of the victim. A new-born child is protected by the law of murder once he or she has an existence independent of the mother. The legal test of death has in the past been determined by heartbeat and breathing, but in some cases where a life-support machine is used these tests are now questionable. It is probable that the courts will adopt the medical tests for 'brain death'. The courts have placed much emphasis on the act/omission distinction in order to distinguish between murder and acceptable medical treatment of the dying.

Summary cont'd

9.3 The *mens rea* of murder is malice aforethought. This includes an intent to kill (express malice) and an intent to cause grievous bodily harm (implied malice). Grievous bodily harm is defined as serious bodily harm, which need not endanger life.

9.4 Both express and implied malice require intention, which is tested subjectively. Foresight by the accused that the result will almost certainly occur is evidence that he intended the result. The courts have had difficulty in deciding whether violent risk-takers should be guilty of murder; the present position leaves much to the discretion of juries, as intention is largely undefined. The defendant must intend to cause death or grievous bodily harm to the victim or a group of people including the victim, although the prosecution can also rely on the doctrine of transferred *mens rea*.

9.5 If convicted of murder, the judge must impose a mandatory life sentence on the defendant. If the conviction is for manslaughter, the judge has a wide range of possible sentences. The sentencing consequences may have affected the development of the law on murder and manslaughter.

9.6 The Law Commission has recommended the creation of two degrees of murder. First degree murder would be cases where there is an intention to kill. Second degree murder would cover other very bad killings.

Further Reading

For readings on intention see Further reading in Chapter 5 and Goff. The structure of the law of murder is examined in Ashworth and Wilson (2000, 2006). On the meaning of death see Devlin and also Dickens. On the legal and moral status of the foetus there is a huge volume of material, including Dworkin, Herring, and Kaufman. On the life sentence for murder see the Criminal Law Revision Committee and also the House of Lords.

Ashworth, 'Principles, Pragmatism and the Law Commission's Recommendations on Homicide Reform' [2007] CrimLR 333.

Devlin, *Easing the Passing* (Oxford University Press 1986).

Dickens, 'Death', in Kennedy and Grubb (eds), *Principles of Medical Law* (Oxford University Press 1998).

Dworkin, *Life's Dominion* (HarperCollins 1993).

Goff, 'The Mental Element in the Crime of Murder' (1988) 104 LQR 30.

Herring, 'The Caesarean Section Cases and the Supremacy of Autonomy', in Freeman and Lewis (eds), *Law and Medicine* (Oxford University Press 2000).

House of Lords, Report of the Select Committee on Murder and Life Imprisonment (HL 1988–89, 78-I).

Kaufman, 'Legal Recognition of Independent Fetal Rights' (1997) 17 Ch LRJ 20.

Law Commission, *Murder, Manslaughter and Infanticide* (Law Com No 304, 2006).

Tadros, 'The Homicide Ladder' (2006) 69 MLR 601.

Wilson, 'Murder and the Structure of Homicide', in Ashworth and Mitchell (eds), *Rethinking English Homicide Law* (Oxford University Press 2000).

Wilson, 'The Structure of Criminal Homicide' [2006] CrimLR 471.

Case Notes

▶ *A-G's Ref (No 3 of 1994)* [1997] 3 WLR 421. House of Lords

The defendant stabbed his girlfriend, who was pregnant, intending to cause injury to the unborn child. The baby was in due course born, but died shortly after its birth owing to the injuries suffered as a result of the defendant's actions. The Court of Appeal stated that although at the time the accused stabbed the mother the foetus was not a person in law, the foetus could be seen as part of the mother. He therefore intended to cause injury to the mother and caused the death of the child once it was born, and using the doctrine of transferred malice the defendant could be convicted of the murder of the child. The House of Lords disagreed and stated that the foetus was an organism *sui generis* and not just part of the mother. The doctrine of transferred malice could not be relied upon as it involved a double fiction – that the intention directed to the mother be transferred to the foetus and that the foetus be deemed to be born so that it could be a person for the purposes of the law. However, the death could be seen as manslaughter using the offence of constructive manslaughter as there was an unlawful act (the stabbing of the mother) which was dangerous (to the mother) and it caused the death of someone (the foetus).

▶ *Cunningham* [1982] AC 566. House of Lords

The appellant was convicted of murder. He struck the victim on the head with a heavy chair, and the victim died from a fractured skull. He denied that he had intended to kill the victim. The trial judge directed the jury to convict of murder if it was sure that the accused intended to do the victim really serious harm. Both the Court of Appeal and the House of Lords upheld the conviction on the ground that malice aforethought could be implied where the accused intended to inflict grievous bodily harm. Lord Hailsham held that the law on this point had been laid down by *Vickers and Hyam v DPP*, and there was no reason to change the law.

▶ *Howe* [1987] AC 417. House of Lords

See Chapter 16 Case notes.

▶ *Malcherek and Steel* [1981] 2 All ER 422. Court of Appeal

See Chapter 4 Case notes.

▶ *Moloney* [1985] AC 905. House of Lords

The appellant was convicted of murder. He had shot his stepfather with a shotgun in the early hours of the morning. Both the appellant and the victim had been drinking and had started an argument as to which one was faster at loading and shooting a shotgun. The appellant claimed that he had not intended to injure the victim. The trial judge directed the jury that in law a man intends the consequence of his act where he desires it to happen, or where he foresees that it will probably happen, whether or not he desires it. An appeal against conviction was dismissed by the Court of Appeal, but on appeal to the House of Lords the conviction was quashed, and a conviction for manslaughter substituted. Lord Bridge recognised that the decision in *Hyam v DPP* had caused some confusion in the law. He held that, as a general rule, the jury did not need to be directed on the meaning of intention, but that in cases where some reference to foresight of consequences was necessary it must be made clear that such foresight was not equivalent to intention, but was evidence from which intention might be inferred. A jury would be entitled to infer intention in a case where the consequence was 'natural' in the sense that 'in the ordinary course of events a certain act will lead to a certain consequence unless something unexpected supervenes to prevent it'. Lord Bridge also rejected the suggestion of Lord Hailsham in *Hyam v DPP* that in cases of murder the act of the accused must be aimed at a specific person.

▶ *Powell and English* [1999] AC 1. House of Lords.

See Chapter 17 Case notes.

▶ *Woollin* [1999] 1 AC 82. House of Lords

See Chapter 5 Case notes.

Chapter 10

Manslaughter

Key Terms

- **Diminished responsibility** – the defendant was suffering an abnormality of mind which lessened his responsibility for the killing.
- **Involuntary manslaughter** – the defendant lacks the mental element required for murder, but can be convicted on the basis of constructive or gross negligence manslaughter.
- **Voluntary manslaughter** – the defendant would be guilty of murder but has successfully raised a defence such as provocation or diminished responsibility.

10.1 Distinguishing between voluntary and involuntary manslaughter

There are two basic types of manslaughter, usually referred to as voluntary and involuntary manslaughter. In the case of involuntary manslaughter the accused lacks malice aforethought, the *mens rea*, for murder. Voluntary manslaughter is different; it arises in cases where both the *actus reus* and *mens rea* of murder exist, but an additional factor is present which operates as a partial defence to murder, reducing it to manslaughter. There are three partial defences: provocation, loss of control and suicide pact. These special defences fall between ordinary defences (such as self-defence) which exonerate completely and mitigating factors which make no difference to criminal liability (legal guilt or innocence), but which can be taken into account by the judge at the sentencing stage. They are needed in the case of murder because murder is an offence with a mandatory sentence of life imprisonment, and therefore no sentencing discretion is available to the judge. It is not only the question of sentence which is important; voluntary manslaughter also removes the stigma of a conviction of murder.

There are three forms of involuntary manslaughter: constructive manslaughter, gross negligence manslaughter and reckless manslaughter. We shall consider these first.

10.2 Constructive manslaughter

Constructive manslaughter arises in cases where the accused lacks the *mens rea* of murder but kills the victim in the course of committing an unlawful and dangerous act. It is called constructive manslaughter as the offence is constructed from a less serious crime. The House of Lords in *A-G's Ref (No 3 of 1994)* [1997] 3 WLR 421 has set out the four requirements for constructive manslaughter. Lord Hope explained:

> The only questions which need to be addressed are (1) whether the act was done intentionally, (2) whether it was unlawful, (3) whether it was also dangerous because it was likely to cause harm to somebody and (4) whether that unlawful and dangerous act caused the death.

We will now consider these requirements separately.

10.2.1 Intentional act

It is necessary to show that the defendant intended to do the act which is the basis for the constructive manslaughter conviction; that is, that the defendant's act was voluntary and not accidental (see Chapter 3).

10.2.2 Unlawful act

What is an unlawful act for these purposes? In the past there was some doubt over whether the act needed to be criminally unlawful or whether it was sufficient for the act to be contrary to the civil law (for example, a breach of contract). It is now clear that the act does need to be criminal (*Kennedy* [2007] UKHL 38). In *Lamb** [1967] 2 QB 981, Sachs LJ said that the act must be unlawful 'in the criminal sense of that word'. In *Andrews v DPP** [1937] AC 576, Lord Atkin held that the unlawful act must be a criminal one which requires more than negligence on the part of the accused. This was in order to preserve a distinction between constructive manslaughter and gross negligence manslaughter. So a negligence-based or strict liability crime is not sufficient as the basis of a constructive manslaughter conviction. Neither is a crime to which a defendant has a defence (for example, self-defence as in *Scarlett* [1993] 4 All ER 629). The unlawful act need not be a serious criminal offence; a common assault or affray (*Carey* [2006] EWCA Crim 17) will do. This can combine with the rules of causation, such as the 'thin-skull rule' (see Section 4.4.2), to produce liability for manslaughter in cases where death was unforeseen and was not even reasonably foreseeable by the accused.

Some commentators take the view that constructive manslaughter is limited to criminal actions and does not include omissions. There is some authority for this in *Rv Lowe* [1973] 1 QB 702, and indeed cases where death is caused by an omission are usually charged as gross negligence manslaughter (see Section 10.3 below). That said, there seems no reason in principle why death caused by an unlawful omission should not lead to a charge of constructive manslaughter.

Some cases are problematic as the courts have not clearly identified the precise offence which caused the death. In the House of Lords decision in *Newbury and Jones** [1977] AC 500 the accused had thrown a paving-stone off a railway bridge, hitting a train and killing the guard. Unfortunately it is not clear from the judgments in the House of Lords exactly what form the unlawful act took; it was merely assumed that the accused had committed an unspecified unlawful act. However, defenders of the decision in *Newbury and Jones* point out that the existence of an unlawful act was not an issue disputed before their Lordships, and it would not have been too difficult to find the offence on the facts (for example, offences contrary to the Criminal Damage Act 1971).

The House of Lords in *Newbury and Jones* held that it was not necessary for the accused to have foreseen the risk of causing harm to any person as a result of his unlawful act. This does not mean that constructive manslaughter has no *mens rea* at all. In order to prove the unlawful act it is necessary to prove both the *mens rea* and *actus reus* of the offence (*Jennings* [1990] Crim LR 588).

10.2.3 Dangerous act

The unlawful act must be objectively dangerous. It does not need to be shown that the act may cause the death of the victim; it is enough if it may cause an injury to the victim. The defendant does not need to realise that his act is dangerous if a reasonable person would have done so. The classic statement of this rule is found in *Church** [1966] 1 QB 59, where Lord Edmund Davies said:

> an unlawful act causing the death of another cannot, simply because it is an unlawful act, render a manslaughter verdict inevitable. For such a verdict inexorably to follow, the unlawful act must be such as all sober and reasonable people would inevitably recognise must subject the other person to, at least, the risk of some harm resulting therefrom, albeit not serious harm.

There needs to be only a risk of harm; there does not need to be a likelihood of harm (*Carey*). 'Harm' in this context was defined by the Court of Appeal in *Dawson, Nolan and Walmsley** (1985) 81 Cr App R 150 to be limited to actual physical injury and not to include terror. However, this was before the House of Lords' interpretation of actual bodily harm in the Offences Against the Person Act as including psychological illnesses (*Ireland and Burstow**). Whether *Dawson, Nolan and Walmsley* must now be reconsidered on this question is a matter of debate. In *Carey* the Court of Appeal suggested that the risk of shock would render the act dangerous, but not a risk of emotional upset. It accepted that the difference between the two was a 'gray area'. In *Johnstone* it was held that spitting and throwing insults could not be regarded as a dangerous act.

The other issue raised by *Dawson, Nolan and Walmsley* was whose perspective should be used when deciding whether the act was objectively dangerous? In this case the defendants had committed an armed robbery against the victim, who had a weak heart. Knowing that the victim had a weak heart, the act of subjecting him to an attempted armed robbery was clearly dangerous. However, the court said that the dangerousness of the act had to be judged from the viewpoint of a reasonable bystander, not someone having any special knowledge (*Ball* [1989] Crim LR 730). Thus the jury could have decided that the robbery here would not have been dangerous to a reasonable on-looker, that it did not involve a risk of harm. In a later case, *Watson* [1989] 2 All ER 865, the defendant broke into the house of an elderly man, who later died from a heart attack. This time the court said that the act of burglary became dangerous as soon as a reasonable person in the defendant's shoes (note, not a bystander) would have realised that the act was dangerous. So in that case the act would have become presumably dangerous as soon as the accused realised that the resident was an elderly person. The court added that if the defendant had special knowledge which would not have been known to the reasonable person in the defendant's shoes (for example, if he had been told by a friend that an elderly person lived in that flat) then that knowledge was to be attributed to the reasonable person in deciding whether the reasonable person would think the act dangerous.

In *Dalby* [1982] 1 All ER 916, Waller LJ suggested that the unlawful and dangerous act must be 'directed at the victim'. However, the 'aimed at' requirement is not part of the law in the light of *A-G's Ref (No 3 of 1994)* which stated that there is no need for the unlawful act to be dangerous to the victim, as long as the act is dangerous to someone. In that case it was sufficient for constructive manslaughter that the unlawful act was dangerous to someone (the mother), even if it caused the death of someone else (the child).

10.2.4 Act caused the death

The unlawful and dangerous act must cause the death of the victim. This is a straightforward question of causation using the normal rules (see Chapter 4), although it may cause problems where it is unclear whether an unlawful act of the defendant or a lawful one caused the death (see *Dhaliwal** [2006] EWCA Crim 1139; *Kennedy*). As we have just noted, there is no need to establish that the actual victim was the intended victim, or that the victim was the person to whom the act was dangerous.

10.3 Gross negligence manslaughter

The second form of manslaughter is gross negligence manslaughter. This was considered by the House of Lords in the case of *Adomako** [1995] 1 AC 171. Gross negligence manslaughter can involve a wide range of cases from the master of a schooner alleged to be sailing unsafely and so causing the ship to founder (*Litchfield*) to a landlord not maintaining the proper repair of gas fires in his flats (*Singh*). The test for gross negligence manslaughter requires proof of the following:

▶ A duty of care;
▶ A breach of the duty;
▶ That the breach of the duty caused the death; and
▶ That the breach of the duty was so gross as to justify a criminal conviction.

These will be now examined separately.

10.3.1 A duty of care

The requirement of a duty of care is essentially a civil law concept found in the law of tort (*Wacker** [2003] QB 1207). We owe a duty of care not to injure anyone whom we could reasonably foreseeably injure (*Winter* [2010] EWCA Crim 1474). Applying that to this context, there is a duty of care if there was a risk that an act or omission of the defendant might kill the victim. As the concept of a 'duty of care' is a legal concept it is for the judge to decide whether a set of facts gave rise to a duty of care (*Wacker; Evans** [2009] EWCA Crim 650; *Winter*).

There is a possibility of confusion here. If the defendant is charged with gross negligence manslaughter by an omission, it must be shown that he owed the victim a a duty of care and that he was under one of the duties to act (see Section 3.3.1) which is always required in order to convict in respect of an omission. That said, if there is a duty to act there will always be a duty of care too.

10.3.2 A breach of the duty

The second requirement, breach of the duty, requires that the defendant acted in a way that a reasonable person would not have acted. If the defendant is purporting to exercise some special kind of skill then the defendant must act as a reasonable person possessing that skill. For example, in *Adomako* the question was whether a reasonably qualified anaesthetist (not an ordinary person) would have realised what was wrong with the patient and have intervened to help him. The test is therefore objective. Adomako's defence that his training was inadequate and that he was exhausted from overwork was irrelevant in deciding whether he had breached a duty. He had not acted as a reasonable anaesthetist would have done, and that was that.

10.3.3 The breach of the duty caused the victim's death

The third requirement is that the breach caused the death. This involves applying the normal rules of causation. It must be stressed that it is not enough to show that the defendant caused the death of the victim; it must be shown that his negligence did. So, in *Singh*, it was not enough to show that the landlord had acted negligently in not summoning expert help to ensure that the gas fires were working properly after his tenants had complained about them. It had to be shown that, had the defendant not acted negligently (that is, had he summoned help), the victims would not have died.

In the majority of cases, if the defendant did an act which caused someone else's death then the first three requirements are made out. Almost always there will have been a duty of care owed to the victim and a breach of that duty. Therefore much weight is placed on the fourth requirement.

10.3.4 The defendant's negligence was gross

This fourth requirement is satisfied if the jury decides that the negligence was sufficiently gross to justify a criminal conviction. As Lord Mackay, in *Adomako*, put it:

> The essence of the matter ... is whether having regard to the risk of death involved, the conduct of the defendant was so bad in all the circumstances as to amount in their judgment to a criminal act or omission.

Essentially this leaves the jury with a discretion: to decide in their judgment whether the defendant deserves a conviction for manslaughter. So what kind of factors will a jury be likely to take into account when considering whether the negligence is gross or not? Of course, the issue is entirely up to the jury, but these are some of the factors the jury are likely to take into account:

1. How far below the standard of the reasonable person was the defendant's conduct?
2. Had the defendant foreseen the risk of death?
3. Did the defendant have a good explanation for his behaviour?
4. Had the victim put his trust in the defendant to exercise special skill?

There were some ambiguous phrases in Lord Mackay's judgment in *Adomako* which suggested that it had to be shown that the defendant was aware of the risk of death. However the Court of Appeal in *A-G's Ref (No 2 of 1999)* [2000] 1 QB 796 has since made it clear that the jury are entitled to convict a defendant of gross negligent manslaughter even though he did not foresee that the victim would be killed or even injured. Clearly in considering whether the negligence is gross, the jury will consider whether the defendant foresaw that the victim might die or be seriously injured as a result of his or her act (*A-G's Ref (No 2 of 1999)*). That said, the jury might be reluctant to convict a person of gross negligence unless the defendant at least foresaw the possibility of death. It should be recalled that in order to establish a duty of care it must be shown that death was foreseeable. In *Winter* not only did the defendants unlawfully store fireworks without a licence; when a fire broke out they misled the fire team as to the contents of the factory. The jury convicted them of gross negligence manslaughter, perhaps because of the misleading information they provided.

In *Misra* [2005] Crim LR 234 it was argued before the Court of Appeal that the definition of gross negligence was so vague that it contravened the defendant's rights under Article 6 of the European Convention on Human Rights. The Court of Appeal disagreed. It also rejected an argument that the offence of gross negligence needed to be redefined in the light of the decision in G [2003] UKHL 50 to reject *Caldwell* [1982] AC 341 recklessness for being too objective. While you can understand the reluctance of the Court of Appeal to accept that their Lordships in G had implicitly overruled their decision in *Adomako*, the definition of gross negligence does not sit very happily with the statement in G about the importance of finding a subjective *mens rea*.

10.4 Reckless manslaughter

There may be a crime of reckless manslaughter, that is where the defendant causes the death of the victim, aware that there is a risk that the victim may die. In such cases the defendant would be guilty of constructive manslaughter or gross negligence manslaughter. It is because of this that reckless manslaughter has not been directly referred to by the courts in a reported case. There is therefore doubt whether it exists, but if it does, the offence is primarily of academic interest only. Notably, reckless manslaughter was not mentioned in Lord Hope's thorough analysis of the different forms of manslaughter in *A-G's Ref (No 3 of 1994* [1997] 3 WLR 421).

10.5 Killing while driving

If someone kills another by driving a car, there is nothing to stop her being charged with manslaughter (*Jennings v US Government* [1983] 1 AC 624). However, juries tend to be very reluctant to convict people who kill in driving 'accidents'. Maybe they can relate more easily to a driver than other kinds of killers and there is a sense of 'there but for the grace of God go I'. As a result of the low rate of conviction of killers while driving, Parliament enacted legislation to create a special offence of killing while driving dangerously. A manslaughter or murder conviction is likely to be sought only where a defendant has used the car in effect as a weapon and driven deliberately into someone.

The offence of killing by dangerous driving is found in s 2A Road Traffic Act 1988 and reads:

> A person who causes the death of another person by driving a mechanically propelled vehicle dangerously on a road or other public place is guilty of an offence.

Dangerousness here is an objective requirement and the question is simply whether the conduct falls below the standard of the ordinary careful and competent driver. There is no *mens rea* requirement. There is no need to show that the defendant was aware she was driving dangerously. The driver can be convicted even if the accident occurs because of a sudden illness (in contrast to the old offence of causing death by reckless driving, discussed in *Reid*). However, a defendant will have a defence if she can show that she was an automaton and hence not 'driving' (see Section 3.5). The offence is interesting for two particular reasons. First, it shows the significance that the law can attach to the consequences of an action. Dangerous driving which does not cause death is a relatively minor crime and often goes unpunished. The fact that it causes death dramatically increases the potential sentence, without there being any increase in the blame attached to the defendant. Second, as we have already mentioned, the existence of the offence shows the effect that society's attitudes can have on the criminal law. Car crimes are generally seen as less serious than equally dangerous and blameworthy conduct involving, say, guns or knives.

There are also special offences of causing death by careless driving or while driving under the influence of illegal drugs or alcohol, which are not covered in this book.

10.6 Voluntary manslaughter

The special nature of voluntary manslaughter has an important result. Because it is relevant only where the *actus reus* and *mens rea* of murder are present, it cannot be charged as a separate offence by the prosecution. The charge must be for murder, and then the accused may put forward a plea of guilty to manslaughter on the ground of (for example) loss of control. This plea will either be accepted by the prosecution, in which case there is no trial and the judge will proceed to sentence, or it will be rejected, in which case the trial for murder will continue, with the accused putting in evidence of loss of control to be considered by the jury. In the case of diminished responsibility, the plea will often be accepted by the prosecution, and so not contested before the jury. However, the prosecution may refuse to accept the plea and counter with its own evidence that the accused is severely mentally ill, so as to come within the legal definition of insanity, or that the accused is not suffering from any kind of illness at all and should be convicted of murder.

10.7 Loss of control

Loss of control is only a defence to a charge of murder. Even if it is raised successfully the defendant will still be guilty of manslaughter. The defence was created by s 54, Coroners and Justice Act 2009. It replaced the old defence of provocation.

To use the defence of loss of control the defendant must show:

1. that his or her acts or omissions resulted from a loss of self-control resulting from a 'qualifying trigger'; and that
2. a person of the defendant's age and sex, with normal powers of tolerance and self-control, in the defendant's circumstances would have responded to the trigger in the same or a similar way.

These requirements will need to be considered in more detail. The following issues need to be considered:

10.7.1 The defendant must lose his or her self-control

The defence of loss of control is only available if the defendant at the time of the killing had lost self-control. To understand the notion of loss of control remember that the defence is only available to those otherwise guilty of murder, in other words people who intended to kill or cause grievous bodily harm. If the defendant got so angry that he did not know what he was doing he would be not guilty of murder as he would lack the *mens rea*. So the law is imagining a person who knows what he is doing and has some control over his act, but his ability to control himself is severely impaired. Section 54(4) explains clearly that a defendant who acts out of desire for revenge cannot rely on the defence.

10.7.2 The defendant must lose self-control as the result of a qualifying trigger

It is not enough for the defendant just to show she lost self-control. She must show this was as a result of a 'qualifying trigger'. In *Acott* [1997] 1 WLR 306, a case decided under the old law of provocation, it seemed the defendant suddenly flipped and in a frenzy killed his mother. Although it was clear he had lost his self-control he could not explain why. He would not be able to use the defence of loss of control.

Under the law prior to the 2009 Act it had to be shown that the loss of self-control was 'sudden and temporary'. However, s 54(2) makes it clear that there is no need for the loss of self-control to be sudden. So if Simon says something very provocative to Cheryl and she goes away and thinks about it, becoming increasingly upset, and then some time later loses her self-control and kills Simon, she will be able to use the defence. However, the longer the time between the qualifying trigger and the killing the more difficult it will be for the defendant to show that she lost self-control as a result of the trigger. Indeed the jury may decide that the defendant acted out of revenge.

The 2009 Act lists two possible qualifying triggers: having a fear of serious violence and being seriously wronged. We will consider these separately.

10.7.3 Fear of serious violence as a qualifying trigger

Section 55(3) of the Coroners and Justice Act 2009 sets out the circumstances when this trigger arises:

> This subsection applies if D's loss of self-control was attributable to D's fear of serious violence from V against D or another identified person.

Notice that this trigger applies where there is a *fear* of serious violence. There does not need to be actual violence. Indeed it could apply where the defendant was mistaken in believing that there was about to be violence. The wording of the section restricts the trigger to violence against a person. Violence against property will not be sufficient. Crucially it must be serious violence. So it is unlikely that fear of a slap will amount to a qualifying trigger. However, the violence need not be directed towards the defendant. If the defendant loses his self-control in seeing the victim threaten his child, the defence would be available.

One important limitation on this trigger is found in s 55(6)(a) which states that the defendant cannot rely on this trigger if what caused the fear of violence was 'a thing which D incited to be done or said for the purpose of providing an excuse to use violence'. This is designed to deal with this kind of situation: Steven wants to kill Brian. He knows Brian has a knife. He punches Brian and Brian pulls out his knife. Steven then kills Brian. Even if Steven could show that he had lost his self-control as a result of fear of violence from the knife (which would be difficult), he could not rely on the defence of loss of control because he had deliberately tried to get Brian to attack him.

It is unlikely this trigger will be often used. The simple reason is that in many cases where the defendant is facing a threat of serious violence and kills he or she will be able to use the defence of self-defence (see Chapter 15). In many cases where a defendant responds to a serious threat by killing, it will be preferable to use self-defence, because that is a complete defence. That inevitably raises the question of when a defendant might use this qualifying trigger rather than self-defnece. It seems the only case would be where the killing of the victim was not a reasonable use of force. As we shall see in

Chapter 15 to be able to use the defence of self-defence it must be shown that the degree of force was reasonable. If it was not, but the defendant did lose self-control, then this qualifying trigger will be relied upon. In *Ahluwalia** [1992] 4 All ER 889 a husband who had been repeatedly violent to his wife warned her that he would injure her the next day. She killed him in his sleep. Although self-defence would probably not be available because she was not facing an imminent threat, under the new law she could seek to rely on loss of control. Another example would be where a householder found a burglar in his house and fearful the burglar was going to hit him and losing self-control killed the burglar. If the use of force was not reasonable (for example, it was well in excess of the threat posed by the burglar) the defence of loss of control could be invoked.

10.7.4 Being seriously wronged as a qualifying trigger

Section 55(4) of the Coroners and Justice Act 2009 sets out the circumstances in which this qualifying trigger arises:

> (4) This subsection applies if D's loss of self-control was attributable to a thing or things done or said (or both) which –
>
> (a) constituted circumstances of an extremely grave character, and
> (b) caused D to have a justifiable sense of being seriously wronged.

This trigger only applies where the defendant is facing circumstances of an 'extremely grave character'. That suggests that a minor taunt or irritation will not be sufficient. Having someone jump in front of you in a queue is unlikely to be regarded as a circumstance of an extremely grave character.

It must also be shown the circumstances created a justifiable sense of being seriously wronged. It is not enough to show that the defendant felt he was wronged, he must be justified in feeling seriously wronged. So, if a homophobe saw two men kissing and lost his self-control and killed one of the men he would not be able to use this trigger, for quite a number of reasons. The circumstances could hardly be described as 'extremely grave'. Even if they were, it is not clear he could be said to be *wronged* (unless perhaps the men were kissing in order to deliberately insult him). Even then, he could not claim to have a *justifiable* sense of being seriously wronged. Under the old law of provocation there was the case of *Doughty* (1986) Cr App R 319 which assumed that the crying of a baby could constitute a provocative act. That decision would not be followed under the new provisions. However annoying the crying might be it would not create a justifiable sense of being seriously wronged. Indeed these restrictions on what will count as a qualifying trigger suggest the defence will only rarely be available.

The statute offers two other restrictions on what can be a qualifying trigger under this heading. Section 55(6)(c) specifically provides that sexual infidelity is not a thing said or done that can amount to a qualifying trigger. This provision was introduced because it was felt that juries were being too sympathetic to men who killed their partners on discovering that their partners were being unfaithful. Of course, there could be a case where D killed V after she was unfaithful to him, but he could point to some other trigger which justified him having the defence. Section 55(6)(b) makes it clear that D cannot rely on something said or done if he incited it for the purpose of providing an excuse. So if D asked V to say the most insulting thing that V could think of in order to provide him with an excuse for killing V, he could not rely on this as a qualifying trigger for the purposes of the defence.

To complete the picture on qualifying triggers s 55(5) explains that a defendant can rely on a combination of both triggers. So, a defendant can claim that he lost self-control in part due to a fear of violence and in part due to a sense of being wronged.

10.7.5 Would a person with normal tolerance and self-restraint have acted as the defendant did?

In order to use the defence of loss of control it is not enough for the defendant to show that he lost his self-control as a result of a qualifying trigger. He must also show that a 'person of D's sex and age, with a normal degree of tolerance and self-restraint and in the circumstances of D, might have reacted in the same or in a similar way to D'. This is a question the jury must decide.

The jury must consider how a person with a normal degree of tolerance and self-restraint would have acted. This means that if the defendant is particularly prejudiced or particularly short-tempered he will not be able to use the defence if a reasonable person in his shoes would not have acted as he did. Generally that might seem fair enough. The short-tempered and intolerant do not deserve our sympathy. However, it may be that the defendant suffers short-temper as a result of a mental disorder. In such a case the defendant will be better off relying on the defence of diminished responsibility.

The reference to normality may be relevant here. The jury are to consider what degree of tolerance and self-restraint we can expect from a normal person not a *Guardian*-reading tolerant chilled out dude. Maybe juries will accept that even normal people can be a little short-tempered and even slightly intolerant.

It remains to be seen whether the jury in considering the response of the normal person are to consider the characteristics of the defendant. Section 54(3) of the Coroners and Justice Act 2009 explains that the reference to the defendant's circumstances 'is a reference to all of D's circumstances other than those whose only relevance to D's conduct is that they bear on D's general capacity for tolerance or self-restraint.' That suggests that the defendant's characteristics can be relevant in assessing whether the provocation was grave. Burning a copy of the Koran would be a graver provocation to a Muslim defendant than it would be to an atheist. So the defendant is permitted to argue that his characteristics made the circumstances graver than they would be for other people. However, s 54(3) states that the defendant cannot argue that their characteristics entitled them to have a lower level of self-restraint than other people. An Italian defendant, for example, could not argue that being Italian he was hot blooded and only needed to show the level of self-restraint of an Italian! That said, age and sex are mentioned as relevant characteristics. So a 15-year-old is only expected to show the level of self-restraint and tolerance that one can expect of a person of that age. It is not at all clear what the reference to sex is meant to indicate. Is the jury to take it that men have less (or more?) self-restraint or tolerance than women? That seems very dubious.

Section 54(1)(c) states that the jury should consider how the person of D's age and sex and in the circumstances of D would reacted. The significance of this is that it allows the jury to take into account the circumstances the defendant was in. One consequences of this is that the nature of the trigger must be seen in the light of the defendant's history. This means that what might appear to be a minor wrong, when seen in the light of the history of the event, is in fact a grave wrong. For example, if Paul has repeatedly sexually abused his daughter, Susan, and one day calls her 'dirty and immoral', this is a far graver wrong to Susan, in the context of their relationship, than it would be if he said those words to a stranger. Here the law accepts that an relatively minor remark can be the last straw and in fact be a grave wrong when seen in the context of the history of the parties' relationship.

A final point to make is that the jury must consider whether the normal person would have reacted in the same or a smilar way to the defendant. This suggests that the jury should consider how the defendant killed. If a defendant was gravely wronged, lost self-control and tortured his victim to death they might be denied the defence if the jury concluded that although the normal person would have lost self-control he would not have tortured the victim.

10.7.6 Loss of control and victims of domestic violence

One issue which greatly troubled the courts in the old law of provocation were cases where a victim of domestic violence had killed his abusive spouse. Such defendants often tried to rely on the defence of provocation, but failed (*Ahluwalia*). The new law on loss of control may prove more fertile ground. As we have seen there is now no need to show the loss of self-control was sudden and temporary, a requirement which proved problematic in the past. The new possibility of relying on fear of violence may also be available when a woman kills her sleeping partner who has threatened further abuse. A problem will still be showing the loss of self-control. In *Ahluwalia* the defendant waited until her husband was asleep and then set fire to him. If that case were to be heard today, although she may well be able to establish a qualifying trigger it would still be difficult for her to show she had lost her self-control. Her actions in finding petrol, pouring it over him and setting it alight, would appear to the court to indicate that she was in control of her actions.

10.8 Diminished responsibility

Diminished responsibility is only available to a charge of murder. It does not provide a defence to any other charge. The defence has the effect of reducing murder to manslaughter, thereby enabling the trial judge to exercise discretion in sentencing (a discretion which the judge does not possess on a conviction of murder, where the mandatory life sentence applies). In the case of attempted murder there is a peculiarity. If a defendant attempts to kill the victim while suffering from diminished responsibility, she will be convicted of attempted murder, even though, had she succeeded, she would have been convicted of manslaughter. This is an oddity, but the wording of the 1957 Homicide Act s 2 is based on the clear presumption that the offence applies to murder, but not attempted murder (*Campbell*).

Diminished responsibility is a popular defence for those charged with murder. The prosecution will often accept a plea of guilty to manslaughter on the basis of diminished responsibility. It is only in cases where the prosecution either refuses to accept the plea of diminished responsibility or counters with evidence of insanity that the scope and application of diminished responsibility will be argued before the court. Diminished responsibility must be proved on the balance of probabilities by the party raising it. The law was recently reformed by the Coroners and Justice Act 2009 and it may be that the defence will as a result be harder to raise.

10.8.1 What is diminished responsibility?

Section 2 Homicide Act 1957 defines diminished responsibility:

> "(1) A person ('D') who kills or is a party to the killing of another is not to be convicted of murder if D was suffering from an abnormality of mental functioning which –
> (a) arose from a recognised medical condition,
> (b) substantially impaired D's ability to do one or more of the things mentioned in subsection (1A), and
> (c) provides an explanation for D's acts and omissions in doing or being a party to the killing.
> (1A) Those things are –
> (a) to understand the nature of D's conduct;
> (b) to form a rational judgment;
> (c) to exercise self-control.
> (1B) For the purposes of subsection (1)(c), an abnormality of mental functioning provides an explanation for D's conduct if it causes, or is a significant contributory factor in causing, D to carry out that conduct."

The burden of proof rests on the defence (s 2(2)). This is consistent with Article 6(2) of the European Convention on Human Rights because the prosecution must prove the elements of murder and the burden of raising the defence rests on the defendant if she wishes to raise it (*Ali* [2001] 2 WLR 211).

There are four requirements that must be met if a defendant wishes to rely on diminished responsibility:

1. he or she was suffering from an abnormality of mental functioning;
2. the abnormality of mental functioning was caused by a recognised medical condition;
3. as a result of the abnormality the defendant's ability to understand the nature of her conduct, form a rational judgement, or exercise self-control, was substantially impaired
4. that the abnormality of mental functioning provided an explanation for the defendant's conduct, in that it was a significant contributory factor in carrying it out.

There are three key elements of the defence.

10.8.2 Abnormality of mental functioning

Under the law before the 2009 reforms, it was only necessary to prove an abnormality of mind. *Byrne* [1960] 3 All ER 1 held that it only needed to be shown that the defendant's mind was sufficiently different from a normal mind to be described as abnormal. That had led to a very liberal approach with a wide range of states of mind falling within the defence. Under the new law it must be shown that the defendant has a 'recognised medical condition'. So it unlikely that the defendant in *Vinagre* [1979] 69 Cr App R 104, who under the old law succeeded in using the defence when it was found he suffered from 'morbid jealousy' would succeed under the new law. It is also clear that intoxication alone will not amount to an abnormality of mental functioning (see Section 10.8.5 below).

10.8.3 The effect of the abnormality

It must be shown that the the effect of the abnormality of mental function was to substantially impair one of the following: the defendant's ability to understand the nature of his conduct, to form a rational judgement or to exercise self-control. We shall consider these separately. The inclusion of the defendant not understanding the nature of his conduct is rather odd. We are dealing with defendants who are proved to have committed murder. It is hard to see how a defendant could have an intention to kill or cause serious harm and yet fail to understand the nature of his act. It is more likely, therefore that defendants will claim that their disorder meant they could not exercise rational judgement or self-control.

Notice that for all three of these impacts of the abnormality, it needs to be shown that there is a substantial impairment in the defendant's ability. So a mental condition that slightly impacts on, for example, the defendant's self-control will not be sufficient.

10.8.4 Explanation for the acts

Section 2(1)(c) requires proof that the defendant's abnormality of mental functioning 'provides an explanation for D's acts and omissions in doing or being a party to the killing'. This is a rather strangely worded provision. Presumably it is designed to ensure that not only does the defendant suffer an abnormality of mental functioning, but that it is a cause of the killing. Without this provision a defendant might have killed while suffering from a mental abnormality, but the abnormality might not, in fact, have anything to do with the killing.

10.8.5 Diminished responsibility and intoxication

In the case law there has been some difficulty in dealing with voluntarily intoxicated defendants who claim that they suffer diminished responsibility. It is clear that intoxication on its own will not amount to an abnormality of mental functioning (*Wood* [2008] EWCA Crim 1305). However, the position is more complex where intoxication is combined with a mental disorder or when the defendant suffers from alcohol dependency syndrome, which the courts have recognised as a mental abnormality (*Stewart* [2009] EWCA Crim 593). It is necessary to distinguish three kinds of cases:

1. The defendant has brain damage as a result of his alcohol misuse. In such a case the brain damage can be included as abnormality of mental functioning.
2. The defendant's taking of alcohol was involuntary. This may be because, for example, her drink was spiked. It may also be because the defendant was an alcoholic who had no control over his or her drinking. In such a case the mental condition caused by the drink can be regarded as an abnormality of mind for the purposes of the defence of diminished responsibility (*Tandy* [1989] 1 All ER 267). However, it will be very difficult for someone suffering addiction to alcohol to show that their drinking was involuntary. In *Tandy* it was suggested that it needed to be shown that the all of the drinking, including the first drinks were involuntary. However, more recently the courts have taken a more liberal approach. In *Woods* the Court of Appeal accepted that a defendant suffering from alcohol dependency syndrome may have control over some drinks, but not others. In such a case the jury could take the impact on the defendant of the involuntary portion of the drinking as an abnormality of mental functioning. It will not be easy for a jury to decide whether the drinking was involuntary or not. To be involuntary the defendant must have been unable to resist the impulse to drink (*Stewart*). Even harder for the jury will be a case where some of the defendant's drunking was involuntary and some was not.

Then they will need to assess the impact of the involuntary drinking. No doubt, the prosecution and defence will seek to introduce expert evidence on these issues to assist the jury.

3. The defendant suffered a mental abnormality (for example, depression) and was voluntarily intoxicated at the time. The House of Lords in *Dietschmann* [2003] 1 All ER 897 has issued guidance on the issue. In such a case the jury must consider whether the impact of the abnormality (and not the intoxication) was sufficient to substantially impair the defendant in the ways referred to in s 2(1A). If it was they can rely on the defence of diminished responsibility. The fact they were also drunk at the time does not rob them of the availability of the defence. Section 2(1B) makes it clear that as long as the defendant's abnormality of mental functioning was a 'significant contributory factor in causing, [the defendant] to carry out that conduct'. This indicates that a defendant can rely on diminished responsibility even if drunk at the time of the killing, as long as the abnormality in mental functioning was a significant cause of the killing.

10.8.6 Why is diminished responsibility a defence?

The justifications for the defence of diminished responsibility have been challenged. There are two main grounds of complaint. The first is that the defence exists simply because of the mandatory life sentence for murder. This is to some extent true, but given the existence of the life sentence it makes sense to have this defence to avoid what may otherwise be an inappropriate life sentence. The second and more substantial criticism is that it either is or is not true that the defendant acted in the way he did because of his illness or condition. If the defendant would still have killed had he not been suffering from the abnormality then the abnormality should have no effect on his liability. However, if the defendant would not have killed had he not suffered from the abnormality then the defendant should be seen as blameless. In other words, the defence should either be complete and be available for all offences, or not exist at all. This criticism argues that the present law on diminished responsibility is an illogical halfway house.

10.9 Suicide pact

It is not a defence to a charge of murder that the victim has asked the accused to kill her. Hence voluntary euthanasia is classed as murder or manslaughter (see Hot topic, Chapter 5). However, if the defendant killed the victim intending to go on and kill herself as part of a suicide pact then it is possible for the defendant to plead the defence of suicide pact to a charge of murder (s 4 Homicide Act 1957). If successful, the defence will reduce the charge to manslaughter, and open up the discretion in sentencing that is appropriate in such sad cases. The onus of proof in establishing the defence is on the defendant. It should be added that if the defendant did not herself actually kill the other party to the pact, she may be found to have aided or abetted their suicide, which is an offence under s 2(1) Suicide Act 1961.

10.10 Infanticide

Infanticide is an offence which can be charged when a mother wilfully kills her recently born child (*Gore*). It is also a defence which such a woman can raise if she is charged with murder. Its requirements are set out in s 1(1) Infanticide Act 1938. Infanticide is available where:

(i) the mother has killed her own child;
(ii) the child is under the age of 12 months;
(iii) the mother does not have a younger child;
(iv) and 'the balance of her mind was disturbed by reason of her not having fully recovered from the effect of giving birth to the child' or by reason of the effects of lacerations consequential upon the birth.

The maximum sentence is life, but the most common sentence is a probation order. The offence has been criticised for allowing the mother to rely only on a disturbance of mind resulting from the birth or resultant lacerations but not on the social and economic consequences which may follow a birth. This restriction may reflect the law's general refusal to permit a defendant's socio-economic background to be considered. It should be added that the reference to lacerations is based on a now discredited medical opinion as to the causes of post-natal depression. This led the Court of Appeal in *Kai-Whitewind* to describe the law on infanticide as unsatisfactory and outdated.

At one time the defence was thought to be justified on the basis of the argument that to kill a child less than one year old was less serious than to kill an older child. Nowadays the defence is seen as analogous to diminished responsibility. The mother who kills her child while suffering from post-natal depression is less culpable than a person who calmly plans the killing.

Some commentators argue that a father should be able to use the defence. However, it seems more appropriate for him to use diminished responsibility, as it is unlikely that he would suffer any form of mental illness directly linked to the birth rather than related to social problems or a pre-existing mental condition.

10.11 Causing or allowing the death of a child or vulnerable adult

Section 5 of the Domestic Violence, Crime and Victims Act 2004 has created a new offence of causing or allowing the death of a child or vulnerable adult. It is particularly useful in cases where a child or vulnerable adult has died at home, but it is unclear which of those looking after the victim caused the death. In such a case both can be charged with the section 5 offence on the basis that they either killed the victim or failed to protect the victim. The offence can also be used where even if it is clear it was not the defendant who killed the victim, the defendant can be blamed for failing to protect the victim from the risk of death. The section 5 offence is committed if the following are proved:

1. V (the child or vulnerable adult) has died as a result of an unlawful act of a person who was in the same household as the victim and had frequent contact with him;
2. there was a significant risk of serious physical harm being caused to V by the unlawful act;
3. either:
   (a) D was the person whose act caused V's death; or
   (b) D was or ought to have been aware that there was a significant risk of serious physical harm being carried out to V by an unlawful act and D failed to take such steps as he could reasonably have been expected to have taken to protect V from the risk;
4. the killing of V occurred in circumstances which D foresaw or ought to have foreseen.

It is to be noted that its *mens rea* is negligence. The test focuses on what D knew or ought to know and what D could reasonably be expected to have done to protect the victim (*Khan*). The offence was justified as a means of guaranteeing the rights of children and vulnerable adults to protection from abuse. In a case where there has been domestic violence the courts will bear in mind that it might be extremely dangerous for a mother, say, to contact the police about fears over what her abusive partner will do to their child (*Khan* (2009), although see the article by Herring).

10.12 Criticisms of and reform of involuntary manslaughter

The present law on murder and manslaughter has come under heavy criticism. The two most serious complaints are as follows. First, manslaughter can be committed when the defendant has only a low level of *mens rea*. If the defendant lightly punches the victim on the nose, and the victim then falls over and bangs his head and dies, the defendant may be guilty of constructive manslaughter. For gross negligence manslaughter, it does not need to be shown that the defendant foresaw death, or even any harm at all to the victim (*A-G's Ref (No 2 of 1999)*).

The second and linked point is that the label 'manslaughter' covers a wide range of killings, from a defendant who only just falls outside the band of murder to an act which may be regarded as little more than a careless accident. The present distinction between constructive manslaughter and gross negligence does not help in dividing the offence into less serious and more serious forms. It is not possible to state whether a constructive manslaughter is necessarily more serious than a gross negligence manslaughter.

It is not surprising, then, that the Law Commission has proposed reform. It suggests two versions of manslaughter. The first is gross negligence manslaughter if:

1. a person by his or her conduct causes the death of another;
2. a risk that his or her conduct will cause death would be obvious to a reasonable person in his or her position;
3. he or she is capable of appreciating that risk at the material time; and
4. his or her conduct falls far below what can reasonably be expected of him or her in the circumstances.

The third point is interesting because it deals with the issue which arose in *Stone and Dobinson** [1977] QB 354, that a person could be guilty of gross negligence manslaughter even though he or she was not capable of living up to the required standard. However, critics complain that the proposed definition still means that a person can be found guilty of manslaughter even though he or she had no intention or foresight of death and that the definition is too vague to properly guide juries.

The second form of manslaughter proposed by the Law Commission is 'criminal act manslaughter'. This involves killing another person either 'through the commission of a criminal act intended by the defendant to cause injury' or 'through the commission of a criminal act that the defendant was aware involved a serious risk of causing some injury'. Notably, unlike the current law, the Law Commission's proposed offence requires the defendant to have foreseen a risk of physical harm. Critics will still complain that a person should not be guilty of the serious offence of manslaughter if all he or she foresaw was a minor injury.

Hot Topic – Battered women who kill

In recent years, women who have killed their abusive husbands or partners have struggled to find a defence to a charge of murder. Before looking at the particular difficulties these defendants have faced, it is interesting to note that the vast majority of murders by women are committed by those who have killed their abusive partners. The fact that they have not neatly fallen into an established defence lends force to the arguments of feminist commentators who have complained that the law has been based on a male norm. In other words, the offences and defences are built up with men rather than women in mind. We will return to this point at several times in this discussion.

In the past decade, the courts have sought to develop the established defences to enable a battered woman to have access to a defence. The courts have been particularly influenced by medical evidence of 'battered women's syndrome'. This 'syndrome' is caused by lengthy experience of abuse and produces a variety of symptoms, including a feeling of helplessness so that the option of leaving the relationship does not appear viable and sudden outbursts of desperate violence can occur. Interestingly, in *Hobson*, the conviction of a battered woman many years ago was overturned because there was a lack of awareness of battered women's syndrome at that time.

So, let us imagine a woman, Eve, who has suffered months of abuse and mistreatment at the hands of her husband. One night, while he is asleep, she pours petrol over him and sets it alight, killing him. Is this a clear case of murder, or can Eve raise any defences?

1. *Loss of control.* In a number of cases, battered women have killed their abusive partners and have sought to use provocation. Eve will face three main problems:

   (a) The first is that Eve must show that she suffered a loss of self-control. The case of *Cocker* [1989] Crim LR 74, although on very different facts, illustrates the potential problem. As mentioned above, Mr Cocker was thought by the Court of Appeal not to have lost his self-control, but to have acted in a calm and deliberate way. The prosecution would argue that finding petrol, pouring it and setting it alight was just like the calm conduct of Mr Cocker in placing the pillow over his wife's face. Hence it could not be

   said that when Eve set her husband alight she was suffering a sudden and temporary loss of self-control.

   (b) Eve must point to a qualifying trigger if she is to use the defence. Either that she feared serious violence or that she had a justifiable sense of being seriously wronged. The court are likely to accept that persistent domestic violence creates 'circumstances of an extremely grave character' which give Eve a justifiable sense of being wronged. She might also be able to show that she feared serious violence.

   (c) The third problem concerns battered women's syndrome itself. It seems from the wording of s 54 Coroners and Justice Act 2009 that the courts will not accept that battered women's syndrome can affect the level of tolerance or self-restraint expected. However, she might argue that the history of domestic violence is part of the circumstances which the jury should take into account when deciding how a normal person would respond.

   Before leaving loss of control, it should be emphasised that provocation is a defence only to murder and so will provide no assistance to a battered woman who injures, rather than kills, her partner. Also the defence is only partial and so, if it succeeds, the defendant will still be convicted of manslaughter.

2. *Diminished responsibility.* Like provocation, diminished responsibility is a defence only to murder and is only a partial defence. Diminished responsibility has a higher chance of success, especially if Eve can introduce medical evidence that she suffered from battered women's syndrome. It appears to be now generally accepted that a defendant who kills while suffering from battered women's syndrome will be able to use diminished responsibility (*Ahluwalia* [1992] 4 All ER 889, *Thornton (No. 2)* [1996] 2 All ER 1023). That said, to rely on diminished responsibility may appear demeaning to Eve. Far from reacting in a mentally disordered way, she may feel she acted in a reasonable way, under the appalling circumstances.

3. *Self-defence.* Self-defence will provide a complete defence and so will lead to an absolute

acquittal. It is therefore an attractive defence. However, Eve will face severe difficulties in using this defence. First, it must be shown that she was facing an imminent threat (see Section 15.3.1). Eve will not be able to show that she was facing such a threat, because her husband was asleep when she attacked him. Second, it needs to be shown that the use of force was necessary and reasonable. A jury may feel that a battered woman could escape the violence by leaving her husband and that killing could not be seen as necessary or reasonable. The second point could be resolved by a reference to *Williams (Gladstone)* and battered women's syndrome. *Williams (Gladstone)* stresses that whether the defendant's response was reasonable and necessary must be assessed on the facts as the defendant believed them to be. As explained earlier, battered women's syndrome can lead a sufferer to believe that escape is impossible and to see no way out of the violence. On that version of the facts, the attack could be seen as reasonable.

Some argue in favour of a change in the law on self-defence. It is argued that if the battered woman can use force to protect herself only when facing an imminent attack, the defence is of little use because in the face of her abuser she is physically unable to defend herself or prevent the attack. It is only when she is not under attack, for example when the abuser is asleep, that she has an opportunity to prevent the abuse continuing.

4. *No* mens rea. Eve could claim that she lacked the *mens rea* for murder (an intent to kill or cause grievous bodily harm). Such a defence may succeed where the defendant acted in a frenzied way. In Eve's case it is unlikely that she can successfully deny that she had the relevant intention.

5. *Creation of a new defence.* Some commentators have suggested that there should be a new defence created to deal specifically with battered women who kill. For example, McColgan suggests a defence where a person kills for the purpose of sustaining his or her autonomy while facing the unlawful and brutally oppressive conduct of another.

Summary

10.1 Voluntary manslaughter exists where the accused has committed the *actus reus* of murder, with malice aforethought, but an additional factor operates to reduce liability to manslaughter. There are three of these factors: provocation, diminished responsibility and suicide pact, the latter two created by the Homicide Act 1957.

10.2 Constructive manslaughter is a common law offence. It consists of causing the death of the victim by an unlawful and dangerous act. The unlawful act should be a crime, but it probably need not be directed at another person. The accused needs not know that the act is unlawful, but if the unlawful act requires *mens rea* then this must be proved by the prosecution. 'Dangerous' means that an ordinary person in the defendant's shoes would appreciate the risk of causing some physical injury to another. There is no need for the accused to foresee the risk of injury; negligence as to causing injury is sufficient.

10.3 Gross negligence manslaughter is established when it can be shown that the defendant owed the victim a duty of care and broke that duty in a way which caused the victim's death, and the jury think that the defendant's conduct was sufficiently serious to justify a criminal conviction.

10.4 Reckless manslaughter may exist but it has never been used in a reported case. Any defendant who is guilty of reckless manslaughter would also be guilty of either constructive or gross negligence manslaughter.

10.5 Causing death by dangerous driving is a statutory offence, now found in s 1 Road Traffic Act 1988. The requirement for dangerousness is entirely objective.

10.6 Voluntary manslaughter occurs where the defendant has the *mens rea* for murder, but the defendant introduces evidence of provocation or diminished responsibility, for example.

Summary cont'd

10.7 The defendant can establish the defence of loss of control if he can show that he killed having lost his self-control as a result of a qualifying trigger and that a person with normal tolerance and self-restraint would have done the same thing. Loss of control is a defence only to a charge of murder and, if successful, reduces the charge to manslaughter.

10.8 Diminished responsibility is only available to murder. It has the effect of reducing the charge of murder to manslaughter. It is based on an abnormality of mental functioning, arising from a recognised medical condition, which provides an explanation for the killing. This may include an inability to exercise will-power to control physical actions.

10.9 If the defendant killed someone as part of a suicide pact, this will provide a defence to murder, but the defendant may still be guilty of manslaughter.

10.10 A mother who kills her child (under one year old) as a result of a disturbed mental state caused by the birth may be able to rely on the defence of infanticide. The mother will still be liable to be sentenced as if convicted of manslaughter.

10.11 The Law Commission has proposed reform of the current law, although even under its proposals it will be possible to convict a defendant who did not foresee the defendant's death.

10.12 There has been much criticism about the law on manslaughter. In particular that it can be committed even though the defendant has a low mens rea.

Further Reading

The law on manslaughter is discussed in Clarkson and Cunningham, Herring and Palser. Reform of involuntary manslaughter is discussed in Mitchell (2008, 2009). The defence of loss of control is analysed in Edwards and in Norrie. Diminished responsibility is examined in Griew, Mackay (1995, 2010) and Mitchell (2009). Defences available to battered women are considered in Chan and McColgan.

Chan, *Women, Murder and Justice* (Palgrave 2001).

Clarkson and Cunningham, *Criminal Liability for Non-Aggressive Death* (Ashgate 2008).

Edwards, 'Anger and Fear as Justifiable Preludes for Loss of Self-control' (2010) 74 J Crim L 223.

Griew, 'The Future of Diminished Responsibility' [1988] Crim LR 75.

Herring and Palser, 'The Duty of Care in Gross Negligence Manslaughter' [2007] Crim LR 24.

McColgan, 'In Defence of Battered Women Who Kill' (1993) 13 OJLS 508.

MacKay, *Mental Condition Defences in Criminal Law* (Oxford University Press 1995).

Mackay, 'The Coroners and Justice Act 2009 – Partial Defences to Murder (2) The new Diminished Responsibility Plea' [2010] Crim LR 290.

Mitchell, 'Minding the Gap in Unlawful and Dangerous Act Manslaughter: A Moral Defence of One-punch Killers' (2008) J Crim L 537.

Mitchell, 'More Thoughts about Unlawful and Dangerous Act Manslaughter and the One-punch Killer' [2009] Crim LR 502.

Norrie 'The Coroners and Justice Act 2009 – partial defences to murder (1) Loss of control' [2010] Crim LR 275.

Taylor, 'The Nature of "Partial Defences" and the Coherence of (Second Degree) Murder" [2007] Crim LR 345.

Williams, 'Drugs Manslaughter and Unorthodox Doctrine on Causation' (2005) 64 CLJ 537.

Wilson, 'Murder and the Structure of Homicide', in Ashworth and Mitchell (eds), *Rethinking English Homicide Law* (Oxford University Press 2000).

Case Notes

▶ *Adomako* [1995] 1 AC 171. House of Lords

The appellant was an anaesthetist who failed to notice that a patient's tube had become disconnected during an operation, and as a result the patient died. The House of Lords, dismissing the appellant's appeal against his conviction, referred to the test for negligence in *Andrews v DPP* and confirmed that it represented the law. Lord Mackay confirmed that it was necessary to show that there had been a duty of care owed by the accused to the victim, that the duty had been breached, that the breach had caused the victim's death, and that the breach had been gross enough to justify a criminal conviction. His speech also made it clear that there had to be a risk of death from the accused's acts if a conviction was to be established. He suggested that a trial judge could direct a jury to consider whether the defendant was 'reckless' in the normal sense of the word, but that it would be inappropriate to attempt to give a full legal definition of that word.

▶ *A-G's Ref (No 3 of 1994)* [1997] 3 WLR 421. House of Lords

See Chapter 9 Case notes.

▶ *Ahluwalia* [1992] 4 All ER 889. Court of Appeal

The accused had entered an arranged marriage with her husband, who abused her over several years. One night she poured petrol over him while he was asleep and lit it, causing a fire which killed him. The court stated that it was necessary to show that she had suffered a sudden and temporary loss of self-control, although it was not necessary to show that the killing had been immediate upon a provocative act. The court also confirmed that battered women's syndrome was a relevant characteristic which could be given to the reasonable person when considering how a reasonable person would have reacted. Battered women's syndrome could also form the basis of a manslaughter verdict on the basis of diminished responsibility, and it was on this ground that the accused's murder conviction was overturned and replaced with a manslaughter conviction.

▶ *Andrews v DPP* [1937] AC 576. House of Lords

The appellant was convicted of manslaughter and his appeal against conviction was dismissed by both the Court of Appeal and the House of Lords. He had killed a pedestrian while driving his van. Lord Atkin in the House of Lords held that for manslaughter a very high degree of negligence was required. 'Reckless' was an appropriate description, suggesting an indifference to risk, but manslaughter also covered the person who appreciated the risk and intended to avoid it, but showed a high degree of negligence in the means adopted to avoid the risk. The simple lack of care sufficient for civil liability was not enough, and manslaughter cannot be based on an unlawful act requiring simple negligence, such as driving without due care and attention.

▶ *Church* [1966] 1 QB 59. Court of Criminal Appeal

The appellant was acquitted of murder, but convicted of manslaughter. He had a fight with the victim, knocking her unconscious. He concluded that she was dead, and put her in a river. She died as a result. The Court of Criminal Appeal dismissed the appeal. Edmund Davies J held that in a manslaughter case it was not enough merely to prove that the accused had committed an unlawful act which caused the death. The unlawful act must have been such that all reasonable people would inevitably realise that the victim was subjected to the risk of at least some harm, albeit not serious harm.

▶ *Dawson, Nolan and Walmsley* (1985) 81 Cr App Rep 150. Court of Appeal

The appellants were convicted of manslaughter. They had attempted to rob a petrol filling station using a replica gun. The attendant had pressed the alarm button and the appellants fled, but the attendant had then collapsed and died of a heart attack. The trial judge ruled that in the context of the test laid down by Edmund Davies J in *Church* (see above), 'harm' included emotional or physical disturbance. The Court of Appeal allowed the appeal and quashed the convictions, holding that emotional disturbance alone cannot constitute 'harm'. However, the test would be satisfied if all sober and reasonable people would have realised that the accused's act would cause emotional disturbance or shock, and that the shock would cause physical injury.

▶ *Dhaliwal* [2006] EWCA Crim 1139. Court of Appeal

The defendant was said to have subjected his wife to physical, emotional and psychological abuse which led her to committing suicide. The defendant was convicted of unlawful act manslaughter and appealed on the basis that it could not be said that an unlawful act of his caused his death. The Court of Appeal explained that if it could be shown that he had caused his wife to suffer a recognisable psychological illness (such as battered women's syndrome) and this had caused her to commit suicide then this could amount to constructive manslaughter. If, however, as appeared to be the case here, the wife suffered emotional upset but no recognised condition, then there was no unlawful act which caused her death. The causing of emotional upset is not *per se* an offence (see Chapter 7, *Chan-Fook*). The court added that if it could be shown a physical assault directly caused her to commit suicide a manslaughter conviction might be available too.

▶ *Evans* [2009] EWCA Crim 650.

See Chapter 3 Case notes

▶ *Ireland and Burstow* [1998] AC 147. House of Lords

See Chapter 7 Case notes.

▶ *Lamb* [1967] 2 QB 981. Court of Appeal

The appellant was convicted of manslaughter. He had pointed a revolver at his friend as a joke and pulled the trigger; the gun fired and the friend was killed. The appellant had thought that the gun would not fire, as he did not understand the mechanism of a revolver. The trial judge directed the jury that firing the gun was an

unlawful act, even if there was no intent to harm or frighten the victim. The Court of Appeal allowed the appeal and quashed the conviction. The act of the appellant could not be unlawful in this context unless there was an assault, and this required proof of the *mens rea* of assault: an intent to frighten. With respect to gross negligence or reckless manslaughter, Sachs LJ held that the jury would need to consider whether the appellant thought that what he was doing was safe, and whether this view was formed in a 'criminally negligent way'.

▶ *Newbury and Jones* [1977] AC 500. House of Lords

The appellants were convicted of manslaughter. They had pushed a piece of paving-stone over a railway bridge onto a train passing underneath. The stone hit and killed the guard of the train. Both the Court of Appeal and the House of Lords dismissed their appeal. The House of Lords held that in the case of manslaughter by an unlawful and dangerous act, it is unnecessary for the accused to foresee that his act might cause harm to another. The test of dangerousness is objective: it depends on whether a reasonable person would recognise the risk of harm to another, and not on the foresight of the accused.

▶ *Stone and Dobinson* [1977] QB 354. Court of Appeal

Stone (who was nearly blind and of low intelligence) and Dobinson (who was 'ineffectual and inadequate') were convicted of manslaughter and appealed. Stone's sister lived in the appellants' house, and suffered from anorexia nervosa. She refused to see a doctor or to leave her room, and eventually died of toxaemia. The appellants made some effort to help her by trying to trace her doctor, and by washing and feeding her, but failed to make contact with her doctor. The appellants argued on appeal (i) that there was insufficient evidence that they had undertaken the care of the victim, and (ii) that the jury had been misdirected on the recklessness required for manslaughter which, it was argued, involved foresight of the possibility of death or serious injury. It was held (i) that they had been under a duty to summon medical help for the victim if they could not care for her themselves; there was evidence on which the jury were entitled to find that a duty of care had been assumed by them and that they had failed to discharge this duty; (ii) 'that indifference to an obvious risk and appreciation of such risk, coupled with a determination nevertheless to run it, are both examples of recklessness'. However, mere inadvertence is not enough: there must be a 'reckless disregard of danger to the health and welfare of the infirm person'. Their appeals were therefore dismissed.

▶ *Wacker* [2003] QB 1207. Court of Appeal

The defendant was convicted of the gross negligent manslaughter of 58 people who were attempting to enter the UK illegally. The defendant had put them in the back of his lorry and closed the single ventilation hole for long periods of time. This had caused nearly all of those in the lorry to be suffocated. He appealed on two main grounds. The first was that the victims had consented to being placed in the lorry without ventilation and therefore he could not be convicted of their manslaughter. The Court of Appeal held that the victims' consent provided no defence in the light of *Brown* (1993) (see Section 7.7.2). The second was that there is a special rule in tort law that people embarking on criminal activities together do not owe each other a duty of care. The Court of Appeal held that although normally the duty of care for gross negligence manslaughter was exactly the same as that in tort law, it was not in the context of this special *ex turpi causa* rule. The public policy objections which justified the absence of a duty of care in tort did not apply in the criminal context.

Part III

Offences against property

Chapter 11

Theft

Key Terms

▶ **Appropriation** – the assumption by the defendant of one of the owner's rights over a piece of property.
▶ **Dishonesty** – the defendant acts in a way regarded as dishonest by the standards of the community, and he or she is aware of that.

11.1 Property offences

Property offences are some of the most complex in the criminal law. Initially this is surprising – property offences are less serious than offences against the person, so we need be less concerned about careful gradations of liability. However, there are two particular reasons why this area has caused so many problems.

The first is that the criminal law on property offences has to interact with the civil law on ownership of property (for example, the law of contract). For instance, many commentators believe that it would be unsatisfactory if the civil law were to say A has validly transferred this property to B, but the criminal law were to say B has stolen this property from A. The problem is that different principles underlie these different areas of the law. Expediency and certainty carry greater weight in civil law than in criminal law. Yet an interaction between the two areas of the law is inevitable. The property offences forbid the harming or taking of property 'belonging to another', and it is largely the complex civil law which determines whether property belongs to another.

The second problem is the structuring of property offences. The offences against the person are generally distinguished on the basis of the severity of the harm caused to the victim (for example, distinguishing between death, grievous bodily harm and actual bodily harm). However, this approach is not entirely suitable for property offences. The value of the property lost does not necessarily reflect the severity of the offence: stealing a pensioner's life savings of a few hundred pounds may be thought more serious than stealing several thousand pounds from a millionaire. So property offences tend to focus not on the severity of the loss, but on the way that the loss was caused, for example by force, deception or subterfuge.

The offences against property are largely in statutory form, the major statutes being the Theft Act 1968, Fraud Act 2006, Theft Act 1978, and the Criminal Damage Act 1971. The Fraud Act 2006 replaced a range of deception offences in the 1968 and 1978 Acts. These had proved complex and difficult to use in practice. The Fraud Act creates a single offence of fraud, which simplifies matters to some extent, although, as we shall see in Chapter 13, creates problems of its own. In this chapter we shall focus on the offence of theft.

11.2 The definition of theft

Theft is the central offence against property and its definition occupies the first six sections of the Theft Act 1968. It is subject to a maximum sentence of seven years' imprisonment. In drafting the Theft Act 1968 a decision was taken to change the basis of theft from 'interference with possession' to 'interference with ownership'. 'Ownership' is a wider concept more suitable for dealing with intangible property and the different types of interest in property, but it is also a more technical concept. The basic definition of theft is found in s 1 Theft Act 1968:

> (1) A person is found guilty of theft if he dishonestly appropriates property belonging to another with the intention of permanently depriving the other of it; and 'thief' and 'steal' shall be construed accordingly.
> (2) It is immaterial whether the appropriation is made with a view to gain, or is made for the thief's own benefit.
> (3) The five following sections of this Act shall have effect as regards the interpretation and operation of this section ...

The offence of theft can then be divided into five elements, the first three making up the *actus reus*, the last two being the *mens rea*:

1. Appropriation
2. Property
3. Belonging to another
4. Dishonesty
5. The intention of permanently depriving another of property.

11.3 Appropriation

We start with the definition of appropriation given in s 3(1) Theft Act 1968:

> Any assumption by a person of the rights of an owner amounts to an appropriation, and this includes where he has come by the property (innocently or not) without stealing it, any later assumption of a right to it by keeping or dealing with it as owner.

Appropriation is therefore an assumption by a person of the rights of an owner. Taking possession of another's property is a common form of appropriation, and perhaps the most obvious 'assumption of the rights of an owner', but there are other ways of appropriating property. Destroying property is an appropriation (as well as an offence under the Criminal Damage Act 1971), and so is selling property (as in *Hircock** (1978) 67 Cr App R 278, where the accused dishonestly sold a car which was the subject of a hire-purchase agreement). Offering another person's property for sale amounts to an appropriation, even though the accused never takes possession of the property (*Pitham and Hehl** (1976) 65 Cr App R 45). This broad definition of the *actus reus* indicates that the Theft Act 1968 has moved beyond preventing one person taking another's property to a more general notion of interference with the enjoyment of the property. However in *Briggs* [2004] Crim LR 495 it was held that deceiving the victim into arranging money to be paid to solicitors who were acting for the defendant in buying a house did not amount to appropriation. The defendant did not perform an act in relation to the property and could not in any sense be said to have taken it. All the dealings with the property had been done or arranged by the victim.

The latter half of s 3(1) makes it clear that it is possible for the thief to appropriate property already in his possession as long as it came into his possession without being stolen. If it were not for this proviso, a thief would commit endless offences of theft every time he dishonestly used the stolen property. In *Hircock*, for example, the accused appropriated a car by selling it; the car was already lawfully in his possession as he had obtained it (by deception) under a hire-purchase agreement. Because of s 3(1) he could be held to have appropriated the property.

The courts have been troubled by a number of key questions about the notion of appropriation and we will consider these now.

11.3.1 Is it necessary for a defendant to appropriate all of the owner's rights?

Appropriation of the rights of the owner involves usurpation of an owner's rights. This means that the defendant is doing something which the owner is entitled to do. The House of Lords has held in *Morris** [1984] AC 320 that property is appropriated when any one of the owner's rights is assumed. It is not necessary to show that all of the owner's rights have been assumed. A piece of property may, then, be appropriated even though it is still in the victim's hands. Changing the price label on goods in a shop was held to be an appropriation because the right to put labels on items for sale is one of the owner's rights. Indeed, in the same way, merely touching the item would be to appropriate it, because one of the rights of the owner of a piece of property is to touch it. This means that there is a huge range of methods of appropriating property. An owner has the right to touch, move, sell, lend, use, destroy or consume his or her property. Doing any of these will amount to appropriation; although, of course, there will be no theft unless the other elements of the offence are made out.

The benefit of this interpretation is that it enables the court to convict a defendant who manipulates a victim's property rights without ever fully possessing the property. For example, if a defendant offered his neighbour's car to a friend as a gift and the friend drove it away, the defendant could be convicted of the theft of the car, even though he never fully possessed the car, or even touched it. Critics of this aspect of the decision in *Morris* argue that it has stretched the meaning of theft too widely. Consider Ben, who sees a car that he is interested in stealing and then puts his hand on the door handle, but then runs off because he sees the owner approaching. Ben's touching would amount to theft, although most people would regard this as more naturally labelled attempted theft. More than this: is the touching of the car door handle properly regarded as a harm of sufficient seriousness to justify the intervention of the criminal law (see Section 1.4.1)?

11.3.2 Is it possible to appropriate by omission?

Consider the following: while in a supermarket, Emma's toddler (Wilfred) picks up an item and, unknown to Emma, Wilfred hides the item, which as a result is not paid for. Once Emma arrives home, she discovers what Wilfred has done but decides to keep the item. Is this theft, assuming it is dishonest? There is little doubt that if Emma in any sense touches the item or uses it this will amount to appropriation and so a charge of theft could lie. But what if once she has discovered what has happened she does nothing with the item? The law is unclear. One view is that she is under a duty to return the item to the shop (*Miller*-type reasoning could be used: see Chapter 3) and in the light of this duty the omission could be liable to criminal punishment (see the New Zealand case of *Subrizky* [1990] 2 NZLR 717). An alternative view is that if no act is done there can be no appropriation (*Broom v Crowther* (1984) 148 JP 592).

11.3.3 Is it possible to appropriate property honestly?

The issue behind this question is whether the notion of appropriation in effect contains an element of *mens rea*. Lord Roskill in *Morris* appeared to suggest that the notion of appropriation did involve an element of *mens rea*. He stated that a practical joker who switched labels on goods in a supermarket would not have appropriated the items, although if a rogue did the same things, hoping to profit from so doing, he would have appropriated the property. In *Gomez* [1993] AC 442, Lord Keith rejected this conclusion. He explained that both the joker and the rogue had assumed the rights of the owner and had therefore appropriated the goods. Their different motivations were relevant to the question of dishonesty, but not to appropriation. Their Lordships in *Gomez* saw appropriation as a neutral concept, not necessarily indicating wrongdoing, but just a word describing an act of the accused.

11.3.4 Can appropriation only involve the defendant acting without the consent of the owner?

The definition of appropriation in the Theft Act 1968 does not contain words to the effect that the appropriation must be without the owner's consent, as the previous definition of theft had done. However, the conception of theft among the general public would involve acts which took place without the owner's consent. The lack of precise words in the statute has generated a confused series of cases. The arguments have centred on whether the act of appropriation had to be unauthorised by the owner; or whether an outwardly innocent act, performed with the consent of the owner, could be transformed into an appropriation, and therefore theft, if done with dishonest intent. For example, a person in a supermarket takes a wire basket provided by the shop and puts several items into it. Overtly, nothing has been done to which the supermarket manager would take exception. Suppose, however, that when putting the items in the basket, the shopper intended to avoid paying for them: is this act an appropriation and does this dishonest intent turn the otherwise lawful act into an offence of theft before the shopper has even left the shop?

The question resulted in conflicting decisions in the House of Lords: *Lawrence** [1972] AC 626, which suggested that an act could constitute appropriation even if it was consented to; and *Morris*, which said it could not. However, the issue has now been settled by the House of Lords in *Gomez**: an act can amount to appropriation even if it has been consented to or authorised by the victim. This means that any customer in a supermarket who touches an item will thereby appropriate the property (the customer is assuming a right of the owner by touching it); however, she will not be guilty of theft unless she dishonestly intends permanently to deprive the owner of it. In so deciding, the majority judgment in *Gomez* did not rely on key legal principles, but simply stated that *Lawrence* was binding and the statement in *Morris* requiring an unauthorised act was *obiter*. Although *Gomez* has resolved the uncertainty in the law, it has been strongly criticised by some commentators. There are three main grounds of complaint:

1. The first is that relied upon by Lord Lowry in his dissenting judgment in *Gomez*, namely that the majority decision is not in line with the view of the Criminal Law Revision Committee, whose report formed the basis of the Theft Act 1968. Supporters of *Gomez* may reply that the House of Lords is in no way bound to

accept the interpretation of a statute given by such a committee, especially if, as the majority suggested, that interpretation would be unworkable.

2. The second ground of complaint is that as a result of the decision in *Gomez*, the offences in s 1 (theft) and fraud (or as it was at the time of the *Gomez* decision, the offence of obtaining property by deception contrary to s 15 Theft Act 1968, which has now been abolished). If a defendant deceives a victim into handing over her property this will be fraud. After *Gomez*, it can also be theft. This is not a particular problem because there are often overlaps of this kind in criminal law. All offences involving grievous bodily harm involve actual bodily harm, for example.

   More significantly the argument can be made that theft should involve taking something from someone and that deceiving someone into handing over their property is a different kind of wrong from that involved in theft. It has been argued that there is a fundamental moral distinction between manipulating the mind of the victim and persuading her to hand property over (which is fraud) and taking property from her (which should be theft). Therefore, it is said, fraud involves a different invasion of the victim's personal autonomy from that of theft, and so obtaining property by fraud is not just a serious kind of theft but a different kind of property offence altogether. Supporters of *Gomez* would reply that it is not clear that this distinction is watertight as many thefts involve a fraud (and manipulation of the victim's mind) in order to enable the theft to occur (for example, lying to the victim in order to distract his attention so that the defendant can steal from his pocket).

3. The third complaint is that as a result of *Gomez*, theft is committed when there is no outwardly wrong act. For example, it is said, it would be harsh to convict defendants, such as those in *Eddy v Niman* [1981] Crim LR 501, who had picked up items from a supermarket shelf intending to steal them, but changed their minds and left the items in the shop and run off, as they had not clearly demonstrated their intention to do wrong. However, on the other side of the argument, *Gomez* does enable the police to intervene at an early stage and protect the victim's property. In the case of international financial frauds where money in bank accounts can be transferred abroad in seconds this may be very important.

Turning to the arguments in favour of *Gomez*, perhaps the strongest is the difficulty in finding any alternative test. Suggestions have included distinguishing consent and authorisation (*Dobson* [1990] 1 QB 274), or between voluntary and involuntary acts of the victim (Shute and Horder), or by asking whether the act was 'manifestly thefteous' (Fletcher); but all of these distinctions could be very difficult for juries or magistrates to draw. *Gomez* is certainly easy to understand and apply. It also avoids having to acquit a defendant simply because he has been charged with an offence of theft, rather than fraud. The decision in *Gomez* also helps in cases where a director is alleged to have stolen from a company. Under the *Morris* approach, it could have been argued that there was no appropriation as the company, through its directors, authorised the act. After *Gomez* such consent would be irrelevant.

Perhaps because of the opposition it has faced, the Court of Appeal in some subsequent cases has been unwilling to interpret *Gomez* literally. In *Gallasso* [1993] Crim LR 459, a nurse took a mentally ill patient's cheque and placed it in a bank account which she had opened in the patient's name. However, she did so intending at some later point to take the money for herself, but before she could she was arrested. *Gomez* would suggest that she had appropriated the money by placing the cheque into the account. The fact that she was permitted to do this by the patient was irrelevant as she had the necessary *mens rea*. However, the Court of Appeal overturned her conviction, arguing that to establish an appropriation it was necessary to show there had been a 'taking', and as there was no such taking her conviction was overturned. The requirement of 'taking' seems clearly contrary to the authority of *Gomez*, and *Gallasso* should be regarded as being wrongly decided. More recently in *Briggs* the Court of Appeal again suggested that for an appropriation there needed to be a taking of possession, but it did so without referring to *Gomez* and so that case may also be incorrectly decided.

As we shall see shortly, the House of Lords in *Hinks* [2000] 4 All ER 833 has recently reconfirmed its decision in *Gomez*. Therefore, despite its critics, *Gomez* represents the law unless Parliament decides to change it.

11.3.5 Can there be appropriation where the transaction constituted a valid gift?

The House of Lords was required again to consider the nature of 'appropriate' in *Hinks**. The case concerned a gullible man of limited intelligence who had been befriended by the appellant and had handed over large sums of money to the appellant. It could not be shown that there was duress or undue influence, and so it appeared the gifts were valid gifts in law. Could the appellant be convicted of theft in such a case? Could there be an assumption of the rights of the owner where the owner entered into a transaction regarded as effective under civil law?

The majority of the House of Lords, by three to two, held 'yes', if the defendant was acting dishonestly. The majority rejected an argument that the reasoning in *Gomez* (that there could be an appropriation even if the owner of the property consented to the defendant's actions) applied to cases where the victim's consent was obtained by deception and did not apply where the consent was obtained by duress or undue influence. Lord Steyn, for the majority, applied *Gomez* in the most straightforward of ways:

> It is true of course that the certified question in *Gomez* referred to the situation where consent had been obtained by fraud. But the majority judgments do not differentiate between cases of consent induced by fraud and consent given in any other circumstances. The ratio involves a proposition of general application.

In *Hinks*, the fact that the victim consented to the handing over of the property was irrelevant to the issue of appropriation. It is important to note that s 2 (as we shall see) states that a defendant who believes he has a right in law to appropriate the property or believes that the owner is consenting to the appropriation will not be regarded as dishonest. Therefore if the defendant is given a gift by someone and the defendant believes she is entitled in law to the gift, it will not be dishonest for her to take it.

If *Gomez* received a torrent of criticism, *Hinks* has received a waterfall. Here are some of the main criticisms:

1. The decision sets up a conflict between the criminal law and the civil law. In the eyes of contract law the gifts are regarded as valid and the appellant can keep the property, while in the eyes of the criminal law the transaction is regarded as a criminal offence. For two branches of the law to have such different responses is an unacceptable contradiction. This is a strong argument, but there are responses. The response given by Lord Steyn was that if there is a conflict between contract law and

criminal law it is the fault of contract law. If contract law allows someone to obtain property through dishonesty from vulnerable people then it is contract law which has got things wrong, not criminal law. Critics of *Hinks* reply that it is the role of criminal law to protect property rights. Property rights are to be determined by civil law. It is meaningless to say that criminal law should seek to protect property rights which do not exist in civil law. An alternative response is that it is arguable that the aims and justification of criminal law and contract law are different. Contract law may be more concerned to ensure that there is certainty as to who owns which property and to uphold contracts whenever possible; whereas criminal law may be far more concerned with protecting vulnerable victims from dishonest offenders. A third response, but one which cannot be dealt with here, is that civil law in fact would not accept the gift as valid whenever there was dishonesty, relying on the notion of unconscionability.

2. The case leads to some highly undesirable results. Lord Steyn considers the following example:

> P sees D's painting and, thinking he is getting a bargain, offers D £100,000 for it. D realises that P thinks the painting is a Constable, but knows that it was painted by his sister and is worth no more than £100. He accepts P's offer. D has made an enforceable contract and is entitled to recover and retain the purchase price.

Lord Steyn appears to accept that, following *Hinks*, D could be convicted of theft if the jury decided that D had been dishonest. The difficulty is that if this is correct, what are the limits of the criminal law? Must double-glazing companies ensure that people are paying a fair price for their products? Must lawyers ensure they are not presenting clients with excessive fees? And must pop stars ensure their concert tickets are not being charged at too high a rate? In all these cases, if the jury decides there is dishonesty then a conviction of theft could follow. Supporters of *Hinks* would reply that the Crown Prosecution Service can be relied upon to ensure that the offence is charged only in reasonable cases.

3. There are serious difficulties in deciding how it can be said that at the time of the appropriation the property belonged to another. If receiving the gift was the act of appropriation and the gift was a valid one under civil law at the time when the property was received, did it not cease to belong to another? The position seems to be that at exactly the same time there was appropriation and the ownership changed hands. The majority seemed willing to accept that if the appropriation took place at the moment ownership changed hands, this was sufficient to amount to appropriation of property belonging to another.

In the light of the opprobrium, can anything be said in favour of *Hinks*? This would be what supporters of *Hinks* might say:

1. The key argument in favour of *Hinks* is that conduct which was found by the jury to be dishonest was punished. Quite simply, the result was right. Do opponents of *Hinks* really think that there should be no punishment for this kind of behaviour? Lord Steyn argued that if a narrow understanding of appropriation were accepted, this would lead to the acquittal of defendants who were undoubtedly dishonest. This argument has been strongly criticised by Simester and Sullivan: 'It is wrong, a profound violation of the Rule of Law, to reinterpret the law in order to convict a particular defendant who deserves the label of criminal'. Lord Hobhouse, dissenting, made a similar point. But we have seen in the discussion of *R v R* [1992]

1 AC 599 on marital rape that the House of Lords is willing to ensure that criminal law must move with the times. Wives must be protected from husbands who wish to have sexual intercourse without their consent. In *Hinks*, their Lordships offered protection to the elderly and vulnerable from those who seek dishonestly to deprive them of their property.

2. The effect of *Hinks* is that the key question in cases of this kind is whether the defendant is dishonest. Supporters of *Hinks* will argue that asking the jury to consider whether there is dishonesty will produce better justice than asking whether the gift was valid under civil law. The dishonesty approach is easier for juries to apply, will lead to quicker and cheaper trials and will focus the jury's mind on the important question (was there dishonesty?), rather than the less significant question for criminal lawyers of the civil law effect of the transaction. As indicated above, the main (some would say only) benefit of *Gomez* is its ease of use. Had *Hinks* been decided differently, this advantage would have been lost.

11.3.6 Does a defendant continue to appropriate property whenever he assumes the rights of an owner?

Another question which has received conflicting answers from the courts is whether appropriation can be a continuing process or whether it is a one-off occurrence. In *Atakpu* [1994] QB 58, the most recent case on the topic, it was recognised that one can appropriate an item any number of times until all the ingredients of theft occur together, at which point the offence of theft is committed, and after that there can be no more thefts or appropriations. For example, if a defendant absent-mindedly picks up a toenail clipper and walks out of a shop with it without paying, lacking the *mens rea* of theft, he is seen as continuing to appropriate it, although there is no theft. If, some time later when using the clippers, he realises what he has done but decides to keep the item, then at that point the *mens rea* comes into existence and he commits theft. But he commits theft only at that point in time, and he does not continue to appropriate or steal the clippers every time he clips his toenails.

11.3.7 Does a purchaser of stolen property appropriate it?

Section 3(2) Theft Act 1968 provides that a person who buys stolen property for value in good faith will not be said to appropriate the property when he realises that the property is stolen:

> Where property or a right or interest in property is or purports to be transferred for value to a person acting in good faith, no later assumption by him of rights which he believed himself to be acquiring shall, by reason of any defect in the transferor's title, amount to theft of the property.

This subsection applies only where the transferee has given 'value'. This does not mean that the true market value must have been paid; merely that the property must not have been received as a gift. The subsection thus protects from liability for theft the figure familiar to property lawyers, the 'bona fide purchaser without notice' (bona fide meaning good faith).

It is worth noting, however, that the protection extends only to theft; if the transferee decides to sell the goods once he has discovered that he does not have a good title to them, and does not inform the buyer of that fact, he will probably be guilty of fraud.

If he does inform the buyer that he does not have good title, the buyer will probably be guilty of receiving stolen goods and the original transferee will then become an accessory to that offence (see the discussion of *Bloxham** [1982] 1 AC 109 in Section 12.6). The protection of s 3(2) is therefore of real value only if the transferee merely keeps the property.

11.4 Property

There are two issues here. The first is the definition of the term 'property' and the second the requirement that the indictment with which the defendant is charged specifies which property it is alleged the defendant has stolen. Normally there is little difficulty with the property requirement. It is usually obvious that what the defendant has taken is property. Where there is a dispute over the issue, a defendant may seek to raise an argument either that the item is not regarded as property in the eyes of the law; or that, even if it is regarded as property, it is excluded from the ambit of theft by s 4. These arguments will be considered separately.

11.4.1 The item is not property in the eyes of the law

Property is defined in s 4 Theft Act 1968 as including 'money and all other property, real or personal, including things in action and other intangible property'. Some of these terms require explanation:

▶ 'Real property' includes buildings and land, but there are special provisions relating to land in s 4(2);
▶ 'Personal property' (that is, property other than real property) may be tangible or intangible (that is, things that can or cannot be touched physically);
▶ A 'thing in action' is intangible property which gives rise to a right to sue someone in the courts: for example a copyright, a debt or a bank credit (*Hilton* [1997] 2 Cr App R 445). Such things cannot be touched but are regarded as property and can be stolen.

So what is not regarded as property in the eyes of the law? Clearly a complete list cannot be given, but here are some of the items which have come before the criminal courts and found not to be property.

1. *Information*. It was held in *Oxford v Moss* (1978) 68 Cr App R 183 that information itself is not capable of being stolen, so that borrowing an examination paper to look at the contents could not be theft of the information on the paper. It was fortunate for the student that he returned the examination paper, because that meant that he could not be guilty of stealing the piece of paper on which the examination was printed. This is because he could argue that he had no intention permanently to deprive the university of the piece of paper itself.
2. *Electricity*. It has also been held that electricity is not property and so cannot be stolen (*Low v Blease* [1975] Crim LR 513). However a specific offence of unauthorised and dishonest abstraction of electricity deals with this in s 13 Theft Act 1968.
3. *Bodies*. A body cannot be stolen, and that is true whether the person is dead or alive, although in certain circumstances a part of a body can be stolen. The traditional view of the law has been that bodies and parts of bodies are not property, whether the body is dead or alive. However, in recent times the courts have been more willing

to accept that some cases body parts may become property. In *Kelly* [1999] QB 621 it was accepted that if someone has exercised special skill on a body part (for example by embalming it) it can become property. In *Bristol v North Bristol NHS Trust* [2009] EWCA 37 the Court of Appeal accepted that the law needed to change its approach to body parts. In that case men could be said to have property interests in sperm they had asked a hospital to store. But they did not set down any general principles as to when a body part can be property. It will be interesting to see how the law develops in the future.

4. *Services*. Services cannot be property; you cannot steal a haircut or a train ride. The Fraud Act 2006 (see Section 13.4) deals with the obtaining of services by fraud.

11.4.2 Where an item is property but cannot be stolen because of s 4

Section 4 provides that two kinds of property are not property for the purposes of the 1968 Theft Act.

1. *Land*. Parliament decided that it should not be possible to steal land, partly because of the difficulties this may cause for land law. So s 4(2) provides that land (or things forming part of land and severed from it, such as trees or minerals) can be stolen only in certain limited circumstances:

    (a) Where a trustee, a personal representative, a person authorised under a power of attorney or a liquidator appropriates the land 'by dealing with it in breach of the confidence reposed in him' (s 4(2)(a)). Thus a trustee, who is the legal owner of the trust property, will be guilty of theft if he dishonestly sells land that was subject to a trust.

    (b) When a person in possession of the land under a tenancy appropriates a fixture (for example, taking a kitchen sink away from a flat), this will be theft of the fixture. The technical definition of land includes fixtures on the land. It is, of course, also theft for anyone to steal a movable object on the land (for example, a table).

    (c) The Act deals with things forming part of land and which may be severed from it, such as plants, trees or minerals. If a person who is not in possession of land cuts down trees or digs up plants or bushes then this can be theft (s 4(2)(b)). However, merely picking apples, fruit or foliage from plants growing wild on someone else's land is not theft unless it is done for a commercial purpose (s 4(3)). So it would not be theft to pick blackberries from a hedgerow unless the fruit were to be sold in a local market. The same rule applies to mushrooms. What the law is seeking to do here is to distinguish casual picking (for example, picking a wild strawberry while out on a walk) from commercial picking or the digging up of plants.

2. *Wild animals*. Section 4 also deals with 'wild creatures, tamed or untamed'. These are property but cannot usually be stolen as they do not 'belong to' anyone (s 4(4)). However, if the wild creature is ordinarily kept in captivity then it can be stolen. Likewise, if the creature has 'been reduced into possession' (caught) by another person and possession has not since been lost (the animal has not escaped), then the creature can be stolen from that person.

    A tame animal, such as a cat or a dog, is the property of its owner (as are domesticated animals such as horses, cows and sheep) and a dishonest appropriation will be theft. The aim of the law here is to avoid treating poaching as theft, as poaching is governed by separate statutes, for example the Night Poaching Act 1828. However, the taking of pets or farm animals is to be regarded as theft.

11.5 Belonging to another

Normally there is little dispute about whether the property belonged to another. In a typical shoplifting case the defendant is unlikely to dispute that the items belonged to the supermarket. Any dispute over whether property belonged to another should be resolved by applying the rules of contract and property law (*Marshall*). However the requirement can give rise to some difficult issues in the following cases:

11.5.1 The property belongs to no-one

The definition of theft provides that the property must belong to another at the time of the appropriation. It is possible to convict an accused of theft even though it is impossible to ascertain who owned the property as long as it is clear that it was someone other than the defendant. It is not necessary to show that any victim has suffered a financial loss as the result of the theft (*Chan Man-sin* [1988] 1 All ER 1). Some property cannot be stolen, because no-one has any proprietary interest in it. This is true, under the common law, of a corpse (*Sharpe* (1857) Dears & B 160), and also arises where property has been truly abandoned (and not merely lost) by its owner. Property left out for the dustman is not abandoned (*Williams v Phillips* (1957) 41 Cr App R 5). Property dumped in a remote place may be regarded as abandoned and owned by no-one.

11.5.2 Where the victim has a right of possession or control

It is crucial to appreciate that it is not necessarily a defence for an accused to demonstrate that he owned the property in question. The issue is whether it belonged to another. The significance of this way of putting it is that sometimes the law recognises that the defendant owned the property, but that it also belonged to another.

The phrase 'belonging to another' is defined in s 5(1):

> Property shall be regarded as belonging to any person having possession or control of it, or having in it any proprietary right or interest (not being an equitable interest arising only from an agreement to transfer or grant an interest).

There are three concepts here: possession, control and proprietary interest. For property to 'belong to' a person, he or she need have only one of these – possession alone would be enough, for example. The meaning of 'proprietary interest' will be discussed below.

The significance of the fact that property is treated as belonging to a person having possession or control of it is that the owner of a piece of property can appropriate and indeed steal that property if he takes it from a person who possesses it. In *Turner (No. 2)** [1971] 2 All ER 441, the accused was convicted of stealing his own car; he had left his car at a garage to be repaired but later drove it away without paying for the repairs which the garage had carried out. Lord Parker CJ held:

> there is no ground whatever for qualifying the words 'possession or control' in any way. It is sufficient if it is found that the person from whom the property is taken... was at the time in fact in possession or control.

The Court of Appeal did not decide whether the possession or control must be lawful. However, in a later case, *Meredith* [1973] Crim LR 253, the court held that an owner who took his car from someone who had no right to retain possession of it as against the owner was not guilty of theft. This case can therefore be distinguished from *Turner (No. 2)*, where the garage had a right to possess the car as against the owner until he paid the bill.

Possession and control are not synonymous: property may be in the possession of one person while being in another person's physical control. For example, if you invited a friend round for a cup of tea, your friend for a while may control the tea cup, even though it will remain in your possession. It is therefore possible for the person in control to steal from the person in possession, though it is difficult to imagine cases where there would be the necessary dishonesty. In general in the criminal law, possession is taken to require some degree of knowledge: the possessor must know that he has something in his possession (see Section 14.7 and *Warner v MPC** [1969] 2 AC 256). It has been held that control does not require such knowledge: the occupier of a disused factory surrounded by fencing to exclude trespassers was in control of scrap metal on the site because he was in control of the whole site, even though he did not know that the scrap was there, and so someone who took the metal was held to steal from the occupier of the factory (*Woodman*). The advantage of this wide definition of 'belonging to another' is that there is no need to specify who actually owned the goods, which may be hard to ascertain, for example if goods are stolen from a lorry on its way from one factory to another.

11.5.3 The victim has a proprietary right or interest

Section 5(1) explains that property is treated as belonging to a person who has a proprietary right or interest in it. This means that not only will the legal owner be regarded as owning the property, but so will those who have an equitable interest (for example, a right of a beneficiary under a trust).

Section 5(1) makes an exception of 'an equitable interest arising only from an agreement to transfer or grant an interest'. This is a reference to the equitable interest of a person who has agreed by contract to buy, for example, land or shares; in both cases the buyer may enforce the specific performance of the contract against the seller. If the seller dishonestly sells the property to a third party, this will be a breach of contract but not a theft from the buyer. So, if Richard enters a contract to sell to Cedric his hot air balloon but decides not to fulfil the contract and instead sells it to Al, this is not theft.

11.5.4 The victim is a company, partnership or trust

What about property owned by a partnership or a company? In the case of a partnership, each partner has a sufficient proprietary interest in the partnership property, so that one partner can steal from the others (*Bonner* [1970] 1 WLR 838). In the case of a company, even where the directors are the sole shareholders, it has been held that the directors can steal from the company (which has a separate legal personality) if they dishonestly appropriate company property (*Attorney-General's Reference (No. 2 of 1982)* [1984] 2 All ER 216).

11.5.5 Where ownership passes in circumstances suggesting that the defendant was dishonest

Many of the difficulties which have arisen in the interpretation of the phrase 'belonging to another' result from the requirement that 'the appropriation', 'dishonesty' and 'property belonging to another' must all coincide in time. In cases where the ownership of property passes from the victim to the thief, it will often be crucial to know and be able to prove precisely when the rights in the property were transferred and when the dishonest appropriation took place. If the former occurs before the latter (as in *Edwards v Ddin** [1976] 1 WLR 942) then there will be no theft. Unfortunately, even an ordinary shop transaction can cause difficulty, as the facts of *Kaur** [1981] 1 WLR 578 reveal. It has proved necessary to create a new offence, 'making off without payment', to fill the gap in the law revealed by *Edwards v Ddin* and other cases of 'bilking' (s 3 Theft Act 1978; see Section 13.6).

Fortunately there are few situations where the difficulties outlined above cause problems. If A transfers ownership of property to B in circumstances of dishonesty, there are four ways in which the law may still convict B:

1. B may be guilty of theft if he is under a personal legal obligation with respect to the property transferred, in which case the property is deemed to belong to another for the purpose of the law of theft under s 5(3) which provides:

   > Where a person receives property from or on account of another, and is under an obligation to the other to retain and deal with that property or its proceeds in a particular way, the property or proceeds shall be regarded (as against him) as belonging to the other.

   The obligation referred to must be a legal obligation (*Gilks* [1972] 3 All ER 280); a purely moral obligation will not be enough. In cases of this sort, where one person receives property on behalf of another, the property is frequently money. The subsection will apply only where the obligation is to retain that money and deal with it in a particular way; it does not apply where the obligation merely creates a creditor/debtor relationship between the parties. For example, in *Hall* [1972] 2 All ER 1009 it was held that s 5(3) did not apply to a travel agent who received money from clients for air tickets. The obligation was to produce the air tickets. There was no obligation to use the actual money given by the clients in a specific way. By contrast, in *Davidge v Bunnett* [1984] Crim LR 296 the accused had an agreement with her flatmates to share the gas bills; she spent the money received from them on other things, and her conviction for theft was upheld by the Divisional Court. Section 5(3) did apply: the accused's flatmates had given her cheques on the understanding that she would use the proceeds of the cheques to pay the bills It is also clear that the obligation to deal with the money need not be to the 'victim' as long as the defendant is under an obligation to someone to deal with the money in a particular way (*Floyd v DPP* [2000] Crim LR 411).

2. B may be guilty of theft if he is obliged in law to return the money to A, that is, if s 5(4) applies. This states:

   > Where a person gets property by another's mistake, and is under an obligation to make restoration (in whole or in part) of the property or its proceeds or of the value thereof, then to the extent of that obligation the property or proceeds shall be regarded (as against him) as belonging to the person entitled to restoration, and an intention not to make restoration shall be regarded accordingly as an intention to deprive that person of the property or proceeds.

This subsection was included in order to deal with the situation which arose in *Moynes v Cooper* (1956) 79 Cr App R 72, decided before the Theft Act 1968, in which an employee, overpaid by a wages clerk and not discovering the mistake until later, kept the overpayment, and was held to have committed no offence by the Divisional Court. In a case with similar facts (wages were paid by direct debit into the accused's bank account in error), the Court of Appeal held that s 5(4) should apply (*A-G's Ref (No 1 of 1983)** [1984] 3 All ER 369) and the accused was convicted. The overpaid employee was under an obligation to restore to her employer the value of the 'thing in action' (the overpayment in her bank account) as soon as she realised that a mistake had been made. However, the Court of Appeal also felt that 'such cases should normally be resolved without resort to the criminal courts'.

3. It may be that B does not in fact receive ownership of the property and it still belongs to A, therefore he is guilty of theft. This occurs where the contract, which is to transfer the property from A to B, is void. If the contract is void there is no difficulty in saying the property belongs to A; it does and always did. For example, in *Williams** [1980] Crim LR 589 the accused exchanged some obsolete Yugoslav banknotes at a *bureau de change* and received sterling in return. In the view of the Court of Appeal, it was not necessary to rely on s 5(4); the mistake made by the *bureau de change* (that the obsolete notes were valid currency) was so fundamental that there was no valid contract between the accused and the *bureau*. The bureau did not part with ownership of the sterling currency, which therefore belonged to another (that is, the *bureau*) when it was appropriated by the accused. The circumstances in which a contract is void involve complex aspects of contract law and cannot be explained here.

4. It may be that although B becomes the owner of the property in common law he has to hold it on trust for A. This would usually be a special kind of trust called a constructive trust. The law on constructive trusts is still being developed by the courts and it is not clear when they will arise. Lord Browne-Wilkinson has stated: 'when property is obtained by fraud equity imposes a constructive trust on the fraudulent recipient' (*Westdeutsche Landesbank v Islington* [1994] 4 All ER 890). If a constructive trust is imposed, this will mean that s 5(2) can apply as A will still have an equitable interest in the property. If B spends the money he can be guilty of theft (*Shadrockh-Cigari*).

11.6 Dishonesty

The *mens rea* of theft, the state of mind which must accompany the appropriation, has two parts: dishonesty; and the intention of permanently depriving the owner of the property. There are two elements of the law's understanding of dishonesty: s 2 Theft Act 1968 and the well-known *Ghosh* [1982] QB 1053 direction on dishonesty which applies when s 2 does not cover the case.

11.6.1 Section 2(1) Theft Act 1968

Section 2 does not contain a definition of dishonesty. Instead s 2(1) provides three examples of states of mind which are not to be regarded as dishonest. Section 2(1) reads:

A person's appropriation of property belonging to another is not to be regarded as dishonest

(a) if he appropriates the property in the belief that he has in law the right to deprive the other of it, on behalf of himself or of a third person; or

(b) if he appropriates the property in the belief that he would have the other's consent if the other knew of the appropriation and the circumstances of it; or

(c) (except where the property came to him as trustee or personal representative) if he appropriates the property in the belief that the person to whom the property belongs cannot be discovered by taking reasonable steps.

The three subsections will be considered separately.

1. *Claim of right: s 2(1)(a)*. Section 2(1)(a) incorporates what is known as the 'claim of right' defence. The accused is not dishonest if he believes that he has a better legal right to the property than the other person. He may believe that he is the owner or that in law he has a right to take the property from the victim. For example, in *Robinson* Crim LR 173 a belief that the accused was entitled to take from the victim a sum of money which the victim owed him was held to excuse, as a claim of right. There appears to be no requirement that the belief be a reasonable one, as long as it is honestly held (*Holden* [1991] Crim LR 478). But the belief must be a belief in a legal, as opposed to a moral, right to the property. This is one of the rare circumstances in which a mistake of law can provide a defence. The explanation is that the essence of theft is the interference with the owner's legal property rights; if the defendant is unaware that he is interfering with these rights then the defendant will be said (at least by subjectivists) to lack *mens rea*.

   Lord Hutton, one of the dissentients in *Hinks* [2000] 4 All ER 833, argues that s 2(1)(a) necessarily implies that where the defendant in fact has a claim of right he or she cannot be dishonest. This was rejected by the majority. So if a defendant in fact has a 'claim of right' but does not realise this then he can still be regarded as dishonest by the jury. This means that it can be dishonest to assert one's legal rights, which is another surprising result of the decision in *Hinks*.

2. *Belief in consent: s 2(1)(b)*. Section 2(1)(b) explains that a defendant who believed that the owner consented to what he was doing would not be dishonest. So borrowing your brother's clothes is not dishonest if you believed he had or would have consented. Again, the subsection requires a belief in a true consent, honestly obtained (*Attorney-General's Reference (No. 2 of 1982)* [1984] 2 All ER 216). Such a belief need not be a reasonable one, but must be a genuine one.

3. *Inability to discover owner: s 2(1)(c)*. Under s 2(1)(c), believing that you cannot discover the owner of a piece of property by reasonable means is a defence. Again there is no requirement that such a belief be based on reasonable grounds. If therefore Lucy after a party finds a toothbrush in her bathroom and decides to keep it because she cannot reasonably find out whose it is she will not commit theft. If, however, a week later Alex tells her that he has lost his toothbrush, but Lucy decides not to mention her discovery and to keep his toothbrush then she may be guilty of theft. There may be appropriation relying on s 3(1) (see Section 11.3 above) and the jury may decide she is dishonest, relying on the *Ghosh* test (see Section 11.6.3 below).

11.6.2 Section 2(2) Theft Act 1968

Section 2(2) Theft Act 1968 states:

A person's appropriation of property belonging to another may be dishonest notwithstanding that he is willing to pay for the property.

This subsection does not provide a definition of dishonesty. Instead it prevents a line of argument that a defendant may seek to raise. It is no defence to a charge involving dishonesty that one intended to pay for the item. Thus taking a neighbour's garden gnome and pushing a cheque through her door for its value does not negate dishonesty. Such a case would need to be resolved by the *Ghosh* test, to which we now return.

11.6.3 The common law interpretation of dishonesty

If the defendant is not dishonest because he or she falls under s 2(1) then that is the end of the case: the defendant is not dishonest. But if the case does not fall under s 2(1), the judge must give further guidance to the jury. The present position is summarised in the leading cases of *Feely** [1973] 1 All ER 341 and *Ghosh**. In the judgment of Lord Lane CJ in *Ghosh*:

> In determining whether the prosecution has proved that the defendant was acting dishonestly, a jury must first of all decide whether according to the ordinary standards of reasonable and honest people what was done was dishonest. If it was not dishonest by those standards, that is the end of the matter and the prosecution fails. If it was dishonest by those standards, then the jury must consider whether the defendant himself must have realized that what he was doing was by those standards dishonest... It is dishonest for a defendant to act in a way which he knows ordinary people consider to be dishonest, even if he asserts or genuinely believes that he is morally justified in acting as he did.

This direction can be broken down into two stages:

1. First the jury must decide whether in all the circumstances of the case, including the defendant's motives and beliefs, he is dishonest judged by the standards of reasonable and honest people. If the jury decide that the defendant is not dishonest then this resolves the issue: the defendant is not dishonest. If the jury decide that the defendant was dishonest by the standards of ordinary people then the jury must move on to the second stage.
2. The jury must decide whether the defendant was aware that his conduct was dishonest by the standards of ordinary people. If the defendant was so aware then he is dishonest; if he was not aware then he is not dishonest.

The test is therefore neither entirely subjective nor objective. This is demonstrated by the following examples:

(i) Grace, a particularly virtuous woman, regards her conduct as dishonest, but most people would not. Applying the *Ghosh* direction, Grace would not be regarded as dishonest.

(ii) Nicki, an animal rights protester take animals from a laboratory. He gives evidence, believed by the jury, that he thought a majority of people were against animal testing and would not regard his conduct as dishonest. Applying the *Ghosh* direction, Nicki would not be regarded as dishonest.

(iii) Pete, an anti-fur protester, takes fur coats from a shop. He gives evidence, accepted by the jury, that he believes he was acting honestly, although he accepts that most people would not agree with him. Applying the *Ghosh* direction, Pete would be dishonest (assuming that the jury found taking the coats to be contrary to the standards of honesty of ordinary people). It should be noted that the jury in this case must not ask themselves whether as individuals they believe Pete's conduct is dishonest, but rather what ordinary people would think. So an anti-fur juror may himself or herself approve of Pete's conduct, but the juror should ask what ordinary people would think.

There is no need for the judge to give the *Ghosh* direction in every case. It is not necessary if the conduct is obviously dishonest (*Forrester* [1992] Crim LR 792), and there is no need to use it if the defendant does not raise the possibility that he thought the conduct was honest (*Brennan* [1990] Crim LR 118). In these cases it is enough simply to ask the jury to consider whether the conduct was honest according to the standards of ordinary people. However, the Court of Appeal has confirmed that the *Ghosh* test should be applied, if necessary, whenever the concept of dishonesty is used in the criminal law. This includes, for example, the offences in the Fraud Act 2006, the common law offence of conspiracy to defraud, and other offences involving fraud (*Lockwood* [1986] Crim LR 244).

Following the decisions of the House of Lords in *Gomez* [1993] AC 442 and *Hinks*, the *actus reus* requirement for theft has been greatly reduced. Much weight will therefore be thrown onto the *mens rea*, and especially the *Ghosh* test for dishonesty. Whether the *Ghosh* test will be able to play the crucial role it is now expected to play, time will tell. The test has attracted considerable criticism from commentators who dislike the resulting uncertainty. Indeed inconsistent verdicts may occur with different juries disagreeing over the standards of 'reasonable and honest people'. This would not be surprising when many doubt whether, given the variety of religious, cultural and moral values in our society, there are such things as 'generally accepted standards'. One of the difficulties is that it is virtually impossible to correct wrong decisions, as Professor Griew (1985) has pointed out in this context:

> A jury without stars or compass cannot be accused of bad navigation. The direction it takes may be deplorable but cannot be wrong.

See the Hot topic for further discussion. Despite these concerns it is clear that any change in the definition of the meaning of dishonesty would require legislation or a decision of the House of Lords, which has not yet been asked to rule on the question. In *Patni, Dhunna, Soni and Poopalarajah* [2001] Crim LR 570 an argument that the *Ghosh* test was so vague that it infringed Article 7 of the European Convention on Human Rights was rejected.

11.7 Intention of permanently depriving

As well as dishonesty, the other part of the *mens rea* of theft is an intention of permanently depriving the owner (or other person to whom the property 'belongs' within s 5 1968 Act) of the property. This means that borrowing is not theft. Borrowing a friend's dress intending to return it the next day, even knowing that she does not consent, will not amount to theft. This is a controversial position for the law to take. Borrowing property can cause the owner great inconvenience and can be seen as a clear infringement of the owner's property rights. Imagine if someone took all your criminal law books and notes and returned them to you after you had sat your criminal law exam. However Parliament has taken the view that borrowing property is too minor a harm to justify the full force of the criminal law and that remedies in civil law are sufficient.

This is not to say that no borrowing can be theft. There are some statutes which make specific forms of borrowing a criminal offence: taking and driving away a conveyance without the owner's consent (s 12 Theft Act 1968, see Section 14.4), and the removal without lawful authority of articles kept for display in places open to the public (such as museums and stately homes; s 11 1968 Act), for example.

It will usually be clear whether or not a person has an intention of permanently depriving. A jury will be very unlikely to believe a pickpocket who claims that he would have returned the wallet had he not been arrested by the police. There are however some cases where the issue is less obvious. We will now discuss two of these.

11.7.1 Borrowing money

Taking money belonging to another, intending to repay, will involve an intention of permanently depriving the other of the particular notes and coins that were taken and so will be theft (*Velumyl* [1989] Crim LR 299). Such a taking will be theft if it is dishonest. In considering dishonesty in such a case, it should be borne in mind that s 2(2) explains that paying for the item taken will not negate dishonesty (see Section 11.6 above); although if the defendant believes that the victim would have consented to the taking, this may negate dishonesty under s 2(1)(b).

11.7.2 Conditional intent

Imagine Nigel is found rifling through Rosie's handbag. By touching the bag and its contents he appropriates them. However he may believably claim that he did not form an intent permanently to deprive Rosie of any particular item. In such a case it is necessary to distinguish three possible states of mind:

1. There is no difficulty if it could be shown that Nigel was looking for a particular piece of property, for example a credit card. He could be charged with theft of the credit card or an attempt to steal the credit card if he had not managed to appropriate it.
2. If Nigel had not yet decided whether or not to take anything, it seems he must be acquitted. Lord Scarman has said (in *DPP v Nock* [1978] AC 979), 'if a man be in two minds whether to steal or not, the intention required by the statute is not proved'.
3. If Nigel had decided to take anything that was of value, this is known as 'conditional intent'. The phrase was defined by the Law Commission:

   > Conditional intent... means that the accused does not know what he is going to steal but intends that he will steal whatever he finds of value or worthwhile stealing.

A person with conditional intent can be charged with attempted theft, although the prosecution will have to exercise care in drafting the indictment. An allegation of an intent to steal specific named property will fail because it cannot be proved that the accused had the intent to steal that property. In the case of *Husseyn* (1978) 67 Cr App R 55, for example, the accused and a friend were found trying to get into a van which contained sub-aqua equipment, and the indictment charged them with attempting to steal this sub-aqua equipment. Their conviction was quashed by the Court of Appeal, as it was not shown that they intended to steal sub-aqua equipment. In *Easom** [1971] 2 All ER 945, the accused had picked up a handbag, examined its contents and put it down, having discovered that it contained nothing of value. He was charged with theft of the handbag and certain identified contents. His conviction was quashed. In *Attorney-General's References (Nos 1 and 2 of 1979)** [1979] 2 All ER 143, Roskill LJ explained these decisions on the basis of the over-precise wording of the indictment.

In both cases the accused had a general intention to steal and this would be sufficient provided the indictment did not refer to specific objects. Roskill LJ said:

> we see no reason in principle why... a more imprecise method of criminal pleading should not be adopted... as for example attempting to steal some or all of the contents of a car or some or all of the contents of a handbag.

11.7.3 Borrowing and returning property in a less valuable state

We mentioned earlier that borrowing something is not theft and gave the example of borrowing a friend's dress for the evening. But what if the dress was returned damaged, would this alter the position? This situation is dealt with in s 6 Theft Act 1968, which reads:

> (1) A person appropriating property belonging to another without meaning the other permanently to lose the thing itself is nevertheless to be regarded as having the intention of permanently depriving the other of it if his intention is to treat the thing as his own to dispose of regardless of the other's rights: and a borrowing or lending of it may amount to so treating it if, but only if, the borrowing or lending is for a period and in circumstances making it equivalent to an outright taking or disposal.
> (2) Without prejudice to the generality of subsection (1) above, where a person, having possession or control (lawfully or not) of property belonging to another, parts with the property under a condition as to its return which he may not be able to perform, this (if done for purposes of his own and without the other's authority) amounts to treating the property as his own to dispose of regardless of the other's rights.

Section 6 is designed to elucidate the meaning of the phrase 'intention of permanently depriving', but is so obscure that it may be more of a hindrance than a help. It is perhaps reassuring, then, that the section is hardly ever needed. Lord Lane CJ takes the view that 's 6 should be referred to in exceptional cases only. In the vast majority of cases it need not be referred to or considered at all' (*Lloyd, Bhuee and Ali** [1985] 2 All ER 661). Soon after the Theft Act 1968 came into force, Edmund Davies LJ warned that s 6 must not be interpreted as in any way 'watering down' the definition of theft, which includes the intention of permanently depriving; it merely gives illustrations of such an intention and clarifies its meaning (*Warner* (1970) 55 Cr App R 932). This approach has been broadly adopted by other judges; Lord Lane in *Lloyd, Bhuee and Ali* summed up the section by saying 'it must mean, if nothing else, that there are circumstances in which a defendant may be deemed to have the intention permanently to deprive, even though he may intend the owner eventually to get back the object which has been taken'.

So, how does the section help in cases where the defendant is returning damaged property? It should be noted that s 6 appears to draw a distinction between 'property' and 'the thing itself'. This distinction is not explained in the Act, but means that there will be occasions where 'the thing itself' is returned to the owner in such an altered form that the 'borrowing' is treated as 'equivalent to an outright taking' of the property. In a debate in Parliament, the Government Minister gave the example of a person who 'borrows' a season ticket and uses it: he is guilty of theft (if dishonest) because he is acting as owner of the ticket; it will make no difference that he intends to return the ticket ('the thing itself') after it has expired. As far as the owner is concerned, the property has been deprived of all its virtue and the act is therefore 'equivalent to an outright taking'. Lord Lane said:

> Borrowing is 'ex hypothesi' not something which is done with an intention permanently to deprive. This half of the subsection, we believe, is intended to make it clear that a mere

borrowing is never enough to constitute the necessary guilty mind unless the intention is to return the 'thing' in such a changed state that it can truly be said that all its goodness or virtue has gone.

An attempt was made in *Lloyd, Bhuee and Ali* to apply the 'using up' principle to video piracy, but the Court of Appeal held that the borrowing of the films in order to make illegal copies of them had not deprived the films of their intrinsic value: they could still be shown to paying audiences. This case illustrates well the restrictive approach of the courts. A freer interpretation of 'an intention to treat the thing as his own to dispose of regardless of the other's rights' might well have included the copying of film tapes in breach of copyright.

Examples of the use of s 6 given in *Lloyd, Bhuee and Ali* include the taking of a railway ticket, intending that the ticket should be returned after use (when its value has gone), and the taking of an electric battery, such as a torch battery, intending to return it only when all its power has been used up. It is unclear whether in order for s 6 to be available it is necessary for the item to lose all of its virtue – would the offence be committed where the defendant took a season train ticket and used all bar a few days? Lord Lane suggested *obiter* in *Lloyd, Bhuee and Ali* that all the value needed to be removed, and this seems correct if the phrase 'equivalent to outright taking' is interpreted strictly. In *DPP v SJ, PI, RC* [2002] EWHC 291 the defendant took the victim's headphones, snapped them and returned them. This, it was held, could amount to theft because the property had lost its practical usefulness, even if its goodness had not been completely exhausted.

Another issue yet to be resolved by the courts is whether the test of value is to be subjective to the victim. If the victim's wedding dress is stolen the day before the wedding and returned the day after, could it be argued that to the victim the dress has lost 'all its goodness'? Or is the answer that it still has the same monetary value as when it was taken and therefore s 6 does not enable a theft conviction.

11.7.4 Treating property as your own

According to s 6, a defendant is treated as having an intention permanently to deprive the victim of their property if he has an intention 'to treat the thing as his own to dispose of regardless of the other's rights'. A remarkably broad definition of this phrase was given by the Divisional Court in *Lavender* [1994] Crim LR 297. There the defendant moved the victim's door from one part of the victim's building to another. This was seen as the defendant treating the door as his own to dispose of regardless of the victim's rights. It is surprising that moving the door was regarded as 'disposing' of the door. If this is correct, it is hard to see why any moving of the victim's property could not similarly be regarded as treating it as the defendant's own. In which case, there is really no problem with the borrowing cases and most appropriations can be regarded as treating the property as one's own. It is hard to believe that *Lavender* can be interpreted so widely, especially given the view of the Court of Appeal in *Lloyd, Bhuee and Ali* that s 6 should have a minimalist role. A similarly wide interpretation of the phrase can also be found in *Fernandes* [1996] 1 Cr App R 175, where a solicitor put a client's money into an unauthorised risky investment. It was held that this could count as 'treating the property as his own' for the purpose of s 6. However, in *Davies* [2008] EWCA Crim 980 it was held that taking a car and abandoning it a couple of miles away with its hazard lights on could not be regarded as disposing of the property for the purposes of s 6.

In short, it is hard to predict what conduct a court may interpret as treating 'the thing as his own to dispose of regardless of the other's rights'.

11.7.5 'Kidnapping' property

This heading deals with what is colloquially but inaccurately described as 'kidnapping' property. What if a defendant takes the victim's goat and then tells the victim that he can have his goat back if he pays the defendant £100? Is this theft of the goat? Can the defendant claim he never intended permanently to deprive the victim of his goat because he intended the victim to pay the ransom demand and to return the goat? Lord Lane explained in *Lloyd, Bhuee and Ali* that s 6 covered such a case:

> [the] first part of s.6(1) seems to us to be aimed at the sort of case where a defendant takes things and then offers them back to the owner for the owner to buy if he wishes. If the taker intends to return them to the owner only on such payment, then, on the wording of s.6(1), that is deemed to amount to the necessary intention permanently to deprive.

This is sometimes referred to as the 'ransom' principle, and covers not only straightforward ransom cases but any case in which the taker makes his own terms and conditions for the return of the property, whether these are known to the owner or not (*Raphael* [2008] EWCA 1014). In *Scott v MPC* [1975] AC 819, for example, the accused took a pair of curtains from a department store without paying for them and then returned them, alleging that he had bought them the previous day and asking for a refund. He was treating the property as 'his own to dispose of regardless of the other's rights' and was guilty of theft.

11.7.6 Gambling with or pawning another's property

Section 6(2) deals with the situation where a person borrows another's property and gambles with it or pawns it. Section 6(2) explains that such a person cannot claim he or she had no intent permanently to deprive because they intended to win the gamble or intended to buy back the pawned property.

Hot Topic – **Finding treasure**

In 2007 the boat MSC Natoli grounded off the South Devon coast (see Glover for a full discussion. The contents of the boat were spilled and washed ashore on Branscombe beach. This led to over one thousand people turning up to salvage or loot (depending on your point of view) the property, which included cars, wine and nappies. Although it was widely thought that theft charges could have been brought no arrests were made.

One reason why no prosecutions were brought was that it was doubtful whether or not a theft charge could be brought. Was it dishonest to turn up on a beach and remove cargo from a stricken

vessel. The fact that so many people did so, and were willing to do so in the full view of the media, reveals it is not a clear cut issue.

The start of the analysis must be s 2. If any of those on beach believed he had a right to take the material then they would not be dishonest. However, it seems unlikely any of those on the beach believed that. Especially as early on the police made it clear people did not have a legal right to take the property. So the focus falls on the *Ghosh* [1982] QB 1053 test.

Remember the *Ghosh* test requires the jury to consider whether or not the acts were dishonest according to the standards of honest people and whether the defendant believed their conduct to be dishonest by those standards. It is difficult to know whether what the people on the beech were doing was dishonest according to the standards of ordinary people. In part because this is a rare event and so the jury cannot consider how most people would react. In part also because there would be a range of views among ordinary people: some would think it dishonest and others would not. There may be a further difficulty here in that people who live by the sea may have a different attitude to the issue than 'landlubbers'. So in this case should the jury consider what reasonable and honest people living by the sea would think?

Even if the jury did decide that the conduct was dishonest, it is still necessary to consider whether the people on the beach believed that ordinary honest people would regard their conduct as dishonest. It may be that, especially given the crowds engaging in the same behaviour, they could claim to believe that their conduct would not be so considered.

The complexities that we have been discussing lead some to complain that the current law is too uncertain. We cannot know what a jury will make of a case like this. Our society is not hemogenous and talk of a consistent standard of honesty is a fiction. The *Ghosh* test fails to provide the jury with clear guidance and fails to provide citizens with a clear statement of what conduct is, or is not, against the law.

However, the *Ghosh* test can be defended against these complaints. The key point to recall is that the prosecution must prove its case beyond reasonable doubt. In a case like this where the standards of honesty across society are unclear in fact the operation of the *Ghosh* test is straightforward: the jury should acquit. They cannot be sure beyond reasonable doubt that the conduct is dishonest. Once this is appreciated much of the alleged uncertainty surrounding the *Ghosh* test falls away.

Summary

11.1 The basic definition of theft is found in s 1 Theft Act 1968. An attempt was made to use clear and uncomplicated language but the complexities of the law of property and contract create inevitable difficulties in defining the scope of theft. Many of the concepts which are used in theft appear in other property offences.

11.2 The offence of theft is made up of five core elements: appropriation, property, belonging, dishonesty and intention permanently to deprive.

11.3 Appropriation is defined in s 3 Theft Act 1968 and includes any assumption by a person of any one of the rights of an owner in the sense of an adverse interference with or usurpation of the owner's rights. Section 3(2) protects a person who buys stolen property in good faith: no later use of the property will amount to theft. Whether the owner consents to the act of usurpation is irrelevant in deciding whether or not there is appropriation.

11.4 Property is defined very widely in s 4 Theft Act 1968 and includes 'things in action' such as a credit balance in a bank account. 'Land' is property which can be stolen only in certain very limited circumstances. Confidential information is not property within s 4.

11.5 The property must belong to another at the time of the appropriation. Property belongs to any person having possession, control, or any proprietary right or interest (s 5(1)) in it. The timing can cause difficulty, particularly if property rights pass as a result of the transaction. If all proprietary rights, as well as possession and control, pass before the act of appropriation, there can be no theft. A new offence has been created (s 3 Theft Act 1978) to deal with 'bilking' cases. The requirement of belonging to another has been given an extended meaning in s 5. Section 5(3) applies where all rights in property are transferred to the thief but he is under a legal obligation to retain and deal with the property in a particular way. Section 5(4) applies where property has been handed over under a mistake and there is a legal obligation to return the property.

11.6 Dishonesty is an important part of the *mens rea* of theft. Section 2 Theft Act 1968 gives some guidance on the meaning of dishonesty, but the concept is not defined and it has been

Summary cont'd

held to be primarily a matter for the jury or magistrates. The jury should ask themselves two questions. First, was the conduct dishonest according to the standards of reasonable and ordinary people? Second, was the accused aware that what he was doing was, by those standards, dishonest?

11.7 The other element of *mens rea* in theft is an intention of permanently depriving another of property. Borrowing property is not theft. There is no bar to conviction for attempted theft in cases where the accused intends to steal anything of value but is arrested before finding anything to steal (even if in fact there is nothing to steal), as long as the indictment is worded in sufficiently general terms. An attempt is made in s 6 Theft Act 1968 to clarify the meaning of the phrase 'intention of permanently depriving'. The section is difficult to construe, and in most circumstances will be redundant. It covers 'ransom' cases, where the accused is prepared to return the property of another only on the performance of some condition. It also covers the cases of 'using up', where the property is returned to the owner, but in circumstances such that its value has completely gone. In these cases, even though the accused may intend to return the 'thing itself', he is deemed to have an intention of permanently depriving the owner of the property.

Further Reading

On the nature of appropriation and disputes over *Gomez* and *Hinks* read Beatson and Simester, Bogg and Stanton-Ife, Gardner, Shute, and Shute and Horder. Elliot, Griew, and Halpin discuss dishonesty. Issues surrounding what is property for the purposes of theft are considered by Cross. Permanent deprivation is examined in Spencer and also Williams.

Beatson and Simester, 'Stealing One's Own Property' (1999) 115 LQR 372.

Bogg and Stanton-Ife, 'Theft as Exploitation' (2003) 23 LS 402.

Cross, 'Protecting Confidential Information under the Criminal Law of Theft and Fraud' (1991) 11 OJLS 264.

Elliot, 'Dishonesty in Theft: A Dispensable Concept' [1982] Crim LR 395.

Gardner, 'Appropriation in Theft: the Last Word' (1993) 109 LQR 195.

Gardner, 'Property and Theft' [1998] Crim LR 35.

Glover, 'Can Dishonesty Be Salvaged? Theft and the Grounding of the MSC Napoli' [2010] J Crim L 53.

Griew, 'Dishonesty: The Objections to Feely and Ghosh' [1985] Crim LR 341.

Halpin, 'The Test for Dishonesty' [1996] Crim LR 283.

Shute, 'Appropriation and the Law of Theft' [2002] Crim LR 450.

Shute and Horder, 'Thieving and Deceiving: What is the Difference?' (1993) 56 MLR 548.

Simester and Sullivan, 'The Nature and Rationale of Property Offences', in Duff and Green (eds), *Defining Crimes* (Oxford University Press 2005).

Spencer, 'The Metamorphosis of Section 6' [1977] Crim LR 653.

Williams, 'Temporary Appropriation should be Theft' [1981] Crim LR 129.

Case Notes

▶ **Attorney-General's References (Nos 1 and 2 of 1979) [1979] 2 All ER 143. Court of Appeal**

Two questions were referred to the Court of Appeal arising out of two cases in which the trial judge had directed an acquittal. The Court of Appeal was asked whether the accused's intention of stealing anything of value which he might find in a building amounted to an intention of stealing necessary for a conviction of burglary or attempted burglary. The Court held that this intention was sufficient, as long as the indictment did not allege that the accused intended to steal specific items. The same principles would apply to theft and attempted theft.

▶ **Attorney-General's Reference (No. 1 of 1983) [1984] 3 All ER 369. Court of Appeal**

The accused received an overpayment of wages by direct transfer of money from her employer (the Metropolitan Police). She knew of the overpayment but did nothing. She was charged with theft of the overpayment. The trial judge directed an acquittal, but it was held in the Court of Appeal that this was a case where s 5(4) Theft Act 1968 applied. The overpayment in the accused's bank account was a debt and a thing in action; she was under an obligation to make restoration of the value of that thing in action when she found that the mistake had been made. The property therefore notionally belonged to another person.

▶ **Bloxham [1982] 1 AC 109. House of Lords**

See Chapter 12 Case notes.

▶ **Easom [1971] 2 All ER 945. Court of Appeal**

The appellant was convicted of theft of a handbag and its contents. He had taken the bag in a cinema, looked through it and, finding nothing of value, had put it back by the owner. His appeal was allowed, and the Court of Appeal held that he could not in those circumstances be convicted of theft or attempted theft because there was no evidence

that he had an intention of permanently depriving the owner of the specific property named in the indictment.

▶ **Edwards v Ddin [1976] 1 WLR 942. Divisional Court**

The accused was charged with theft of petrol from a garage. He had asked the garage attendant to fill the tank of his car with petrol and had then driven away without paying for it. The magistrates held that this was not appropriation of property belonging to another because ownership of the petrol transferred to the accused when it was put into his car. The Divisional Court upheld this decision on the ground that under the Sale of Goods Act 1893 this was a contract where ownership in goods passed to the buyer before payment. When the accused drove away from the garage, therefore, the petrol in his car belonged to him and not to the garage.

▶ **Feely [1973] 1 All ER 341. Court of Appeal**

The appellant was convicted of theft of a sum of money from his employers. He had taken about £30 out of the till, leaving an IOU. He said that his employers owed him about £70 and that he had intended to pay the money back. The jury was directed that his intention to pay back the money was irrelevant to the question of dishonesty in theft. The court allowed the appeal, holding that dishonesty related to the state of mind of the accused; whether or not a person was dishonest was a question of fact for the jury, and the jury should apply the current standards of ordinary decent people.

▶ **Ghosh [1982] QB 1053. Court of Appeal**

The appellant was convicted of obtaining money by deception contrary to s 15 Theft Act 1968. He was a surgeon who had allegedly claimed payment for operations carried out either by another person or under the National Health Service. The court held that there had been a misdirection on the meaning of dishonesty, but dismissed the appeal, applying the proviso to s 2(1) Criminal Appeal Act 1968. It was held that dishonesty was a state of mind of the accused. The jury should first ask itself whether what was done by the accused was dishonest by the ordinary standards of reasonable and honest people, and then whether the accused realised that it was dishonest by those standards.

▶ *Gomez* [1993] AC 442. House of Lords

The accused was employed as the assistant manager of a shop. He persuaded the manager of the shop to accept two building society cheques from a customer in exchange for some electrical goods. He was aware that the cheques were worthless but told the manager that they were 'as good as cash'. He was convicted of theft of the goods. He appealed to the House of Lords, arguing that if the victim authorised the handing over of property there could be no appropriation. The House of Lords, by a four to one majority, held that the fact that the manager had authorised the handing over of the goods was irrelevant to the issue of appropriation. All that needed to be shown for an appropriation was an assumption of any of the rights of the owner, and so the conviction was upheld.

▶ *Hinks* [2000] 3 WLR 1590. House of Lords

The appellant befriended John Dolphin, a naïve, gullible 53-year-old man of limited intelligence. It was alleged that the defendant had persuaded Dolphin to hand over £60,000 from his building society account and some other property. The appellant claimed that the man had voluntarily handed over the property as valid gifts or loans. The majority of the House of Lords held that even if the transfers were valid gifts under contract law, they were appropriations. If they were dishonest, they could be the basis of a conviction of theft. The minority believed that this created an unacceptable conflict between the civil and the criminal law.

▶ *Hircock* (1978) 67 Cr App Rep 278. Court of Appeal

The appellant was convicted of obtaining a car by deception (contrary to s 15 Theft Act 1968) and of theft of the same car. He had obtained the car on hire purchase, using a false name,

and had then sold it. The convictions were upheld by the court, which held that when the appellant obtained the car this was not a theft, as the owner had consented. There was therefore no bar to his conviction for theft on the basis of the later dishonest selling of the car.

▶ *Kaur* [1981] 1 WLR 578. Divisional Court

The appellant was convicted of theft of a pair of shoes. She had taken them from a rack in a shop and noticed that the shoes were each marked with a different price. The higher price was the correct one. She presented them to the cashier without mentioning this difference and was charged the lower price, which she paid. On leaving the shop with the shoes she was arrested and charged with theft. The court allowed the appeal, holding that at the time when she walked out of the shop and appropriated the shoes, they were her own. She had paid for them, and the mistake as to the price was not sufficiently fundamental to render the contract of sale void *ab initio*.

▶ *Lawrence* [1972] AC 626. House of Lords

The appellant was convicted of theft of £6. He was a taxi driver who, when offered £1 for a 10s 6d fare, told the victim, who was an Italian on his first visit to England, that it was not enough and took a further £6 out of his wallet. The victim did not object to this money being taken, but there was no evidence that he intended to pay the appellant more than the correct fare. The appellant argued on appeal that the victim had consented to the taking of the money, and that this consent had operated to transfer ownership of the money to the appellant, so that when the appellant took the money it no longer belonged to the victim. These arguments were rejected by both the Court of Appeal and the House of Lords. Viscount Dilhorne in the House of Lords held that there was no reason to add the words 'without the consent of the owner' to s 1 Theft Act 1968. He also held that the money belonged to the victim at the time when the appellant appropriated it, even though the act of appropriation itself may have transferred the ownership. It was also held that ss1 and 15 Theft Act 1968 are not mutually exclusive, and conduct which falls within s 15 may also amount to theft within s 1.

▶ *Lloyd, Bhuee and Ali* [1985] 2 All ER 661. Court of Appeal

The appellants were convicted of conspiracy to steal. They had taken video-tapes of films from the cinema in which Lloyd worked in order to make pirated copies of the films for sale. The films were returned promptly to the cinema in order to avoid detection. The appellants appealed against conviction on the ground that the trial judge should not have directed the jury in terms of s 6(1) Theft Act 1968. The appeal was allowed and the convictions quashed. It was held that s 6 should be referred to in exceptional cases only. It was designed to deal with two kinds of case: (1) where the accused takes property intending to offer it back to the owner for payment; (2) where the accused intends to return the 'thing' in such a changed state that all its goodness or virtue has gone. In this case, the planned copyright swindle would adversely affect the commercial interests of the owners but would not affect the value of the films themselves, which could still be shown to paying audiences.

▶ *Morris* [1984] AC 320. House of Lords

The appellant was convicted of theft of goods from a supermarket. He had changed the price labels on the goods for labels showing a lesser price, paid the lower price at the checkout, and was then arrested. In a second case which was consolidated on appeal (*Anderson v Burnside*), the facts were similar although the appellant was detected at the checkout before paying the lower price. It was argued on appeal that dishonest label switching did not in itself amount to an act of appropriation. The House of Lords dismissed the appeals on the ground that the label switching was a sufficient appropriation: it amounted to an assumption of one of the rights of the owner, which was to determine the price at which goods should be sold. Lord Roskill held that an appropriation in theft required an adverse interference with, or usurpation of, one of the owner's rights.

▶ *Pitham and Hehl* (1976) 65 Cr App Rep 45. Court of Appeal

See Chapter 12 Case notes.

▶ *Turner (No. 2)* [1971] 2 All ER 441. Court of Appeal

The defendant left his car at a garage for repairs. Once the repairs were complete, but not paid for, the defendant drove the car away. The court held that the garage was the possessor of the car and so even though the defendant was the owner of the car, he could be held guilty of theft. The decision is rather unfortunate as it is not clear on the basis of the right to possession. The court said that it was not necessary to discuss the lien (a form of property right which would have arisen following the performance of work on the car until payment), but this seems the best explanation of the right of possession.

▶ *Warner v MPC* [1969] 2 AC 256. House of Lords

See Chapter 6 Case notes.

▶ *Williams* [1980] Crim LR 589. Court of Appeal

The appellant was convicted of theft. He had exchanged obsolete Yugoslav banknotes at a *bureau de change* in a department store for sterling currency, and had been charged with theft of the sterling as well as obtaining the currency by deception. The trial judge ruled that there was insufficient evidence of the false representations alleged to support the charge of obtaining by deception, but the appellant was convicted of theft, the jury having decided that he was dishonest. On appeal it was held that the appellant had, by offering the obsolete banknotes for sale at a *bureau de change*, represented that they were valid currency. The theft conviction was upheld on the ground that there had been no sale of the sterling currency to the appellant. His fraud rendered any such contract void, and the sterling therefore remained throughout the property of the *bureau de change*.

Chapter 12

Offences connected to theft

Key Terms

- **Robbery** – the use of force combined with the offence of theft.
- **Burglary** – entering a building as a trespasser either with intent to commit certain offences or, having so entered, committing certain offences.

12.1 Robbery

All the offences discussed in this chapter are broadly connected to the offence of theft and are found in the Theft Act 1968. The first to be considered is robbery. Robbery is a form of aggravated theft. It involves theft combined with the use of force. The offence covers a wide range of conduct, from 'bag snatching' to an armed gang forcing cashiers at a bank to hand over large sums of money. It is subject to a maximum punishment of life imprisonment, in contrast to a maximum of seven years for theft. Section 8 Theft Act 1968 describes the offence of robbery:

> (1) A person is guilty of robbery if he steals, and immediately before or at the time of doing so, and in order to do so, he uses force on any person or puts or seeks to put any person in fear of being then and there subjected to force.
>
> (2) A person guilty of robbery, or of an assault with intent to rob, shall on conviction on indictment be liable to imprisonment.

The essence of robbery is the combination of two elements:

12.1.1 Theft

Unless every element of theft is made out, a conviction for robbery is impossible; this includes the *mens rea* of theft. It will therefore be a defence to robbery to argue lack of dishonesty for one of the reasons set out in s 2(1) Theft Act 1968, such as the claim of right. It is not necessary for the accused to believe that he had the right to take the property by force (*Robinson* [1977] Crim LR 173), as long as he honestly believed that he had a legal right to the property. Therefore the dishonesty question is linked to the appropriation, not the use of force. It is tested, in the absence of one of the states of mind specified in s 2(1), by the test laid down in *Ghosh** [1982] QB 1053 (see Section 11.6.3).

12.1.2 Force

The defendant must have used or threatened to use force. The courts have left the definition of force to the jury, making it clear that a relatively small degree of force may be enough – there is certainly no need for actual injury, but presumably there must be more than a mere touching. In *Hale** (1978) 68 Cr App R 415, it was said that 'the jury were at liberty to find the appellant guilty of robbery relying on the force used when he put his hand over [the victim's] mouth to restrain her from calling help'. In *Dawson*

(1978) 68 Cr App R 170, the jury decided that jostling the victim in order to pick his pocket was capable of amounting to force, and the Court of Appeal thought the jury were entitled to take that view. The force or threat of force need not be directed at the victim of the theft (the person to whom the property belongs); it may be used on a bystander, a hostage or a security guard, for example. Nor does it matter whether the force is applied to a piece of property rather than aimed at a person (*Clouden* [1987] Crim LR 56). This is a surprising decision as it blurs the division between theft and robbery. The decision could be supported on the basis that, if the defendant is aggressively tugging on a piece of property, this will often put the victim in fear of violence. It will be noted that a threat of force is sufficient. So an accused who passes a note to a bank cashier threatening violence unless money is handed over may be convicted of theft if the money is indeed supplied. It does not need to be shown that the victim was frightened by the force. In *B and R v DPP* [2007] EWHC 739 (Admin) the victim was startled, but not frightened by the force. The Court was willing to uphold a conviction for robbery, because fear by the victim was not required.

The force (or threat of force) must be used in order to steal. It will normally be possible to infer from the fact that the use of force assisted the theft, that the force was used in order to steal. The force may take the form of snatching the property from the victim or distracting the victim to enable the theft to take place. The timing of the force is important: it must occur at the time of the theft itself or just before it. So it will not be robbery to use force in order to escape after the theft is over (although the separate offences of theft and assault may be charged in such a case). Nor would it be robbery if the defendant assaulted the victim and then noticed the victim's watch and took it. It is therefore important to know when the theft is complete, and this will depend on the understanding of appropriation (see Section 11.3). The attitude of the courts has been flexible: on the one hand, it has been held that the theft was complete, and robbery committed, on the basis of a momentary appropriation. For example, in *Corcoran v Anderton* (1980) 71 Cr App R 104, the two accused attacked a woman, pulling at her handbag so that she dropped it. They then ran away leaving the handbag on the ground, but it was held that the appropriation, the 'assumption of the rights of an owner' (s 3 Theft Act 1968), had occurred by tugging the handbag, and so they were guilty of theft. On the other hand, in *Hale*, Eveleigh LJ in the Court of Appeal said that although a theft had been committed when the accused seized a jewellery box, 'the act of appropriation does not suddenly cease. It is a continuous act and it is a matter for the jury to decide whether or not the act of appropriation had finished.' In this case, the theft was held still to be continuing when the accused tied the victim up after seizing the jewellery box, and so the conviction was upheld. The Court of Appeal has suggested that the appropriation continues while the accused can be said to still 'be on the job', but once the theft is complete there can be no further thefts of that piece of property by the defendant (*Atakpu* [1994] QB 58).

The *mens rea* of robbery includes the requirement that the force was used for the purpose of enabling theft. So a defendant who accidentally used force while stealing would not commit the offence of robbery.

12.2 Assault with intent to rob

As implied in s 8(2) Theft Act 1968, it is an offence to assault with intent to rob. This offence is also punishable with life imprisonment. It involves proof of an assault, performed with an intent to commit robbery. As robbery itself has not been committed it is surprising that no distinction is made in the sentence.

12.3 Burglary

Burglary is regarded as a particularly unpleasant crime as it typically involves an invasion of a home, a place where people are meant to feel secure and safe. The definition of burglary is in fact wider than commonly perceived, as it is not limited to dwelling houses or to offences involving stealing. In fact, burglary is a complicated offence because it can be committed in so many different ways.

12.3.1 The essence of burglary

The essence of burglary is trespass into a building (such as a private house or a factory) for some criminal purpose. Section 9 Theft Act 1968 provides:

(1) A person is guilty of burglary if –
   (a) he enters any building or part of a building as a trespasser and with intent to commit any such offence as is mentioned in subsection (2) below; or
   (b) having entered any building or part of a building as a trespasser he steals or attempts to steal anything in the building or that part of it or inflicts or attempts to inflict on any person therein any grievous bodily harm.
(2) The offences referred to in subsection (1)(a) above are offences of stealing anything in the building or part of a building in question, of inflicting on any person therein any grievous bodily harm, and of doing unlawful damage to the building or anything therein.

The maximum punishment for burglary is 14 years if the building involved was a dwelling, and 10 years if it was any other kind of premises (for example, a factory). In addition there is an aggravated offence of burglary with a firearm, which is subject to life imprisonment (s 10 Theft Act 1968).

12.3.2 The two kinds of burglary

There are essentially two kinds of burglary. Both involve proof that the defendant entered a building or part of a building as a trespasser, but the requirements differ:

1. Section 9(1)(a) requires that the defendant entered with intent to commit one of the offences listed in s 9(2). There is no need for the defendant actually to commit any of the offences.
2. Section 9(1)(b) requires that the defendant actually committed theft or inflicted grievous bodily harm. The purpose of s 9(1)(b) is to cover the defendant who enters a building not intending to commit any offence but once inside the building decides to do so.

The elements of the offence are as follows:

▶ Entry
▶ A building
▶ As a trespasser
▶ Awareness of being a trespasser
▶ Intent to commit a crime (s 9(1)(a)) or commission of crime (s 9(1)(b))

These factors will now be considered separately.

12.3.3 Entry

The leading case on burglary is *Collins** [1973] QB 100. The accused climbed naked up a ladder to the bedroom window of a girl he knew slightly, intending to have sexual intercourse with her. It was the middle of the night and the girl was asleep in bed, but when she saw the accused at the window she jumped to the conclusion that he was her boyfriend and invited him into the room. They then had sexual intercourse. Collins was convicted of burglary with intent to rape, under s 9(1)(a). (Rape used to be one of the offences listed in s 9(2), but it was removed by the Sexual Offences Act 2003, to be replaced with a new offence discussed in Section 12.5 below, of trespassing with intent to commit a sexual offence.) His appeal was allowed on the basis of the uncertainty over whether he had entered as a trespasser: if the victim had invited him into the room before he had entered it then, according to the court, he would not have been a trespasser. If, however, he had entered the room before the invitation then he would have committed the offence.

The key issue in *Collins* was the meaning of the term 'entry'. Edmund Davies LJ said that the entry must be 'effective and substantial'. In *Brown* [1985] Crim LR 212, the Court of Appeal preferred to use just the word 'effective' and refused to interpret this to mean that the whole of the body must be in the building. It has recently been held that putting an arm and head through a window amounted to 'entry' (*Ryan* [1996] Crim LR 320). It might be thought that the use of the word 'effective' means that it is necessary to show that enough of the body was inserted into the building to enable the theft to be carried out. However in *Ryan* this interpretation was rejected. In *Ryan*, although the defendant had not put enough of himself into the building to enable him to steal, he was still found to have entered. So we are left with the conclusion that the entry must be effective, but it is not clear what effective means.

It is possible to use an innocent agent (for example, a young child) to burgle (*Wheelhouse* [1994] Crim LR 756), and presumably it could be burglary to insert an object though a window to remove an item.

12.3.4 Building or part of a building

The word 'building' is not defined, although inhabited vehicles and vessels are expressly included by subsection (3). 'Building' is to be given its ordinary meaning, but it requires a construction which has a degree of permanence. The word is not restricted to homes, but can include offices, factories and outbuildings (*B and S v Leathley* [1979] Crim LR 314). Vehicles do not count as buildings unless they are inhabited (for example, a houseboat). This is made clear in s 9(4).

Burglary can be committed where either a building or part of a building is entered by a trespasser. This is significant where buildings such as banks and shops are generally open to the public but have sections reserved to those with express permission to enter. Entering one of those private parts will be entry into part of a building as a trespasser, even where entry into the building itself is permitted. What amounts to a separate part of a building will be a question of fact for the jury. In *Walkington** [1979] 2 All ER 716, it was held that an area of a shop floor behind a three-sided counter was a separate part of the building, from which the public was excluded. It is the absence of any authority to enter which sets this 'part' of the building apart from the public area although, as Geoffrey Lane LJ accepted, the physical characteristics of the building were also relevant.

There needs to be some visible sign or marking which separates the part of the building not open to the public; for example, a 'no entry' sign would be sufficient.

12.3.5 As a trespasser

The concept of entry 'as a trespasser' has proved to be one of the most controversial aspects of burglary. Trespassing is a civil law concept, but is adopted as part of the criminal law definition of burglary. A trespasser is a person who lacks authority for his presence – he lacks either express or implied permission from the owner to enter. It is crucial to the offence that the accused must enter the building (or part of the building) as a trespasser. It is not enough to enter with permission but become a trespasser at some later stage (for example, on being asked to leave), unless he then enters a separate part of the building.

If the permission to enter is obtained by a misrepresentation then the permission may be seen as invalid, but it is unclear when this is so. It may be that mistakes as to identity negate the effectiveness of permission. The question was not properly addressed in *Collins*, but may depend on the court's interpretation of the facts – was the invitation issued to her boyfriend or the man standing on the window sill?

12.3.6 Awareness of being a trespasser

It was held in *Collins* that trespass contains within it a *mens rea* element. Edmund Davies LJ said:

> In the judgement of this court, there cannot be a conviction for entering premises 'as a trespasser' within the meaning of s.9 of the Theft Act 1968 unless the person entering does so knowing that he is a trespasser and nevertheless deliberately enters, or, at the very least, is reckless whether or not he is entering the premises of another without the other party's consent.

This statement appears to require that the defendant was aware that when entering the building he might be a trespasser. This does not mean it must be shown that the defendant was aware that he fell into the legal category of a trespasser, but rather that he knows the facts which render him a trespasser at law.

It is unfortunate that in a subsequent case the importance given to the *mens rea* of trespass in *Collins* has been expanded so much that the mental element threatens to take over the concept of trespass altogether. In *Smith and Jones** [1976] 3 All ER 54, two boys decided to steal two television sets from the house of the father of one of the boys. The Court of Appeal held that the very fact that they had entered the house with the intention of doing something which they knew they had no authority to do (stealing the television sets) made them trespassers. James LJ said that a person would be a trespasser for the purposes of s 9:

> if he enters the premises of another knowing that he is entering in excess of the permission that had been given to him, or being reckless as to whether he is entering in excess of the permission that has been given to him to enter, providing the facts are known to the accused which enable him to realise that he is acting in excess of the permission given or that he is acting recklessly as to whether he exceeds that permission.

It has been argued that this decision, although it purports to follow *Collins*, is in fact inconsistent with it. Applying the *Smith and Jones* doctrine, *Collins* would still have been a trespasser in spite of the invitation, because the accused's intent to rape was certainly 'in excess of the permission given', and he must have known this. If this was correct, there was no need for the court to spend so much time considering whether Collins had entered. Some argue that Collins might have thought the invitation indicated that the victim was consenting to sexual intercourse. This interpretation, although a possible reading of the facts, was not mentioned by the Court of Appeal, and so clearly it could not have seen this as important.

The possible conflict with *Collins* gives some support to those who dislike the implications of the decision in *Smith and Jones* and would like to see it overruled. Applied rigorously, the decision would mean that every person who enters a building with what Glanville Williams calls 'burglarious intent' (an intent to commit one of the offences listed in s 9(2)) automatically becomes a trespasser, and so guilty of burglary under s 9(1)(a). The would-be shoplifter who enters a shop with the intention of stealing therein becomes a trespasser and therefore a burglar. This would widen the scope of the offence enormously and unnecessarily. *Smith and Jones* is also not easily reconcilable with the subsequent decision in *Walkington*. There Geoffrey Lane LJ stressed the fact that the accused had entered a separate part of the shop which the public had no general permission to enter, and it was that which rendered him a trespasser. However, his Lordship need not have stressed this if the accused's intention to steal had made him a trespasser when entering the shop, as *Smith and Jones* seems to imply. Further case law clarifying the ambit of *Smith and Jones* is badly needed.

12.3.7　The intent to commit a crime: s 9(1)(a)

For a conviction under s 9(1)(a) it must be shown that, on entering the building, the defendant intended to commit one of a number of offences specified in s 9(2). The most common form of burglary under s 9(1)(a) involves an intent to steal. The offence is complete as soon as the accused entered the building; it is irrelevant that he had not been able to do anything to further his intent, and it is also irrelevant that the property he would have liked to steal was not in the building (*Walkington*).

For a time, the problem of conditional intent bedevilled burglary under s 9(1)(a) as well as theft (see Section 11.7.2). There were several acquittals of alleged burglars who could not be said to intend to steal a specific piece of property, because they intended to steal anything they might find in the building that was worth stealing. The Court of Appeal has ruled that if the indictment alleged an intent to steal specific items an intent to steal those items would need to be proved. However, there was no objection to drafting the indictment more widely without stating specific items (for example, 'entering as a trespasser with intent to steal'). In such a case, so-called conditional intent is no bar to a conviction for burglary (*A-G's Ref (Nos 1 and 2 of 1979)** [1979] 2 All ER 143).

12.3.8　The commission of a crime: s 9(1)(b)

For the commission of an offence under s 9(1)(b) it must be shown that the defendant entered a building as a trespasser. These requirements are as discussed above. Unlike s 9(1)(a), where the burglary is complete as soon as the accused has entered the building with the necessary *mens rea*, under s 9(1)(b) a further element of *actus reus* is required. The accused must either steal or attempt to steal something in the building, or inflict or attempt to inflict grievous bodily harm on any person in the building.

The infliction of grievous harm in s 9(1)(b) does not in itself refer to a specific offence under s 18 or s 20 Offences Against the Person Act 1861. But it is very likely that grievous bodily harm would be interpreted in line with ss 18 and 20 to mean serious bodily harm. It has been held (*Jenkins** [1984] AC 242) that 'inflict' does not necessarily imply assault, although in practice an assault will usually be involved. It is not clear what, if any, further *mens rea* is required, but it is likely that recklessness as to inflicting grievous bodily harm would be needed. It seems a little odd that a defendant who enters a building without an intent to commit a crime but then commits criminal damage is not guilty of burglary, although the defendant will still be guilty of plain criminal damage.

The difference between the *actus reus* of s 9(1)(a) and that of s 9(1)(b) has an important consequence for the timing of the *mens rea*. Since the offence under s 9(1)(a) is complete on entry into the building, the *mens rea*, both the knowledge that the accused is a trespasser and the further intent, must exist at the time of entry. In the case of s 9(1)(b), although the accused must actually be a trespasser on entry, it will normally be sufficient if the accused realises that he is a trespasser by the time the further offence (the theft or infliction of grievous bodily harm) is committed. However, if the accused is a trespasser only by virtue of the *Smith and Jones* doctrine, he must have *mens rea* from the moment of entry into the building or part of the building, since it is this *mens rea* that makes him a trespasser and without it he will not have 'entered as a trespasser'.

12.4 Aggravated burglary

Aggravated burglary is a more serious form of burglary (burglary under s 9(1)(a) or s 9(a)(b)). Under s 10 Theft Act 1968, aggravated burglary is punishable with life imprisonment if, at the time of the burglary, the accused has with him a firearm, imitation firearm, or weapon of offence or explosive. It is worth noting that 'weapon of offence' is defined in s 10(1)(b) as 'any article made or adapted for use for causing injury to or incapacitating a person or *intended by the person having it with him for such use*' (emphasis added). An 'innocent' object such as a screwdriver could therefore be regarded as a weapon of offence, depending on the intent of the accused. In *Kelly* (1992) 97 Cr App R 245, the accused had a screwdriver and used it to open a window and later to poke the victim. He was found guilty of an offence under s 10(1)(b). There is no need to show that the defendant intended to use the innocent item in a particular burglary as long as he had it with him as a weapon to use against someone at some time (*Stones* [1989] 1 WLR 156). It is also sufficient if the accused intended to use the weapon should the need arise (*Kelly*).

The difference between the *actus reus* of s 9(1)(a) and that of s 9(1)(b) is important for aggravated burglary, as it affects the time at which the firearm or weapon must be in the possession of the accused: in the case of s 9(1)(a) it will be the time of the entry; whereas for s 9(1)(b) it will be the time at which the further offence is committed. Thus in *O'Leary* (1986) 82 Cr App R 341, the accused entered a house and found a knife in the kitchen. He later used it to threaten the occupant during a theft. As he used the knife in the course of a stealing this was sufficient, even though he did not have the knife at the point of entry to the building. Had he never actually used it during the burglary he would not have committed aggravated burglary. In *Francis* [1982] Crim LR 363, a conviction under s 10 was quashed on these grounds; the prosecution, having alleged a s 9(1)(b) type of burglary, had not proved that the accused had the weapons of offence (sticks) with them when they stole (they had discarded them at the door of the house).

12.5 Trespassing with intent to commit a sexual offence

Under s 63 Sexual Offences Act 2003 if a person is a trespasser in any structure, part of a structure, or any land and intends to commit a sexual offence or does commit any sexual offence he commits an offence. This is similar to burglary, but is not limited to buildings, and includes any land. It would therefore include a man who has trespassed onto a school playing field, intending to rape or commit some other sexual offence.

12.6 Handling stolen goods

The offence of handling stolen goods is concerned with those who help thieves dispose of stolen property. The offence is justified on the basis that 'there would not be so many thieves if there were no receivers' (*Battams* (1979) 1 Cr App R (S) 15). It is because people are willing to buy stolen goods that theft and burglary are so prevalent. Section 22(1) Theft Act 1968 provides:

> A person handles stolen goods if (otherwise than in the course of the stealing) knowing or believing them to be stolen goods he dishonestly receives the goods, or dishonestly undertakes or assists in their retention, removal, disposal or realisation by or for the benefit of another person, or if he arranges to do so.

Handling stolen goods is subject to a maximum sentence of 14 years. It is therefore seen as at least potentially more serious than theft. This is understandable when one considers that some handlers operate on a very large scale, sometimes 'commissioning' thieves to work for them.

The following elements make up the offence:

12.6.1 Goods

'Goods' is widely defined in s 34(2)(b) Theft Act 1968. The term excludes land but includes money and every other description of property (including things severed from land, such as timber or minerals). In *A-G's Ref (No. 4 of 1979)* it was stated that things in action could be included in this definition of goods for the purposes of this offence.

12.6.2 Stolen

The goods at the time of the handling must be 'stolen', although this is given a wide definition in the Act. There are three situations in which the goods will be considered 'stolen':

1. *Goods which have actually been stolen.* The difficulty for the prosecution is often in proving beyond reasonable doubt that the goods have been stolen. The prosecution can prove this in several ways. The most obvious is to show that someone else has already been convicted of stealing the goods (s 74 Police and Criminal Evidence Act 1984; it is not usually possible for the thief to be a handler, as we will see). Failing a previous conviction, the prosecution could rely on circumstantial evidence that the goods handled by the accused were in fact stolen. It is important not to allege that the goods must have been stolen just because the handler thought that they were (*Overington* [1978] Crim LR 692). There needs to be evidence independent of the accused's own beliefs, such as the circumstances in which the accused came by the goods, their price, or evidence of goods of the same description having been

reported stolen (*McDonald* (1980) 70 Cr App R 288). The definition of stolen goods also includes goods stolen outside England provided that the stealing either was an offence under the Theft Act 1968 or amounted to an offence where, and at the time, the goods were stolen.

2. *Goods obtained by robbery, burglary and fraud, and goods obtained by blackmail.* (s 21 Theft Act 1968)

3. *The proceeds of the goods falling into 1 or 2.* This means that if the thief sells the stolen goods (for example, a car) the money he receives in exchange for the car will also be considered stolen. If the thief passes the money on to another person that person could be convicted of handling the 'stolen' money. In order for proceeds to become stolen goods under s 24(2) two conditions must be fulfilled:

   (a) First, the proceeds must be in the hands of either the thief or a handler. This means that proceeds which have been through innocent hands cannot be stolen goods. For example, if Ronnie steals a Rolls-Royce and sells it to Andrew for £2,000 but tells Andrew to pay the money to his grandmother then, if the grandmother knows nothing about the stealing of the Rolls-Royce, the money is not stolen in her hands. Even if the grandmother later gives the money to her friend, Charles, who knows all about the source of the money, it is still not stolen property in Charles' hands. This is because the money has passed from an innocent person's hands and therefore cannot be stolen property.

   (b) The second requirement is that the proceeds must represent directly or indirectly the original stolen goods. So if Ronnie sells the stolen Rolls-Royce for £2,000, uses the £2,000 to buy shares and later sells the shares and buys a Rover car, then the Rover will be stolen goods, as one could trace the Rover back to the stolen Rolls-Royce through the shares. The result of these rules could be that from one stolen item there might be several pieces of property that were 'stolen' for the purposes of the statute. For example, if Ronnie sells the stolen Rolls-Royce to Andrew for £2,000, who sells it to Imogen for £2,400, all of them aware of the origin of the car, then the £2,000 in Ronnie's hands, the £2,400 in Andrew's hands and the Rolls-Royce in Imogen's hands are all deemed 'stolen property'. (See *A-G's Ref (No 4 of 1979)* for the even more complex position where money is paid into a bank account.)

A separate difficulty concerns the possibility of stolen goods ceasing to be 'stolen' for the purposes of s 22. This is covered by s 24(3), which provides that goods will no longer be regarded as stolen once they have reached either (i) the original owner, (ii) an innocent person or (iii) lawful custody (for example, the police). This last category can be difficult to define, especially if the police discover some stolen property but while they are making inquiries someone takes the property away. Whether goods are in the custody of the police often depends on the intentions of the police officers involved (*A-G's Ref (No 1 of 1974)** [1974] 2 All ER 899). It will not always be easy to draw the line between an investigation of the goods and a decision by the police to take charge of the goods.

Goods will also cease to be stolen under s 24(3) where the person from whom they were stolen loses any right to restitution of them. This is a matter of civil law and rarely arises. It is most likely to occur when the goods were originally obtained by fraud, and the owner on discovering the fraud nevertheless decides to ratify the disposal of the goods.

12.6.3 The different ways of handling stolen goods

The definition of handling stolen goods in s 22 specifies 18 different ways of handling. It is easiest to list these:

1. receiving stolen goods;
2. undertaking the retention of stolen goods for the benefit of another;
3. undertaking the removal of stolen goods for the benefit of another;
4. undertaking the disposal of stolen goods for the benefit of another;
5. undertaking the realisation of stolen goods for the benefit of another;
6. assisting in the retention of stolen goods by another;
7. assisting in the removal of stolen goods by another;
8. assisting in the disposal of stolen goods by another;
9. assisting in the realisation of stolen goods by another;
10–18 arranging to do any one of the above.

When the indictment is drafted, the prosecution is not expected to specify in exactly which of the 18 ways the accused is alleged to have handled the goods. The crucial requirement is that the accused knows in enough detail the case he has to meet in order to prepare his defence. The large number of ways in which it is possible to commit the offence indicates that the section is casting a wide net to make it as difficult and profitless as possible to dispose of stolen property (*Tokeley-Parry* [1999] Crim LR 578). In the important case of *Bloxham** [1982] 1 AC 109, Lord Bridge said that s 22 creates in essence two offences: one of receiving (or arranging to receive) and the other covering all the other forms of handling. All offences except receiving need to be carried out 'by or for the benefit of another person'. Most of the forms of handling are self-explanatory – retaining, removing, disposing, realising, undertaking and assisting. These words are to be given their normal meaning. However, something needs to be said here about the terms 'receiving', 'assisting' and 'by or for the benefit of another'.

1. *'Receiving'*. 'Receiving' takes place when the goods are taken into the possession or control of the accused. This means that the accused must be aware that she has possession or control of the items (*Hobson v Impett* (1957) 41 Cr App R 138). No offence will be committed if at the time of receiving the accused lacks *mens rea* for handling (defined below) at the moment of receipt. A subsequent discovery that the goods are stolen will not turn the receiver into a handler. Likewise the goods must be stolen at the time of receipt, and it is worth noting that this applies also to arranging to receive stolen goods: the goods must already be stolen at the time the arrangement is made. If they are not yet stolen, the 'arrangement' will amount to a conspiracy to handle stolen goods, but not the complete offence of handling.

2. *'Assisting'*. 'Assisting' has been held to involve an element of help or encouragement. It was not enough in *Sanders* for the accused merely to use the stolen property left in his father's garage. The use did not help or encourage the person retaining the goods. Also, in *Brown* [1970] 1 QB 105, it was held that a failure to inform the police of the presence of stolen goods in the accused's flat did not by itself amount to assisting in the retention of the goods. However, there was evidence that the accused had 'provided accommodation' for the goods, and this was sufficient to be assistance. If the police ask an accused about the presence of stolen goods and the accused tells lies about the existence of the goods then she may be guilty of assisting in the

retention of stolen goods. But she will not have committed an offence by keeping silent or refusing to answer questions (*Kanwar*).

3. *'By or for the benefit of another'*. If the defendant is not alleged to have received the property and one of the other forms of handling is relied upon, it must be shown that the defendant acted for the benefit of another. In *Bloxham*, it was held by the House of Lords that selling goods did not amount to a disposal 'for the benefit of' the buyer. The accused had bought a stolen car without realising that it was stolen. On becoming certain that it was stolen he sold the car to an innocent third party. He was charged with handling the car by undertaking its disposal or sale for the benefit of another person (the innocent third party). Lord Bridge supported the common-sense view that a sale is undertaken by the seller primarily for his own benefit. People rarely sell property for altruistic reasons. A sale could be regarded as for the benefit of another only if it was carried out on behalf of someone else. This might arise where a defendant was acting as the agent of someone who had stolen the property. This means that a *'bona fide* purchaser' such as Bloxham cannot be charged with either receiving or handling by disposal. He cannot be charged with theft either, as a result of s 3(2) Theft Act 1968 (Section 11.3). However, as Lord Bridge pointed out, if the bona fide purchaser sells the stolen goods once he discovers that they are stolen, as Bloxham did, he will almost certainly be guilty of an offence: either fraud (if he does not inform his purchaser that the goods were stolen) or being an accessory to the receiving offence committed by his purchaser (if he does enlighten him).

It is not clear from Lord Bridge's judgment whether or not the *Bloxham* principle applies only to those who sell the goods on to another. Could it be said that a person who gives away stolen goods does so for the benefit of the recipient? It is arguable, although it does not seem right, to distinguish between the person who gives away the goods and the person who asks a very low price.

12.6.4 Dishonesty

There are two *mens rea* elements in handling stolen goods: the act of handling itself must be dishonest; and the accused must, at the time of that act, know or believe that the goods are stolen. There has been little discussion of the meaning of dishonesty in s 22, largely because it will be unusual for a person to know or believe the goods to be stolen and yet not be dishonest. In fact, in *Roberts* (1987) 84 Cr App R 117 it was held that a person who receives stolen goods knowing that they are stolen and then sells them must be dishonest. The requirement of dishonesty seems to add little, although lack of dishonesty may provide a defence to a person who knowingly receives stolen goods, intending to return them to the owner or to lawful custody such as the police. It is clear from *Roberts* that the *Ghosh* test for dishonesty applies to s 22, although it was held that the full *Ghosh* direction (see Section 11.6.3) need not be given unless the issue of dishonesty is raised on the facts or by the accused.

12.6.5 Knowledge or belief that the goods are stolen

The requirement of knowing or believing the goods to be stolen has given rise to a large number of cases going to appeal. The law is still not completely certain, partly because the courts have been content to leave the definition of knowledge and belief to the 'common sense of the jury' (Waller LJ in *Reader* (1977) 66 Cr App R 33). Guidelines have been largely restricted to a series of statements of what knowledge and belief are not. The best that can be said is that knowledge and belief should be given their normal meanings (*Forsyth*). Certain points are clear, however:

1. The knowledge or belief of the accused is tested subjectively (*Atwal v Massey* [1971] 3 All ER 881). It is a question of the accused's actual state of mind, not what he or she ought to have known, or what a reasonable person would have believed in the circumstances.
2. While belief must fall short of knowledge (otherwise there would be no point in the statute using both words), belief is not the same thing as suspicion. Nor is 'turning a blind eye' equivalent to a belief that the goods are stolen (see, for example, *Bellenie* [1980] Crim LR 437 and *Moys* (1984) 79 Cr App R 73). Something approaching more useful guidance has now been given by the Court of Appeal in *Hall** (1985) 81 Cr App R 260. Lord Lane CJ held that a person would 'know' goods were stolen when told that they were by a person with first-hand knowledge, such as the thief. Belief, on the other hand, could be said to be the state of mind of a person who says to himself, 'I cannot say I know for certain that those goods are stolen, but there can be no other reasonable conclusion in the light of all the circumstances of all that I have heard and seen'. This supports Glanville Williams's view that belief amounts to being 'virtually certain', adding very little to actual knowledge.
3. The jury are entitled to infer knowledge or belief from the fact that the accused was in possession of goods which had recently been stolen. This is the so-called doctrine of recent possession, but it is important to realise that it is only one factor which the jury may take into account; it is in no sense a conclusive proof of *mens rea*, which must be based on the actual state of mind of the accused.

12.6.6 Handling and theft

Is it possible to steal property which has already been stolen? Property which has been stolen can be stolen again, though not by the original thief (see s 3(1) Theft Act 1968; and Section 11.3). The statute states that the handling must be otherwise than in the course of the stealing, and this has been held to mean the original theft (*Sainthouse* [1980] Crim LR 506 and *Devall* [1984] Crim LR 428). Many acts of handling, such as receiving, will also amount to an appropriation of property belonging to another, and so a new theft. There is nothing to prevent two counts, alleging theft and handling respectively, on the indictment, although the Court of Appeal has said that a jury should be directed not to convict for both theft and handling (*Shelton** (1986) 83 Cr App R 379).

Not all acts of handling will be theft: some types of handling (such as arranging to receive) may not amount to an appropriation. If the goods are 'stolen' by virtue of having been obtained by fraud, or because they are proceeds, ownership of the goods may be transferred to the handler. This does not affect liability for handling, but it does mean that the goods no longer belong to another, a requirement for theft. In both these cases, an element of the *actus reus* of theft is missing. However, it will be very unusual for a person to possess the *mens rea* of handling but lack the *mens rea* of theft.

The original theft will not be an act of receiving because of the requirement in s 22 that the handling must be 'otherwise than in the course of the stealing'. While 'the stealing' is still occurring, no handling can take place. Only once the theft is completed can the goods become stolen, and then the subject of a handling charge. Following the wide interpretation of appropriation in *Gomez* [1993] AC 442 (see Section 11.3) and the fact that a piece of property once stolen by a defendant does not continue to be stolen every time it is appropriated (see *Atakpu* [1994] QB 58, and Section 11.3) mean that handling can take place very shortly after the thief first touched or dealt with the property (*Pitham and Hehl** (1976) 65 Cr App R 45). To summarise, this rule, that the handling must be otherwise than in the course of the stealing, means that the thief cannot be guilty of handling unless an act of handling is committed once the stealing is over.

Hot Topic – The wrongs of burglary

Here we will discuss why burglary is a specific offence. Although burglary is a well-established criminal offence, its justification is not straightforward. There are two separate issues, depending on the kind of burglary involved: first, s 9(1)(a): entering a building as a trespasser with intent to commit one of the listed criminal offences. Here the question is why is an intention to commit theft suddenly a serious offence if it is held while entering a building as a trespasser? We do not normally punish intentions to commit crimes unless the defendant has gone so far as to commit an attempt (see Chapter 18). Why not just rely on the civil law on trespass and the law on attempts to deal with the situation? It is notable that entering a building intending to commit theft (that is, burglary) carries a higher maximum sentence than actual theft. This is surprising when it is remembered that simply entering a building as a trespasser is not a criminal offence and that in this form of burglary no theft need have actually taken place.

Second, s 9(1)(b): committing one of the listed offences while being a trespasser in a building. Here the question is why is burglary not treated simply as a form of theft or inflicting grievous bodily harm? We do not have special offences of shoplifting or pickpocketing. These offences are simply regarded as forms of theft. So why single out burglary as a particular kind of theft? This issue is part of a much wider debate about how precisely we should define criminal offences (see Section 1.4).

Some commentators such as Simester and Sullivan seek to justify both these offences with an overarching explanation. They can be conceived of as an invasion of a person's private and family life. To many people what makes a home is not so much the building and the possessions in it, but the sense of security and peace that is offered there. It is this sense of security and peace that to many

is extremely important. Therefore an uninvited person entering a home and committing a crime or intending to commit a crime destroys the one place where people find security and peace. Simester and Sullivan explain:

> It is hardly surprising that house burglary, in particular, causes victims great distress even if they were absent at the material time. The victim of such a burglary is unable to live assured of her safety even in her own home. Most people, when their safety cannot be taken for granted, are no longer free. One of the foundations of autonomous life is destroyed.

Such an explanation is convincing, but not unproblematic. First, it presents a rather 'home-made apple pie' image of a home. Victims of domestic violence and parents caring for constantly screaming babies or rebellious teenagers may not recognise the description of a home as a haven of peace, but rather see home as a prison. Indeed there is strong evidence that women are more likely to face violence in the home than outside it. Nevertheless, that image of home is one shared by many, as an ideal if not in reality. Second, it does not explain why invasions of office buildings and garden sheds are regarded as burglaries. It is, however, noticeable that in sentencing burglaries of homes are not treated as more serious than burglaries of commercial premises.

Another explanation for the existence of the offence of burglary is that it is more likely to lead to violence. A person who finds a burglar in his home may well resort to violence (see the controversial case of *Tony Martin*), and is more likely to do so than in a case of pickpocketing for example. In particular, in burglary the victim has nowhere safe to run to, to escape from any feared attacker. This argument would then be that this is a form of conduct which is particularly likely to lead to serious violence, and for that reason should be prohibited.

Summary

12.1 Robbery is theft accompanied by the use or threat of force. The force must occur at the time of, or immediately before, the theft, and for the purpose of stealing.

12.2 Assault with intent to rob is also an offence. There must be an assault or battery made with the intent to commit robbery.

12.3 There are two main types of burglary. Both require entry into a building as a trespasser. A person who enters without authority is a trespasser. It has been held that a person is a trespasser if he enters a building for a purpose which is outside the scope of the permission given, expressly or impliedly, by the owner. The accused must know or be reckless that he is a trespasser. One type of burglary requires that the accused entered the building with the intention of committing a further offence, such as stealing something in the building. The offence was complete as soon as the building was entered with the necessary intent. Burglary may also be committed by stealing or inflicting grievous bodily harm once inside the building. In this case the offence is not complete until the further act has been committed.

12.4 It is aggravated burglary to commit burglary with a firearm, explosive or weapon of offence.

12.5 It is an offence to trespass with intent to commit a sexual offence.

12.6 Handling stolen goods requires that the goods be stolen at the time of the act of handling. 'Stolen' means appropriated by theft or obtained by fraud or blackmail. Goods are also 'stolen' if they are the proceeds of stolen goods and have represented the stolen goods in the hands of the thief or a handler. Goods may cease to be stolen if they are returned to their owner or other lawful custody. There are two main ways of handling stolen goods: handling by receiving; and handling by retaining, removing, disposing or realising the goods. The second form of handling must be done to assist, or for the benefit of, another. A sale of stolen goods is not undertaken for the benefit of the buyer. An act of handling cannot be committed at the same time as the original theft, but may amount to a separate theft in respect of the same goods. All forms of handling require dishonesty, and the fact that the handler knew or believed the goods to be stolen. Belief is not the same as suspicion; it amounts to being virtually certain that the goods are stolen. If the accused has a recent conviction for theft or handling, this can be used to prove knowledge or belief that the goods were stolen.

Further Reading

Ashworth discusses robbery and Mawby and Pace burglary, while the other articles consider aspects of the law on handling stolen property.

Ashworth, 'Robbery Reassessed' [2002] Crim LR 851.

Mawby, *Burglary* (Willan 2001).

Pace, 'Burglarious Trespass' [1985] Crim LR 716.

Shute, 'Knowledge and Belief in the Criminal Law', in Shute and Simester (eds), *Criminal Law Theory* (Oxford University Press 2002).

Spencer, 'Handling and Taking Risks – A Reply to Professor Williams' [1985] Crim LR 440.

Spencer, 'Handling, Theft and the Mala Fide Purchaser' [1985] Crim LR 92.

Sullivan, 'Knowledge, Belief and Culpability', in Shute and Simester (eds), *Criminal Law Theory* (Oxford University Press 2002).

Williams, 'Handling, Theft and the Purchaser Who Takes a Chance' [1985] Crim LR 432.

Case Notes

▶ *A-G's Ref (No 1 of 1974)* [1974] 2 All ER 899. Court of Appeal

The accused was acquitted of handling stolen goods at the direction of the trial judge. A police officer had found an unlocked car containing clothing which he suspected was stolen. He immobilised the car and waited until the accused returned and tried to start the engine. He then questioned the accused and arrested him, as he was not satisfied with his explanation. At the trial the judge accepted the defence submission that the clothing was no longer stolen at the time of the act of handling, since it had been taken into lawful custody by the officer. The Court of Appeal was asked for its opinion on whether goods are restored to lawful custody when a police officer suspects them to be stolen and keeps them under observation with a view to tracing the thief or handler. The court held that goods would cease to be stolen once they had been taken into the possession of a police officer acting in the execution of his duty. If the officer was merely watching the goods, and was of an open mind as to whether he would take them into possession, they would remain stolen. This would depend primarily on the intention of the officer. The issue should therefore be left to the jury to determine.

▶ *Attorney-General's References (Nos 1 and 2 of 1979)* [1979] 2 All ER 143. Court of Appeal

See Chapter 11 Case notes.

▶ *Bloxham* [1983] 1 AC 109. House of Lords

The appellant was convicted of handling stolen goods. He had bought a car from an unidentified third party without realising that it was stolen. When the seller disappeared without producing the registration papers, the appellant realised that the car was stolen; he then sold it to another person who was prepared to buy it without registration documents. The appellant argued at the trial, and on appeal, that his disposal of the car had been for his own benefit, and not for the benefit of 'another person' as required by s 22(1) Theft Act 1968. The House of Lords agreed with this argument and allowed the appeal. Lord Bridge held that a purchaser

of stolen goods was not 'another person' for whose benefit the seller acted.

▶ *Collins* [1973] QB 100. Court of Appeal

The appellant was convicted of burglary contrary to s 9(1)(a) Theft Act 1968. It was alleged that he had entered, as a trespasser and with intent to rape, the bedroom of a girl whom he knew slightly. His appeal was allowed on the basis that it was unclear whether or not he was in fact a trespasser when he entered the room. There was evidence that the girl, mistaking him for her boyfriend, had invited him into the room before he entered it. It was also held that being a trespasser requires an element of knowledge, or at least recklessness, on the part of the accused as to whether or not he is entering the building without permission.

▶ *Ghosh* [1982] QB 1053. Court of Appeal

See Chapter 11 Case notes.

▶ *Hale* (1978) 68 Cr App Rep 415. Court of Appeal

The appellant and another were convicted of robbery, contrary to s8 Theft Act 1968. They had entered the victim's house and the appellant had taken a jewellery box while his companion tied the victim up. It was argued on appeal that the force was used on the victim after the theft was complete, and was not therefore immediately before or at the time of the theft, as required by s 8. The appeal was dismissed on the ground that an appropriation might continue over a period of time. It was for the jury to decide whether the appropriation had ceased.

▶ *Hall* (1985) 81 Cr App Rep 260. Court of Appeal

The appellant was convicted of handling stolen goods. He was an antique dealer and had been found with the goods, in company with two other men who later pleaded guilty to burglary. He claimed that he had not been told by the other two men that the goods were stolen, but had become very wary and refused to purchase them. He appealed against conviction on the ground that the trial judge had not sufficiently emphasised the distinction between belief and suspicion. His appeal was dismissed on the ground that the trial judge had not misled the jury by confusing belief and suspicion. The court held that 'belief' fell short of knowledge – it was the state of mind of a person who was not certain that goods were stolen, but who felt that there was no other reasonable conclusion in all the circumstances. However, mere suspicion was not enough to amount to 'knowledge or belief'.

▶ *Jenkins* [1984] AC 242. Court of Appeal

The appellant and others were charged with burglary, contrary to s 9(1)(b) Theft Act 1968 (entry of a building as trespassers and inflicting grievous bodily harm on a person in the building). The jury, after a direction from the trial judge, acquitted the appellants of burglary but convicted them of assault occasioning actual bodily harm. They appealed against conviction and the appeals were allowed on the basis that 'inflict grievous bodily harm' in s 9 Theft Act 1968 had the same meaning as in s 20 Offences Against the Person Act 1861.

▶ *Pitham and Hehl* (1976) 65 Cr App Rep 45. Court of Appeal

The two appellants were convicted of handling stolen goods. They had agreed to buy some furniture from a third man. The appellants were aware that the third man was not the true owner of the goods (who was in prison). They went to the victim's house in a furniture van. They appealed against conviction on the ground that their alleged act of handling had been committed 'in the course of stealing'. The appeals were dismissed. It was held that the third man had stolen the furniture by offering to sell it to the appellants. and this was an assumption of the rights of the owner. The appropriation was then complete. Any later dealing by the

appellants was therefore not 'in the course of stealing'.

▶ *Shelton* (1986) 83 Cr App Rep 379. Court of Appeal

The appellant was convicted of theft and obtaining by deception. He had obtained money on cheques taken from a chequebook which had been stolen that day. He had also been charged with handling, and had submitted at the trial that he should be acquitted of both theft and handling if the jury were not sure which offence he had committed. The trial judge directed an acquittal on the handling charge and left the theft charge to the jury. The appeal was dismissed. The Court held that it was proper to charge with both theft and handling in the alternative, but the jury should be told that the accused could not be convicted of being both a thief and a handler in respect of the same transaction. A conviction for theft may be based on the original appropriation from the victim, or on a later appropriation by the accused from someone else, if the indictment is sufficiently widely drafted.

▶ *Smith and Jones* [1976] 3 All ER 54. Court of Appeal

The appellants were convicted of burglary contrary to s 9(1)(b). They had entered the house of Smith's father and taken two television sets. They appealed against conviction on the basis that Smith had general permission to enter his father's house, and could not therefore be a trespasser. The appeals were dismissed. The court held that it was trespass to enter a building for a purpose that was outside the permission given if the accused realised or was reckless as to whether he was entering outside that permission.

▶ *Walkington* [1979] 2 All ER 716. Court of Appeal

The appellant was convicted of burglary, contrary to s 9 (1)(a) Theft Act 1968. He had gone behind a three-sided counter in a department store and attempted to steal money from the till, which was open but empty. At the trial, the accused submitted that there had been no trespass, but the trial judge ruled that if the jury were satisfied that the area behind the counters was prohibited to customers, and that the accused realised this, then this was a trespass. The appeal was dismissed. The court held that the question of trespass was rightly left to the jury; it was a question of fact whether the public was excluded from the area behind the counters. It was also held that the fact that the till might be, and was, empty did not affect the appellant's intention to steal money from it if he could.

Chapter 13

Fraud

Key Terms

▶ **Deception** – an untruthful representation.
▶ **Representation** – a communication by words or deeds

13.1 The fraud and deception offences

Why has the law treated offences where a defendant has acquired another's property by deception or other fraud differently from cases where the defendant has taken the victim's property? Could not theft and the fraud offences all be treated as examples of wrongful interference with a person's property interests? It is submitted that there is a strong case for regarding deception offences as different from theft and the taking of property. First, a fraud involves not only the interference with the defendant's property but also a manipulation of the victim. By the fraud, the defendant has persuaded the victim to hand over his property or perform a service. In a way, the defendant has treated the victim as a puppet, and has certainly infringed his autonomy. A victim's autonomy is not infringed in the same way if theft is committed. Second, the ownership of property and the free transfer of property by buying, selling, giving and receiving are important aspects of our society. In acquiring property or services by a fraud, the defendant is undermining this crucial aspect of our society. The fraud offences are therefore there to protect society, as well as to highlight the special harm that the victim has suffered as a result of the deception.

The law on fraud offences is now found in the Fraud Act 2006. We shall focus on the offences created by that legislation. Under the Fraud Act there are three ways of committing fraud:

▶ Fraud by false representation
▶ Fraud by failing to disclose information
▶ Fraud by abuse of position.

There is no need for the prosecution to prove which of the three means was used, as long as the jury are convinced that at least one of them was used. However, of these three it is fraud by false representation which is the most common, and so we will address it first.

13.2 Fraud by false representation

Section 2(1) Fraud Act 2006 states:

A person is in breach of this section if he:

(a) dishonestly makes a false representation, and
(b) intends, by making the representation –
    (i) to make a gain for himself or another, or
    (ii) to cause loss to another or to expose another to a risk of loss.

The offence can be broken down into the following elements:

13.2.1 A false representation

A representation can be made by words, writing or conduct. An example of a representation of fraud by conduct is *Barnard* (1837) 7 C&P 784. A man came dressed in a university cap and gown and was granted credit facilities. It was held that by wearing this garb he was representing that he was a member of Oxford University. The representation by conduct need not involve a disguise. If a person went to a wedding reception to which he had not been invited and ate the food, the very act of walking into the room where the reception was taking place and eating the food might be taken as representing that he was an invited guest. In *Ray* [1974] AC 370, the House of Lords held that the accused, who remained seated in a restaurant after having finished a meal, thereby represented that he was an honest customer who intended to pay for his meal before leaving. The accused had apparently intended to pay at the outset, but had changed his mind; the continuing representation became a deliberate deception. This case indicates that the courts can be quite creative in deciding whether there is a deception by conduct.

Section 2(3) Fraud Act 2006 states that a representation will be false if it is 'untrue or misleading'. So, if the defendant makes a statement which is literally true, but implies a statement which is untrue, then this may amount to a false representation. An example of an implied deception is *Williams** [1980] Crim LR 589, where it was said that the presentation of obsolete Yugoslav banknotes at a bureau de change involved an implied representation that the notes were valid currency. The deception may be implied from the surrounding circumstances as well as the conduct of the accused. The jury should ask themselves how a reasonable person in the victim's shoes would have understood the defendant's statements.

Another important example of an implied deception is where a person provides a cheque as payment, aware that the cheque will be 'bounced' by the bank. Here by presenting a cheque a person is taken to imply that they believe the cheque will be honoured (*MPC v Charles** [1977] AC 177). If that implied statement is false they could be guilty of fraud. Similarly presenting a credit card as payment impliedly represents that one is authorised to use it (*Lambie** [1982] AC 449).

Section 2(3) makes it clear that the representation can be as to fact, law or a person's state of mind. A statement of opinion can be deceptive if what is said is not truly the speaker's opinion. In *King v DPP*, the car dealer stated that the odometer reading 'may not be correct'. This implied that he was not sure whether it was correct. In fact he knew it was incorrect, and so the statement of opinion amounted to a misrepresentation. A similar point can be made about representations concerning intentions. But it should be stressed that the fact that the speaker changes her mind and so does not carry out her intention does not make the original statement of intent itself untrue.

Section 2(5) makes it clear that the offence applies to frauds carried out on machines or computers. So a person who by fraud gets money out of a cash machine, or a chocolate bar from a chocolate bar machine, will have committed the offence. Further using fraud to get a computer to transfer money into your bank account would fall within the offence.

13.2.2 The false representation must be made by the defendant

This requirement means that this version of fraud will not be established where the defendant knows that the victim is labouring under a misapprehension caused by someone else. So if Luke was aware that Rex had told Jennifer that Luke's car was in good working order and took advantage of that and sold Jennifer his car, there would be no fraud by false representation (although there may be fraud by failure to disclose).

13.2.3 The defendant must know that the statement is or may be untrue or misleading

This requirement is found in s 2(2)(b). This means that if the defendant genuinely believes that what he or she is saying is true there is no fraud. However, if he or she knows that what they are saying may be untrue, then the offence is established.

13.2.4 The statement is made with the intention to make a gain or a loss

It is very important to note that this offence does not require proof that the defendant in fact made a gain or caused a loss. It is enough if that was the defendant's intention. So if a man stopped people in the street, saying untruthfully 'I have lost my wallet, please give me some money', he could be convicted of fraud even though no one had in fact given him money. It would be enough that he intended to make a gain from his statements. Similarly an e-mail sent asking people to send money to an account could amount to the offence even if everyone who received the e-mail just deleted it. This offence is, therefore, really about lying with an intent to make an economic gain, rather than obtaining property.

This requirement also means that if a person makes a false statement with no intention to gain by the statement he or she will have a defence. If, therefore, a stallholder in a market shouts out, 'These are the best cucumbers in the world', he or she could have a defence if they persuade the jury they did not think anyone would actually hand over money on the basis of such a palpably false statement.

The terms 'gain' and 'loss' in the section refer to a financial gain or loss. So using a false representation to persuade someone to have sex is not included. Nor is a statement which is just designed to cause distress.

13.2.5 The defendant is dishonest

The Fraud Act 2006 does not define dishonesty, so presumably the *Ghosh** ([1982] QB 1053) test (see Section 11.6) will be used. Note that the provisions dealing with dishonesty in s 2 Theft Act 1968 do not apply to the fraud offences.

13.3 Fraud by failing to disclose information

Section 3 Fraud Act 2006 states:

A person is in breach of this section if he –

(a) dishonestly fails to disclose to another person information which he is under a legal duty to disclose, and
(b) intends, by failing to disclose the information –
  (i) to make a gain for himself or another, or
  (ii) to cause loss to another or to expose another to a risk of loss

This offence deals with 'deception by silence' cases, but only where there is a legal duty to disclose. It is important to be aware that a person selling a piece of property is not under an obligation to inform a buyer of any defects. So if a person buying a car asks 'is there anything I should know about' and the seller replies 'no', even though the brakes do not work, this would not fall under s 3 because there is no duty to disclose. However, it might well fall under s 2 for being a misleading answer or a false statement about someone's intention. In a case where there is no duty to disclose but the police believe there is manifest dishonesty, the better charge may be theft. The kinds of cases where there is a legal duty to disclose include where the contract is one of the 'utmost good faith' (for example, insurance contracts) or where there is a statutory obligation to make a disclosure (as there is in the case of company prospectuses).

13.4 Fraud by abuse of position

Section 4(1) Fraud Act 2006 states:

A person is in breach of this section if he –

(a) occupies a position in which he is expected to safeguard, or not act against, the financial interests of another person,
(b) dishonestly abuses that position, and
(c) intends, by means of the abuse of that position –
   (i) to make a gain for himself or another, or
   (ii) to cause loss to another or to expose another to a risk of loss.

This offence applies where a person is in a legal position of trust in relation to another. That will include the position of a trustee; a professional person and client; and an employer and employee (*Gayle* [2008] EWCA Crim 1344). It remains to be seen whether this section applies only where the civil law recognises a special obligation of trust, or whether it may apply where there is a moral obligation, but not one the civil law would recognise.

13.5 Obtaining services dishonestly

Section 11 Fraud Act 2006 creates the offence of obtaining services dishonestly. It states:

(1) A person is guilty of an offence under this section if he obtains services for himself or another –
   (a) by a dishonest act, and
   (b) in breach of subsection (2)
(2) A person obtains services in breach of this subsection if –
   (a) they are made available on the basis that payment has been, is being or will be made for or in respect of them
   (b) he obtains them without any payment having been made for or in respect of them or without payment having been made in full, and
   (c) when he obtains them, he knows –
      (i) that they are being made available on the basis described in paragraph (a), or
      (ii) that they may be,
   but intends that payment will not be made or not be made in full.

The following are the key elements of this offence.

13.5.1 Obtaining services for himself or another

This offence is concerned with the obtaining of services rather than receiving goods. So it would cover obtaining a haircut, watching a film or even sexual services by fraud. The offence can be committed over the internet as well as in person. Illegally downloading music would appear to be covered. The offence, unlike the fraud offences, requires the service actually to have been provided.

13.5.2 The services must be available on the basis that they will be or have been paid for

This offence is committed only where the dishonesty is used to obtain services which will be paid for. So, it would apply if Kevin persuaded Olivia to collect his child from school, untruthfully saying he had an injured foot. If Olivia collected the child she will have provided a service, but not on the expectation that it will be paid for, and so the s 11 offence will not be covered.

13.5.3 Dishonesty

The Fraud Act 2006 does not define dishonesty, so presumably the *Ghosh* test (see Section 11.6) will be used.

13.5.4 Intention that payment will not be made

The offence is committed only if the defendant does not intend to pay in full for the service. So if a 15-year-old by a fraud managed to get in to see an 18 rated film at a cinema, the s 11 offence would not be committed if he or she had paid the full price to see the film. This requirement also means that a person who lies and says that they have enough money to pay when they do not may have a defence if they can show that they did intend to pay, even though they were short of money when they requested the services.

13.6 Making off without payment

This offence is found in s 3 Theft Act 1978. It was created to fill a gap which had become apparent some years after the Theft Act 1968 was enacted. Conduct known as 'bilking' – leaving without paying for goods or services – did not easily fall within either theft or any of the deception offences. The difficulties arose where the defendant obtained ownership of the goods or provision of the services before she was obliged to pay (for example, she had eaten a meal before being presented with the bill). If then the defendant, after receiving the goods or services, decided not to pay, there was grave difficulty in obtaining a conviction. There was no theft, as the dishonesty existed only once the ownership in the goods had passed, and so at that point the goods were not 'property belonging to another'. Similarly, for a deception offence it could not be said that the goods or services had been obtained by the deception (although see *Ray* [1974] AC 370, which shows that the courts were willing to go to some lengths to avoid this difficulty). The prosecution's job in such a case is easier now because s 3 Theft Act 1978 creates a specific offence which requires neither a deception nor the appropriation of property belonging to another.

Section 3 Theft Act 1978 provides:

(1) Subject to subsection (3) below, a person who, knowing that payment on the spot for any goods supplied or service done is required or expected from him, dishonestly makes off

without having paid as required or expected and with intent to avoid payment of the amount due shall be guilty of an offence.

(2) For purposes of this section 'payment on the spot' includes payment at the time of collecting goods on which work has been done or in respect of which service has been provided.

(3) Subsection (1) above shall not apply where the supply of the goods or the doing of the service is contrary to law, or where the service done is such that payment is not legally enforceable.

The offence can be separated into the following elements.

13.6.1 Goods supplied or service done

There is no definition of 'service', but presumably the definition of 'services' in s 1(2) Theft Act 1978 would be used. By s 5(2) Theft Act 1978 the definition of 'goods' given in s 34(2)(b) Theft Act 1968 is used:

'goods' except in so far as the context otherwise requires, includes money and every other description of property except land and includes things severed from the land by stealing.

Probably the most common examples of the s 3 offence are people leaving restaurants, petrol pumps or taxis without paying the amount due. There is some doubt whether goods are supplied when an accused takes them from a self-service supermarket. Griew has argued that such goods are not supplied but 'exposed for sale', while Smith argues that they are supplied in the sense that they are 'made available for sale'. In reality, most takings from supermarkets are easily charged using theft, and so the question is unlikely to trouble the courts too much.

13.6.2 Payment on the spot is required or expected

It is implied in s 3 that payment on the spot must be not only required or expected by the supplier, but actually legally due from the accused. A conviction under s 3 was quashed on this ground in Troughton. The accused, after a dispute with a taxi driver, apparently left without paying the fare. It was held that he was under no obligation to pay the driver because he had not been taken to the correct destination and the driver was therefore in breach of contract. The expectation of payment in the mind of the taxi driver was not enough.

The goods must be supplied or the service provided on the understanding that there will be payment on the spot. Payment on the spot must be taken to include (though again this is not made explicit) cases where payment by cheque or credit card is acceptable. This is debatable because, where there is payment by credit card, the restaurant (for example) will in fact receive the money from the credit card company only some time later. However, it is widely accepted that payment by cheque or credit card should be regarded as payment on the spot. If this were not so, the offence would be useless in practical terms since all establishments at risk from the 'bilker' are prepared to accept credit cards and most will accept cheques.

13.6.3 Makes off

The accused must 'make off', and this has been held to mean that he must leave the spot where payment is required (Brooks and Brooks). Often in s 3 cases the defendant will try to leave the place surreptitiously, for example leaving a restaurant through a toilet window. However, this is not required by the offence. As the Court of Appeal explained, a making-off may 'be an exercise accompanied by the sound of trumpets or a silent stealing away after the folding of the tents'. So boldly walking out of a restaurant in full view of everyone will involve a making-off.

More difficult are cases where the victim has consented to the defendant leaving. Michael enjoys a pleasant meal at Moira's restaurant, but when presented with the bill he explains to Moira that he has left his wallet at home. He provides Moira with a false name and address, promising to return later that week to pay. Moira is taken in and waves him goodbye as he leaves the restaurant. Could it be said that Michael has 'made off'? The case law as yet does not provide an answer. However, Spencer has usefully suggested that 'making off' be defined as 'disappearing or leaving in a way that makes it difficult for the debtor to be traced'. If this definition was used, Michael could be said to have made off, although he could not if the address was correct.

The defendant must have made off from the spot where payment is expected. If therefore the defendant makes a dash for the door of the restaurant, but is apprehended by a waiter before he reaches it, he may not have committed the s 3 offence because payment would be expected anywhere inside the restaurant (McDavitt). In such a case, the correct charge would be an attempt to commit the s 3 offence. The Divisional Court has held that if the victim offers two places to pay – one where people are meant to pay and a second for anyone who forgot to pay the first time – it will be only once the second place is passed that the defendant will have gone past the spot where payment is expected or required (*Moberley v Alsop*, *The Times*, 13 December 1991).

13.6.4 Without having paid as required or expected

The defendant must make off 'without having paid as required or expected'. It is interesting that the statute uses the word 'or' here. It may be that the law is concerned about someone who eats an unsatisfactory meal at a restaurant and is so unhappy with it that he pays only half of his bill and walks out. If he is entitled under contract law to do this, he may have 'paid as required' (although not 'as expected') and so not have committed an offence. Where a defendant had by deception persuaded hotel owners to let him pay at some time in the future he had not committed the offence because he had paid as expected (that is, he had paid nothing at the time of deception, as expected) (*Vincent* [2001] Crim LR 488).

There is some doubt about whether a defendant who leaves a worthless cheque for payment can be said to have 'paid'. As such a defendant would commit an offence under s 2(1)(b) Theft Act 1978, the issue may be of limited significance. In Hammond, Morrison J suggested that a worthless cheque would be regarded as being payment, although he also suggested that counterfeit money would not. On the other hand, Smith (1997) argues that a worthless cheque is not payment 'as expected'.

13.6.5 Knowledge that payment on the spot is required or expected

The *mens rea* for s 3 includes knowledge that payment on the spot is required or expected, and must coincide in time with the making-off. So, there is no offence under s 3 if the defendant absentmindedly walks out of a restaurant, even if he remembers some time later that he forgot to pay, but does not return to the restaurant. At the time he made off he was not aware that payment was required or expected.

13.6.6 Dishonestly

This will be given its usual meaning in property offences (that is, as in the *Ghosh* direction: see Chapter 11).

13.6.7 Intent to avoid payment

There is an additional element to the *mens rea*: the intent to avoid payment of the amount due. Initially there was some doubt precisely what this phrase meant but the point has been resolved by the decision of the House of Lords in *Allen** [1985] AC 1029. The accused left a hotel without paying a bill of over £1,000. He claimed that he genuinely expected to be able to pay the bill and intended to do so at some point. It was held in the House of Lords that an 'intent to avoid payment' means an intent to make permanent default or never to pay, and not merely an intent to avoid payment on the spot or to defer payment. The decision is however controversial as it will be difficult for the prosecution to prove beyond reasonable doubt that the defendant did not intend to return to pay his bill. The decision also creates some overlap between s 3 and s 2(1)(b) Theft Act 1978.

Hot Topic – Has the Fraud Act 2006 improved the law?

There is one sense in which the Act has certainly improved the law: it is simpler to understand. Previously there were a host of offences dealing with different ways in which a person might acquire goods or release from debts by a deception. Many a law student spent many an unhappy week staring blankly at s 2 1978 Theft Act and the desperate attempts of textbook writers to explain the law in simple terms. Now with the one offence of fraud, albeit with three ways of committing it, there is no chance of the wrong offence being charged by the prosecution, as there was under the old law.

Another important benefit of the Fraud Act is that there is no need to show that anyone has been deceived or that any deception operated on the mind of the victim. These problems bedevilled the earlier cases. Under the 2006 Act the mind of the victim is irrelevant; indeed there does not need to be a victim as such. The offence involves the use of fraud with a view to making a gain. An indirect benefit of this approach is that there is now no problem in using fraud to prosecute cases where the victim was a 'computer', as there was under the old law.

Although the Fraud Act 2006 has definite advantages over its predecessors, there are certainly problems with it. David Ormerod (2007) argues that the offence has criminalised lying. This is a deliberate over-exaggeration – not all lies are made with a view to making a financial gain. But it does mean that the scope of the law has been extended. Perhaps more worryingly it does so without it being quite clear what the parameters of the new offence are. Notably fraud is not defined in the act. Precisely what may be regarded as a misleading statement is uncertain. The offence includes where the defendant knows the statement is 'or might be untrue or misleading'. This could be very broad. If I am selling my car and state that it is in good working order and it turns out that statement is untrue, I may have to admit that I could not have known for certain that the car was in good working order, especially as I am not very knowledgeable about cars. Therefore I would have to admit that I knew the statement might be untrue. It is, perhaps, the notion of dishonesty which protects the offence becoming ridiculously wide in this regard, but that is a notoriously uncertain concept. Auction houses have expressed concern that if they state a picture is an original but it turns out not to be, they can be found to have committed the offence.

Section 6 makes it an offence to possess an article which could be used for the commission of a fraud. Even this book could fall into that definition. So could a computer, or even a pen and paper. Much will depend on the notion of dishonesty again.

As we have seen, the new Act is potentially very wide and some of its terminology can be said to be ambiguous. Two things may determine whether or not the new offence is regarded as a success. The first is whether it is used sensibly by prosecutors to charge cases only where there is clearly fraud of a nature which should be criminal. As drafted it could be used for the most petty kinds of lies, but maybe we can trust the prosecution authorities to ensure that does not happen. Second, the notion of dishonesty will play a key role in policing its bounds. The current definition of dishonesty is controversial. Time will tell whether it is up to the job.

Summary

13.1 The fraud offence is found in the 2006 Fraud Act, which has replaced the previous complex law on deceptions.

13.2 Fraud by false representation occurs when a defendant dishonestly makes a representation by words or conduct with intent to make a gain or cause a loss. The offence includes implied statements and false statements of opinion or intention.

13.3 Fraud by failure to disclose arises where a defendant is under a legal obligation to make a representation and fails to do so dishonestly, with intent to make a gain or cause a loss.

13.4 Fraud by abuse of position is committed when a person has a legally recognised position of trust in relation to another and dishonestly misuses that.

13.5 The offence of obtaining services dishonestly requires proof that the defendant used dishonest means to persuade another to provide a service. However, it must be a service provided on the understanding that it would be paid for.

13.6 It is an offence under s 3 Theft Act 1978 to make off without payment for goods or services knowing that payment on the spot is required or expected. The accused must intend never to pay, not merely to defer payment.

Further Reading

Campbell, 'The Fraud Act 2006' (2007) 18 KCLJ 337.
Green, *Lying, Cheating and Stealing* (Oxford University Press 2007).
Ormerod, 'The Fraud Act 2006 – Criminalizing Lying' [2007] Crim LR 193.
Ormerod and Williams, *Smith on Theft* (Oxford University Press 2007).

Case Notes

▶ *Allen* [1985] AC 1029. House of Lords

The appellant was convicted of making-off without payment. He had left a hotel without paying his bill of over £1,000. He claimed that he had genuinely hoped to be able to pay the bill. His conviction was quashed by the Court of Appeal, and the House of Lords agreed. It was held that the words 'with intent to avoid payment of the amount due' in s 3 Theft Act 1978 should be interpreted to mean with intent never to pay.

▶ *Charles* [1977] AC 177. House of Lords

The appellant was convicted of obtaining a pecuniary advantage by deception: being allowed to borrow by way of overdraft contrary to s 16 (2)(b) Theft Act 1968. He had paid for gaming chips at a club with a cheque backed by a cheque card, knowing if the cheque were honoured his account would be overdrawn without authority. The manager of the club gave evidence that if a cheque card was used, he did not enquire into the creditworthiness of the drawer of the cheque. The appeal was dismissed, on the ground that the appellant had impliedly represented that he was entitled to use the cheque card to back a cheque for that amount, and that the manager had been induced to accept the cheque by this false representation.

▶ *Ghosh* [1982] QB 1053. Court of Appeal

See Chapter 11 Case notes.

▶ *Lambie* [1982] AC 449. House of Lords

The appellant was convicted of obtaining a pecuniary advantage by deception. She had used a credit card to make purchases in a shop, although she knew that she was over the credit limit and the issuing bank had asked her to return the card. It was argued on appeal that any representation she had made as to her authority to use the card was not operative, since the shop was guaranteed payment on the transaction as a result of the contract between the shop and the issuing bank. Her appeal was dismissed. The House of Lords followed *Charles* (above), and held that the jury were entitled to find that the manager of the shop would not have accepted the card had she known that the appellant had no authority to use it, and that the deception was therefore operative.

▶ *Williams* [1980] Crim LR 589. Court of Appeal

See Chapter 11 Case notes.

Chapter 14

Other offences against property

Key Terms

- ▶ **Arson** – damaging property through fire.
- ▶ **Blackmail** – making an unwarranted demand with menaces with a view to gain or to cause loss to someone.
- ▶ **Damage** – impairing the usefulness or value of an item.

14.1 Criminal damage

The Criminal Damage Act 1971, like the Theft Acts, protects property interests from harmful interference from others. It contains the offences relating to the destruction of and damage to property. The most important criminal damage offences are found in s 1 of the Act, which provides:

> (1) A person who without lawful excuse destroys or damages any property belonging to another intending to destroy or damage any such property or being reckless as to whether any such property would be destroyed or damaged shall be guilty of an offence.
>
> (2) A person who without lawful excuse destroys or damages any property, whether belonging to himself or another –
>   (a) intending to destroy or damage any property or being reckless as to whether any property would be destroyed or damaged; and
>   (b) intending by the destruction or damage to endanger the life of another or being reckless as to whether the life of another would be thereby endangered; shall be guilty of an offence.
>
> (3) An offence committed under this section by destroying or damaging property by fire shall be charged as arson.

This section creates three offences: ordinary criminal damage in subsection (1); dangerous damage in subsection (2) and arson in subsection (3). Dangerous damage and arson are punishable with life imprisonment, while simple criminal damage is punishable with 10 years' imprisonment. In addition to s 1, the Criminal Damage Act creates separate offences of threatening to destroy or damage property (s 2) and possession of anything (such as petrol, matches, stones, a knife or a crowbar) with the intention of destroying or damaging property (s 3), but these will not be discussed in detail here.

14.1.1 Ordinary criminal damage

The offence of criminal damage is found in s 1 Criminal Damage Act 1971, quoted above. The offence contains the following elements:

1. *Destruction or damage.* The central element in the actus reus is the destruction of or damage to property. It is generally agreed that to destroy something is to damage it, and so most of the cases concern what it means to damage property.

   The word 'damage' should be given its ordinary meaning. What constitutes damage will depend on the nature and use of an item (*Roe v Kingerlee* [1986] Crim

LR 735). Hence splattering mud on a parked car may not constitute damage, but it may be damage to put mud on a painting. Probably the most useful test to ascertain whether or not property has been damaged is to ask whether the defendant's act has impaired the value or usefulness of the item (*Morphitis v Salmon** [1990] Crim LR 48). The removal from a car of a wheel clamp by the owner of the clamped car may constitute criminal damage to the wheel clamp, as the wheel clamp is now of diminished usefulness (*Lloyd v DPP* [1991] Crim LR 904). Scratching a scaffolding pole neither impairs its usefulness nor reduces its value, and is therefore not to be regarded as damaging it (*Morphitis v Salmon*).

The damage need not be permanent. In *Hardman* [1986] Crim LR 330, graffiti which would eventually have been washed away by the rain were held to amount to damage, but if the impact of what the defendant did can be easily removed then it is less likely to constitute damage. For example, in *R v A* [1978] Crim LR 689 it was held that spitting on a policeman's coat did not damage it. In one case a defendant was arrested on the point of painting over a piece of National Front graffiti with white paint. This was found not to be criminal damage, partly on the ground that the wall was being returned closer to its intended (original) state (*Fancy* [1980] Crim LR 171).

Damage is not restricted to breaking an item. It can be damage to attach something to a piece of property (for example, dumping rubbish onto a piece of land (*Henderson and Battley* (1984), Unreported)) or to remove something (for example, taking away an essential part of a machine (*Tacey* (1821) Russ. & Ry. 452)). Controversially it has been held that wrongfully wheel-clamping a car does not damage it (*Drake v DPP* [1994] Crim LR 55) because there has been no 'intrusion into the integrity of the object'. Although the wheel-clamping had affected the car's usefulness, it could (on payment) be quickly and easily removed without any long-term effects (unlike the land in *Henderson and Battley*). Perhaps the better charge in Drake would have been theft of the car, if dishonesty could be shown (see Section 11.6).

2. *Property*. 'Property' is defined in s 10(1) Criminal Damage Act 1971 and is expressly restricted to tangible property. The term therefore includes land, but excludes patents, copyrights, etc. Otherwise the definition is similar to that found in s 4 Theft Act 1968. In *Cox v Riley* [1986] Crim LR 460, the defendant erased a computer program from a printed circuit card. Convictions were upheld because the damage was to the card itself and not to the programs, which were intangible property and so not protected by the Act.

3. *Belonging to another*. You cannot be convicted of ordinary criminal damage to your own property. If you want you may rip up this book, if it is yours (although it will be noted that the offence of dangerous criminal damage can be committed against your own property). A person who destroys his own property in the belief that it belongs to someone else could face the further annoyance of being convicted of attempted criminal damage of property belonging to another (see Chapter 18).

The phrase 'belonging to another' is defined in s 10(2) to include any person having custody, control, any proprietary right or interest, or a charge on the property. So you cannot destroy property which you own if someone else has a proprietary interest in it, for example. There are provisions relating to trust property and the property of a corporation which are counterparts to the provisions in s 5(2) and (5) Theft Act 1968 (see Section 11.5).

4. *Intention or recklessness.* The *mens rea* for s 1(1) requires intention or recklessness as to causing damage to property belonging to another. It is enough if the defendant intended or was reckless as to the damaging of some property belonging to another, even if it was not the property which was actually damaged. In other words, the doctrine of transferred *mens rea* can apply to these offences (see Section 5.7). The accused must intend or be reckless as to damaging property and intend or be reckless as to the property belonging to another (*Smith* [1959] 2 All ER 193). The meaning of 'recklessness' is now governed by *R v G** [2003] UKHL 50, and is discussed in Section 5.4.2.

5. *Without lawful excuse.* The criminal damage offences do not contain that element of *mens rea* which is so typical of the Theft Acts: dishonesty. However, some of the elements of dishonesty are found in the requirement that the damage caused must be 'without lawful excuse'. The Criminal Damage Act 1971 contains in s 5 a partial definition of the phrase 'lawful excuse':

> (2) A person charged with an offence to which this section applies shall, whether or not he would be treated for the purposes of this Act as having a lawful excuse apart from this subsection, be treated for those purposes as having a lawful excuse –
>   (a) if at the time of the act or acts alleged to constitute the offence he believed that the person or persons whom he believed to be entitled to consent to the destruction of or damage to the property in question had so consented, or would have consented to it if he or they had known of the destruction or damage and its circumstances; or
>   (b) if he had destroyed or damaged ... the property in question
>   (c) ... in order to protect property belonging to himself or another or a right or interest in property which was or which he believed to himself or another or a right or interest in property which was or which he believed to be vested in himself or another, and at the time of the act or acts alleged to constitute the offence he believed –
>   (i) that the property, right or interest was in immediate need of protection; and
>   (ii) that the means of protection adopted or proposed to be adopted were or would be reasonable having regard to all the circumstances.
> (3) For the purposes of this section it is immaterial whether a belief is justified or not if it is honestly held.
> (4) For the purposes of subsection (2) above a right or interest in property includes any right or privilege in or over land, whether created by grant, licence or otherwise.
> (5) This section shall not be construed as casting doubt on any defence of dishonesty recognised by law as a defence to criminal charges.

There are two main defences in this section:

(a) *The defendant believes that the owner consented to the damage.* The defence covers the defendant who believes that the owner consented to the damage, even if in fact the owner did not. The belief that the owner consented or would have consented provides a defence even if it is an unreasonable belief (s 5(3)) and even if the mistaken belief is caused by the defendant's drunkenness (*Jaggard v Dickenson* [1981] QB 527). A defendant who argued that he believed God owned the property and that God authorised him to damage the property did not have a defence (*Blake** [1993] Crim LR 586). The court did not explain why this was so. The best explanation was that the defendant did not really believe that God owned the property in law or that God had the legal authority to consent to the damage. It is not clear whether there is a defence if, unknown to the defendant, the owner has consented to the damage. In light of the *Dadson* (1850) 4 Cox CC 358 principle (see Section 16.1) it is unlikely that this 'unknown justification' provides a defence.

(b) *The defendant was acting in order to protect his own or another's property.* The defence in s 5 also covers damage done in order to protect other property. To be successful, the accused must believe both that the other property is in immediate need of protection and that the means of protection adopted are reasonable in the circumstances. It does not need to be shown that the threat to the property which the defendant is seeking to avert is unlawful (*Jones and Milling* [2005] Crim R 121). In order to be able to rely on this defence the courts have developed a rather complicated twofold test:

    (i) Using a subjective test, did the defendant believe that the property was in immediate need of protection and that the means he used were reasonable (Johnson (1994))?

    (ii) Using an objective test, could the defendant's acts be said to be performed in order to protect the property (based on the facts as the defendant believed them to be)?

These may make more sense when applied to some cases. In *Ashford and Smith* [1988] Crim LR 682, where the defendants were found outside a nuclear base armed with a pair of wire cutters, they tried to argue that they believed that by cutting the wire and getting into the military base to protest they would lessen the chance of a nuclear war with its resulting damage to property. The defendants were prevented from using the s 5 defence as the court decided that, even taking the facts as the defendants believed them to be, it could not be said that *cutting the fence* would protect property. They believed that shutting down the base would protect property, but not cutting the fence. This suggests that it is necessary to show a clear causal link between the damage done and the anticipated protection of property (see also *Jones and Milling*). In *Hunt* [1977] Crim LR 740, the defendant set fire to property in sheltered housing to demonstrate the lack of fire precautions and to persuade the owners to install better fire prevention facilities. He was held not to have acted in order to protect property by that act (that is, the setting fire to the property). In both *Ashford and Smith* and *Hunt* the defendants were acting in order to protect property, but they were not intending to protect other property directly by damage, but by actions which would follow from the damage.

In order to rely on s 5, the defendant must show that he believed that the property he was acting in order to protect was in need of immediate protection. This is judged subjectively on the defendant's state of mind. This is a further reason why the defendants in *Blake*, *Ashford and Smith* and *Hunt* all faced difficulties. In *Ashford and Smith*, for example, it would be unlikely that the defendants believed a nuclear war was imminent. It also explains why a defendant cannot rely on the defence if she cuts off a wheel clamp placed on her car, even if she believes she has been wrongfully clamped (*Mitchell* [2004] Crim LR 139). The common law defences, which include self-defence, automatism and insanity (see Chapters 15 and 16), are also available to charges under the Criminal Damage Act 1971, as is made clear by s 5(5).

14.1.2 Dangerous criminal damage

In the case of dangerous criminal damage two elements are required:

1. There must be ordinary criminal damage, with two provisos. First, it is possible to commit dangerous criminal damage to your own property, the reasoning being that although you should be free to destroy or damage property which belongs to you, you should not do so in such a way as to endanger other people. This proviso also

has consequences for the *mens rea* for this requirement. In the case of dangerous damage, only intention or recklessness as to damaging property is required. There is no need to have any *mens rea* as to the ownership of the property. Second, the lawful excuse defences explained in s 5 do not apply. The defendant may, however, still rely on the general defences, such as duress or lawful defence.

2. Dangerous damage also requires intention or recklessness in relation to endangering the life of another person by the destruction or damage. The person whose life is endangered does not have to be the owner of the property (although it could be), but it cannot be the accused him- or herself. The mad scientist who blows up his garden shed and almost himself in an ill-fated experiment does not commit the offence unless another person's life was thereby endangered. It should be stressed that there is no need for there in fact to be an endangerment of someone's life. What must be shown is that there was intention or recklessness as to the endangerment. Thus, in *Sangha* [1988] 2 All ER 385, the defendant lit a fire in his room and left the house. The Court found he was guilty of dangerous criminal damage even though unknown to him the building was very well fireproofed, and so in fact there was no danger to anyone living near by.

In *Steer** [1988] AC 111, the House of Lords held that there had to be a link between the damage to property and the endangering of life. It was not enough under s 1(2) to prove both recklessness as to the damage and recklessness as to endangering life; it had to be proved that there was at least recklessness as to endangering life by the damage to property. For example, where a defendant threw a brick through a car windscreen it was necessary to show that he was reckless that life was endangered by the damage to property (that is, the shattering of the windscreen – be it by obscuring the driver's vision or by the driver being hit by pieces of glass) and not by the driver being hit by the brick. That would not be endangering life through criminal damage, but an offence under s 47 or s 20 Offences Against the Person Act 1861 (*Webster and Warwick** [1995] 2 All ER 168).

Some commentators have complained that the offence is too widely drafted. *Merrick* [1996] 1 Cr App R 130 demonstrates this concern. The defendant, acting with the consent of the homeowner, removed a television signal-receiving box from the side of a house. While doing this he left an electric cable exposed for six minutes. The defendant was convicted of dangerous damage. J. Smith has noted that the decision looks dubious because there is no offence of laying a dangerous cable. So why is there an offence of cutting a cable (with the owner's consent) in a dangerous way?

14.2 Arson

The serious offence of arson requires no additional *mens rea* to that for simple criminal damage. What must be shown is that the destruction or damage was caused by fire. The charge may be brought under either s 1(1) or s 1(2), together with s 1(3). The lawful excuse defence in s 5 does apply, although the defendant may rely on the general defences, such as duress or lawful defence.

14.3 Blackmail

According to s 21(1) Theft Act 1968:

A person is guilty of blackmail if, with a view to gain for himself or another or with intent to cause loss to another, he makes any unwarranted demand with menaces. ...

The section goes on to say that such a demand will be unwarranted unless:

the person making it does so in the belief –

(a) that he has reasonable grounds for making the demand; and
(b) that the use of menaces is a proper means of reinforcing the demand.

The maximum sentence for this offence is 14 years' imprisonment. The offence is therefore made up of the following elements.

14.3.1 Making an unwarranted demand

The jury will have to use their common sense in determining whether the statement is a demand or not. The demand can be in writing or oral, and can be expressed or implied from the circumstances, tone of voice, physical gestures, etc. There is obviously a fine line between an offer (which cannot form the basis of a blackmail charge) and a demand (which can). 'Give me £20 and I will make your life worthwhile' may be seen as an offer, but in some circumstances it may be a threat, by including the implied threat that unpleasant consequences will follow if you do not give me the money.

In a case of blackmail, a demand must be made. A victim of a crime would not commit blackmail if his assailant made an unsolicited offer to hand over money in return for not reporting the crime (although the assailant might be guilty of incitement to commit an offence under s 5 Criminal Law Act 1967: see Section 18.2). Another consequence of the requirement that the demand needs to be made is that it seems to be irrelevant whether or not the victim actually hears or receives the demand (*Treacy* [1971] AC 537). If a letter containing a demand with menaces is lost in the post, the offence is still committed by the sender even though the intended victim did not receive the letter.

The demand may be that the victim or someone else acts or omits to act in a particular way. It need not be that specific money or property be handed over, but the demand must involve a financial gain or loss (s 34(2)(a)). Thus a demand that you be given a lucrative job would suffice, but not a demand to be appointed to an unpaid position in a voluntary organisation.

14.3.2 Menaces

The second element of the *actus reus* is that the demand must be made with menaces. The term 'menace' is not defined in the Act, but it is to be given its 'normal meaning' involving the 'threats of any action detrimental to, or unpleasant to, the person addressed. There is no need to show the threat is aggressive, it could be 'suave and gentle' (*Lambert* [2009] EWCA Crim 2860). It may also include a warning that in certain events such an action is intended (*Lawrence and Pomroy* (1971) 57 Cr App R 64). Again, the menace can be expressed or implied from the circumstances. It does not matter whether the threat is that unpleasant consequences will befall the victim or someone else (*Lambert*, 2009).

The menace must not be so trivial that it has no effect on the person threatened. Thus, the sale of a poster which exempted shops from 'rag activities' during a student fund-raising event was held not to constitute a menace (*Harry* [1974] Crim LR 32). Normally it is enough for a judge to direct a jury that the threat involves menaces if that is how a reasonable person would interpret the words. However, there are two circumstances in which the judge will need to give further direction. The first is where the victim is not troubled by the menaces, even though a reasonable person would have been. This may be because the victim is unusually robust or because, unknown to the defendant, the facts are such that the threat is ineffective (for example, John threatens to persuade Sue's employers to sack her, even though, unknown to John, Sue has just handed in her notice). In these circumstances, the words are still threats with menaces despite the fact that they have no effect on the victim (*Clear* [1968] 1 QB 670).

The second situation in which the judge will need to give a further direction is where the victim interprets the words as menaces even though a reasonable person would not have done so. Then, as long as the defendant was aware of the effect that his words would have on the victim, the threat can still be seen as menace (*Garwood*). Thus threatening to send the victim a bunch of flowers can amount to a menace if the defendant is aware that the victim is allergic to flowers. These decisions may sit a little uneasily with the rule that a threat does not need to be communicated to the victim, but the policy seems to be that if words are spoken by the defendant and she is aware of their potential effect, she cannot hide behind the victim's unlikely response.

14.3.3 Unwarranted

The definition of an unwarranted demand focuses on whether the defendant believed that there were reasonable grounds for his demand, not whether there were reasonable grounds. A demand will be unwarranted unless the defendant believes that '(a) he keeps reasonable grounds for making the claim' and (b) 'that the use of menaces is a proper way of enforcing the demand'. Consideration of (a) will focus on the legitimacy of the gain and of (b) will focus on the means used to obtain the loss or gain. These are expressed as *mens rea* to be proved by the prosecution, rather than defences for which the defence would need to introduce evidence. Let us consider these two elements separately.

First, when considering whether the defendant believes he has reasonable grounds for making the claim, she is to be judged on the facts as she believed them to be and by what she believes are the standards of the community (*Harvey* (1981) 72 Cr App R 139). So the question is whether, on the facts as the defendant believed them to be, the defendant thought that ordinary people would say her demand was proper. The demand is 'proper' if the defendant believes that she is morally entitled to make the claim, even if there is not full legal entitlement. If Bob dies, leaving nothing to his son in his will, the son may believe he is morally entitled to some of Bob's estate, even though there is no legal entitlement. Therefore if the son demands a part of the estate, the demand is not improper.

Second, it must be shown that the defendant believed that the use of menaces is a proper way of enforcing the demand. This is usually a more difficult requirement for the defendant to satisfy. Although a defendant may readily persuade the jury that he believed that the victim owed him money, it will be more difficult to persuade a jury that he believed threats of violence were a proper way of enforcing the demand. The courts have decided that if a defendant is threatening to do an illegal act and the defendant is aware that it is an illegal act then he cannot claim that that was a proper way of enforcing the demand (*Harvey*).

An important consequence of the fact that the defendant must show that he thought both the demand and the method of enforcing the demand were reasonable is that a blackmail charge can lie where the defendant is threatening to do something lawful. For example, if Mark catches Maria committing theft and says that he will report her to the police unless she gives him £100, this amounts to blackmail. Although Mark is entitled to report Maria to the police, the making of the demand is improper.

14.3.4 Intention to make unwarranted demand with menaces with a view to gain for oneself or another, or cause loss to another

The *mens rea* requirement of blackmail is an intention to make the unwarranted demand with menaces, with a view to gain for oneself or another, or cause loss to another. As stated earlier, the view to a gain must be to one of property or money either for oneself or another. It is not necessary to show that the primary motivation is to receive money or property so long as it is a factor influencing the defendant in making the demand (*Bevans** [1988] Crim LR 236).

Section 34(2) defines 'gain' as including 'a gain by keeping what one has as well as a gain by getting what one has not', and a loss as including 'a loss by not getting what one might get, as well as a loss by parting with what one has'. A threat to tell the victim's husband about her adultery could not therefore form the basis of a blackmail charge as there was to be no gain or loss of monetary value. There is some dispute over whether 'a view to a gain' includes payment of a debt. An accountant might say that it is no gain to receive money legally owed to you, as it simply means that the money is recorded in the part of your accounts listing the money you actually have rather than in the part of your accounts detailing the money owed to you, but there is no judicial authority for this view. In reality, given the unreliability of creditors, most people would see it as a gain to receive payment, and there is some authority for this view (*Parkes* [1973] Crim LR 358).

14.3.5 Why is blackmail an offence?

There has been much discussion over why blackmail is unlawful, especially when the defendant threatens to do what is lawful, or indeed to do what may be one's legal duty. Consider this example. Huw and Clare are co-workers. Clare catches Huw defrauding their employer. Clare says that she will report Huw to their boss unless Huw pays her £1,000. Here Clare's threat (to report Huw) is lawful – indeed it may even be her legal duty – and simply asking for £1,000 is lawful. So how can the two lawful acts combine to create a criminal offence? Perhaps the best explanation is that the core wrong in blackmail is not just the making of a threat, nor just the acquiring of another's property. It is the combination of the two: the threat of coercive force in order to obtain a financial gain. The offence is therefore similar to the crime of deception, where the victim's mind is manipulated in order to persuade him to hand over property. The difference is that in blackmail it is a threat (rather than deception) which is used to manipulate the victim's mind. An alternative understanding of the offence is to liken blackmail to an assault, putting the victim in fear of what the defendant is about to do.

14.4 Taking a conveyance

It will be recalled that one of the elements of theft is that the defendant intended permanently to deprive the owner of the property. Therefore, it is normally no offence to borrow something, even without the owner's permission. Although there is some dispute over whether such borrowing should generally constitute theft, it is clear that borrowing cars (joy-riding, as it has become known) is a particular social problem. Hence it is a specific offence under s 12 Theft Act 1968:

> ...a person shall be guilty of an offence, if, without having the consent of the owner or other lawful authority, he takes any conveyance for his own or another's use or, knowing that any conveyance has been taken without such authority, drives it or allows himself to be carried in or on it.

Notably there is no need to show an intention permanently to deprive the owner of the conveyance. The offence contains the following elements.

14.4.1 Conveyance

Conveyance here includes a car, motorbike, boat and indeed 'any conveyance constructed or adapted for the carriage of a person or persons whether by land, water or air, except that it does not include a conveyance constructed or adapted for use only under the control of a person not carried in or on it'. This definition would include as well as the obvious wheelchairs and hang-gliders. It excludes supermarket trolleys (which are not designed to convey people and anyway do not 'carry' the driver) and horses (which are not 'constructions' (*Neal v Gribble* [1978] Crim LR 500)). There is a specific offence relating to bicycles in s 12(5).

14.4.2 'Taken'

The word 'taken' could be interpreted widely to include taking possession of a car, or narrowly to mean taking in the sense of causing the conveyance to move. The courts have accepted the narrow interpretation. The argument in favour of this interpretation is to contrast the word 'take' with 'use' later on in the section. If 'take' had been intended to have the wider meaning then the section could have been drafted 'to use the conveyance for his own or another's use'. So the present law is that starting the engine of a vehicle but not actually causing it to move does not amount to a taking, although it may constitute an offence of interfering with a motor vehicle with the intent that an offence under s 12(1) shall be committed (s 9 Criminal Attempts Act 1981; *Bogachi* [1973] QB 832). However, there could be a taking even if the vehicle were moved only a few feet (*Marchant v MacCallister* (1984) Cr App R 361). There is no need for the conveyance to be moved on its own motion in order to be taken; it is sufficient if it is towed away, for example (Pearce). It is possible for a defendant to take a car which had already been taken by someone else and abandoned (*Spriggs* [1958] 1 QB 270).

The offence can also be committed by someone who drives or allows herself to be carried in a conveyance which has been taken for the purposes of s 12 if she knows that the conveyance has been so taken. 'Carried' here requires a movement of the conveyance (*Miller* [1983] 2 AC 161).

14.4.3 'For his own or another's use'

This phrase has been interpreted to mean that it must be taken for use *as a conveyance* (*Bow** (1976) 64 Cr App R 54). Thus where a man, as a 'practical joke', pushed his ex-girlfriend's car round a corner so that she would think it had been stolen, it was held that the car was not taken for use as a conveyance (*Stokes* [1982] Crim LR 695). By way of contrast, where two people pushed a car round a corner intending to return later in the day and drive it away, the offence was committed (*Marchant v MacCallister*). Similarly, if a car's handbrake was released and it travelled down a hill, but without carrying passengers, then again the taking would not be a taking as a conveyance; it was not being used to convey anyone. In *Bow*, the defendant moved a car 200 yards as he felt the vehicle was obstructing his way down a track. The court felt the question was one of fact, and on the facts of the case the car had been taken as a conveyance, although moving a car which was an obstacle for a couple of yards would not be. This decision seems dubious, as it is hard to see how he was using the car as a conveyance in this case. The defendant was not using the vehicle to convey himself or another anywhere. Indeed it took him out of his way, and he was using it so as to enable him to drive his own car down the track. It has also been argued that the court's interpretation of the section as requiring the car to be taken for use as a conveyance is an unduly restrictive reading of the offence. The loss to the victim is the same whether the car is taken as a form of transport or towed away to form the basis of a bonfire or for a prank.

14.4.4 'Without having the consent of the owner'

It is not enough to show that the owner would have consented if he had known of the circumstances; the owner has to consent at the time of the taking (*Ambler* [1989] RTR 217), although, as we shall see shortly, the defendant can raise a defence based on the fact that she believed that the owner would have consented to the taking. The prosecution will need to prove the owner's lack of consent only if the defence raises it as an issue at the trial (*McPherson* [1973] Crim LR 191).

What if the owner had been deceived into giving his consent? The decided cases have not been very satisfactory, but the present position is as follows. If the defendant persuaded the owner to consent to lending the conveyance by a lie or deception, the offence is not committed and the owner is seen as consenting to the taking. This was stated in *Whittaker v Campbell* [1984] QB 318 where the court thought to decide otherwise would involve the court in having to distinguish between fundamental and non-fundamental mistakes, a complex question of civil law, and that if a 'common-sense' definition of consent is used there is consent even if it is induced by a deception. So, if the defendant obtains the consent of the owner to take the car by lying about his age, there is no offence under s 12. However, it is necessary to distinguish this from where the owner gives consent only for a specific use and the defendant uses the car outside the terms of permission, in which case he will be acting without the owner's consent. So the offence would not be committed if the accused asked the owner if he could take the car as he needed to go to Reigate for a wedding and the owner had said 'you can borrow the car', but the accused drove to Newcastle. However, the offence would have been committed if the owner had said 'you can borrow the car but only to go to Reigate and nowhere else'. In practice this distinction may be hard to draw. Thus, if the owner gives a general consent for the defendant to take the car after the accused has lied about where he is going, this will not be seen as taking the vehicle without the owner's consent because the owner consented to the general taking at the moment when the defendant first drove off (*Peart* [1970] 2 QB 672). However, if the owner agrees to the defendant taking the car on a specific journey and the defendant completes that journey but then departs on a new journey, the court has held that there is a second taking at the point when the driver departed from the agreed route. As this second taking is without the owner's consent, the defendant has committed the offence (*McGill* [1970] Crim LR 290). That said, 'not every brief, unauthorised diversion from his proper route' is sufficient to constitute a new journey and a new taking (*McKnight v Davies* [1974] Crim LR 62). It is difficult, if not impossible, to find a sensible rationale behind these decisions.

14.4.5 Defence based on belief that the owner would consent

It should be noted that there is a specific defence to show that the defendant believed that the owner would consent to the taking or that he had lawful authority (s 12(6)). No doubt if a defendant took his friend's car to get his pregnant wife to hospital, the defendant would easily persuade the jury that he believed that his friend would have agreed to him taking the car. The test is subjective: it does not depend on whether the defendant's belief was reasonable, but simply on whether there was such a belief. It may even be that a drunken and unreasonable belief will suffice (by analogy with *Jaggard v Dickenson* [1981] QB 527).

14.4.6 An intent to cause movement of the conveyance

The *mens rea* for the offence is an intent to cause movement. Therefore if the defendant accidentally caused a vehicle to move there is no offence (*Blayney v Knight* [1975] Crim LR 237). The crime is one of basic intent, and so drunkenness is inadmissible as evidence of lack of intent (*McPherson*).

14.5 Aggravated vehicle-taking

The Aggravated Vehicle-Taking Act 1992 added a new s 12A to the Theft Act 1968, thereby creating a more serious form of the s 12 offence. This Act was introduced to combat behaviour which has been called 'joy riding', but which has led to death, serious injury and damage. Section 12A provides:

(1) Subject to subsection (3) below, a person is guilty of aggravated taking of a vehicle if –
  (a) he commits an offence under section 12(1) above (in this section referred to as the 'basic offence') in relation to a mechanically propelled vehicle; and
  (b) it is proved that, at any time after the vehicle was unlawfully taken (whether by him or another) and before it was recovered, the vehicle was driven, or injury or damage was caused, in one or more of the circumstances set out in paragraphs (a) to (d) of subsection (2) below.
(2) The circumstances referred to in subsection 1(b) above are –
  (a) that the vehicle was driven dangerously on a road or other public place;
  (b) that, owing to the driving of the vehicle, an accident occurred by which injury was caused to any person;
  (c) that, owing to the driving of the vehicle, an accident occurred by which damage was caused to any property, other than the vehicle;
  (d) that damage was caused to the vehicle.
(3) A person is not guilty of an offence under this section if he proves that, as regards any such proven driving, injury or damage as is referred to in subsection (1)(b) above, either –
  (a) the driving, accident or damage referred to in subsection (2) above occurred before he committed the basic offence; or
  (b) he was neither in nor on nor in the immediate vicinity of the vehicle when that driving, accident or damage occurred.

In summary, aggravated vehicle-taking arises where, in addition to the straightforward s 12 offence, one of the harms listed in s 12A(2) occurs. Probably the most common form of the offence is where a defendant takes a vehicle contrary to s 12 and then drives the vehicle dangerously. Driving dangerously requires proof that 'it would be obvious to a competent and careful driver that driving in that way would be dangerous' (s 2A(1)(b) Road Traffic Act 1988). Notably, these further harms do not require proof that the defendant intentionally or recklessly caused them. In *Marsh* [1997] 1 Cr App R 67, the defendant took a car without the owner's consent and then ran over the victim who ran out into the road in front of the defendant. His conviction under s 12A was upheld. The court in *Marsh* explained that 'the policy of this statute is to impose heavier sanctions on those who take vehicles unlawfully and then cause an accident, whether or not the accident involves fault in the driving'. It is only necessary to show that the car's movement caused the accident which led to injury or damage. All those in the car are liable to conviction 'even though the passenger has protested at the driving which has caused damage to the vehicle' (Davies (2000)).

14.6 Computer crime

It is, of course, possible to commit all kinds of crime using a computer. The most obvious is obtaining property by deception, but Smith and Hogan even suggest one could commit murder by computer if one hacked into an air-traffic controller's computer system and caused aircraft to crash, with the intent to kill the passengers. Here we will discuss crimes which specifically relate to computers. Not surprisingly, these are relatively recent creations of statute.

14.6.1 Computer Misuse Act 1990

There is no general crime of looking at other people's personal information, for example by looking inside their private diaries. However, the Computer Misuse Act 1990 is designed to protect information kept on computers. The previous law was seen as inadequate following a House of Lords decision where it was held that 'hacking' (gaining unauthorised access into a computer) was not *per se* a criminal offence. There are four particular reasons given by the Law Commission which suggest why it might be thought that information held on computers needs special protection by the criminal law. First, it is very hard to safeguard information stored on a computer, particularly as often the information is intended to be accessed by a number of authorised people. By contrast, information on paper can be kept in a safe or other secure place. Second, the ease of destroying or corrupting data on a computer means it deserves protection, particularly as it is not always possible for the owner of the computer to realise that the data have been looked at. Third, the highly confidential nature of the kind of information kept on computers (often concerning many members of the public) is such that it needs particular protection. Fourth, it may be sensible to deter people from searching for confidential information because of the temptation to use it for fraudulent purposes once they have found it. The Act was amended by the Police and Justice Act 2006.

The term 'computer' is not defined in the Act. No doubt any attempted definition would rapidly become out of date. In practice this is unlikely to create any problems as the term's meaning is generally understood. The courts appear to have taken a broad interpretation of the word 'computer', and it has been held to include machines which are not normally referred to as computers, such as electronic personal organisers, boxes attached to televisions which control access to cable television channels (Maxwell-King) and cash registers (*A-G's Ref (No 1 of 1991)* [1993] QB 94).

14.6.2 Unauthorised access to computer material

This offence is set out in s 1 of the Act and is designed to punish people who try to gain access to unauthorised data:

> 1(1) A person is guilty of an offence if –
>> (a) he causes a computer to perform any function with intent to secure access to any program or data held in any computer or to enable such access to be secured;
>> (b) the access he intends to secure or enabled to be secured is unauthorised; and
>> (c) he knows at the time when he causes the computer to perform the function that that is the case.
>
> (2) The intent a person has to have to commit an offence under this section need not be directed at –
>> (a) any particular program or data;
>> (b) a program or data of any particular kind; or
>> (c) a program or data held in any particular computer.

The *actus reus* and *mens rea* of this offence will be examined separately:

1. *The* actus reus *of the s 1 offence.* The *actus reus* of the offence is simply causing a computer to 'perform any function'. It seems that this could even include switching a computer on. It would not cover simply looking at a computer screen because this does not involve causing the computer to perform a function. There is no need to show that the defendant actually reached unauthorised material, only that he intended to do so.

2. *The* mens rea *of the s 1 offence.* The *mens rea* requirement can be broken down into three elements:

   (a) An intention to secure access to any program or data on any computer. The phrase 'secure access' is narrower than may be at first assumed. Section 17(2) states:

   > A person secures access to any program or data held in a computer if by causing a computer to perform any function he –
   >
   > (a) alters or erases the program or data;
   > (b) copies or moves it to any storage medium other than that in which it is held or to a different location in the storage medium in which it is held;
   > (c) uses it; or
   > (d) has it output from the computer in which it is held (whether by having it displayed or in any other manner);
   >
   > and references to access to a program or data (and to an intent to secure such access) shall be read accordingly.

   This seems to mean that simply looking at unauthorised data on a computer does not infringe s 1. Once seeing the data, the defendant must do one of the four things with the data, using a computer. Writing down the data seen would not be regarded as copying it under (b), because the copying is not done by causing the computer to perform a function. 'Using' under (c) is restricted by the requirement that the computer must use the data. So finding confidential information on a database and then using it to blackmail someone would not be sufficient unless 'by causing a computer to perform any function he... uses it'. It is made clear in s 1(2) Computer Misuse Act that there is no need to prove an intent to obtain access to any particular program or data. In other words, the offence is committed if a defendant is entering the computer just to see what she can find. Further, it does not matter whether the defendant is trying to reach data on the computer she is using, or attempting to reach data on another computer using her own computer (*A-G's Ref (No 1 of 1991)*). Section 1 could be used to protect copyright in computer software, although it is not clear that the section was intended to do this. If someone received an unlicensed copy of some software and used it on her computer then this would seem to breach the terms of s 1 of the Act.

(b) The access to the data must be unauthorised. To be authorised to access data it must be shown that the defendant was either himself entitled to control access to those data, or he had been given authority to access the information by a person who was able to control access to it (s 17(5) Computer Misuse Act). It may be that a defendant is permitted access to some parts of a computer's database, but this would be no defence if she were attempting to reach parts of the database which she was not permitted to access. For example, in *R v Bow Street Metropolitan Stipendiary Magistrate ex p Government of the USA** [2000] 2 AC 216 an employee of a credit-card company was allotted certain customers and access to data held about them on her company's computer. She accessed information about other customers. This would have constituted an offence under s 1 of the Act. It was no defence that she was authorised to access other customers' data; she was not authorised to access the data referred to in the charge.

Similarly, it may be that a defendant is authorised to access data for one purpose but not another. So, if a defendant is permitted access to data only for work purposes but accesses the data for her own reasons then this will be seen as unauthorised access (*R v Bow Street Metropolitan Stipendiary Magistrate ex p Government of the USA*). Further, a person may be entitled to view certain data, but not to amend them. In such a case, amending the data could infringe s 1. It is also submitted that a person may be authorised to access data only in a particular way (for example, by using an office computer) and that accessing those data in an unauthorised manner (for example, by using a computer from home) could infringe s 1. However, the courts are yet to address this question.

In *DPP v Ellis* [2001] EWHC Admin 362, an employee of a university used computers which he was not entitled to use because they were restricted for use to certain staff. He simply used the computer to view web pages. It was held in the Divisional Court that he was not authorised to use the computer and that he was therefore not authorised to access the web-browser program on the computer. This was so, even though the web-browser program was widely available and the web pages did not contain secret information. The simple fact that he was unauthorised to use that computer meant he was not authorised to use the programs on the computer.

(c) The defendant knows that he or she is not authorised to access the program or data. It should be noted that this knowledge is based on a subjective test. There will therefore be borderline cases where a person is unsure whether he is authorised or not to access the data. If the defendant believes that access is unauthorised but in fact it is not, he will not have committed the offence although he may have committed an attempted offence. It must also be shown that the knowledge existed at the time when he caused the computer to perform a function. So if the defendant, believing he is authorised, enters a database and a message flashes on the screen that he is not authorised to use the data then he will not have committed an offence if he just watches the screen. He will however commit the offence if he then causes the computer to perform a function with the relevant intent.

14.6.3 Unauthorised access with intent

The offence in s 2 is a more serious one than that in s 1. It requires proof that a defendant committed an offence under s 1, and in addition that he intended to commit or facilitate the commission of a serious arrestable offence (see Chapter 2). The most common example of an arrestable offence in this context is likely to be a deception offence or theft. It is made clear in subsection 2(3) that there is no need for an intention that the serious arrestable offence is committed on the same occasion as the s 1 offence. Therefore a defendant who obtains data which he intends to use at some point in the future to commit an offence of obtaining property by deception will still be guilty of the s 2 offence. Further, according to s 2(4), it is not a defence that the arrestable offence he hopes to commit will in fact be impossible to commit. This is in line with the general law on 'impossible crimes' (see Chapter 18).

14.6.4 Unauthorised modification of computer material

This offence is defined in s 3 Computer Misuse Act as follows:

(1)   A person is guilty of an offence if –
    (a)   he does any unauthorised act in relation to a computer; and
    (b)   at the time when he does the act he has the requisite intent and the requisite knowledge.
(2)   For the purposes of subsection (1)(b) above the requisite intent is an intent to do the act in question and by so doing –
    (a)   to impair the operation of any computer,
    (b)   to prevent or hinder access to any program or data held in any computer, or
    (c)   to impair the operation of any such program or the reliability of any such data, whether permanently or temporarily.
(3)   The intent need not be directed at –
    (a)   any particular computer;
    (b)   any particular program or data; or
    (c)   a program or data of any particular kind.
(4)   For the purposes of subsection (1)(b) above the requisite knowledge is knowledge that the act in question is unauthorised.
(5)   In this section –
    (a)   a reference to doing an act includes a reference to causing an act to be done;
    (b)   'act' includes a series of acts…

The *actus reus* of this offence, under s 3(1), is 'any act which causes an unauthorised modification of the contents of any computer'. The *mens rea* is:

an intent to cause a modification to the contents of any computer and by so doing –

(a)   to impair the operation of any computer;
(b)   to prevent or hinder access to any program or data held in any computer; or
(c)   to impair the operation of any such program or the reliability of any such data.

It is also necessary to show that the defendant knew that the modification which was intended was unauthorised. Thus a defendant has a defence if he was authorised to modify a program to some extent but by mistake modified much more than he intended.

This section is clearly aimed at people who alter computer data with intent to corrupt a program or alter a database. The intent does not need to be directed towards any particular computer or data. Modification is defined as including removal of any program or data on a computer and includes adding to the contents or erasing them. It also includes temporary modification (s 3(5)). Section 3 appears to cover sending someone a disk with a virus on it which was intended to damage the working of the computer. In *DPP v Lennon* [2006] EWHC 1201 (Admin) it was held that sending over five million e-mails over the course of a weekend would be an offence under this section. It could not be argued that the victim, by having an e-mail account, was consenting to receiving so many e-mails.

14.6.5 Criminal damage of computers

Some cases have suggested that to damage computer software may be an offence under the Criminal Damage Act 1971. The information on software itself cannot be damaged under the Act as it is intangible property and so not covered by the Act. However, if the defendant is charged with damaging the computer or a disk then it seems that this may be an offence under the Act (*Cox v Riley* [1986] Crim LR 460). Under s 3(6) Computer Misuse Act criminal damage can be charged in relation to computers only if there has been a change in the physical condition of the computer. It is clearly intended that prosecutions involving corruption of data should be brought under the Computer Misuse Act. However, the wording of s 3(6) is rather vague, and the higher sentences and *mens rea* requirement of the Criminal Damage Act may persuade some prosecutors still to use the Criminal Damage Act in this area. Such a prosecution would involve expert witnesses arguing over whether changing information on a computer hard-drive, for example, involves a physical change in the computer.

14.7 Possession offences

Several statutory offences have been created requiring possession, for example, of offensive weapons (Prevention of Crime Act 1953); drugs (Misuse of Drugs Act 1971); and articles for use in burglary, theft or deception (s 25 Theft Act 1968). The major difficulty with these offences has been to decide whether possession involves any *mens rea* element. In the leading case of *Warner v MPC** [1969] 2 AC 256, the defendant picked up two boxes which he thought contained perfume. In fact they contained drugs and he was charged with possession of drugs. The House of Lords held that if you possess a box or container then you possess the items in the container. The House of Lords has recently confirmed this ruling in *R v Lambert** [2001] 3 WLR 206. Lord Clyde explained:

> Where the drug is in a container, it is sufficient for the prosecution to prove that the defendant had control of the container, that he knew of its existence and that there was something in it, and that the something was in fact the controlled drug which the prosecution alleges it to be. The prosecution does not require to prove that the accused knew that the thing was a controlled drug.

There are two exceptions to this rule. The first is if the item has been placed in the defendant's pocket or handbag without her knowledge and she has not had an opportunity to discover that the item has been placed there. The second is if the accused believed that the box contained something completely different from what it actually held. However, in *Warner v MPC* perfume was said not to be wholly different from drugs, which is a surprisingly narrow and rather harsh interpretation of the second exception. It seems that the burden of proof of either of these exceptions is on the defendant (*McNamara* (1988) 87 Cr App R 246). However, these are evidential, rather than legal, burdens of proof (see Chapter 2 for explanations of these terms) and therefore do not infringe the Human Rights Act (*Lambert*: see Chapter 2).

Hot Topic – Is graffiti criminal damage?

At first, it might seem that graffiti will always be damage. In *Hardman* [1986] Crim LR 330 graffiti was held to be damaged, even though it would have been readily washed away by rain. However, there may be some very minor graffiti which could so easily be removed that it is equivalent to the spit on the coat in *R v A* [1978] Crim LR 689, which was found not to amount to damage.

More interesting is an argument that graffiti might be said to improve the property rather than damage it. Consider for example, graffiti by the artist known as Banksy, which could render the property very valuable (see Edwards).

Some sociologists have distinguished between art graffiti and vandalism graffiti. Certainly the description of graffiti as art has been debated by some. However, it is the work of Banksy in this country, which has been represented in leading art galleries, which has meant it is hard to deny that some graffiti has clear artistic merit. Banksy himself (quoted by Edwards) has stated:

Modern street art is the product of a generation tired of growing up with a relentless barrage of logos and images being thrown at their head every day, and much of it is an attempt to pick up these visual rocks and throw them back. Suppression of graffiti is part of society's 'headlong march into bland conformity'.

There is no defence in the Criminal Damage Act 1971 that the act has artistic value. So the only defence could be that the act is not damage, or he did not foresee it could be damage.

Perhaps the strongest case for graffiti not being damage in where the graffitied property has been left derelict or left to rack and ruin. In such a case if the graffiti turns the ugly wall, say, into an attractive one, then there may be an argument there is no damage. In such a case it might be said that the graffiti has not impaired either the value or the usefulness of the property. Nevertheless the court may take the view that if the owner sees the need to remove the graffiti that is likely to involve cost and therefore the graffiti has affected the value of the item. Where, however, the owner decides to sell the graffitied wall it may seem hard to argue its value has been impaired.

An alternative argument for the graffiti artist is to argue that there is no intention or recklessness to damage the property. It is not clear how the court will interpret this element of the offence. If the defendant claims he did not intend or foresee that his artwork could be regarded as damage, is that a defence? Or will the court argue that the defendant intended to do the act, and the court assesses whether the act amounts to damage or not. There is no case law on that issue, but it is likely the court will rule that it is for the court to determine whether an act is damage and the *mens rea* requires intention or recklessness to do the act which amounts to damage.

Summary

14.1 Criminal damage is the offence of intentionally or recklessly destroying or damaging property belonging to another. There is also a separate offence of destroying or damaging property with intent to endanger life or being reckless as to whether life is endangered. Recklessness has been held to include the state of mind of the person who foresees an obvious risk that property will be destroyed or damaged, or life endangered. It also includes the state of mind of the person who fails to foresee that risk.

14.2 Arson occurs where property is destroyed or damaged by fire.

14.3 The essence of blackmail is the making of unwarranted demands, with menaces, with a view to gaining something for oneself or someone else. Whether words or acts are demands with menaces is determined by considering all the circumstances, and the threat can be express or implied. The gain must be financial.

14.4 It is an offence for the accused to take a conveyance for her own or another's use. 'Take' means that the conveyance must be taken in the sense of being moved. It must also involve taking the conveyance as a means of transporting someone and not for some other use. It is a defence if the owner consented to the taking.

14.5 Aggravated vehicle taking arises when a person takes another car and causes death or serious injury.

14.6 Computers can be used to commit all kinds of crimes, although there are some specific crimes designed for computers set out in the Computer Misuse Act 1990. This Act prohibits gaining unauthorised access to computer material, and contains a more serious offence of doing this with the intent to commit another offence. There is also an offence of modifying computer material in an unauthorised way. It is possible to be guilty of criminal damage to computers if there has been a physical change to some component of the computer.

14.7 There are various offences relating to possession of particular items. The notion of possession has been held not to include a *mens rea* requirement. One is held to possess an item found on one's body unless one thought the item was different in substance, or one lacked the opportunity to ascertain that one was in possession of an item.

Further Reading

Blackmail is discussed by Aldridge and Lamond. Elliot and Edwards considers criminal damage, Spencer the 1992 Aggravated Vehicle-Taking Act and Wasik computer crimes.

Aldridge, 'Attempted Murder of the Soul: Blackmail, Privacy and Secrets' (1993) 13 OJLS 368.
Edwards, 'Banksy's Graffiti: A Not-so-simple Case of Criminal Damage?' (2009) J Crim L 345.
Elliot, 'Endangering Life by Destroying or Damaging Property' [1997] Crim LR 382.
Lamond, 'Coercion, Threats and the Puzzle of Blackmail', in Simester and Smith (eds), *Harm and Culpability* (Oxford University Press 1995).
MacEwan, 'The Computer Misuse Act 1990: Lessons from Its Past and Predictions for Its Future' [2008] Crim LR 955.
Spencer, 'The Aggravated Vehicle-Taking Act 1992' [1992] Crim LR 699.
Wasik, *Crime and the Computer* (Oxford University Press 1991).

Case Notes

▶ *Bevans* [1988] Crim LR 236. Court of Appeal

The defendant, who suffered from osteoarthritis, took a gun to his doctor's surgery and threatened to kill a doctor unless he was given a pain-relieving drug. He was convicted, and appealed, arguing that he had not made a demand for financial gain. The Court of Appeal upheld his conviction, holding that his demand was to be given the drug, which was property. The fact that his motive was to relieve his pain rather than make a financial gain was immaterial.

▶ *Blake* [1993] Crim LR 586. Divisional Court

The accused wrote slogans opposing the Gulf War in felt-tip pen on a concrete pillar. He was charged with criminal damage, but attempted to argue that his conduct was justified by s 3 Criminal Law Act 1967. This argument failed because the writing did not constitute 'force'. He also argued that he believed that God owned the pillar and consented to the damage. The court rejected this argument, claiming that such questions were outside the provenance of the court.

▶ *Bow* (1976) 64 Cr App R 54. Court of Appeal

The Crown alleged that the appellant and his brother were poaching when gamekeepers approached them. The head gamekeeper parked his Land Rover so as to obstruct the only escape route for the appellant's car. The appellant got into the driver's seat of the Land Rover, released the handbrake and coasted 200 yards without switching on the engine. The appellant was convicted of taking a conveyance contrary to s 12 Theft Act 1968. He appealed and argued before the Court of Appeal that he had not taken the conveyance as a means of transport. The Court of Appeal decided that the motive of the appellant was irrelevant and he could be said to have taken the vehicle as a conveyance.

▶ *R v Bow Street Metropolitan Stipendiary Magistrate ex p Government of the USA* [2000] 2 AC 216. House of Lords

Ojomo was an employee of the American Express credit-card company in the United States of America. Although she was able to access the accounts of any customer on her work computer, she was authorised to access only the accounts of certain customers assigned to her. She accessed the accounts of customers who had not been assigned to her. In proceedings to extradite her to the United States, the issue arose whether she had committed an offence under UK law and in particular s 1(1) Computer Misuse Act 1990. She argued that s 1(1) dealt with hackers, 'outsiders' entering a database, not insiders who were entitled to enter part of the database. The House of Lords rejected such a distinction. As Ojomo was not entitled to have access to the part of the database which she accessed, she had committed the offence, even though she was authorised to access other parts of the database.

▶ *R v G* [2003] UKHL 50. House of Lords

See Chapter 5 Case notes.

▶ *R v Lambert* [2001] 3 WLR 206. House of Lords

See Chapter 2 Case notes.

▶ *Morphitis v Salmon* [1990] Crim LR 48. Court of Appeal

The defendant removed a scaffolding clip from a barrier erected by a neighbour and was charged with causing criminal damage to the clip. He had scratched the clip, but this was held not to be damage as scratch marks occurred as part of normal use of these clips. The court suggested that a conviction might have succeeded had he been charged with damage to the barrier as a whole.

▶ *Steer* [1988] AC 111. House of Lords

The appellant was convicted of criminal damage, being reckless as to endangering the life of another person, contrary to s 1(2)(b) Criminal Damage Act 1971. He had fired a rifle at the door and bedroom window of a house. The trial judge held that under s 1(2), the danger to life need not come from the damage to property (in this case the damage to the door and window), but that it was sufficient if the danger came from the act of the accused which caused the damage (in this case the rifle shots). The Court of Appeal allowed the appeal and the House of Lords dismissed a further appeal by the prosecutor. It was held that under s 1(2) it was necessary that the accused should intend to endanger (or be reckless as to endangering) life by the destruction of, or damage to, the property itself.

▶ *Warner v MPC* [1969] 2 AC 256. **House of Lords**

See Chapter 6 Case notes.

▶ *Webster and Warwick* [1995] 2 All ER 168. **Court of Appeal**

The Court of Appeal heard two cases together. Webster and some others threw a stone from a railway bridge onto a passenger train. The stone crashed into the roof and showered the passengers with fibreglass. Warwick threw a brick at the rear window of a police car. In both cases the appeal concerned the correct direction on the *mens rea* of dangerous damage. The Court of Appeal stressed that it had to be shown that the recklessness as to endangerment of life was endangerment by criminal damage. In other words, it needed to be shown that Webster foresaw that passengers would be threatened by the splintering roof, not the stone itself, and that Warwick foresaw that the police officer would be endangered by the broken glass, not the brick itself. The Court of Appeal found that, in each case, although the trial judges had misdirected the juries, it was clear from the evidence and the juries' verdicts that the appellants were reckless as to whether the life of another would be endangered, and so convictions on that basis under s 1(2) Criminal Damage Act would be substituted.

Part IV

Defences

Chapter 15

Denial of elements of offences

Key Terms

- ▶ **Exemption** – an exclusion from the ambit of the criminal law because a person lacks the capacity to comply with the law.
- ▶ **Insanity** – the defendant suffers from a defect of reason caused by a disease of the mind, which means they are not aware of what they are doing or not aware that what they are doing is wrong.
- ▶ **Self-defence** – the defendant uses a reasonable level of force in response to a person who is posing an unjust threat to him or her.

15.1 Defences

A defendant who faces a criminal charge and wishes to plead not guilty has essentially four courses open to her:

1. *To claim an exemption from liability.* Some defendants are excluded from the ambit of the criminal law altogether, however heinous their crime, for example those under the age of criminal responsibility and those who are insane. Such defendants are exempted from liability because they lack a core requirement of criminal liability: they are people who lack the capacity to comply with the requirements of the criminal law. To punish infants or the insane would contravene profound principles which underlie the criminal law by punishing people who are not capable of being responsible for their actions. As Horder (1996) explains:

    > in a civilized legal system, only those who have the intellectual and moral capacity to understand the significance of their conduct will fall to be judged under its rules of criminal responsibility.

2. *To deny that the* actus reus *has been proved.* A defendant can argue that the prosecution has not proved beyond reasonable doubt that the defendant's acts amounted to the *actus reus*. This may be a simple claim that the defendant was not present at the scene of the crime but somewhere else (an alibi); that she was at the scene of the crime but did not do the relevant act (for example, she did not pull the trigger, but someone else did); or that her act did not cause the injury. A less obvious way of denying the *actus reus* is to admit that the defendant did the act which caused the injury, but argue that it was not an unlawful act; for example the defendant acted in self-defence. The courts have (rather oddly) seen unlawfulness as an aspect of the *actus reus*, and so a claim of self-defence is in fact a claim that the defendant acted lawfully and thus a denial of the *actus reus*. Alternatively, the defendant may seek to argue that she did not really act but was an automaton at the time when the crime happened. This also is a denial of the *actus reus* – a denial that the defendant acted in the legal sense (see Section 3.5).

3. *To deny that the* mens rea *has been proved.* The defendant may claim she did not have the required *mens rea*. This can be the straightforward claim that, for example, she

did not intend the injury, or that she did not foresee that the injury might be caused, and so she was not reckless. Two particular ways of denying *mens rea* arise when the defendant claims that she lacked the necessary *mens rea* because she was intoxicated or had made a mistake.

4. *To rely on a defence.* A defendant may admit that she performed the *actus reus* with the necessary *mens rea*, but seek to argue that she has a special defence, for example that she acted under duress (*Fisher* [2004] Crim LR 938) or with the consent of the victim. If successful, these will result in an acquittal. When facing a charge of murder, the defendant can use a partial defence (for example, loss of control) which, if successful, reduces the conviction from murder to manslaughter.

There are many different ways of classifying these defences. One way is to analyse them as is done in this book (as exemptions, denial of *actus reus* or *mens rea*, or special defences). This method has the benefit of distinguishing those claims which argue that the wrong of the crime was not present (that is, there was no *actus reus* or no *mens rea*) and those claims which admit the wrongness of the act but argue that in all the circumstances the defendant should still not be blamed for it (that is, by relying on an exemption or defence). The classification of defences into '*actus reus* defences' and '*mens rea* defences' is also important because it has implications for the way in which the defences develop and can be used. For example, if the offence is one of strict liability then only *actus reus* defences may be pleaded; lack of *mens rea* is irrelevant if there is no *mens rea* element to the offence. It also has the benefit of being the way in which the judiciary most commonly discusses the defences.

However, to analyse defences in the above way has two drawbacks. First, there can be grave difficulties in deciding into which category a particular defence should fall. For example, the House of Lords has suggested that the consent of the victim (where it is relevant) should (in respect of offences against the person) be seen as a special defence (*Brown* [1993] 1 AC 212). However, many academic commentators believe that it is better to see consent as a denial of the *actus reus*, a denial that the act was harmful at all (see Section 7.7). Second, the analysis may hide the fact that the defences in different categories are closely linked. For example, there is a clear similarity between diminished responsibility and insanity, although in the above analysis they would be placed in different categories.

We have already noted that commentators have suggested some overarching theories which might explain all the defences (for example, the choice theory or the character theory: see Section 1.4). That would be another way of categorising the defences. Another popular method would be to distinguish between justifications and excuses, and we will discuss that distinction at the start of Chapter 16.

Before considering the defences in greater detail it is important to distinguish between a defence and a mitigation. When the defendant is able successfully to raise a defence then he is found not guilty (except in the case of a partial defence where the defendant is convicted of a lesser offence than she would have been without the partial defence). By contrast, mitigation is a factor which becomes relevant at the sentencing stage. The mitigating factors can be so persuasive that only a nominal sentence is imposed (for example, an absolute discharge). But even where that occurs the defendant still has the censure of a criminal conviction, marking the law's disapproval of the accused's actions.

We will try to draw analogies between the defences where appropriate, but will divide the defences up on the basis mentioned earlier: that is, into those which are exemptions from the criminal law, those which deny the *actus reus*, those which deny the *mens rea* and those which admit that the defendant has committed the *actus reus* with the necessary *mens rea*, but seek to use a special defence.

15.2 Exemptions from liability

As explained above, an exemption applies to a person who lacks the moral capacity to be subject to liability under criminal law.

15.2.1 Infancy

Infancy is a clear example of an exemption from criminal liability. There is an age below which children are *doli incapax*, that is they are not responsible for their actions under the criminal law. If not responsible for their actions, children deserve not the censure of a criminal conviction but the assistance of social services. Different societies take different views on the appropriate age of criminal responsibility, and in English law this has changed over the years. It is necessary to discuss two age groups:

1. *Under-10-year-olds.* At present, the age of criminal responsibility is set at 10 years old by s 50 Children and Young Persons Act 1933. If a 9-year-old commits the *actus reus* of a crime, be it the most premeditated, most heinous, most blameworthy of crimes, she cannot be held criminally responsible for it. It is possible for care proceedings to be instigated under the Children Act 1989, which may result in a child being placed in secure local authority accommodation, but those are civil, not criminal, proceedings and are beyond the scope of this book.

   If an under-10-year-old's conduct would, in an adult, amount to the *actus reus* of an offence and it is proved that the child was manipulated by an adult who had the necessary *mens rea* for that offence, then the adult can be convicted of the offence. The child is regarded as the 'innocent agent' of the adult if a causal link can be shown between the conduct of the adult and the *actus reus* of the offence (see Section 4.4).

2. *Children over 10 years old.* It used to be the law that between the ages of 10 and 14 a child was presumed *doli incapax* and so could not be convicted of a crime, but that presumption could be rebutted if the prosecution proved that he had the capacity to differentiate between right and wrong. However, this presumption was abolished by s 34 Crime and Disorder Act 1998:

   > The rebuttable presumption of criminal law that a child aged 10 or over is incapable of committing an offence is hereby abolished.

   Although there had been some debate over the correct interpretation of this provision in *R v JBT* the House of Lords made it clear that the section abolishes the *doli incapax* rule for all children over 10. So a child over the age of ten can be convicted of a criminal offence even if she does not know the difference between right and wrong (provided she has the necessary *mens rea*). In *T and V v UK* [2000] Crim LR 187 the European Court of Human Rights rejected an argument that it was contrary to the Convention to punish children under the age of 14. It should be added that there are special sentencing and criminal procedures for juvenile offenders.

15.2.2 Insanity

There are two ways in which a defendant's sanity may be relevant: if he is insane at the time of the actual trial itself or if he was insane at the time when he committed the offence. The two have quite different justifications. It is unfair to try someone who is insane at the time of the trial (unfit to plead), because if he is unable to understand the proceedings then he will be unable to participate and put forward his case. It is also inappropriate to punish someone who is insane at the time he committed the offence because he was not responsible for his actions. Although such a person may be suitable for compulsory detention, the censure connected with a criminal conviction would not be appropriate. Given those different justifications, it is not surprising that the law regulating these two versions of the insanity defence is quite distinct.

1. *Unfitness to plead.* In relation to unfitness to plead, the law is now governed by the Criminal Procedure (Insanity and Unfitness to Plead) Act 1991. To be found unfit to plead it is necessary to show that the defendant is unable to give, receive or understand communications relating to the trial. So if, because of his disability, the defendant was unable to comprehend the evidence given or to instruct his counsel, he would not be fit to be tried. It seems that a defendant who is able to understand the proceedings but suffers from delusions (for example, that he is convinced he is guilty when he is not; or that the court is influenced by malign powers) will still be fit to stand trial (*Moyle* [2008] EWCA Crim 3059).

   If there is a question over whether the defendant is fit to plead, that question will be the first issue which the jury will have to decide, before hearing any evidence about the crime itself. If the defendant is found fit to plead then the trial will proceed as normal (although with a different jury). If it is decided that he is not fit then there will be a 'trial of the facts' using a different jury. Here the essential question for the jury is whether the defendant committed the *actus reus* of the crime with which he is charged. The jury do not need to consider whether the defendant had the *mens rea* (*Antoine* [2001] AC 340) or could rely on an excuse such as loss of control (*Grant* [2002] 2 WLR 1409). If it is decided that the defendant did not commit the *actus reus*, then obviously he can walk free. But if the defendant did commit the *actus reus* then the judge will have a wide range of orders available, ranging from a discharge, to a supervision order, to compulsory admission to hospital; although in the case of a murder charge, indefinite detention in a special hospital is mandatory. These different orders are available to a judge if the defendant committed the *actus reus*, even if it is not shown that he had the *mens rea* of the crime (*A-G's Ref (No 3 of 1998)* [2000] 1 QB 401). In *R v H* [2003] 1 HRLR 19 the House of Lords rejected a claim that this procedure violated the European Convention on Human Rights.

2. *Insanity at the time of the crime.* The second way in which the issue of insanity could be raised is by introducing proof that the defendant was insane at the time he committed the *actus reus*. This will become relevant only if the defendant is fit to stand trial. This area of the law was until recently overshadowed by the fact that if a defendant was found insane at the time of the crime then the judge would have no alternative but to send him to a hospital where he could be detained without a maximum sentence. This led many who might otherwise have pleaded insanity not to do so, because they would rather be found guilty and receive a sentence which would at least have a maximum duration. Since the Criminal Procedure (Insanity and Unfitness to Plead) Act 1991 the judge has a much wider discretion

on sentencing and she can even order an absolute discharge, except in murder cases where indefinite detention in a special hospital is still mandatory. It was expected that this greater flexibility on sentencing would lead to a greater number of people attempting to use the defence, although in fact this has not occurred. Maybe the stigma of an insanity verdict is still a strong deterrent.

The legal definition of insanity dates back to the *M'Naghten** [1843–60] All ER 229 rules set out in 1873. It is important to realise that insanity here is a legal concept and the legal definition of the term is quite different from any medical or popular understanding of insanity. Some people who are insane under the law would certainly not be regarded as insane in medical terms. For example, courts have found epilepsy, sleepwalking and hypoglycaemia (caused by diabetes) to fall within the legal definition of insanity. Similarly someone who might be regarded as insane by doctors (although medical terminology tends to avoid the use of the term insanity) would not necessarily fall within the legal terminology. A person who heard voices telling him to kill traffic wardens and then did so might not fall within the legal definition of insanity.

Lawton LJ in *Quick** [1973] 1 QB 910 referred to insanity as 'this quagmire of law seldom entered nowadays save by those in desperate need of some kind of a defence'. In *Sullivan** [1984] 1 AC 156, Lord Diplock admitted that 'the nomenclature adopted by the medical profession may change from time to time ... But the meaning of the expression "disease of the mind" as the cause of "a defect of reason" remains unchanged for the purposes of the application of the *M'Naghten* rules.'

The *M'Naghten* rules (as confirmed by the House of Lords in Sullivan) state that there are two requirements which need to be shown in order to establish insanity:

(i)   The defendant suffers from a defect of reason caused by a disease of the mind.
(ii) The defect of reason must mean that either: (a) the defendant is not aware of what he is doing or (b) he is not aware that what he is doing is wrong.

This definition contains the following elements:

▶ Disease of the mind
▶ Defect of reason
▶ The defendant did not know what he was doing or that what he was doing was wrong.

(a) *Disease of the mind.* 'Mind' is used not to mean brain, but in the sense of 'the mental faculties of reason, memory and understanding' (Devlin J in *Kemp* [1956] 3 All ER 249, approved by Lord Diplock in *Sullivan*). So a condition which does not affect the brain as such but does affect the reasoning process could be classified as a disease of the mind. This widens the definition of insanity. This is especially so because a disease of the mind need not be permanent. In *Sullivan*, Lord Diplock explained that if the disease impairs the faculties of reason, memory and understanding, 'it matters not ... whether the impairment itself is permanent or is transient and intermittent, provided that it subsisted at the time of commission of the act'. Lord Diplock thereby cast doubt on dicta of Lord Denning in *Bratty v AG for Northern Ireland** [1963] AC 386, 20 years earlier, who defined a disease of the mind in terms of a 'disorder which has manifested itself in violence and is prone to recur ... At any rate it is the sort of disease for which a person should be detained in hospital rather than be given an unqualified acquittal.' This wide definition of insanity means that epilepsy and conditions caused by diabetes can be classified as forms of insanity.

It is important to distinguish automatism from insanity. The crucial distinction depends on whether the impairment of mental facilities was caused by an 'external factor' or an 'internal factor'. In order to constitute insanity an internal factor must be involved. This distinction has already been discussed in Section 3.5.

(b) *The defect of reason*. The disease of the mind must cause a defect of reason. It was pointed out in Clarke (1972) that confusion or absentmindedness causing a failure to use the power of reasoning or failure of concentration does not amount to a defect of reason. The accused must be deprived by the disease of the power of reasoning, even if temporarily.

(c) *Did not know the nature and quality of his act or that the act was wrong*. The defect of reason must be sufficiently severe that the accused either did not know the nature and quality of his act or did not know that it was wrong. This is a difficult test to satisfy. The Report of the Butler Committee on Mentally Abnormal Offenders (1975, Cmnd 6244) commented:

> Just as a person must generally be very mad indeed not to know what he is doing (the nature and quality of his act) when he is killing a man or setting fire to a building, so he must be very mad not to know that these acts attract the unfavourable notice of the police (his knowledge of wrong).

The 'nature and quality' of an act refers to its physical nature, and covers cases of severe delusions, where the accused believes he is doing something quite different from the act which is in fact done; for example, where the defendant thinks he is killing monsters from outer space when in fact he is killing a human being. It also covers cases where the accused has no control over his physical movements, as in an epileptic fit (*Sullivan*). Lord Diplock in Sullivan suggested that the phrase 'not knowing the nature and quality of his act' be explained to a jury as 'he did not know what he was doing'.

If the accused was aware of the nature of his act, he may still be found to be insane if it is proved that he did not know that it was wrong. 'Wrong' here means legally wrong rather than morally wrong (Windle, Johnson (2007). It should be stressed that the lack of knowledge of the legality of the defendant's acts must stem from her disease of the mind. Generally, ignorance of the law is no excuse.

It will be appreciated that the *M'Naghten* rules mean that a defendant who as a result of insane delusions believes that God has told him to kill people will not be regarded as insane. He will be aware of the nature of his acts and aware that what he is doing is contrary to the law. It would be different if he thought that God had told him that the people were in fact not humans but aliens from outer space whom he should destroy. In such a case the defendant would appear not to know the quality of his acts and would be classified as insane. Whether it is proper to distinguish between delusions in this way is open to debate.

The *M'Naghten* rules also do not cover a person who suffers from what is called an 'irresistible impulse' to act if he knows what he is doing and knows that it is contrary to law. Lord Denning said in *Bratty v. AG* for Northern Ireland, 'when a man is charged with murder, and it appears that he knew what he was doing, but that he could not resist it, then his assertion "I couldn't help myself" is no defence in itself'. In the case of murder, however, irresistible impulse may be evidence of diminished responsibility (*Byrne* [1960] 3 All ER 1).

15.2.2(a) Discussion of the law on insanity

The legal definition of insanity is odd. It bears no relation to how doctors understand mental disorder. Further it seems related to whether or not defendants pose a danger to the public. Although, following the Criminal Procedure (Insanity and Unfitness to Plead) Act 1991 the evidence of two medical experts is required before a finding of insanity can be made, the experts have to use the outdated M'Naughten definition. This can mean not only that people who should not be labelled insane are, it also means that people who need the help of mental health services are not identified.

Three peculiarities of the procedural aspects of the insanity defence should be noted. First, the result of a successful insanity plea is not a straightforward acquittal: it is the 'special verdict' of 'not guilty by reason of insanity'. Second, there is a presumption of sanity, so that, as an exception to the general rule, an accused raising insanity has the burden of proving it on the balance of probabilities (on the burden of proof generally see Section 2.4). This is controversial. Normally the prosecution has to rebut the defendant's claim that he had no *mens rea* beyond reasonable doubt. Where, however, the defendant's claim is that he is insane, the burden switches to the defendant. Third, the prosecution, as well as the defendant, may raise the issue of insanity. This may happen on a plea of diminished responsibility, another defence which puts in issue the accused's state of mind. The prosecution may counter with evidence of insanity in order to ensure detention in a hospital instead of a complete acquittal or a sentence of ordinary imprisonment. Such a situation may result in a change of plea to guilty by an accused who prefers a sentence of imprisonment to the stigma of the special verdict.

15.2.2(b) Insanity and the Human Rights Act

The present law on insanity could be challenged in two ways under the Act. First, it could be claimed that the present law, with its placing on the defendant of the burden of proving that he is insane, contravenes Article 6 of the Convention. This argument would follow the lines made in Section 2.4.2 in relation to reverse onus clauses. The Court of Appeal in *R v M; R v Kerr; R v H* [2002] Crim LR 57 held that Article 6 had no application in cases of insanity, because the finding that a defendant is insane is not a criminal proceeding.

Second, Article 5(1) allows the lawful detention of persons of unsound mind, but only in accordance with a procedure prescribed by law. The European Court of Human Rights has held that unsoundness of mind must be established on objective medical evidence (*Winterwerp v Netherlands* (1979) 2 EHRR 387). The Criminal Procedure (Insanity and Unfitness to Plead) Act 1991 appears to comply with this requirement by insisting on two medical witnesses before a special insanity verdict can be given. However, these witnesses must use the legal definition of insanity and not the medical one. This would mean, as we have seen, that the medical evidence could be used to detain an epileptic. Could this mean that the detention is not established on 'objective medical evidence'? Indeed in the case of an epileptic the evidence would be that the person is not medically insane. Another issue raised by the Court of Appeal, but yet to be resolved, is whether the fact that a person found unfit for trial can be detained is compliant with Article 5, given that the procedure does not involve a finding that the defendant's unfitness requires detention (Grant).

15.3 Denial of *actus reus*

As mentioned earlier, the defendant can seek to mount a defence on the basis that he did not satisfy the *actus reus* of the crime. This can be a straightforward denial that he did the act alleged. In this section we will look at two special ways in which a defendant may allege that he did not commit the *actus reus*.

15.3.1 Self-defence and the prevention of crime

Here we will consider two closely aligned defences:

1. *Section 3 Criminal Law Act 1967*. This provides a defence to a person who is using force to prevent a crime. Section 3 states:

    (1) A person may use such force as is reasonable in the circumstances in the prevention of crime, or in effecting or assisting in the lawful arrest of offenders or suspected offenders or of persons unlawfully at large.
    (2) Subsection (1) above shall replace the rules of the common law on the question when force used for a purpose mentioned in the subsection is justified by that purpose.

    This section will therefore apply where the defendant sees a friend being attacked and uses force to protect his friend.
2. *The common law of self-defence*. Subsection (2) of s 3 makes it clear that where s 3(1) applies, the common law defence of use of force to prevent a crime or to effect or assist in a lawful arrest of offenders can be used. However, subsection (2) does not refer to the defence of self-defence. It is therefore generally assumed that the common law defence that a defendant can use force to protect him- or herself from an unjust threat still exists. In some cases both these defences will apply. If the defendant is attacked by someone and responds with violence, the defendant may be able to rely on either defence: to claim that his use of force was an attempt to prevent further attacks on him and therefore fell within s 3; or to rely on common law self-defence, arguing that the defendant was acting in order to defend himself. One or both of these defences apply to someone who is protecting themselves from an attack; to someone who is protecting someone else who is being attacked; to someone who is protecting her own property from attack; and to someone who is protecting someone else's property from attack.

Despite the similarities between the two defences there are two key differences:

1. Where the attacker is not acting unlawfully (for example, the attacker is a child or is insane) then s 3 does not apply (the defendant is not preventing a crime); but common law self-defence does apply.
2. The common law defence applies only if the defendant is acting in order to protect him- or herself. It does not apply where he or she is acting in order to prevent an attack on another, although s 3 does.

Fortunately, you do not need to get too worried about whether the correct defence to apply is s 3 or the common law defence, because it is generally assumed that the legal rules applying to the two defences are the same (*McInnes* [1971] 3 All ER 295, *A-G for Northern Ireland's Reference (No 1 of 1975)* 2 All ER 686.

The defences are readily justified. A society offers its citizens protection from violence from each other, usually by means of a police force. However, if someone is suddenly attacked, clearly the state cannot provide protection. Thus the law permits people to protect themselves, using force if necessary, to prevent an immediate attack or its continuation. In addition, the law allows a third party to intervene to protect someone from an attack. The law is sometimes justified by using the argument that the attacker forfeits her rights not to have personal violence used against her by attacking someone else. However, this can be a misleading explanation because the law does not permit any amount of force to be used against an attacker; only what is reasonable. Therefore an attacker does not lose all her rights. An alternative way of justifying the defence is to argue that there has been a net gain for society in repelling the attack. In other words, as a result of the defendant's intervention the situation is better than it would have been had the defendant not acted.

There are four main requirements which need to be proved if either defence is to be available:

1. The defendant must respond to an unjustified threat to the defendant or her property or someone else
2. The force used by the defendant was necessary to avoid the threat
3. The force used by the defendant was proportionate
4. The defendant acted in order to defend herself or someone else and not for some other reason.

We will consider these requirements separately.

1. *The defendant must respond to an unjustified threat to the defendant or her property or someone else.* The definition of the kind of attack which can give rise to self-defence has received relatively little attention in law, but it is important to find such a definition in order to distinguish self-defence from duress of circumstance (see Section 16.3). This is particularly true where the latter is not a defence to murder. Uniacke (1994) has suggested that at the heart of the notion of lawful defence is that the victim was posing an unjust threat to the defendant. The notion of an 'unjust threat' involves two elements:

   (a) The victim must pose an unjust threat to the defendant or another (*DPP v, Bayer* [2003] EWHC 2567). Lawful defence applies only where the threat comes from the victim, rather than from elsewhere. Consider Leonardo, who after a shipwreck is clinging onto a piece of wood when Kate tries to pull him off. Leonardo can use self-defence in repelling Kate's attack because she is posing a threat to his well-being. Because there is no reason why she, rather than he, should be entitled to the piece of wood, the threat is unjust. However, Kate is not being unjustly threatened by Leonardo and so she cannot claim to be acting in self-defence in using force against him in her attempt to get hold of the piece of wood. The threats to her welfare come from the inclement elements and the sea, not Leonardo.

   (b) The threat must be an unjust one. It is important to appreciate that this does not require the victim to be blameworthy (*Re A (Conjoined Twins)* [2000] 4 All ER 961: see Hot topic at the end of this chapter). Lawful defence applies, for example, where a sleepwalker or a child uses force against the defendant. Rather than showing that the threatener was blameworthy, it must be shown that the threat was unjust.

It follows that you may not be able to use self-defence if you are responsible for the attack against you. So, for example, if Jack hits Arnold and Arnold responds by pushing Jack away, to which Jack responds by stabbing Arnold, Jack cannot claim that he is using lawful defence in response to Arnold's push, because Arnold's push could not be regarded as unjust because it was an act of self-defence. In *Rashford* [2006] Crim LR 547 the Court of Appeal explained that the key question is whether the victim's reaction to the defendant's initial act entitled the defendant to defend himself. So if (by contrast to the above example) Jack hits Arnold and Arnold responds by pulling out a gun and aims it at Jack, to which Jack responds by stabbing Arnold, then the defence is available. Arnold's response to Jack's initial hit was disproportionate; it could not therefore be a lawful act of self-defence. Therefore Jack could use lawful force to defend himself against it.

One issue which has troubled the courts is where the defendant thinks she is facing an unjust threat, but in fact she is not. For example, a woman is walking home at night and a man comes running towards her. She attacks him, believing that he is on the point of raping her. In fact he is just out for a jog. The leading case is *Williams (Gladstone)** (1983) 78 Cr App R 271. There the defendant thought that he was witnessing a person being mugged. He joined in the struggle and tried to help the victim of the mugging. In fact he had made a mistake and the 'mugger' was a plain-clothes police officer seeking to arrest the 'victim'. The court said that the defendant should be judged on the facts as he believed them to be. As he perceived the facts to be, he was justified in using force, and so the court held he had a defence. Later cases (*Beckford** [1987] 3 WLR 611; *Oatridge* (1992) 94 Cr App R 367; *B v DPP**) have followed this and it has now become a well-established principle. In *Williams (Gladstone)*, Lord Lane explained:

> The reasonableness or unreasonableness of the defendant's belief is material to the question of whether the belief was held by the defendant at all. If the belief was in fact held, its unreasonableness, so far as guilt or innocence is concerned, is neither here nor there. It is irrelevant. Were it otherwise, the defendant would be convicted because he was negligent... In other words the jury should be directed first of all that the prosecution have the duty of proving the unlawfulness of the defendant's actions; secondly, if the defendant may have been labouring under a mistake as to the facts, he must be judged according to his mistaken view of the facts; thirdly, that is so whether the mistake was, on an objective view, a reasonable mistake or not.

In summary, what needs to be shown is that the defendant believed that he or she was responding to an unjust threat, whether or not in fact there was an unjust threat.

2. *The force used is necessary to rebut the threat.* There are some cases which suggest the defence is available only if defendant uses force (*Renouf* [1986] 2 All ER 449). However, in *DPP v Bayer* the Divisional Court held it would be illogical if the defence were not available to those who used peaceful means to avoid a threat.

It must be shown that it was necessary for the defendant to use force in order to avoid the threat. If the defendant could easily have escaped from the attack but instead decides to use violence in return, the defence may not be available. Having said that, the courts are sympathetic to a defendant who is faced with an unjustified threat but fails to see a means of escape. As long as the defendant believes that the use of force is the only effective way to repel the attack and there is no reasonable means of escape, he or she will be able to rely on the defence (*Bird* [1985] Crim LR 388). Where the court determines that the use of force was in retaliation for an attack, rather than to prevent one, the defence will not be available (*Hussain* [2010] EWCA Crim 94).

The law has even been willing to accept that it may be 'necessary' to use pre-emptive force before the aggressor has begun a threatened attack (*Cousins* [1982] 2 All ER 115). In one case, Lord Lane said that it may be considered necessary for the accused to have armed himself in advance of an expected attack if 'his object was to protect himself or his family or his property against imminent apprehended attack and to do so by means which he believed were no more than reasonably necessary to meet the force used by the attackers' (*A-G's Ref (No 2 of 1983)** [1984] 2 WLR 465).

There is, therefore, no absolute rule in English law that in order to plead lawful defence the defendant must have first tried to retreat. However, the possibility of retreat will be taken into account by the jury in deciding whether or not force was necessary. In Julien, Widgery LJ said:

> It is not ... law that a person threatened must take to his heels and run ... but what is necessary is that he should demonstrate by his actions that he does not want to fight. He must demonstrate that he is prepared to temporise and disengage and perhaps to make some physical withdrawal.

In *Bird*, the Court of Appeal considered a direction to the jury based on this passage, and held that it was not necessary for the accused to have demonstrated an unwillingness to fight. However, such a demonstration would provide a convincing rebuttal of any suggestion that the accused was the aggressor or that the force was used in retaliation or revenge, and not in self-defence. In *Burns* (2010) a man who used force to remove a woman he had picked from his car was said not to be justified in removing force because she had said she would leave if he took her back to the place he had picked her up.

3. *The force must be reasonable.* This requirement is now explained in s 78 Criminal Justice and Immigration Act 2008:

   (1) This section applies where in proceedings for an offence –
        (a) an issue arises as to whether a person charged with the offence ('D') is entitled to rely on a defence within subsection (2), and
        (b) the question arises whether the degree of force used by D against a person ('V') was reasonable in the circumstances.
   (2) The defences are –
        (a) the common law defence of self-defence; and
        (b) the defences provided by section 3(1) of the Criminal Law Act 1967 (c. 58) or section 3(1) of the Criminal Law Act (Northern Ireland) 1967 (c. 18 (N.I.)) (use of force in prevention of crime or making arrest).
   (3) The question whether the degree of force used by D was reasonable in the circumstances is to be decided by reference to the circumstances as D believed them to be, and subsections (4) to (8) also apply in connection with deciding that question.
   (4) If D claims to have held a particular belief as regards the existence of any circumstances –
        (a) the reasonableness or otherwise of that belief is relevant to the question whether D genuinely held it; but
        (b) if it is determined that D did genuinely hold it, D is entitled to rely on it for the purposes of subsection (3), whether or not –
             (i)   it was mistaken, or
             (ii) (if it was mistaken) the mistake was a reasonable one to have made.

(5) But subsection (4)(b) does not enable D to rely on any mistaken belief attributable to intoxication that was voluntarily induced.

(6) The degree of force used by D is not to be regarded as having been reasonable in the circumstances as D believed them to be if it was disproportionate in those circumstances.

(7) In deciding the question mentioned in subsection (3) the following considerations are to be taken into account (so far as relevant in the circumstances of the case) –

    (a) that a person acting for a legitimate purpose may not be able to weigh to a nicety the exact measure of any necessary action; and

    (b) that evidence of a person's having only done what the person honestly and instinctively thought was necessary for a legitimate purpose constitutes strong evidence that only reasonable action was taken by that person for that purpose.

(8) Subsection (7) is not to be read as preventing other matters from being taken into account where they are relevant to deciding the question mentioned in subsection (3).

(9) This section is intended to clarify the operation of the existing defences mentioned in subsection (2).

(10) In this section –

    (a) 'legitimate purpose' means –

        (i) the purpose of self-defence under the common law, or

        (ii) the prevention of crime or effecting or assisting in the lawful arrest of persons mentioned in the provisions referred to in subsection (2)(b);

    (b) references to self-defence include acting in defence of another person; and

    (c) references to the degree of force used are to the type and amount of force used.

As this section makes clear the force must be a proportionate (reasonable) response to the threat as the defendant believed it to be. In deciding what is a proportional response, a very important factor will be the seriousness of the threat and its object: was it a threat of minor damage to property or a threat to someone's life? In the case of a fight, the jury will consider what weapons were being used. In *McInnes*, for example, Edmund Davies LJ said that in a fist-fight it was 'totally unreasonable' to pull out a knife and deliberately (in the words of the accused) 'let him have it'. Even in the panic of a fist-fight, the defendant should show due regard to human life. If the defendant is aware that his 'attackers' are police officers it is unlikely that the jury will accept that the response was reasonable; although it still may be possible to persuade the jury that the force used was reasonable if the defendant feared that the police were to use more force than they were entitled to under the law (*Burley* [2000] Crim LR 840).

In deciding that the response was reasonable, the use of force must be proportionate to the threat as it was perceived by the defendant. This does not mean that it is up to the defendant to decide whether the response is reasonable. The jury, not the defendant, must decide whether the defendant's response was reasonable on the facts as the defendant believed them to be. As was explained in *Owino* [1995] Crim LR 743 by Collins J:

> The jury have to decide whether a defendant honestly believed that the circumstances were such as required him to use force to defend himself from an attack or a threatened attack. In this respect a defendant must be judged in accordance with his honest belief, even though that belief may have been mistaken. But the jury must then determine whether the force used was reasonable in the circumstances as he believed them to be.

The point was emphasised in the notorious *Tony Martin** [2002] 2 WLR 1 case. There a farmer who found two young men burgling his property shot at them, killing one. The key finding was that Martin was not shooting because he thought he was in danger, but to protect his property. Although he thought it was reasonable to shoot at burglars, the Court of Appeal emphasised that it was for the jury to decide whether on the facts as Martin believed them to be it was reasonable to shoot. The jury decided not. It would have been quite different if Martin had thought that the burglars were going to kill or seriously injure him. Then on the facts as he understood them no doubt a jury would have decided he was acting reasonably.

When deciding whether the response of the defendant was reasonable, the jury should not be unduly strict. Lord Morris in *Palmer** [1971] AC 814 explained:

> If there has been an attack so that defence is reasonably necessary, it will be recognised that a person defending himself cannot weigh to a nicety the exact measure of his necessary defensive action. If a jury thought that in a moment of unexpected anguish a person attacked had only done what he honestly and instinctively thought was necessary that would be most potent evidence that only reasonable defensive action had been taken.

In considering the reasonableness of the defendant's response, the jury can take into account the defendant's physical characteristics but not his psychological condition (*Martin*). So the defendant may be able to argue that his physical frailty meant that it was reasonable for him to use a weapon, rather than fight the attacker with his fists. However, his psychological condition cannot make a disproportionate response reasonable.

If the defendant's response is unreasonable then the defendant is guilty. There is no defence to murder if a defendant uses more force than is proportionate, even if he is a police officer acting in the course of duty (*Clegg** [1995] 1 AC 482). The *Clegg* decision is controversial. If the defendant is attacked and is justified in using some force, but in the heat of the moment misjudges the appropriate level of force and kills, there is a strong case for saying he does not deserve the full censure of murder conviction. In such a case it may be that the defence of loss of control will be available, but only if the defendant can show that he or she did in fact lose control (see Section 10.7)

Where a defendant claims that he was acting in order to protect property it will be rare for a jury to find that a defendant's very violent response was reasonable. However, a low level of violence may be thought to be appropriate (*Burns*). The issue is, of course, to be left for the jury and it may well be that individuals disagree on the appropriate levels of violence to protect property. It may be that the jury will attach weight to the kind of property and whether the property is threatened with damage or the defendant just want to get possession back (*Burns*).

4. *The defendant acts in order to defend himself and not for some other reason.* This is in line with the *Dadson* principle (Section 16.1). It needs to be shown that the defendant was not acting out of revenge or any other motive but acting in order to protect himself or another. This requirement also means that if the defendant injures someone, who unbeknown to him is in fact attacking someone else, he cannot rely on lawful defence as a defence. In *Ayliffe v DPP* [2005] Crim LR 959 protesters entered military bases to protest at the Iraq war. In defence to charges of aggravated trespass and criminal damage they argued that they were seeking to prevent a crime (the, as they saw it, illegal war). The Divisional Court said the defence could not be used because their acts were for protesting and not genuinely in an attempt to prevent the damaged items being used in the war.

15.3.2 The Human Rights Act and self-defence

Ashworth (2000) has argued that the rule in Williams and Beckford that the defendant can rely on an honest (even if unreasonable) mistake as the basis of self-defence or lawful defence may infringe the victim's right to life in Article 2 in a murder case.

Article 2(2) permits killing in self-defence in cases of absolute necessity and this may be thought to justify the Williams rule. However, there have been several cases where the European Court has examined Article 2(2) and restricted its meaning. In *McCann v United Kingdom and Andronicou v Cyprus* (1996) 21 EHRR 97 it was confirmed that the belief of an accused trying to rely on Article 2(2) to justify the killing must be based on 'good reason'. Ashworth argues that following these decisions the Williams and Beckford approach is inconsistent with Article 2(2).

Those who disagree with Ashworth tend to adopt one of two arguments. First, Buxton has argued that the Convention applies only to public officials. Indeed, the two leading cases (*McCann v United Kingdom and Andronicou v Cyprus*) have involved public officials. So although Ashworth's argument could be made where soldiers or police officers (for example) use force against citizens, the Convention has no application to where one citizen uses force against another. There is some support for this view in *NHS Trust A v M; NHS Trust B v H* [2001] 1 FLR 406 where Butler Sloss P suggested that a doctor could not infringe Article 2 because he or she was not acting as an official of the state. Those who oppose Buxton's approach argue that it takes insufficient regard of *A v UK* [1998] Crim LR 892 which establishes that the obligation under Article 3 is not limited to ensuring that the state does not infringe a citizen's rights under Article 3, but extends to protecting one citizen's rights from being infringed by another citizen. The same is surely true of Article 2.

Second, Buxton argues that the existence or otherwise of the defence is not likely to affect the response of the person who believes he is being attacked. In other words, the state's protection of the victim's rights under Article 2 is of the same level whether the Williams defence is part of the law or not. He argues if a person believes he has to kill another to defend himself, he will kill whatever the law says. In other words, the Williams rule does not lessen the protection of citizens' rights to life. Ashworth argues that in A v. UK it would not have been a defence for the UK to argue that changing the law would not stop parents injuring their children in the name of corporal punishment. A v. UK makes it clear that states must ensure that their laws protect the rights of individuals, regardless of the likely effectiveness of those laws.

15.3.3 Damaging property in order to protect people or other property

Damage to property in order to protect property is governed by s 5 Criminal Damage Act 1971 (see Section 14.1). The defendant must believe both that the property is in immediate need of protection and that the means adopted are reasonable in the circumstances. Note that the means adopted do not actually have to be reasonable: it is enough if the accused believed that what was done was reasonable. In the case of damage to property in order to protect oneself or another person, the common law of lawful defence is also available (s 5(5)). That requires that only reasonable measures may be taken (for example, Sears v. Broome). The difference between the statutory and common law rules is an anomaly.

15.3.4 Automatism

This is another particular way of denying that the defendant performed the *actus reus*, by claiming that he did not act in the legal sense. Automatism has already been discussed in Section 3.5.

15.4 Denial of *mens rea*

As mentioned above, the defendant may simply deny that he intended or foresaw a consequence as required for the *mens rea* of the offence. Here we will deal with two more complex ways of denying a *mens rea*.

15.4.1 Mistake

One way of denying that the prosecution has made out its case is to say that the defendant is mistaken about a fact which is an aspect of the *actus reus*. Such a mistake will succeed only if the effect of the mistake is such that the defendant did not have the appropriate *mens rea*. This means that there is no defence of mistake as such. It is rather that some mistakes will lead to a finding that the defendant has no *mens rea*. So when will a mistake mean that the defendant lacks *mens rea*? This is answered by the following points:

1. *The mistake must relate to an aspect of the* actus reus. For example, if the defendant has sexual intercourse with Jane, a non-consenting woman, believing she is called Susan, this belief affords no defence. That is because the *mens rea* of rape does not require proof that the defendant was aware of the name of the victim. If, however, the defendant was reasonably mistaken about whether the victim was consenting, this would be a relevant mistake because the lack of consent of the victim is part of the *actus reus*. In *DPP v B* [2000] 2 AC 428 and *R v K** [2001] UKHL 41 the House of Lords has confirmed that there is a presumption that a mistake as to any element of the *actus reus* provides a defence, unless there is a statutory provision making it clear that such a mistake does not provide a defence (see Chapter 6, *R v G*).
2. *The mistake does not need to be reasonable.* Lord Hailsham explained in *Morgan** [1976] AC 182:

   > I believe that 'mens rea' means 'guilty or criminal mind', and... to insist that a belief must be reasonable to excuse it is to insist that either the accused is to be found guilty of intending to do that which in truth he did not intend to do, or that his state of mind, though innocent of evil intent, can convict him if it be honest but not rational.

   This approach was recently confirmed by the House of Lords in *B v DPP* and *R v K*. This is, however, subject to an exception. If the offence is a statutory one which makes it clear that only a reasonable mistake affords a defence, or indeed that no mistake will provide a defence, then that provision governs the law. So if the offence is a strict liability one or a partial one (see Chapter 6), the mistake will provide no defence. Notably in relation to rape the Sexual Offences Act 2003 requires the defendant's belief that the victim is consenting to be reasonable if he is to be acquitted of rape on that basis.
3. *The mistake must be one of fact, not law.* So far we have only considered mistakes of fact. Is it possible for a mistake as to the law to be a defence? There is a well-known maxim that ignorance of the law is no excuse: it will do the accused no good to argue that he did not know that having sexual intercourse with a woman without her consent was a crime; or that 'stolen goods' for the purpose of the offence of handling stolen goods includes goods obtained by deception.

So, a mistake as to the content of the criminal law does not affect liability. On the other hand, a mistake as to the civil law may do so. For example a mistake as to whether property belongs to oneself or another will be relevant to liability for theft (s 2(1)(a) Theft Act 1968 makes this clear), and this mistake may be based on an inaccurate view of the civil law of contract or sale of goods. As with mistakes of fact, the mistake must relate to an element of the *actus reus* which requires *mens rea*.

15.4.2 Intoxication

Strictly speaking, there is no defence of intoxication, however keen students seem to be to talk of it. Rather in some cases it is possible to introduce evidence of intoxication to support a defence of no *mens rea*. In such a case the defence is of 'no *mens rea*', rather than being a defence of intoxication. This is not surprising. It would be most peculiar if the law were to say: because you were drunk we will provide you with a defence.

In order to understand the law on intoxication it is necessary to distinguish cases where the defendant was voluntarily intoxicated and where he was involuntarily intoxicated. To decide whether a defendant was voluntarily or involuntarily intoxicated, the key question is: did the defendant knowingly take alcohol or illegal drugs?

If the answer is 'yes', the defendant knowingly took alcohol or illegal drugs (for example, heroin or cannabis) realising what they were then the defendant will be voluntarily intoxicated. It is no defence for a defendant to claim that he was unaware of the strength of the alcohol in the drink (even if he believes that it is a low-alcohol drink: *Allen* (1988)). Likewise it is no defence for an accused to claim that he was unaware of the effect that alcohol or drugs would have on him.

If the answer is 'no', if the drink was non-alcoholic or the drugs were legal (for example, those prescribed by a doctor), or the defendant believed them to be, then the question will be whether the defendant was aware that the drugs might have the effect of causing him to lose control over his behaviour. If he did then he is voluntarily intoxicated; if he did not then he is involuntarily intoxicated. Common examples of involuntary intoxication arise where the defendant's non-alcoholic drink is (unknown to the defendant) spiked with alcohol. In *Hardie** [1984] 3 All ER 848, the defendant took Valium (an anti-depressant drug) which had been prescribed by a doctor to a friend. The defendant went on to set fire to a room. It was found that the defendant believed that the Valium would have the effect of calming him down or sending him to sleep, but not of exciting him. He was therefore said to be involuntarily intoxicated. Had he been aware of the potential effect of the drug then he would have been voluntarily intoxicated.

Now we can consider the law in cases where the defendant is intoxicated.

1. *Voluntary intoxication*. In the leading House of Lords' case on voluntary intoxication, *Majewski**, a distinction was drawn between crimes of 'specific intent' and 'basic intent':
   (a) *Crimes of specific intent*. In crimes of 'specific intent', the defendant can introduce evidence of intoxication to deny that he had the necessary *mens rea*. This is not to mean that in crimes of specific intent just because the defendant is intoxicated he should be found not guilty. Rather, as the courts regularly confirm, 'a drunken intent is still an intent' (for example, *Kingston** [1995] AC 355). Rather, the jury should consider all the evidence, including the defendant's intoxicated state, to decide whether or not he really had the *mens rea*.
   (b) *Crimes of basic intent*. In crimes of 'basic intent', the defendant cannot introduce evidence of voluntary intoxication to rebut a claim that he had the necessary *mens rea*.

So how do we know which crimes are crimes of specific intent and which are crimes of basic intent? Although there is much dispute over the exact meaning of these phrases, the best interpretation is that 'basic intent' means recklessness, while 'specific intent' means intention. It may help to remember that a specific intent crime requires proof that something specific was intended; a basic intent crime does not. Occasionally an offence may have some aspects which involve 'specific intent' and some which involve 'basic intent'. Rape is an example. There intoxication would be relevant in deciding whether the defendant intended to penetrate (an issue of 'specific intent'), but not in deciding whether he reasonably believed the victim was consenting (an issue of 'basic intent'). Although this is the general approach taken, there do seem to be exceptions. In *Heard** [2007] Crim LR 654 the Court of Appeal thought the offence of sexual assault in s 3 Sexual Offences Act 2003 was an offence of basic intent, despite its requirement of an intention to touch.

So how might the law work in practice? First, consider a specific intent crime such as murder. The facts of *Moloney* [1985] AC 905 provide a useful example. There the defendant and his step-father were both very drunk and decided to embark on a game involving guns. The defendant shot his step-father, but gave evidence that he did not mean to shoot him, but pulled the trigger to win the game. As murder is a specific intent offence, the evidence of his intoxication could be introduced. It was therefore up to the jury, considering all the evidence including the defendant's drunkenness, to decide whether he intended to kill or cause grievous bodily harm to his step-father. The fact of the drunkenness is crucial here because otherwise it would have been unbelievable that a sober man shooting a gun a few feet away from his step-father did not intend seriously to injure him. However, taking into account the drunkenness, the defendant's story becomes believable and it would be possible for a jury to decide that the defendant did not have the necessary intention.

Second, looking at a crime of basic intent, requiring proof of recklessness, we have already seen that a defendant who is voluntarily intoxicated cannot introduce evidence of his intoxication to rebut a claim that he was. This will mean that if the risk was obvious, the jury is bound to assume that the defendant foresaw the risk and so he was reckless; unless perhaps he can provide some other reason (apart from the intoxication) why he did not foresee the obvious risk (for example, he was blind).

2. *Involuntary intoxication.* If the defendant was involuntarily intoxicated, she can introduce evidence of her intoxication to rebut an allegation of recklessness (basic intent), and to argue that she did not foresee the consequences of her actions. As with voluntary intoxication, she can also introduce evidence of intoxication to show she did not intend a consequence (have specific intent). However, it must be stressed that if, after taking into account the involuntary intoxication and other evidence, the jury decides that the defendant did have the relevant *mens rea*, the defendant has no defence based on the involuntary intoxication. This was stressed in *Kingston* where the defendant, who had paedophilic desires, was lured into his enemy's flat. The enemy laced the defendant's cup of coffee with a drug. The defendant was taken to a room where there was a drugged naked boy. The defendant claimed that because of the drugs his inhibitions were removed, and although normally he would have been able to resist such a temptation, he committed an indecent assault on the boy. The House of Lords decided involuntary intoxication was only relevant in deciding whether the defendant had the necessary *mens rea*. Having decided that

the defendant did intend to commit the assault, it was irrelevant that he did so only because drugs were administered against his will. This case stresses the point that there is no such thing as a defence of intoxication; it is simply that intoxication can be evidence supporting a defence of no *mens rea*. *Kingston* was a harsh decision, but the court seemed concerned that a defence of involuntary intoxication would be easy for a defendant to raise and difficult for the prosecution to disprove.

3. *Intoxication and defences.* What if a drunken defendant is seeking to raise a defence? Unfortunately the law has developed in a rather haphazard way and a general principle cannot be found. All we can do is discuss the individual defences separately.

(a) *Mistake.* What if the defendant, because of his drunken mistake, was not aware of an element of the offence? The correct view, it is submitted, is to follow the approach outlined above. For voluntary intoxication, the mistaken belief can be introduced as evidence of no *mens rea* in cases of specific intent, but otherwise will not provide a defence. So in a murder case, if the defendant was so drunk that he thought the victim was a deer and shot him, this could provide a defence: there was no intent to kill or seriously injure a person. This defendant would still be convicted of manslaughter. In cases of involuntary intoxication, the drunken mistake can provide a defence if that mistake negates *mens rea*. This approach is logical. If the law does not allow a voluntarily intoxicated defendant a defence to an offence of recklessness based on the fact that he did not foresee the consequences of his action because he was drunk, why should a drunken mistake as to the circumstances in which he acts provide a defence?

Unfortunately there are two cases which suggest that a drunken mistake as to a circumstance can provide a defence. In *Jaggard v Dickenson* [1981] QB 527, the very drunk defendant damaged a house. She argued that she believed that the house was owned by her friend, who would have consented to the damage. In fact the house was not her friend's, but in her drunken state she had made a mistake. Section 5(2) Criminal Damage Act provides a defence if the defendant believed that the owner would consent to the damage. Mustill J stated that the section provided a defence even if the belief was a drunken one. In *Richardson and Irwin* [1999] 1 Cr App R 392, the defendant believed that the victim was consenting to rough horseplay and therefore consented to the force. He therefore was not aware that his act was without the consent of the victim. This was held to be a defence to a charge of maliciously inflicting grievous bodily harm.

In the light of these two cases, therefore, the law cannot be stated with certainty. The better view is that *Jaggard* and *Richardson* are incorrectly decided and that a voluntarily intoxicated defendant cannot use evidence of intoxication to deny recklessness (basic intent), be that by denying foresight of consequences or awareness of circumstances. An alternative view is that an intoxicated belief as to the circumstances in which he acts can provide support for a no *mens rea* defence to any criminal charge; although a drunken mistake as to the consequences of a defendant's actions cannot provide support to a charge of basic intent.

(b) *Self-defence or prevention of crime.* As explained above, in *Gladstone Williams* it was held that a defendant can use the defence of self-defence or the prevention of crime even though there was in fact no threat, as long as the defendant honestly believed that he was facing such a threat. However, this is not true where the defendant, because he is intoxicated, incorrectly believes that he or another is being attacked. So if the defendant believes, because of his voluntary intoxication, that he is being attacked he cannot rely on a defence of self-defence. This was established in *Hatton** [2006] Crim LR 353. In cases of specific intent, the judge needs to direct the jury carefully here. The defendant can use his drunken beliefs as evidence that he had no intent to kill, but not as evidence that he was acting in self-defence.

(c) *Duress*. If a defendant believes that there is a threat to life or of serious injury because he is intoxicated then this belief cannot form the basis of a duress claim, because the defendant must show that he has reasonable grounds for his beliefs that a threat has been made and will be carried out (see Section 16.2). Similarly, the defendant will not be able to argue that because he was intoxicated he gave in to the threat; he is required to show the level of firmness of a reasonable sober person.

(d) *Automatism*. If the defendant commits a crime, having fallen over and banged his head while in an intoxicated condition, he may try to plead automatism. If he was in a state of automatism, Stripp indicates that the key question is whether the defendant's state was caused predominantly by his intoxication or by his concussion. If it was the concussion then he would be able to plead automatism; if it was his voluntary intoxication then he would not (*Burns; Lipman* [1970] 1 QB 152).

(e) *Diminished responsibility*. The relationship between diminished responsibility and intoxication is discussed in Section 10.9.

(f) *Insanity*. The leading case on insanity and intoxication is *Lipman*. There the defendant took LSD and (he claimed) as a result had a hallucination in which he was attacked by a many-headed monster. He killed the monster. On recovering, he discovered that in fact he had killed his girlfriend. He was not permitted to plead insanity because it was his voluntary intoxication, rather than any disease of the mind, which had caused him to be unaware of the nature of his acts. If, however, a person can show that, although he was intoxicated, it was his mental condition which primarily caused his lack of awareness then insanity may be available (*Burns*).

4. *Discussion of the law on intoxication*. There has been much dispute over the logic and policy which underlie the present law on intoxication. Understandably, the courts have been very unwilling to absolve completely from criminal responsibility those who incapacitate their mental processes with alcohol or drugs, and then go on to cause injury to other people or property. In Majewski, several of their Lordships accepted that their position owed more to policy than logic. Lord Salmon put it like this:

> A man who by voluntarily taking drink and drugs gets himself into an aggressive state in which he does not know what he is doing and then makes a vicious assault can hardly say with any plausibility that what he did was a pure accident which should render him immune from any criminal liability ... In strict logic this view cannot be justified. But this is the view that has been adopted by the common law of England which is founded on common sense and experience rather than strict logic.

This argument was expressed in differing ways by the judges in Majewski. Lord Simon of Glaisdale said:

> There is no juristic reason why mental incapacity (short of M'Naghten insanity), brought about by self-induced intoxication, to realise what one is doing or its probable consequences

> should not be ... a state of mind stigmatised as wrongful by the criminal law, and there is every practical reason why it should be.

This view suggests that although intoxication may render a person incapable of forming a specific intention, such as an intent to kill, intoxication itself provides the *mens rea* necessary for a certain basic level of criminal culpability. Put this way, intoxication is seen as an alternative form of *mens rea*, rather than as an aspect of the rules on evidence, which is how we have explained the law in this section. This would mean that even if the defendant could prove that, had he been sober, he would not have foreseen the risk (for example, because he was blind), he would not have a defence. This is how Lord Elwyn-Jones explained in *Majewski* [1977] AC 443 why assault was a 'basic intent' crime:

> If a man of his own volition takes a substance which causes him to cast off the restraints of reason and conscience, no wrong is done to him by holding him answerable criminally for any injury he may do while in that condition. His course of conduct in reducing himself by drugs and drink to that condition in my view supplies the evidence of mens rea, of guilty mind, certainly sufficient for crimes of basic intent. It is a reckless course of conduct and recklessness is enough to constitute the necessary mens rea in assault cases.

Mens rea is here regarded as a general requirement of culpability, rather than a precise state of mind such as intention or knowledge. This explanation for the law appears to be that if the accused takes illegal drugs or alcohol he is at that point reckless. He must be aware that he may go on to commit a crime because, once intoxicated, no-one can be sure how they will behave. The law presumes that everyone is aware of this potential effect of illegal drugs or alcohol. As was stated by GriffithsLJ in *Bailey* [1983] 1 WLR 760, 'it is common knowledge that those who take alcohol to excess or certain sorts of drugs may become aggressive or do dangerous or unpredictable things'. This explanation of the law has been criticised on two main grounds. First, it does not explain why those who drink a very small amount of alcohol or a low-alcohol drink should be seen as reckless. Second, the *mens rea* of foreseeing that one may go on to commit some kind of criminal act is not a sufficient *mens rea* for many crimes. For example, for a conviction under s 20 Offences Against the Person Act it has to be shown that the defendant foresaw that his act might cause some harm to the victim. Evidence that the defendant foresaw that he might commit some kind of crime would be insufficient. In any event, such a *mens rea* is not contemporary with the *actus reus*. One solution is to regard the whole sequence of events as one indivisible 'series of acts' under the doctrine of *Thabo Meli* [1954] 1 All ER 373 (see Section 5.8). This was the approach of Lord Denning in *Gallagher** [1963] AC 349, a case where the link was clear because of evidence of a preconceived plan formulated before the accused got drunk, but this case involved an exceptional set of facts.

It may be that the law on intoxication represents a policy choice. Many crimes of violence are committed by those who are intoxicated. It is interesting to note that the Law Commission in its working paper suggested wholesale reform of the law in the light of the theoretical difficulties. However, as a result of the reaction to the working paper, and particularly the argument that the general public would not accept the acquittal of drunken defendants on the ground of lack of *mens rea*, the Commission decided in its final report to propose retaining the present law, albeit on a statutory footing.

Hot Topic – Home owners killing burglars and self-defence

In recent years there has been much discussion about members of the public who use force to defend their homes or property, only to find that they are then prosecuted for an assault or even murder. In the Tony Martin case a man who had been persistently troubled by burglars shot two young men who had just burgled his property. Section 78 Criminal Justice and Immigration Act 2008 (see Section 15.3.1 above) was enacted to clarify the law on when a person can use force to defend themselves against attacks on themselves or their property. In discussing these cases it is useful to distinguish two kinds of mistakes that a defendant could make.

The first is where she has made a mistake of perception: the defendant thinks she is being attacked but she is not. The second is where the defendant has made a mistaken judgement of value: the defendant correctly perceives the facts but decides to respond with an inappropriate level of violence. The test developed by the courts is that a defence is available if, on the facts as the defendant believed them to be, the level of force used was reasonable. In other words, the law is sympathetic to a mistake of perception which will not lead to a denial of the defence; while the law is less sympathetic to a mistake of value which will cause the defendant to be unable to rely on the defence. Why are these different kinds of mistakes treated differently?

In relation to mistakes of perception, the courts have relied on an analogy with the case of Morgan. Morgan was interpreted as arguing that it was necessary to show that the defendant had the necessary *mens rea* in respect of each part of the *actus reus*. So a defendant to a rape charge who believed (albeit unreasonably) that a victim was consenting was not guilty as he did not have the necessary recklessness as to the victim's consent, which was part of the *actus reus*. Likewise in *Gladstone Williams*, the court argued that if the defendant believed he was acting in legitimate self-defence then he did not have the necessary *mens rea* for the whole of the *actus reus*. That is because the court argued that it was an aspect of the *actus reus* of an assault that the act was unlawful. This reasoning is controversial. There are three particular difficulties.

First, there is doubt whether it is correct that unlawfulness is a part of the *actus reus*. It has been argued that unlawfulness cannot be part of the *actus reus* as such, because an act is not unlawful until both the *mens rea* and *actus reus* have been proved

(*Simester*). In other words, to call unlawfulness an aspect of the *actus reus* is to put the cart before the horse.

Second, it was clear from their Lordships' speeches in Morgan that they did not intend to change the law on self-defence. Indeed their Lordships in Morgan appeared to assume that the mistake had to be reasonable if it was to be a basis of self-defence.

Third, as moral issues it may be that mistakes in rape and self-defence can be distinguished. Simester argues it is important to appreciate in the case of a mistake over the consent of a victim of rape that the defendant is not aware he is harming the victim. In the case of self-defence one can argue that the defendant is aware that he is harming the victim, but he is claiming that he had good reason for doing so. The significance of this distinction is that the law could legitimately require a defendant who is aware that he is harming another to ensure he has reasonable grounds to believe that he has a good reason for injuring the victim; whereas if a person is unaware that he is harming the victim, the law cannot expect someone to ensure he has a good reason for performing the act. This argument might suggest that the law should be more sympathetic to the mistaken rapist than to the mistaken self-defence case. An alternative argument, made by Horder (1990), is to focus on the emotions which cause or explain the mistake. He suggests that fear of injury is a legitimate reason for making such a mistake (as in self-defence), but that sexual excitement is not a legitimate reason to make a mistake (as in Morgan). Seen this way, the law should be more sympathetic to the mistaken self-defence than to the mistaken rape case. Even though they have contradictory results, both arguments indicate that the two situations are not directly analogous.

Despite these concerns, the House of Lords in *DPP v. B* and *R v. K* has approved the Morgan approach as one of general application, including in relation to self-defence. So, despite the above concerns, the courts appear persuaded by the analogy.

What about mistakes of value? As mentioned above, although the courts have been sympathetic about mistakes of perception, they have not to mistakes of value. In cases like the Tony Martin case, where a home owner shoots a burglar, they may believe that they are justified in doing so to protect their property. Had Tony Martin thought (wrongly) that the burglar was about to kill him, he could have relied on the defence. Perhaps the best explanation of this position is that mistakes of perception are all too common. People mishear or misunderstand things all the time. There is no particular blame that attaches to such a mistake. Where someone believes he is about to be attacked there is no opportunity to double-check that this belief is justified. By contrast, a mistake of value is different. People who have values which are inconsistent with the law (for example, that it is permissible to shoot people dead to protect pieces of property) are not treated like those who mishear things. Adults are seen as responsible for their moral opinions. Such attitudes are themselves not criminal, but once they are put into action they can become so.

Summary

15.1 A defendant who does not want to plead guilty to a criminal charge has a number of options available. She can simply claim that the prosecution has not proved its case – that the *mens rea or actus reus* has not been made out. Alternatively, she can seek to introduce evidence of a special defence, which involves admission of the *actus reus* and *mens rea* but seeks to claim that the defendant falls within one of the situations accepted by the law in which the defendant does not deserve the blame attaching to a conviction.

15.2 Some groups of people are exempt from criminal sanctions, as the criminal law cannot be addressed to them. Infancy and insanity are the two best-known examples. Infancy covers all those under the age of 10. There is a presumption of sanity in all cases. However, insanity can be relevant in two ways. Firstly, if the defendant is insane at the time of the trial (she is unable to understand the trial or give her representative instructions), in which case if it is shown she committed the *actus reus* then the judge has a discretion as to what orders can be made in respect of the defendant. The defendant may also claim that she was insane at the time when she committed the offence. Insanity may be raised by the prosecution as well as the defence. The law on insanity is still governed by the M'Naghten rules, formulated in the nineteenth century and requiring a defect of reason caused by a disease of the mind.

15.3 Self-defence applies where it is necessary to use some force to defend oneself, another person or property, and the degree of force used is reasonable in the circumstances which the accused believed to exist. A person may also use a reasonable degree of force in the prevention of crime or in a lawful arrest, under s 3 Criminal Law Act 1967. Automatism is another way of denying that the accused has the required *mens rea*.

15.4 Two specific ways in which the defendant may argue that she lacks *mens rea* are by claiming she has made a mistake or that she was intoxicated when she committed the crime. A mistake of fact may amount to a denial of the *mens rea* of an offence if it concerns a fact which forms part of the *actus reus*. But the mistake will not excuse if that part of the *actus reus* does not need a mental element. There is no general rule as to whether the mistake has to be reasonable; if the offence requires intention or knowledge there is no need for the mistake to be reasonable. If recklessness is sufficient, the position depends on the type of recklessness applied by the courts to that offence. If the offence is one of negligence then the mistake must be reasonable. Involuntary intoxication which results in the accused not possessing the necessary *mens rea* for the offence charged can form the basis of a defence. Voluntary intoxication will be a defence only to crimes which require intention as part of the *mens rea* (specific intent crimes); it is not a defence to crimes which can be committed recklessly (basic intent crimes). Involuntary intoxication is admissible as evidence of no *mens rea* for either specific or basic intent crimes.

Further Reading

A discussion on the nature of defences is found in Horder (1996), Sullivan, and Wilson. A discussion of insanity is found in Mackay and Kearns, Mackay, Mitchell and Howe, and Mackay. Intoxication is considered in Gardner, Law Commission, and Paton. Mistakes and defences are debated in Horder (1990) and in Simester. Walker considers the criminal responsibility of children. Self-defence is analysed in Horder (1995), Leverick, Smith, and Uniacke.

Ashworth, 'The Human Rights Act and the Substantive Criminal Law' [2000] Crim LR 564.

Gardner, 'The Importance of Majewski' (1994) 14 OJLS 279.

Horder, 'Cognition, Emotion and Criminal Culpability' (1990) 106 LQR 469.

Horder, 'Drawing the Boundaries of Self-Defence' (1995) 58 MLR 431.

Horder, 'Criminal Law: Between Determinism, Liberalism and Criminal Justice' (1996) 49 CLR 159.

Law Commission, *Intoxication and Criminal Liability* (Law Com No 314, 2009).

Leverick, 'Is English Self-Defence Law Incompatible with Article 2 of the ECHR' [2002] Crim LR 347.

Mackay, *Mental Condition Defences in Criminal Law* (Oxford University Press 1995).

Mackay, 'Righting the Wrong? – Some Observations on the Second Limb of the M'Naghten Rules' [2009] Crim LR 80.

Mackay and Kearns, 'An Upturn in Unfitness to Plead? Disability in Relation to the Trial under the 1991 Act' [2000] Crim LR 532.

Mackay and Reuber, 'Epilepsy and the Defence of Insanity – Time for Change?' [2007] Crim LR 782.

Mackay, Mitchell and Howe, 'Yet More Facts about the Insanity Defence' [2006] Crim LR 399.

Simester, 'Mistakes in Defence' (1992) 12 OJLS 295.

Smith, 'The Use of Force in Public or Private Defence and Article 2' [2002] Crim LR 958.

Sullivan, 'Making Excuses', in Simester and Smith (eds), *Harm and Culpability* (Oxford University Press 1995).

Uniacke, *Permissible Killing* (Oxford University Press 1994).

Wilson, 'The Structure of Criminal Defences' [2005] Crim LR 108.

Case Notes

▶ *A-G's Ref (No 2 of 1983)* [1984] 2 WLR 465. Court of Appeal

The accused was charged with having explosives in his possession without a lawful object, contrary to s 4 Explosive Substances Act 1883. His shop had been damaged during rioting and he was worried about another attack. He manufactured some petrol bombs 'as a last resort'. He was acquitted. The trial judge directed the jury that self-defence could be pleaded as a 'lawful object' for the purposes of s 4. The Court of Appeal held that this was correct. It was open to the jury to find that the making of the petrol bombs was a reasonable means of protection for the accused and his property in the face of an imminent apprehended attack.

▶ *B v DPP* [2000] Crim LR 403. House of Lords

See Chapter 6 Case notes.

▶ *Beckford* [1987] 3 WLR 611. Privy Council

The appellant was convicted of murder. He was a police officer who had been sent to arrest the victim who was reported to have been threatening another person with a gun. It was alleged by the prosecution that the appellant had shot the victim when he was unarmed and ready to give himself up. The defence case was that the victim had fired at the police and the appellant had shot and killed the victim in self-defence. The trial judge directed the jury that the killing would be in self-defence if the accused reasonably believed that he was in danger of death or serious injury, and used necessary and reasonable force to resist the attack. The Privy Council allowed the appeal on the ground that the accused would have been acting in self-defence if he had used such force as was reasonable in the circumstances, as the accused honestly believed them to be, even if his belief was not reasonable.

▶ *Bratty v AG for Northern Ireland* **[1963] AC 386. House of Lords**

See Chapter 3 Case notes.

▶ *Clegg* **[1995] 1 AC 482. House of Lords**

Private Clegg was policing a checkpoint in Northern Ireland. He requested the driver of a car to stop but the car increased speed and drove through the checkpoint. He fired several shots at the car. The fourth shot, which killed a passenger, was fired after the car had passed through the checkpoint. The House of Lords upheld his conviction for murder, stating that killing by using excessive force in self-defence was murder. As the car had driven past the checkpoint and was driving away at speed, it could not be argued that the car or its occupants were threatening Clegg or his colleagues or posed an immediate threat to other people. Shooting at the car was an inappropriate amount of force to effect an arrest.

▶ *Gallagher* **[1963] AC 349. House of Lords**

The accused was convicted of murder. He had killed his wife with a knife, having bought the knife together with a bottle of whisky. He pleaded insanity and intoxication. The Court of Criminal Appeal in Northern Ireland quashed the conviction on the ground that the trial judge had directed the jury to consider the state of the accused's mind before he started drinking the whisky. The House of Lords allowed the appeal by the prosecutor and restored the conviction. It was held that drunkenness which impaired the accused's powers of perception, moral sense

or self-control was no defence. Intoxication would be a defence to murder (though not manslaughter) only if the accused was so drunk that he did not know what he was doing and could not form the necessary intention. If intoxication brings on a disease of the mind then the accused may be temporarily insane within the M'Naghten rules, and the insanity defence applies. This was not the case here. He formed the intention to kill while sober, and made preparations to do so. It was no defence that he then got drunk in order to give himself 'Dutch courage' to do the killing.

▶ *Hardie* **[1984] 3 All ER 848. Court of Appeal**

The appellant was convicted of criminal damage. He was depressed after the breakdown of his relationship with the woman with whom he had been living. He took several Valium tablets, and then set light to the bedroom of the flat while the woman and her daughter were in another room. The trial judge directed the jury that since the drug was taken deliberately and not on prescription it was no defence for the accused to argue that as a result of taking the Valium he had no *mens rea*. The Court of Appeal allowed the appeal. The jury should have been directed to consider whether the taking of the Valium itself was reckless, in light of its characteristics as a sedative drug 'wholly different in kind from drugs which are liable to cause unpredictability or aggressiveness'.

▶ *Hatton* **[2006] Crim LR 353. Court of Appeal**

The defendant and victim met at a nightclub and drank together. They returned to the defendant's flat. The defendant claimed that he had killed the victim, drunkenly believing that the victim was attacking him with a stick. The trial judge ruled that it was not open to the defendant to rely on a mistake induced by drunkenness as the basis of a self-defence claim. The defendant's appeal was dismissed by the Court of Appeal. It was held that in a case of self-defence the defendant could not rely on the fact that he drunkenly believed he was about to be attacked.

▶ *Heard* [2007] EWCA Crim 125. Court of Appeal

The defendant was charged with an offence of sexual assault after exposing his penis and rubbing it on the thigh of a police officer. He was heavily intoxicated at the time. He claimed that his intoxication meant he did not intentionally touch the officer, as required in the definition of the offence of sexual assault. The Court of Appeal confirmed that a drunken intent is still an intent. Even if the defendant's touching had been done without 'the mind going with the act' his intoxication did not provide a defence. An offence of specific intent was one where the intention related to something beyond the act itself, such as consequences of the act. The requirement of intentional touching in the offence was therefore one of basic intent. Therefore the intoxication could not be used as evidence of no intention.

▶ *R v K* [2001] UKHL 41. House of Lords

See Chapter 6 Case notes.

▶ *Kingston* [1995] 2 AC 355. House of Lords

The defendant's coffee was spiked with a drug by a man who was seeking to blackmail him. The man then took the defendant to a room where there was a boy who was also drugged. The defendant assaulted the boy. The defendant admitted he had paedophilic inclinations but was normally able to resist any temptation to put them into practice. However, he said that his inhibitions were removed by the spiked drink and he therefore committed the crime. The Court of Appeal suggested that an accused could have a defence where alcohol or drugs were administered against the accused's will by another. The Crown appealed and the House of Lords upheld the appeal. It accepted the principle that intoxication could only be relevant as evidence that the accused did not have the necessary *mens rea* for a crime. Here the accused admitted having the necessary recklessness and so the involuntary intoxication could be relevant only to mitigation.

▶ *Majewski* [1977] AC 443. House of Lords

The appellant was convicted of assault occasioning actual bodily harm and assaulting a police officer in the execution of his duty. He had consumed a large quantity of drugs and alcohol before becoming involved in a fight in a pub. The trial judge directed the jury that the effect of the drugs and drink could not be a defence to the charges. The Court of Appeal and the House of Lords dismissed his appeal. It was held that although self-induced intoxication could be a defence to a crime such as murder which required a specific intent, it was no defence to a crime which could be committed recklessly. Self-induced intoxication is a reckless course of conduct which is itself an integral part of the crime (Lord Elwyn-Jones).

▶ *Martin* [2002] 2 WLR 1. Court of Appeal

The appellant shot two young men who had entered his isolated house at night. He had been repeatedly burgled and was at the end of his tether. Both men were shot and one died from his injuries. He was convicted of murder. On appeal his counsel introduced new evidence that Martin suffered from a psychiatric condition. The Court of Appeal confirmed that in assessing the availability of a lawful defence the jury should consider whether the defendant's actions were reasonable acts of defence on the facts as he or she believed them to be. The Court of Appeal rejected an argument that the jury should consider how a reasonable person with the defendant's mental condition would have reacted. The question was whether the use of force was reasonable. The Court did accept that the defendant's physical disabilities could be relevant. It might be that a disabled person lacked the opportunity to escape or repel a threat, meaning that a use of force was reasonable. The Court of Appeal did however accept that the fresh medical evidence indicated that Martin was suffering diminished responsibility at the time of the killing and therefore substituted a manslaughter conviction for his one of murder.

▶ *M'Naghten* [1843–60] All ER Rep 229. House of Lords

The accused was charged with murder and the jury brought in a verdict of not guilty by reason of insanity. There was medical evidence that the accused suffered from delusions which affected his perceptions of right and wrong, and over which he had no control. The case was debated in the House of Lords and a number of questions were submitted to all the judges for their opinion. The judges said that every person is presumed to be sane and 'to possess a sufficient degree of reason to be responsible for his crimes' until the contrary is proved. A person suffering from partial insane delusions, concerning one or more subjects or persons, would nevertheless be criminally liable if he knew that his action was contrary to law. He should be judged as if the facts with respect to which the delusion existed were real. Lord Tindal CJ stated the terms on which the jury should be directed as to the state of mind of such a person (see Section 15.2.2 above).

▶ *Morgan* [1976] AC 182. House of Lords

See Chapter 8 Case notes.

▶ *Palmer* [1971] AC 814. Privy Council

The appellant was convicted of murder. The judge directed the jury on self-defence that, in deciding whether it was reasonably necessary to have used as much force as was used, the jury should take into account all of the circumstances; if an unreasonable degree of force had been used, the jury should convict of murder. It was argued on appeal that in cases where the jury found that it was necessary for the accused to use some force but the defendant used an excessive, unreasonable amount of force, then it should be open to the jury to convict of manslaughter. The Privy Council dismissed the appeal. Self-defence either succeeds so as

to result in an acquittal or is disproved by the prosecution and therefore rejected. It cannot, unlike provocation, be a partial defence to murder. In deciding whether the force used was reasonable, the jury will recognise that a person defending himself cannot weigh precisely how much force is necessary to defend himself.

▶ *Quick* [1973] QB 910. Court of Appeal

See Chapter 3 Case notes.

▶ *Sullivan* [1984] 1 AC 156. House of Lords

See Chapter 3 Case notes.

▶ *Williams (Gladstone)* (1983) 78 Cr App Rep 276. Court of Appeal

The appellant was convicted of assault occasioning actual bodily harm. He had punched the victim, who he thought was making an unlawful assault on a youth. In fact the victim had seen the youth rob a woman and had been lawfully attempting to prevent the youth from escaping. The Court of Appeal quashed the conviction on the ground that the jury had been misdirected as to the mistake of fact. The Court held that in cases where the accused makes a mistake of fact, he must be judged on the basis of the mistaken facts as he believed them to be. This is so not only in relation to a mistake as to consent (as in *Morgan*) but also where the mistake relates to the use of reasonable force in self-defence or the prevention of crime. If the mistake was genuinely held, its unreasonableness is irrelevant.

Chapter 16

General defences

Key Terms

- **Duress** – a claim that the defendant acted reasonably as a result of a threat of death or serious injury.
- **Excuse** – a claim that the defendant was not to blame for causing a harm.
- **Justification** – an argument that the act is permitted under the law.
- **Necessity** – a claim that the defendant's act was the lesser of two evils.

16.1 Justifications and excuses

When thinking about defences it can be useful to distinguish between justifications and excuses. A claim of justification is essentially an assertion that the act committed was permissible in all the circumstances. It need not necessarily be the most morally appropriate act, but it needs to be an act which is permitted by the law. For example, if the defendant is approached by a 5-year-old child, pointing a gun and at the point of pulling the trigger, shooting the child may be permitted (justified) by the law – even if morally the ideal thing to do would be to let the child shoot. A justification does not deny that the victim was wronged but explains that there were countervailing circumstances which made that conduct justifiable.

A claim of excuse, on the other hand, admits that the act was not justifiable but seeks to argue that in the circumstances the defendant does not deserve the blame attached to a criminal conviction. The claim is that the acts were understandable and excusable, given the defendant's mental state or the circumstances in which the defendant acted. Paul Robinson has neatly summarised the distinction between justifications and excuses: 'acts are justified, actors are excused'.

It is possible for excuses to be partial excuses. That is, the defendant is not fully to blame for the commission of the *actus reus*, but is nevertheless still somewhat to blame. For example, diminished responsibility is a defence to murder which reduces the sentence to manslaughter. A partial defence does not indicate that the defendant is blameless, otherwise there would be an acquittal, but implies that her blame is insufficient for a murder conviction and so can be seen as a partial excuse.

Although this classification of defences into excuses and justifications is conceptually very useful, there are dangers in putting too much emphasis on it. In particular, the law's definition of defences was developed without the classifications of justification and excuse in mind. The law might have been clearer if the distinction between justification and excuse had been relied upon by the courts.

One danger of placing too much weight on the excuse/justification distinction is that there is a temptation to believe that each defence should be classified as either a justification or an excuse. Within the legal definitions of a defence may fall factual situations, some of which are justifications and some of which are excuses. For example, as mentioned above, self-defence is a classic example of 'justification', but within the legal definition of self-defence falls the situation where the defendant makes a mistake and believes that he is being attacked when he is not. In such circumstances some commentators would argue that the defendant is not justified. Can it be said to be permissible for the defendant to use force against a victim who is in fact posing no threat to the defendant? No doubt the defendant would have an excuse. Although some defences cannot be neatly classified as either an excuse or a justification, some defences clearly fall into one category or the other; insanity, for example, is clearly an example of an excuse.

Another danger of putting too much emphasis on whether defences fall into the philosophical categories of justification and excuse is that practical considerations, policy factors and the need to make the law readily comprehensible to juries also influence the rules relating to defences. We should not, therefore, expect the justification/excuse distinction to be the sole influence on the development of the law relating to defences.

So far we have looked at the theoretical distinction between justifications and excuses. What are the practical implications which should follow? Several have been suggested, which will now be discussed, although, as we have just stated, there are many other influences on the law in this area.

16.1.1 The practical significance of the differences between a justification and an excuse

1. *Accessories.* If a third party assists someone who is acting in a justified way then she is not guilty of any crime. This is because she is assisting in the commission of an *actus reus* which is seen as desirable by society. However, an accessory to an excused principal will be guilty as she has assisted in the commission of an undesirable *actus reus* (unless the accessory has her own defence).

2. *Nature of the legal test.* You might at first think that the test to determine the availability of a justification would be wholly objective because the law is considering whether the defendant's act was socially desirable. In contrast, you might expect that the test for excuses would be essentially subjective because the law is considering the defendant's culpability. This is generally accurate but not wholly correct. First, in relation to justifications it is necessary to show that the defendant acted for a justified reason. For example, if Mike sees his enemy George and shoots him but, unknown to Mike, George was about to detonate a bomb in a crowded marketplace and so Mike would have been justified in so acting, Mike cannot rely on that justification. The reason is that when considering whether an act is justified, one considers all the circumstances including the defendant's beliefs. A defendant is not acting as society would wish him to act if he is killing for an inappropriate motive. This is sometimes known as the *Dadson* (1850) 4 Cox CC 358 principle.

   Likewise an excuse sometimes does not rely on a wholly subjective test. Take loss of control: if a defendant is gravely insulted and is so angry that he loses his self-control, he is afforded a partial excuse. However, we may not want to make the defence available to a defendant whose response was totally unreasonable and caused by drunkenness or pride. So the defendant, in order to use loss of control as excuse, must show that his response was reasonable and so worthy of an excuse. This could be explained in two ways: either an example of where a public policy (for example, the desire of the law to protect members of society from those who kill unreasonably following a grave wrong) affects the test which would be used if moral philosophy alone determined the test; or an argument that if the defendant was able to control his anger, but did not have a good reason for not controlling his anger, is blameworthy and cannot claim an excuse.

3. *Self-defence or prevention of crime.* Another practical effect of the distinction between a justification and an excuse is that if a defendant is defending herself against force, she can defend herself against an excused attacker (for example, if the attacker is sleepwalking) but not against a justified attacker (see Section 15.3.1).

4. *Strict liability offences.* It also seems that excuses would be ineffective for a defendant facing a charge of a strict liability offence, but justifications are available to any crime.

5. *Mistakes and defences.* Some commentators argue that there should be a distinction between justifications and excuses where the defendant makes a mistake of perception. If the defendant misinterprets the facts and thinks they permit him to use justified force then he can have a defence even if the mistake is unreasonable. However, if the defendant is relying on excuse, it must have been reasonable for him to make that mistake. The argument for this is that a person who is seeking to rely on an excuse is already admitting that his acts were unjustified, and if he is to deserve an excuse he should be blameless. If he has acted in an unjustified way and made an unreasonable mistake, an excuse should not be available.

We will now consider two defences in which the defendant admits he has the necessary *actus reus* and *mens rea*, but is seeking to rely on a defence.

16.2 Duress by threats

The defence of duress may be pleaded where the accused admits that he committed the offence charged, with the necessary fault element, but claims that he did so only because he was threatened with death or serious injury if he did not comply with the demands of the threatener. The threat may be to harm the accused himself or another person. Like self-defence, duress is a complete defence, resulting, if successful, in an acquittal. However, whereas self-defence is accepted as generally a justification for using force, it is not clear whether duress is also a justification or whether it is regarded primarily as an excuse.

A plea of duress based on justification would seek to argue that the wrong done in obeying the threatener (committing theft or a drug offence, for example) was less than the wrong which would have been done by the threatener (such as death or a serious assault). In other words, the offence committed under duress was the lesser of two evils. The problem with seeing duress as a justification is that the defendant is often ordered to injure an innocent bystander. For example, terrorist groups in Northern Ireland have in the past seized a taxi driver and threatened to kill him and his family unless he drove the terrorists and their weapons to a particular destination. Here the people who will be injured or killed in the explosion are blameless, and some commentators argue that therefore their injury or death cannot be justified. An important contrast is often drawn with self-defence where, as in duress, the defendant is acting to prevent injury to himself or another, but, unlike in duress, the person he injures (the attacker) is blameworthy, having attacked him and so legitimised the use of force against him. In other words, in self-defence the victim is posing a threat to the defendant; in duress he is not. Having emphasised this distinction, it should be remembered that you can use self-defence even where the victim is innocent, for example if there is no real attack but one believes that there is; or if the person who is attacking you is blameless, for example where he is a child. This suggests that the distinction may not be as steadfast as might at first appear.

An alternative argument is to see duress as an excuse. Seen in this way, it could be claimed that the law cannot expect ordinary people to show extraordinary courage in resisting such fearsome threats, and that a person who succumbs to such a threat is not greatly culpable. Thus duress can be regarded as simply a concession to human frailty (Lord Hailsham in *Howe*** [1987] 2 WLR 568), in that most people, when faced with a threat that they or their families would be killed, would commit the crime. A slightly different way of putting the argument is that in the inevitable panic which follows a threat of death or serious injury the defendant is not able to think clearly and so would not be responsible for any decision made. It has sometimes been said that a defendant who acted under duress acted involuntarily. However, this claim must be treated with care. Acting under duress is not at all the same as being unable to control your actions, say because of a spasm. Indeed, in duress the defendant deliberately chose to commit the crime rather than suffer the harm. But the defendant chose to act as he did in circumstances such that the choice should not be seen as one for which the defendant is responsible. So perhaps the best way of expressing the effect of duress as an excuse is to state that the defendant did not have a fair opportunity to comply with the law; that she chose to act as she did, but that she had no morally acceptable alternative.

So is it best to see duress as a justification or an excuse? It may be the legal defence of duress in fact which covers two types of situation: duress as an excuse or duress as a justification. If Harrison, a well-known terrorist, kidnaps Meg and threatens to kill all her family unless she steals a chocolate bar then surely she should steal the chocolate bar. That is what society would want her to do; she could be said to be justified. Indeed, an argument based on excuse – that she was so caught up in the dilemma of choosing between the two evils that she was not responsible for her choice – sounds inappropriate. However, in other cases where a defendant has to kill an innocent person or be killed, it may be that the killing would not be justifiable, but an argument based on the panic of the moment may lead us to excuse or partially excuse the defendant. If this view is correct then some of the difficulties that the law has faced with duress have resulted from the fact that it has failed to realise that in fact there are two different kinds of duress defences lurking under the single heading 'duress'.

It is, of course, possible to explain the existence of the defence without referring to the notions of justification and excuse. For example, it is possible to argue that when a person is faced with a threat of death or serious injury the criminal law cannot hope to influence the behaviour of individuals. In other words, the law cannot have a deterrent effect and so there will be no gains to society in imposing criminal liability.

Enough of the theory. What about the law on duress?

16.2.1 To what crimes is duress a defence?

Duress is available as a defence to all crimes except murder (whether as a principal or an accessory: *Howe*), attempted murder (*Gotts* [1992] 2 AC 412) and some forms of treason. No-one really knows what kind of treason is referred to here as there are few cases to go on. It is clear that duress may be pleaded in at least some types of treason (such as propaganda for the enemy in wartime: *Purdy* (1946)).

The reason for excluding duress as a defence to murder is explained by Lord Hailsham in *Howe* who suggested it would not be:

> good morals, good policy or good law to suggest, as did the majority in Lynch ... that the ordinary man of reasonable fortitude is not supposed to be capable of heroism if he is asked to take an innocent life rather than sacrifice his own. Doubtless in actual practice many will succumb to temptation ... But many will not, and I do not believe that as a 'concession to human frailty' the former should be exempt from liability to criminal sanctions if they do.

The reasoning here sounds justificatory in tone. When faced with a threat, the law expects heroism and the defendant should lay down his own life rather than kill an innocent third party. Thus the law here seeks to uphold the sanctity-of-life principle and protect the innocent victim's life. One difficulty with this reasoning is that it does not cover the situation where the threat is to kill the defendant's family. It is one thing to expect someone to lay down his own life for another; it is another to expect him to lay down the lives of his family. The denial of the defence of duress to murder is particularly strange when it is recalled that the defence is available only if the defendant acted as a reasonable person would, and it would only be in the most unusual cases that the jury would decide that a defendant had acted reasonably if he had killed an innocent third party. Nevertheless, under no circumstances is duress a defence to murder. The harshness of the law's approach was recently demonstrated in *Wilson* [2007] EWCA Crim 1251 where a 13-year-old boy was ordered by his father to help kill his mother. The Court of Appeal upheld his conviction for murder (as an accomplice) and confirmed that duress could not provide a defence to murder.

The argument in favour of allowing duress as a defence to murder was eloquently made by Lord Morris in *Lynch* [1975] AC 653:

> If ... someone is threatened with death or serious injury unless he does what he is told to do is the law to pay no heed to the miserable agonizing plight of such a person? For the law to understand not only how the timid but also the stalwartly may in a moment of crisis behave is not to make the law weak but to make it just. In the calm of the court room measures of fortitude or of heroic behaviour are surely not to be demanded when they could not in moments for decision reasonably have been expected even in the restrained and well disposed. ...

Duress is also not available as a defence to a charge of attempted murder (*Gotts*). The argument persuading the House of Lords was that it can be pure chance whether death results from the defendant's acts or not, and so the availability of duress in attempted murder should be the same as in murder. So the only defence for a defendant who was threatened and is facing a charge of murder or attempted murder is to try to plead a lack of intent. The argument would have to be that the defendant did not have the purpose to kill (but simply to avoid the threat) and, although he foresaw death as a virtually certain consequence of his actions, the jury should still hold back from saying that he had an intention (*Woollin** [1999] 1 AC 82: see Section 5.3). However, although this argument can be made and has some case law support (*Bourne* (1952) 36 Cr App R 125; *Steane* [1947] KB 997), it was stressed in *Howe* that simply because one is acting under duress does not mean that one lacks intent.

16.2.2   What must be shown if the defence is to succeed?

The requirements of the defence of duress were set out in *Graham** [1982] 1 All ER 801 by the Court of Appeal and confirmed by the House of Lords in *Howe* and *Hasan** [2005]

UKHL 222. They are as follows:

1. *The defendant was compelled to act in the way she did by threats of imminent death or serious physical injury.* This is a subjective test. Did the defendant act in the way she did because of the threats? This will be fairly easy to show. It would be only in a most unusual case that the defendant did not commit the crime in response to the threat. If the defendant was ordered to kill his enemy whom he had been looking for an opportunity to kill for a long time, then maybe this requirement would not be made out.

   It should be noted that the threat must be of death or serious injury of the defendant or any other person (*Conway* [1989] QB 290). It used to be thought that the threat had to be of injury to the defendant's family, but it now seems that the threat can be made towards a stranger (*Pommell** [1995] 2 Cr App R 607). However, the closeness of the relationship may be relevant when considering the reasonableness of the defendant's response (requirement **(iv)** below). Any threats short of death or serious injury (such as minor injury; loss of job or reputation or, perhaps most common, to inform the police of some other offence) will not excuse, and can only go towards mitigation of sentence (*Baker and Wilkins* [1999] 2 Cr App R 335). This meant that a defendant who drove while intoxicated to get a pain killer for his daughter who was slightly ill was not able to rely on the defence (*DPP v Hicks* [2002] All ER (D) 285). In *Shayler* [2001] 1 WLR 2206 the Court of Appeal said a vague threat to the public good was insufficient to enable the defendant to rely on duress. Nor in *Jones v Gloucestershire CPS* [2004] EWCA Crim 1981 was duress available to defendants who committed crimes in an attempt to thwart what they regarded as the illegal war against Iraq.

   What about threats to cause serious psychological harm? In *Baker and Wilkins*, it was stated that the threat had to be of physical harm. However, in *Ireland and Burstow*, the House of Lords stated that a clear distinction could not be drawn between physical injury and psychological injury. The House of Lords interpreted the term 'actual bodily harm' in the Offences Against the Person Act 1861 as applying to psychological injuries (see Chapter 7). It is arguable that *Baker and Wilkins* will need to be reconsidered in the light of *Ireland and Burstow*. If other threats accompany the threat of death or serious injury, the accused may still rely on duress (*Valderrama-Vega* [1985] Crim LR 220), as long as it was the threat of death or injury that caused him to commit the offence.

   In *Hudson and Taylor* [1971] 2 All ER 244, one of the issues discussed was the need for the threat to be of immediate harm. The two accused were charged with perjury. They were young women who had been threatened that if they did not give false evidence they would be injured. One of those who had made the threats was seen by the young women in court before they gave evidence. The Court of Appeal held that the crucial question was not whether the threat was capable of being carried out when it was made, but whether the threat was effective at the moment when the crime was committed. A threat of future violence may be too remote, but if the threat is 'sufficient to destroy his will' at the time when the accused has to decide whether or not to commit the offence, duress may be pleaded. In *Abdul-Hussain** [1999] Crim LR 570, the Court of Appeal rejected an argument that the threat had to be of immediate harm, as long as the threat was of imminent harm.

2. *The defendant must have good grounds to believe that the threat had been made.* This is an objective requirement. If a threat has not been made but the defendant unreasonably

believes it has then he cannot rely on the defence (*Hasan*). At present, therefore, the law appears to be that if the defendant had been kidnapped by a terrorist and the defendant unreasonably misheard the terrorist and believed that she was being threatened (but she was not), she will not be able to use the defence. This may seem harsh, as one cannot expect defendants to show great powers of calmness and clarity of perception when placed in such a dilemma. On the other hand, when the jury is deciding whether the mishearing was unreasonable no doubt it will take into account the stressfulness of the accused's situation. Presumably also the defendant would be expected to show only those powers of perception of which she was capable. So a person with hearing difficulties would not be blamed for misunderstanding a threat. There is no case law expressly on this, but no doubt the court would take such disabilities into account.

3. *The defendant must have good cause to believe that the threat will be carried out.* Again, this is an objective test. If an American tourist was kidnapped by a gunman in London who threatened to kill his family who were in the United States, it might be argued that there were no reasonable grounds to believe that the threat could be carried out, and so he would not be able to rely on the defence of duress. In deciding whether there was good cause, the courts will bear in mind the unusual circumstances in which the defendant found herself. Again, presumably a defendant's disabilities can also be taken into account in deciding whether there was good cause to believe that the threat would be carried out.

4. *The defendant must act as a sober person of reasonable firmness would have acted in those circumstances.* This is the part of the test which may be hardest for a defendant to fulfil. The test asks the jury to consider how an ordinary person, not an especially heroic one, would react to the threat. The defendant is expected to show 'the steadfastness reasonably to be expected of ordinary citizens in his situation' (*Graham*). One way of asking this question is to consider whether the defendant's response was proportionate to the threat that he or she was facing (*Abdul-Hussain*). Clearly, the more serious the offence, the greater the threat must be. As Lord Wilberforce explained in *Abbott* [1977] AC 755, 'the more dreadful the circumstances of the [crime], ... the stronger and more irresistible the duress needed before it could be regarded as affording any defence'. *Shayler* went so far as to suggest that the evil done by the defendant must be less than the harm threatened.

   The courts have had difficulty in deciding which of the defendant's characteristics to give to the reasonable person in deciding how she would react. The courts have allowed age, sex, pregnancy, recognised mental illness (for example, learned helplessness or post-traumatic stress disorder: Emery) and serious physical disability as characteristics which can affect the degree of firmness to be expected (*Bowen** [1996] 2 Cr App R 157). It is clear that neither voluntary intoxication (*Bowen*), nor other self-induced characteristics (*Flatt* [1996] Crim LR 576), nor particular vulnerability to pressure (*Horne* [1994] Crim LR 584), nor lack of firmness arising from sexual abuse (*Hirst* (1995) 1 CAR 82), nor emotional instability (*Horne*), nor low IQ (*Bowen*) can be taken into account as affecting the level of firmness required. One underlying principle emerges from *Bowen*, and that is that if a characteristic is to be taken into account it must be one which provides a reason why the defendant cannot be expected to demonstrate a reasonable degree of firmness. Hence sexual orientation is not a relevant factor in duress because there is no reason why someone who is straight should not be as brave as someone who is gay. The courts have not made it clear whether the defendant's characteristics can be taken into account in considering the gravity of the threat, as opposed to the level of firmness expected. Presumably the court would accept that to a concert pianist the threat to remove a finger might be graver than to someone else, but there is no case law on this.

The law here is trying to strike a delicate balance between the subjective and objective camps, attempting to mitigate the rigours of the objective test where it is not the defendant's fault that he is not a reasonable person. It is a shame that *Bowen* did not explain the basis of the distinction between those characteristics which were, and those which were not, relevant. The distinction drawn by the Court of Appeal in *Bowen* could be supported on the ground that there are two categories of characteristics which are not to be assigned to the reasonable person in ascertaining the level of firmness expected. First, excluded are those characteristics which cannot affect the level of firmness (for example, sexual orientation) simply because they are irrelevant. Second, also excluded are those characteristics for which the defendant is to be blamed (for example, drunkenness or cowardice, etc.).

5. *The defendant must not be responsible for the threats.* The defence of duress is not available where it is self-induced. That usually arises where the defendant is threatened by a gang which he has voluntarily joined, in which case, if he was aware that the gang was a violent one which might subject him to threats of violence when he joined it, he cannot rely on the defence of duress (*Hasan*). However, this applies only if the defendant voluntarily joined the gang and knew or ought to know that the gang was of a violent nature, and was likely to threaten him if he tried to leave (*Baker* [2000] Crim LR 700). So it would seem to be no bar to duress if the defendant joined a shoplifting gang which later decided to perform armed robbery and threatened the defendant with violence when he tried to leave the organisation. There also needs to be a close association between membership of the gang and the making of the threat. So where a defendant joined a gang and was later imprisoned, but while in prison he was threatened by a member of the gang, it was held that the threat was not closely related to his membership of the gang (*Lewis*), and so the defence of duress was available.

Self-induced duress is not limited to membership of criminal gangs. A defendant may be thought to have put himself in a position where he would be liable to be threatened in other circumstances. In *Heath* [2000] Crim LR 109, a defendant borrowed money from a drug dealer. When he did not pay the money back, the drug dealer threatened him with violence unless he played a role in transporting drugs. He was not able to rely on duress because he had put himself in a position where he was liable to be threatened by borrowing money from such a person.

In *Hasan* the House of Lords clarified an issue over which there had been a division of authority. It held that for the self-induced duress bar to operate there is no need to show that the defendant foresaw the kind of crime he would be asked to commit. It would be enough if he foresaw, or ought to foresee, that he might be asked to join in some kind of criminal enterprise.

A slightly different issue is where there is a gap in time between the making and the performance of the threat (see *Hudson and Taylor*). In *Abdul-Hussain*, the Court of Appeal stressed that it was not necessary to show that the defendant had reacted spontaneously in response to the threat, but the longer the gap in time between the point when the threat will be enacted and the performance of the crime, the less likely it is that it will be reasonable for the defendant to act in the way he or she did. The Court of Appeal explained that the threat of death or serious harm would have to be imminent, but not immediate. This is largely because the longer the gap in time, the more likely it is that the defendant will be able to find a way to escape from the threat, in particular by obtaining police protection or assistance. Although this will often be the reasonable course of action it is not always available, as in *Abdul-Hussain* where the victims were Shiite Muslims who had hijacked a plane to escape Saddam Hussain's Iraqi regime. By contrast, in *Heath* the defendant was told he would have to help with the transportation of drugs the next day or else face violence. The Court of Appeal felt this gave him enough time to seek police protection.

16.2.3 Reform of the law on duress

Law Commission Consultation Paper 177 has proposed a change in the law to permit duress to be a partial defence to (in their new proposed scheme) First Degree Murder. If duress is successfully raised, the defendant will be guilty only of Second Degree Murder. However, its proposed definition of duress is narrow:

1. there must have been a threat of death or serious violence;
2. the threat must have been directed against the defendant or his/her immediate family or someone close to the defendant;
3. the defendant must have good reason to believe that the threat will be carried out;
4. the offence committed by the defendant must have been directly caused by the threat;
5. the defendant may rely on the defence only if there was no evasive action that he or she could reasonably have been expected to take. The House of Lords has said that the defendant should be expected to take evasive action unless he or she expects the threat to be carried out 'almost immediately';
6. the defendant may not rely on duress to which he or she has voluntarily laid him or herself open, for example by voluntarily joining a criminal or terrorist gang;
7. it must be the case that a person of ordinary courage sharing the characteristics of the defendant might have acted as the defendant did.

16.3 Duress of circumstances

This defence has only recently been recognised by the courts and has developed by analogy with duress by threats. The difference between the two defences is that whereas in duress by threats someone has threatened the defendant, in duress of circumstances there is no threat uttered by anyone else but the circumstances are such that unless the defendant commits a crime someone will be killed or suffer serious injury. For example, in *Conway* [1989] QB 290 the defendant was driving a car, with a passenger who had recently narrowly escaped death in a gun attack by two men. Two more men approached the car and the defendant believed that his passenger was about to be attacked again. He drove off in a dangerous manner, exceeding the speed limit. The court found that he genuinely and reasonably believed that his friend was about to suffer death or serious injury (although in fact the two men were plain-clothes police officers) and could plead the defence of duress of circumstances to a charge of dangerous driving.

A case close to the borderline between the defences of duress by threats and duress by circumstances is *Cole* [1994] Crim LR 582, where the defendant was told by creditors that unless he paid money which was due to them they would cause his family serious harm. The defendant committed a bank robbery. The court decided that this scenario was closer to duress of circumstances than duress by threats, as the defendant was not told that he must commit a particular crime and it was in reality his financial difficulties (a circumstance) which caused him to commit the crime.

The fact that it can be difficult to draw a sharp distinction between duress by threats and duress of circumstances does not need to be of concern, because the defences are identical in their extent and requirements. As with duress by threats, duress of circumstances is not available as a defence to either murder or attempted murder. The test for duress of circumstances is identical to that for duress by threats (*Pommell* [1995] 2 Cr App R 607): was the defendant compelled to act as she did because of the circumstances as she reasonably believed them to be? Did she have good cause to believe that the circumstances threatened her life or presented the likelihood of serious injury, and would a sober person of reasonable firmness have reacted to the circumstances in the same way? One point recently emphasised by the Court of Appeal is that it is not possible for duress of circumstances to be based solely on internal pressures. So a defendant cannot claim to be compelled to act in an illegal way by his own suicidal feelings (*Rodger* [1998] 1 Cr App R 143) or as a result of pain from a medical condition (*Quayle* [2005] EWCA Crim 1415).

It is important for a defendant seeking to use duress of circumstances to show that he committed the crime only for as long as was necessary. For example if he is attempting to use the defence to a charge of drunk driving, he needs to show that he drove for only as long as was necessary to avoid the threat of death or serious injury (*Bell* [1992] Crim LR 176). Once the threat has passed, the defendant should stop driving.

16.4 Coercion

Coercion is a particular form of duress and arises where a wife is threatened by her husband and so she commits a crime. It must be shown that the wife committed the crime because of her husband's threats (*Shortland* [1995] Crim LR 893). It is not necessary for her to show that the threats were of death or serious injury; any threat will be sufficient as long as it compelled her to commit the crime. It must be shown that the pressures were such that she was 'forced unwillingly to participate'. The defence is available only to married couples and not to long-term unmarried partners, nor even to parties to a void marriage (*Ditta, Hussain and Kara* [1988] Crim LR 43). This special rule for wives seems based on the clearly outdated notion that a wife is dominated by her husband (the defence is not available to a husband). Indeed the Law Commission has called for its abolition (Law Commission Report 83). Of course, there is nothing to stop a wife from relying on the defence of ordinary duress, although there seems no advantage in her doing so. Like duress, coercion is not available to a charge of murder or treason; although, unlike duress, it is available as a defence to attempted murder.

16.5 Self-defence and duress of circumstances

In this section we will briefly consider the interrelation of duress of circumstances and self-defence. We have noted that the distinction between duress by threats and duress of circumstances is not exact. This is not of particular concern as the scope of both defences and the rules governing them is effectively identical. It is more difficult to distinguish between duress of circumstances and self-defence. This time the distinction needs to be clear, as duress of circumstances, unlike self-defence, is not available as a defence to murder or attempted murder. Further, if a defendant thinks she is being attacked but is not, self-defence is available; whereas if the defendant thinks the circumstances are threatening her but they are not, duress of circumstances is available only if the mistake was reasonable. Although the law has failed to draw a clear distinction between the two defences, some work on this has been done by commentators. Consider the following hypothetical scenario of Uniacke (as summarised by Horder):

> D and V are locked in a room with a diminishing supply of oxygen. D realises that only if he kills V will the oxygen supply be likely to last long enough for rescuers to save him. So he kills V. On Uniacke's view, this will not be killing in self-defence because V is not herself posing the threat; the threat stems from the lack of oxygen ... It might be different, however, if instead of breathing normally, V began to hyperventilate ... Now we may want to say that V has become part of the threat. V is, albeit involuntarily, assisting or enhancing the threat itself [and so the defence of self-defence may be available].

This is a neat analysis but it may not be sufficient to justify why in one case the defendant can rely on self-defence and commits no crime but in the other is guilty of murder. The fineness of the distinction casts further doubt on the correctness of the ruling in *Howe* [1987] 2 WLR 568, that duress should not be available as a defence to murder.

16.6 Necessity

Unfortunately the term 'necessity' has been used by the courts and commentators to mean different things. Sometimes the courts have called duress of circumstances 'necessity' (for example, *Shayler* [2001] 1 WLR 2206). However, in other cases and in other jurisdictions 'necessity' has been used to refer to a defence of pure justification: where the defendant was placed in a situation in which whatever he did would cause harm to someone and he performed an act which was the lesser of two evils. In *Safi* [2003] Crim LR 721 it was suggested that there was an overarching defence of necessity, of which duress of circumstances and private defence were but examples. To avoid confusion in this book, 'necessity' will be used to refer to the notion of pure justification and not duress of circumstances. So when will necessity in this context provide a defence?

The present position has been summarised by the Court of Appeal in *Pommell* [1995] 2 Cr App R 607, where Kennedy LJ stated in obiter dicta:

> The strength of the argument that a person ought to be permitted to breach the letter of the criminal law in order to prevent a greater evil befalling himself or others has long been recognised (see for example Stephen's *Digest of Criminal Law*), but it has, in English law, not given rise to a recognised general defence of necessity...

The leading case on necessity and murder is *Dudley and Stephens* (1884–5) LR 14 QBD 237. In that case, Lord Coleridge CJ held that necessity was no defence to murder, arguing from the authority of Hale (who wrote in the seventeenth century). The defendants had been shipwrecked and had killed and eaten a boy of 17 after eight days without food and six days without water in an open boat. Lord Coleridge said:

> the temptation to the act which existed here was not what the law has ever called necessity. It is not needful to point out the awful danger of admitting the principle which has been contended for. Who is to be the judge of this sort of necessity? By what measure is the comparative value of lives to be measured? Is it to be strength, or intellect, or what?... We are often compelled

to set up standards we cannot reach ourselves, and to lay down rules which we could not ourselves satisfy. But a man has no right to declare temptation to be an excuse, though he might himself have yielded to it.

As A.W.B. Simpson pointed out in his book on this case (*Cannibalism and the Common Law*, 1986), the reasoning in the case reflects a view of the judicial function which is no longer widely accepted: that of laying down morally correct standards of behaviour. However, in more recent cases judges have been equally doubtful of the defence of necessity, on the ground that it would encourage all sorts of spurious claims.

So there is no general defence of necessity. However, the courts have recognised four circumstances in which necessity provides a defence:

1. An action taken to preserve the life or wellbeing of another person who is unable to consent (Lord Goff in *Re F* [1990] 2 AC 1). The most obvious example is where a doctor operates on a patient who is unable to consent (because, for example, she is unconscious), if that treatment is immediately necessary for her wellbeing. Another example is where one person pulls another out of the way of a moving vehicle when there is no time to obtain the consent of the other. It should be noted that if a person is capable of consenting and wishes to die, treatment cannot lawfully be forced upon that person against her will (*S v St George's* [1998] 3 All ER 673).
2. Where property is damaged in order to save other property then the defence may apply (Lord Goff in *Re F*). An example of this may be where a house is pulled down to create a firebreak and prevent a fire engulfing a whole town.
3. Where property is damaged in order to avoid injury to a person, the defence may be available (Lord Goff in *Re F*).
4. In the Court of Appeal decision of *Re A (Conjoined Twins)** [2000] 4 All ER 961, Ward LJ suggested that necessity may be available on the special facts of that case. It concerned the question whether it was lawful to operate to separate conjoined twins in an operation which would end the life of one twin but would probably save the life of the other. Ward LJ was willing to permit the operation on the basis that it would not be unlawful, because the doctors could rely on the defence of necessity. However, he provided a very narrow definition of when necessity could be available:

> Lest it be thought that this decision could become authority for wider propositions, such as that a doctor, once he has determined that a patient cannot survive, can kill the patient, it is important to restate the unique circumstances for which this case is authority. They are that it must be impossible to preserve the life of X without bringing about the death of Y, that Y by his or her very continued existence will inevitably bring about the death of X within a short period of time, and that X is capable of living an independent life but Y is incapable under any circumstances (including all forms of medical intervention) of viable independent existence.

It is difficult to imagine circumstances, other than cases involving conjoined twins, in which these requirements would be made out. Brook LJ also suggested that necessity was available. He gave a broader definition of necessity. Three circumstances had to be demonstrated:

1. the act is needed to avoid inevitable and irreparable evil;
2. no more should be done than is reasonably necessary for the purpose to be achieved;
3. the evil inflicted must not be disproportionate to the evil avoided.

Controversially Brook LJ states that this kind of necessity provided a defence to murder. As neither of the other judges in the Court of Appeal accepted this definition, it is not binding on a later case. In any event there are difficulties with Brooke LJ's requirements. The core difficulty is that the Court of Appeal approved the decision in *Dudley and Stephens*, even though the three requirements appeared to have been satisfied in that case. (See Hot topic at the end of this chapter for further discussion.) It may be that it also has to be shown that the killing of this victim was the only way of avoiding the death of others. If the killing of another person would also have avoided the death (as was the case in *Dudley and Stephens*, but not in *Re A (Conjoined Twins)*) then maybe the defence is not available.

This is probably not a complete list of the circumstances in which necessity is available. It may be that if a case comes before the court and it feels that the defence should be available it will develop the defence. Professor Bohlander (2006) has considered what the position would be if an aircraft was hijacked and flown towards a city centre. Would a soldier who shot the plane out of the sky be able to rely on a defence of necessity? Quite possibly.

However, the court will not use necessity where the issue is the kind which Parliament has considered and made a policy decision. In *Quayle* [2005] EWCA Crim 1415 defendants who were suffering from painful medical conditions smoked cannabis to alleviate their pain. When prosecuted under the Misuse of Drugs Act the defendants sought to rely on the defence of necessity: smoking the cannabis was a lesser evil than suffering the pain. Their defence failed. In a case on similar facts, *Altham* [2006] Crim LR 633, the defendant again sought to rely on necessity, arguing that in not allowing him to use cannabis the state was breaching his right under Article 3 of the European Convention on Human Rights not to suffer torture or inhuman or degrading treatment. The argument failed. The state was required to protect him from inhuman treatment, but that did not extend to permitting him to commit crimes. Parliament had considered the issues carefully and had set out in the Misuse of Drugs Act when people could use drugs. It was not for the courts to overrule Parliament.

It should be noted that the second and third kinds of necessity listed above, as well as being forms of common law necessity, are also statutory defences under the Criminal Damage Act 1971. This reflects a wider point that in many circumstances where it might be thought that necessity should apply there is in fact a statutory provision which provides a defence. Words such as 'reasonable' can in effect contain a defence where the defendant acts in performing the lesser of two evils. The point can work in reverse, however. In *Cichon v DPP* [1994] Crim LR 918, a defendant tried to use necessity as a defence to a charge under s 1(2)(d) Dangerous Dogs Act 1991 (which made it an offence not to muzzle some dogs under certain circumstances). The accused's argument was that the dog was ill and if the muzzle had been removed then there would be little danger to the public, but the dog's life might have been saved. However, the Divisional Court decided that the defence of necessity was not available, because if Parliament had thought the defence should be available in this scenario then it would have expressly provided for it, as it did in the Criminal Damage Act. This seems to suggest that necessity is not available as a defence to a statutory offence unless the statute expressly states that it is. On other occasions the nature of the *mens rea* may include elements of necessity. But this, suggests *Backshall*, does not mean that the defence of necessity is necessarily unavailable.

There has been much discussion of an incident which occurred during the *Herald of Free Enterprise* disaster. It appears that as the boat began to sink, several passengers were attempting to escape by means of a ladder but one person was so terrified that he was unable to move. After many attempts to persuade him to move, someone pushed him off; he was never seen again. The others were able to use the ladder to escape. Had the other passengers been charged with murder, self-defence would not have been available as a defence because there was no threat posed by the victim; rather the threat was posed by the rising waters. Duress would not be available as it is not a defence to a charge of murder. Loss of control cannot apply because there was nothing said or done which caused a loss of self-control. One possible defence would be a lack of intent. The hypothetical defendant could argue that it was not his purpose to kill the passenger (he would have been delighted if the passenger had managed to swim to safety). The case would therefore fall within the *Woollin* direction. Although the defendant was aware that it was virtually certain that death or serious harm would be caused by his actions, the jury may still be entitled not to find intention (see Section 5.3). More likely to succeed would be the defence of necessity as developed by Brooke LJ in *Re A (Conjoined Twins)*. The three requirements he set out appear to have been satisfied in this case.

16.7　Superior orders

It is no defence to state that you were ordered to commit a crime by a person in a senior position to you (*Yip Chi-Cheung* [1995] 1 AC 111). The most likely circumstances in which this could arise is where a police officer or someone in the armed forces would try to argue that a more senior officer had ordered him to commit the crime. The reason behind the law's approach is the principle of the rule of law; that no-one can escape the umbrella of the law. Even the most senior army officer is bound by the criminal law and cannot give an exemption to others. It is possible that if one were ordered to commit the crime one could then deny having the necessary *mens rea* or seek to rely on duress.

Hot Topic –　Killing one to save the many?

Is it permissible to kill one person to save five? Some people's initial reaction is to say 'yes'; surely if the only options are that one person die or that five people die we should prefer the latter. But such a response is normally a little too quick. Imagine that a doctor has five patients all of whom are in desperate need of a different organ, and if organs are not found soon they will die. Could the doctor kill a nurse so that he could use her organs in order to save the lives of his five patients? Put that way, most people feel rather uncomfortable with the proposition that you can kill one person to save five.

But why not? One response is that each person has a right to life. We cannot take the life of an innocent person, however much good may be produced as a result. Once we start accepting the simple proposition that if the act produces more harm than good it is justifiable we lose respect for

the dignity of each person and open the door to a catalogue of abuse and horrors. History is replete with examples of times when minority groups were persecuted and abused in order to promote a greater good.

The benefit of focussing on a right to life approach is that it explains why self-defence can be used as a defence to murder, but not duress. In a case of self-defence the right to life can be forfeited by an attacker, and hence the use of force against them is justified. However, in a case of duress the victim has done nothing which lessens their entitlement to protection.

The argument based on a right to life may still leave borderline cases. What if, returning to our example of the doctor mentioned above, the doctor had a patient who was in persistent vegetative state, with no hope of recovery. Would it be appropriate to remove their organs? If it would, where do we draw the line? Or, to pose a different question, what if a terrible disease was threatening the lives of millions of people, but one person appeared to have developed an anti-body. Only by killing him could scientists produce a medication which would saves millions of lives. Would it be obvious there that he should not be killed? Or consider the scenario posed by Professor Bohlander (2006) of a hijacked plane heading towards a highly populated city. Could it be justified to shoot it down in order to save the lives of those living in the city? In that case it might be argued that the people on the plane are due to die very soon, whether the plane is shot down or not. This might be used as an argument that shooting the plane down is only a minor infringement of their right to life. By accepting such an argument some people believe we would be taking a dangerous step down a road which led to us not valuing the lives of older or severely ill people as highly as others.

Summary

16.1 Certain defences can be seen as justifications for the conduct of the accused, whereas others are seen as total or partial excuses. English law has not developed with the distinction between justifications and excuses explicitly in mind, but they are useful theoretical tools.

16.2 Duress of threats is pleaded where the accused admits the commission of the act, with the required mental element, but claims that he acted under compulsion. The threat must be effective at the time of the crime, and only a threat of death or serious injury to the accused or another person will suffice. It must be a threat that an ordinary person of reasonable fortitude would have failed to resist. The possibility of avoiding the threat by seeking official protection will be taken into account, as will the immediacy of the threatened violence. A mistake as to the seriousness of the threat is taken into account only if it was reasonable. Duress is no defence to murder or attempted murder.

16.3 Duress of circumstances is available under similar conditions to duress by threats, except that in duress of circumstances the threat to life or serious injury is not made specifically by a particular person, but the circumstances are such that unless the defendant commits a crime there is risk of death or serious injury.

16.4 A wife who commits a crime following threats from her husband can plead a special defence of coercion if the threats compelled her to commit the offence.

16.5 It can be difficult to distinguish between circumstances which give rise to duress of circumstances and those which give rise to self-defence. The key distinction is whether the threat is posed by the victim, by the surrounding circumstances or by third parties.

16.6 Necessity is available in a variety of situations. One is where the defendant is acting in order to promote the best interests of the victim whose life or wellbeing was in danger. Another is where the defendant is preventing a more serious harm and the only way of doing so is by committing an offence.

16.7 It is no defence to a criminal charge to claim that one was acting under orders.

Further Reading

The distinction between justifications and excuses is examined in Alldridge, Duff, Fletcher, J. Gardner, Horder, K. Smith and Wilson, and Tadros. Duress is considered in Buchanan and Virgo, Elliott, Loveless, and K. Smith. Necessity is discussed in Bohlander, Clarkson, S. Gardner, and Ost. Wallerstein discusses superior orders.

Further Reading cont'd

Alldridge, 'The Coherence of Defences' [1983] Crim LR 665.

Bohlander, 'In Extremis – Hijacked Airplanes, "Collateral Damage" and the Limits of Criminal Law' [2006] Crim LR 579.

Buchanan and Virgo, 'Duress and Mental Abnormality' [1999] Crim LR 517.

Clarkson, 'Necessary Action: A New Defence' [2004] Crim LR 81.

Duff, 'Rethinking Justification' (2005) 39 Tulsa L Rev 829.

Elliott, 'Necessity, Duress and Self-Defence' [1989] Crim LR 611.

Fletcher, *Rethinking Criminal Law* (Little Brown 1978).

J. Gardner, 'Justifications and Reasons', in Simester and Smith (eds), *Harm and Culpability* (Oxford University Press 1995).

S. Gardner, 'Necessity's Newest Inventions' (1991) 11 OJLS 125.

S. Gardner, 'Direct Action and the Defence of Necessity' [2005] Crim LR 371.

Horder, *Excusing Crime* (Oxford University Press 2004).

Loveless, 'Domestic Violence, Coercion and Duress' [2010] Crim LR 93.

Ost, 'Euthanasia and the Defence of Necessity: Advocating a More Appropriate Legal Response' [2005] Crim LR 355.

Rogers, 'Necessity, Private Defence and the Killing of Mary' [2001] Crim LR 515.

K. Smith, 'Duress and Steadfastness: In Pursuit of the Unintelligible' [1999] Crim LR 363.

K. Smith and Wilson, 'Impaired Voluntariness and Criminal Responsibility' (1993) 13 OJLS 69.

Tadros, 'The Characters of Excuses' (2001) 21 OJLS 497.

Wallerstein, 'Why English Law Should not Incorporate the Defence of Superior Orders' [2010] Crim LR 109.

Western, 'An Attitudinal Theory of Excuse' (2006) 25 Law Philos 289.

Case Notes

▶ *Re A (Conjoined Twins)* [2000] 4 All ER 961. Court of Appeal

The case concerned two conjoined twins: Jodie and Mary. If the twins were separated Mary would inevitably die, but there was a promising prognosis for Jodie. However, if there was no separation, both twins would die within three to six months. This was because Mary lacked effective organs to pump her blood around her body and was in effect relying on Jodie's organs to live, but Jodie's organs were not able to support two people for any length of time. The children's parents objected to the operation. The Court of Appeal declared that the performance of the operation would not be unlawful. Although the doctors who performed the operation would be said to have intended to kill Mary, the operation would be lawful because the defence of necessity could apply.

▶ *Abdul-Hussain* [1999] Crim LR 570. Court of Appeal

The appellants were Shiite Muslims fleeing from Saddam Hussein's regime in Iraq under which they claimed they faced various forms of persecution. They had escaped to Sudan, but were on the point of being returned to Iraq where they feared they would be killed. They therefore hijacked an aircraft. At the trial, the judge withdrew the defence of duress because the threat was insufficiently immediate. The Court of Appeal held that the key issue was whether the threat was operating on the minds of the defendants. Whether the threat was immediate was a relevant factor in deciding whether the defendants' response was proportionate; duress was not restricted to where the defendants' criminal act was a spontaneous response to the threat. The Court of Appeal repeated calls for legislation to define duress with precision.

▶ *Bowen* [1996] 4 All ER 837. Court of Appeal

The appellant was convicted of obtaining services by deception. He claimed that he had obtained the financial services only because two men in a pub had threatened to petrol bomb him and his family. He was convicted and appealed on the basis that the judge had failed to direct the jury to take into account his low IQ when considering his duress defence. The Court of Appeal dismissed his appeal. It explained that the direction to the jury on the defence of duress involved two tests. First, was the defendant impelled to act as he did because he feared death or serious physical injury? Second, if so, did the defendant respond as a sober person of reasonable firmness sharing the characteristics of the defendant would have done? But in considering the second question not every characteristic of the accused should be taken into account. The mere fact that he was timid or pliable was not a relevant characteristic. Characteristics could be considered if those possessing them as a group were less able to resist threats than others. Age, pregnancy, physical disability and recognised psychiatric conditions could therefore be relevant, but low IQ could not. There was no reason why those with low IQ were less able to resist threats than others.

▶ *Graham* [1982] 1 All ER 801. Court of Appeal

The appellant was convicted of murder. He had assisted in the killing of his wife by another man with whom he had a homosexual relationship. The other man was violent and the appellant said that he had only acted out of fear. It was argued on appeal that the jury had been misdirected on the defence of duress. The Court of Appeal dismissed the appeal. It was held that the applicable test was twofold. First, was the accused taking part in the killing because of a well-grounded (reasonable) fear of death or serious physical injury as a result of his companion's words or conduct? Second, would a sober person of reasonable firmness, sharing the characteristics of the accused, have responded to those words or conduct by taking part in the killing? The effects of voluntary consumption of drink and drugs should be disregarded.

▶ *Hasan* [2005] UKHL 14. House of Lords

The defendant was convicted of aggravated burglary. His defence was that he had participated in the burglary only because S (who was a violent gangster) had threatened to harm him and his family if he did not. The judge directed the jury that if he had voluntarily put himself in the position in which he knew he was likely to be subjected to threats then he could not rely on the defence of duress. The Court of Appeal quashed the defendant's conviction but asked the House of Lords to clarify what kind of knowledge when joining a criminal gang or association with a criminal would exclude the defence of duress. Their Lordships said that that defence would not be available if, as a result of the accused's voluntary association with others engaged in criminal activity, he foresaw or ought to have foreseen the risk of being subjected to any compulsion by threats of violence. There was no need to show that the defendant foresaw what kind of crime he would be compelled to commit. Their Lordships also approved the direction that the defendant could rely on duress if he was facing, or reasonably believed he was facing, a threat of death or serious injury to himself or his family.

▶ *Howe* [1987] 2 WLR 568. House of Lords

The appellant, with another man, was convicted of murder. They had pleaded duress as a defence, claiming that they believed they would themselves be killed if they did not carry out the killing. The trial judge ruled that duress could be raised as a defence only in respect of the first count, in which they were charged as accessories to murder. Their appeals were dismissed by the Court of Appeal and the House of Lords. The House of Lords (departing from *Lynch*, an earlier House of Lords decision) held that duress could not be a defence to murder, whether the defendant is charged as a principal or accessory. With respect to the test to be applied in cases of duress, the decision of the Court of Appeal in *Graham* (see above) was correct. It was also held that it was possible to convict an accessory of murder as long as the accessory had the required intent, in cases where the principal was guilty only of manslaughter because of some special mitigating factor.

▶ *Pommell* **[1995] 2 Cr App Rep 607. Court of Appeal**

The police found the accused in bed with a gun. He explained that he 'took it off a geezer who was going to do some people some damage with it'. He was convicted of unlawful possession of the gun. He was convicted after the trial judge had ruled that the defence of duress of circumstances was not available in the circumstances of the case. The Court of Appeal stated that, if true, the defendant's story could enable him to use the defence of duress of circumstances and quashed his conviction. The defence was available to the same crimes as duress by threats. The court stressed that the defendant might have an uphill task here showing that he took the earliest opportunity to hand the gun over to the police and so stop the commission of his crime.

▶ *Woollin* **[1999] 1 AC 82. House of Lords**

See Chapter 5 Case notes.

Part V

Participation in crime

Key Terms

> ▶ **Accessory** – a person who assisted or encouraged the principal to commit the crime.
> ▶ **Innocent agent** – a person whose conduct satisfies the external elements of the offence, but who is blameless and was caused to act by another.
> ▶ **Principal** – the person who satisfied the external elements of the offence.

17.1 What is an accessory?

Imagine a criminal gang which has three members who decide to commit a robbery, with each member performing a different role. One is the mastermind behind the gang who plans and co-ordinates the robbery; another obtains the gun which is used; and the third actually commits the robbery. It would be unsatisfactory if the criminal law were able to convict only the person who actually carried out the robbery. Indeed, sometimes the 'mastermind' behind such gangs is a greater threat to smociety than the individual who actually carries out the crime. The actual perpetrator may simply be a small cog in a huge machine. So it is not surprising that the law spreads the net of liability wider than to just those who actually commit the crime, by enabling the conviction of those who assist or encourage others in the commission of the crime.

There are two main ways, at a theoretical level, in which the law could deal with accessories (or secondary parties, as they are sometimes known). This issue will be dealt with in greater detail as the Hot topic at the end of this chapter, but a brief summary can be given now. The law could see accessories as guilty of a crime because they have partly caused the commission of the crime – without their assistance or encouragement the crime would not have taken place, at least not at the time or in the manner in which it took place. This view is sometimes known as 'derivative liability' (that is the accomplice's responsibility derives from that of the person who actually carries out the crime). Alternatively, one could punish accessories because the acts of assistance are in themselves harmful to society, independent of any causal link to the commission of the actual crime. Those who adopt this theory tend to draw an analogy between accessory liability and inchoate offences, such as incitement and attempts (see Chapter 18). The most significant difference between these derivative and inchoate theories would be where someone tries to help another commit a crime but the assistance is not used at all. In those circumstances the derivative theory would not attach accessorial liability, as in no sense did the assistance contribute towards the commission of a crime, whereas the 'inchoate theory' would. At present the law adopts elements of both. In fact these theories reflect a strain in the law between two competing concerns: on the one hand the law does not want criminal liability to be too extensive, while on the other it is understandable that the law should attempt to deter people who seek to aid criminal acts.

Before we look at the law, a point on terminology. Courts and commentators have used the terms 'accessories'; 'accomplices' and 'secondary parties' to refer to those who assist another to commit a crime. There is no difference in meaning between these terms. Similarly the person who actually commits the crime can be called the 'principal' or the 'perpetrator'.

17.2 Principals and the doctrine of innocent agency

It is necessary first of all to distinguish a principal from an accessory. There is no requirement for an indictment to state whether the defendant is charged as a principal or an accomplice. For example, a person will simply be charged with murder whether it is alleged that he was the principal or an accessory to murder. Although the charge will be the same, the indictment will specify how the accused is alleged to have participated in the offence. The accessory is liable to the same punishment, although whether the actual sentence differs from that given to the principal will depend on the circumstances of the offence, the degree of involvement of the parties and the personal circumstances of the individual defendant.

Who is a principal? A principal is the person who fulfils the *actus reus* requirements for the crime. There is one exception to this and that is the doctrine of innocent agency, to be discussed shortly. Where the *actus reus* of the crime involves an act such as damaging property or wounding, the principal will be the person who does that act. Where the *actus reus* of the crime involves bringing about a particular consequence, such as the death of another person, the principal will be the person who is the most direct cause of that consequence. It is, of course, possible to have two or more principals. For example, if two people together push a rock from the top of a cliff onto a victim below they will both be joint principals to the killing. If two people were present at the scene of the crime but it is unclear who actually committed the crime, the law has developed a special set of rules. If one of them must have been the principal and the other either a joint principal or an accomplice, even if it is not clear who was which, then both can be convicted of the crime without it being established who actually was the principal. This is possible only as long as they both had the *mens rea* for being either a principal or an accomplice (*Gianetto* [1997] 1 Cr App R 1).

There is one circumstance in which the person who performs the *actus reus* is not the principal, and that is if she is an 'innocent agent'. If the person most intimately connected to the *actus reus* is an innocent agent then the person who caused the innocent agent to act in this way is to be regarded as the principal. Suppose a terrorist plants a bomb which is set to explode the moment someone touches it. A traffic warden touches the bomb, setting it off and killing a passer-by. It would seem odd if the traffic warden were seen as the principal of the crime and the terrorist as an accessory (although in such a case the traffic warden would not be guilty because she had no *mens rea*). In such a case the traffic warden would be regarded as an innocent agent and the terrorist as the principal. A person may be an innocent agent in two ways:

1. She lacks the capacity to commit the crime, for example she is exempt from criminal liability because she is below the age of criminal responsibility (*Michael* (1840) 173 ER 867) or she is insane (*Tyler* (1838) 8 C&P 616); or
2. She lackthe *mens rea* and is unaware of the criminal nature of her acts.

The traffic warden above would fall under heading 2. Another example would be a secretary who types and posts a fraudulent letter dictated by her boss, unaware that it is fraudulent (*Stringer* (1991) 94 Cr App R 13). It appears that someone is not an innocent agent simply because she acts under duress or self-defence.

Although we have referred to the rule here rather grandly as the 'doctrine of innocent agency', in fact it is little more than an application of the rules of causation (see Chapter 4). The traffic warden's act would not be seen as breaking the chain of causation under the rules of causation, as she was not acting in a way which was 'free, voluntary and informed' and so was not a *novus actus interveniens* (see Section 4.4). Similarly when a person can be regarded as an innocent agent, his acts will not break the chain of causation, so the primary cause of the chain of events could be regarded as the principal.

A particularly controversial example of the use of the doctrine of innocent agency is *Cogan and Leak* [1976] QB 217. Mr Leak persuaded his friend, Mr Cogan, to have intercourse with his wife, Mrs Leak. He told Mr Cogan untruthfully that Mrs Leak might appear to resist, but that she would act in this way in order to heighten her enjoyment of the occasion. In fact Mrs Leak did not consent to the sexual intercourse. Mr Cogan was acquitted on a charge of rape of Mrs Leak because he believed that the victim was consenting. However, the Court of Appeal suggested that Mr Leak could be seen as guilty of raping Mrs Leak through the innocent agency of Mr Cogan. This is seen as controversial for two reasons. The first is that Mr Leak at that time (before R: see Section 8.2) could not in law be guilty of raping his wife. It seems odd that he could be convicted of a crime for which he could not have been convicted had he committed the crime himself. Indeed the reasoning in the case would suggest that a woman could be convicted of raping another woman as a principal. Second, the case has been criticised as it is said that some crimes cannot 'linguistically' be committed through an innocent agent. Rape is such a 'physical' crime that it is inappropriate and unrealistic to refer to it as being committed through an innocent agent. Indeed another case has held that one cannot be said to 'drive' a vehicle through the innocent agency of another (*Millward** [1994] Crim LR 527). A conviction for procuring rape would seem more realistic on the facts of *Cogan and Leak*, and was indeed said by the Court of Appeal to be available on the facts. However, despite these criticisms *Cogan and Leak* has not yet been overruled, although in a recent case on similar facts the prosecution relied on the charge of procuring rape rather than using the innocent agency rule (*K and B* [1997] Cr App R 36). Indeed, whenever the innocent agency rule operates, a charge of procuring would be possible (*Wheelhouse* [1994] Crim LR 756).

17.3 The *actus reus* of being an accessory

Having established who is the principal, it is then possible to decide whether anyone can be convicted as his or her accessory. Before outlining the ways in which the law recognises how someone can be an accessory, it is important to emphasise two restrictions on accessorial liability. First, here we are dealing with those who assist or encourage the principal before or during the commission of the crime. Separate rules govern those who assist a principal after the crime is completed (see Section 17.10 below). Second, one can only be an accessory to a crime which has actually been committed. However much assistance or encouragement the accused offers the principal, unless the principal goes on to commit a crime the would-be accessory commits no offence as an accessory. He may, however be guilty of conspiracy or an offence under the Serious Crime Act 2007 (see Chapter 18).

We turn now to the definition of the ways of being an accessory. A person can be an accessory by being a party to a joint enterprise or by acting in one or more of four ways set out in s 8 Accessories and Abettors Act 1861 (the Magistrates Court Act 1980 is in similar terms for summary offences):

> Whosoever shall aid, abet, counsel, or procure the commission of any indictable offence, whether the same be an offence at common law or by virtue of any Act passed or to be passed, shall be liable to be tried, indicted and punished as a principal offender.

The Court of Appeal has said that these four words (aiding, abetting, counselling and procuring) are to be given their ordinary meaning and that the words should be seen as indicating separate concepts (*A-G's Ref (No 1 of 1975)* [1975] 2 All ER 686). However, it is not always easy to distinguish the four concepts. Indeed Potter LJ in *Bryce** [2004] EWCA Crim 1231 stated:

> So far as the charging of secondary parties is concerned, it is frequently advisable (as was done in this case) to use the 'catch-all' phrase 'aid, abet, counsel or procure' because the shades of difference between them are far from clear.

Perhaps not surprisingly then, the case law rarely discusses the differences between the different concepts, but the following definitions appear from it.

17.3.1 Aiding

This is the giving of assistance to a principal. It can range from supplying equipment (for example, *Bainbridge* [1959] 3 All ER 200), to acting as a look-out (for example, *Perman* [1996] 1 Cr App R 24). There is no need to show that the assistance was requested, and indeed there may be no communication at all between the aider and the principal. For example, if an employee left a business premise with the door open, out of spite, and later a burglar wandered in and stole something, the employee could be seen as an aid to the burglary. However, it must be shown that the assistance was actually used in the performance of the crime (*Able* [1984] QB 79). It seems sufficient for the act to be of only a small amount of assistance, although there is little authority on this. In *Bryce*, transporting the killer to a caravan near the victim's house 13 hours before the killing was sufficiently helpful to amount to an act of assistance: the act of assistance was still 'operative'; the crime had progressed in a foreseeable way; and there had been no 'overwhelming supervening event' after the act of assistance, before the killing.

17.3.2 Abetting

To be honest, no-one knows the meaning of abetting. It appears to involve encouragement and support provided to a principal, but probably only if it is given during the performance of the crime. It seems that abetting has no separate role, the concept being covered by aiding or counselling.

17.3.3 Counselling

This involves giving encouragement, advice or information to the principal. There is no need to show that the counselling caused the principal to act as he did, although it is necessary to show that the principal acted within the 'scope of the counselling'. So, if Clare suggests that Ellie kills Alex, and Ellie replies 'don't worry I was about to anyway' and goes on to kill Alex, Clare could still be convicted as an accessory. However, if Ellie went on to rob Alex, Clare could not be convicted as an accessory to robbery. An example discussed in *Calhaem** [1985] 2 All ER 266 by Parker LJ also demonstrates this requirement. If the accused had counselled the principal to kill and

> if the principal offender happened to be involved in a football riot in the course of which he laid about him with a weapon of some sort and killed someone who, unknown to him, was the person whom he had been counselled to kill, he could not, in our view have been acting within the scope of his authority; he would have been acting outside it, albeit what he had done was what he had been counselled to do.

This appears to mean that only exceptionally will the resulting act, if within the terms of the counselling, be considered too remote. The required link under the derivative theory between the assistance and the crime is stretched to its limits here. In *Bryce*, Potter LJ suggested obiter that even in the counselling there needed to be 'some causal connection' between the counselling and the principal's crime. In *Luffman* [2008] EWCA Crim 1379 the Court of Appeal explained that it had to be shown that the defendant said or did something that objectively could encourage the commission of the offence, even if in fact the principal was not encouraged.

17.3.4 Procuring

Procuring has been defined as 'to produce by endeavour. You procure a thing by setting out to see that it happens and taking appropriate steps to produce that happening' (*A-G's Ref (No 1 of 1975)*). This means that there must be a causal link between the act of procuring and the *actus reus*. A common example is where an accessory spikes a principal's drink (for example, by putting alcohol into someone's non-alcoholic drink) and the principal then goes on to drive. In such a case the accessory is seen to be guilty of procuring the drink-driving offence.

17.3.5 Joint enterprise

A joint enterprise arises where two or more people commit a crime together. In order for the doctrine to operate, two or more people must act in concert (*Gnango** [2010] EWCA Crim 1691). So in one case where a man attacked a victim in a car park and a stranger came along and joined in the attack, it was held that there was no joint enterprise, although both were liable as principals for their own acts (*Petters and Parfitt* [1995] Crim LR 501). This is not to say it is necessary for the members of the joint enterprise to agree expressly on a course of conduct, but they need to act together with a common purpose.

If there is a joint enterprise and the group out their plan, all the members will be jointly liable for each other's acts. So, if a gang committing a burglary together will all be guilty of burglary, even if some of the gang stay outside the house as look-outs. Lord Hoffmann in *Rahman** [2008] UKHL 45 called this kind of case a 'plain vanilla' case of joint enterprise.

However, the doctrine of joint enterprise goes beyond the 'plain vanilla' case and applies where the parties have a common purpose to commit one crime, but the principal goes on to commit a different crime. An example of the joint enterprise doctrine at work is where D and P are committing a burglary when they are disturbed by X, the owner, and P kills X. Then D can be liable as an accomplice to murder (providing he has the *mens rea*).

How is a joint enterprise different from other ways of being an aider and abetter? There has been some considerable dispute over whether joint enterprise cases are simply an example of how one can be an accessory or whether it has its own discrete set of rules. Some commentators say it is impossible to draw a hard and fast distinction between joint enterprise and being an accessory. Is a look-out for a burglary a party to a joint enterprise or an aider? To others joint enterprises involve a special scenario and the law should develop special rules for such cases. The argument is that D by joining P in committing a crime has thereby 'lost the sympathy of the law'. We should therefore be more ready to convict him as an accomplice than we would be to convict someone who simply supplied equipment to a principal. The courts have not taken a consistent approach on this issue, but the latest authorities regard joint enterprise as a form of accessorial liability and held that the same rules to joint enterprise as for other forms of accessorial liability (*Mendez* [2010] EWCA Crim 516; *R v A, B, C, D**).

We will now discuss some of the particular issues which have arisen concerning the *actus reus* of being an accessory.

17.4 The mere presence of an accessory

One contentious topic has been whether a person's mere presence at the scene of a crime can amount to the *actus reus* of being an accessory. There are three circumstances in which the law recognises that presence can amount to the *actus reus* for being an accessory:

1. *Presence as encouragement.* Mere presence can itself amount to encouraging (counselling). It must be shown that the principal was actually encouraged by the accused's presence and the accused realised that his presence was encouraging the principal (*Coney* (1882) 8 QBD 534). It is not enough to show that the bystander was willing to intervene should his assistance become necessary, unless that willingness actually encouraged the principal (*Sirat* [1986] Crim LR 245). In *Clarkson* [1971] 3 All ER 344, the accused, a soldier, came across a fellow soldier raping a woman, and stayed and watched. He did nothing to stop the incident. However, he was acquitted on a charge of being an accomplice to rape as it was not shown that the rapist found any encouragement from his presence. Nor was it shown that he had the necessary *mens rea* of being aware that his presence might be an encouragement. By contrast, in *Wilcox v Jeffery* [1951] 1 All ER 464 the accused attended a performance by a saxophonist, an illegal immigrant, whom he had invited to play in England. His act of meeting the saxophonist on his arrival in England and his presence and clapping at the performance were encouragement to the illegal performance. The court suggested that had the accused attended the concert and shouted 'boo', and in other ways tried to disrupt the performance, he might not have been an accomplice. It is possible for a jury to infer assistance from mere presence at the scene of a crime (*Francom* [2001] 1 Cr App R 237), but the law is generally reluctant to do this without further evidence (*Coney*).
2. *Duty to prevent the crime.* If the accused has a duty to intervene to stop the principal committing the crime but fails to do so then this may establish him as an accessory. For example, in *Du Cros v Lamborn* [1907] 1 KB 40 the owner of a car was convicted of speeding. In fact it was not clear whether he was driving the car or was a passenger in it when it exceeded the speed limit. Clearly, if he was the driver then he was guilty

of the offence. It was held, however, that if he was the passenger then he had a duty, as owner, to ensure that his car was not driven illegally. Therefore his presence in the car, together with a duty to stop the crime, could establish him as an accomplice. The Court of Appeal has recently confirmed that having a duty to intervene and failing to do so may constitute being an accessory to the crime, although it added that this would be so only where the defendant made a positive decision not to intervene (*Alford* [1997] 2 Cr App R 326).

3. *Joint entperirse.* If the defendant has joined the principal in committing a crime, during which the principal commits a different crime, then the defendant can be liable as an accomplice to that second crime (providing she has the necessary *mens rea*). Under the doctrine of joint enterprise it is not necessary to show the accomplice helped the principal to commit the second crime, it is enough they were alongside the principal for the purpose of committing some other crime.

17.5 The *mens rea* of being an accessory

17.5.1 The general rules

The *mens rea* for an accessory is far from clear and commentators have divided on how to understand the case law. Fortunately the Court of Appeal has done much to clarify the law in *Bryce* [2004] EWCA Crim 1231, even though it has done so in a controversial way. In that decision the Court of Appeal undertook a thorough consideration of the current law and the case is therefore taken to represent the current law (*Luffman* [2008] EWCA Crim 1379). It summarised what the prosecution has to show to establish that someone is an accessory in four requirements:

1. an act done by D [the defendant] which in fact assisted the later commission of the offence,
2. that D did the act deliberately realising that it was capable of assisting the offence,
3. that D at the time of doing the act contemplated the commission of the offence by [P] [the principal]that is, he foresaw it as a 'real or substantial risk' or 'real possibility' and
4. that D when doing the act intended to assist [P] in what he was doing.

It is useful to say a little bit about each of these:

1. s simply the *actus reus* of being an accessory, as discussed above.
2. the defendant's act of assistance must not be accidental. A security guard who forgetfully does not shut a gate is not an accomplice to the burglary which takes place later that night. Although arguably if the guard later that night remembers he left the gate open but decides that he cannot be bothered to return and shut it, he has decided deliberately to omit to shut the gate. As he is under a contractual duty to keep the building secure, he is under a duty to act and therefore can be liable in respect of the omission (see Chapter 3). The accessory must also be aware that his act was capable of assisting the principal, but in the light of factor (d) that he must intend to assist the principal this requirement is superfluous.
3. emphasises that the key issue is foresight: did D realise that P might commit the offence (*Webster* [2006] EWCA 415). It is not necessary to show that D wanted or intended A to commit the offence (*Gillick v West Norfolk and Wisbech Area Health Authority** [1986] AC 112; *Alford* [1997] 2 Cr App R 326). Nor is it necessary to show

that D and P agree to commit the offence. But D must foresee that there was a real risk, not a fanciful one, that P will commit the offence. When we say D must foresee that P will commit the offence we mean that D must foresee three things.

First, D must foresee the kind of act P does which constitutes the *actus reus*. It is P's act which must be foreseen, not the consequences of that act. So if D foresees that P will stab V and P does so, thereby killing V, D will be an accessory to murder. He foresaw P's act and that is enough. He does not need to foresee that death will result (*Day* [2002] Crim LR 984; *Neary* [2002] EWCA Crim 1736). A famous example of where the accomplice did not foresee what the principal would do is *Saunders and Archer* (1573) Fost 371, where a husband and a friend agreed to poison the husband's wife with a poisoned apple. In the friend's absence, the husband gave the apple to his wife but she gave the apple to their child. The husband kept quiet while the child ate the apple and died. It was held that the friend was not an accomplice to the child's murder as the husband chose not to intervene and stop the child eating the apple, and that had not been foreseen by the friend.

Second, D must foresee the circumstantial aspects of the *actus reus* (*Johnson v Youden* [1950] 1 All ER 300). So to be an accessory to rape it must be shown not only that D foresaw that P would penetrate the victim but also that the victim would not consent. Similarly, to be an accessory to criminal damage D must foresee not only that P will damage property, but also that that property will belong to another.

Third, D must foresee that P will act with the necessary *mens rea* for the offence (*R v A, B, C and D* [2010] EWCA Crim 1622). So if P had foreseen that D might accidentally kill someone, but did not foresee that P might kill intending to cause death or serious injury, then P cannot be liable as an accomplice to murder.

It is not necessary, however, to show that D foresaw all of the details of the offence. If D gives P a piece of equipment which D foresees P will use in a burglary, it is not necessary to show that P foresaw where or when the burglary would take place (*Bainbridge* [1959] 3 All ER 200). Similarly if D gave P a lift to a place where he foresaw that P would commit an offence, but was not sure which of a number of offences it would be, D could be convicted as an accessory if P performed one of the kind of offences D contemplated (*Maxwell** [1978] 3 All ER 1140).

4. It is the requirement that D must intend to assist P which is the most controversial part of *Bryce*. The problem is that it is far from clear exactly what (d) means. Potter LJ in *Bryce* stated the following:

> where a defendant, D, is charged as the secondary party to an offence committed by P...it is necessary for the Crown to prove intentional assistance by D in the sense of an intention to assist (and not to hinder or obstruct) P in acts which D knows are steps taken by P towards the commission of the offence.

He also made it clear that it is not necessary to show that D must intend or want P to commit the crime. But does it make sense to say: 'I did not intend P to murder, but I did intend to assist P in murdering'? The distinction Potter LJ draws between intending to assist and intending the principal to commit the crime seems hard to draw. Here are two ways in which it may be possible to make some sense of the distinction:

(a) Imagine this: P says to D, 'drive me to the scene of the crime or I will kill you' and D does what he is told. In such a case D may be said to intend to assist (in the oblique intention sense: see Section 5.3.2, *Woollin** [1999] 1 AC 82), but not intend the principal to commit the crime. Or take the kind of situation in

National Coal Board v Gamble* [1959] 1 QB 11, where the defendant knew that what he was doing was assisting the principal, but did not care whether the principal was going to go on and commit the offence. Again there may be oblique intention to assist, but not that the principal will commit the crime. If these are the kinds of cases Potter LJ had in mind it would have been clearer to say 'D knew that his act was going to assist P'.

(b) It may be that the key distinction in Potter LJ's statement is in brackets: 'and not to hinder or obstruct'. Is the suggestion that if D is aiding P foreseeing that she will go on to commit a crime then either D is intending to assist or D is intending ultimately to hinder or obstruct the principal (for example, by reporting it to the police)? In other words D will be taken to intend to assist unless she can show she intended to obstruct. The difficulty with this interpretation is that it overlooks the possibility that D could not care less whether P ultimately commits the offence.

Requirement 4 may assist in dealing with a scenario which has troubled some commentators: the 'problem of the generous host'. If a host at a party provides alcohol for her guests, aware that some of those drinking are driving home after the party, is she aiding and abetting their drunk driving? Remember that the fact that it is not her purpose that they should drink-drive seems to be irrelevant. It has been suggested (in *A-G's Ref (No 1 of 1975)* [1975] 2 All ER 686) that the host is not guilty as the decision to drink is entirely up to the driver; although this is not entirely convincing as it is always true that the principal has a choice whether or not to commit the crime whenever there is a principal and an accessory. It may be that as the host does not intend the guest to drive the *mens rea* for being an accessory is not made out.

Having looked at the general rules we will now consider some troublesome issues:

17.5.2 Accomplice foresees the result but not the means

What if the accessory foresees that the principal may cause a particular harm but the principal causes that harm in a way which the accessory did not foresee? In *Rafferty* [2007] EWCA Crim 1846 the defendant was part of a gang punching and hitting the victim. He then ran off. Some of the other members of the gang then drowned the victim. It was held that this way of killing the victim was 'fundamentally' different from what the defendant had foreseen. He was not, therefore, liable as an accessory. This suggests that it is not necessary for the accomplice to foresee exactly the method by which the injury will be inflicted as long as it is similar to a method foreseen by the accomplice. *Rafferty* could be contrasted with *Luffman* where a defendant hired a hit man to kill someone. The hit man decided just to rob the victim, but when the victim protested, the hit man killed him. In that case the killing was said to be not very different from that which the accessory had counselled and so the accomplice was still liable. In *Rahman* [2008] UKHL 45 asking whether the act of the principal was in a 'different league' from that foreseen by the accomplice was a valid way of putting the question. In the context of a case involving death, *Mendez* [2010] EWCA Crim 516 suggested asking whether the act of the principal was 'altogether more life threatening' than what was foreseen by the defendant.

17.5.3 Accessories and returning borrowed property

How should the law deal with a case where a defendant is obliged in civil law to return a piece of property to the owner but is aware that the owner is likely to use the equipment for criminal purposes; for example, where Tim asks Judith to return a gun that he had lent her, but Judith is aware that Tim plans to use the gun to kill someone. In *Gamble* [1989] NI 268, Devlin J suggested that if one is obliged under civil law to return equipment to another then doing so should not attract liability as an accomplice. The idea seems to be that if Tim is in law entitled to have possession of an item then by handing the item over Judith is not doing anything of legal significance. However, in *Garrett v Churchill* [1970] 1 QB 92 the Court of Appeal refused to follow this reasoning and argued that civil law does not require the return of a piece of property which, it is known, is going to be used in a crime. It is certainly undesirable that the complexities of civil law should determine the issue. There is a need for an authoritative decision on how to balance the protection of property interests and the need to discourage crime.

17.5.4 The accomplice foresees the act of the principal but not the *mens rea*

An accessory is only liable if he or she foresaw that the principal might commit the crime they commit, with the necessary *mens rea* (*Powell and English** [1997] 3 WLR 959, *Uddin** [1999] QB 431). So, if the defendant leant his friend a gun, foreseeing that the friend, a clumsy man, might accidentally kill someone, the defendant would not be liable as an accomplice to murder if the friend deliberately killed someone. Although he might have foreseen the act of the friend (the killing) he would not have foreseen the killing with the *mens rea* for murder.

For some time considerable confusion surrounded a scenario where the defendant foresaw that the principal would stab the victim intending to wound, but in fact the principal stabbed the victim intending death. Fortunately we now have clear guidance. To be an accomplice to murder the defendant needs to foresee the kind of act that the principal would do and that the principal had the *mens rea* for murder (that is, that he intended to kill or cause grievous bodily harm). So it is no defence for an accessory to claim that they did not foresee that the principal would act intending to kill, if they did foresee that the principal would intend to cause grievous bodily harm (*Rahman*). If the defendant did not foresee the intention to kill or cause grievous bodily harm, but did foresee the act that caused the death, then a conviction for accessory manslaughter will follow (*R v A, B, C and D*). That will be rare. If the defendant foresaw that the principal would stab the victim, for example, it will be hard to believe he did not foresee that the principal would do so intending death or serious injury.

The significance of these rules is enhanced given the 'weapons rule', which we will consider next.

17.5.5 The weapons rule

If the accomplice is aware that the principal has a weapon, it is presumed that the accomplice foresees that the principal will use it (*Powell and English*). This is so even if the accomplice knew about the weapon only a few seconds before the commission of the crime (*Cairns* [1999] 2 Cr App R 137). The rule means that if the accomplice is assisting the principal in committing a burglary, but is aware that the principal has a knife, and during the course of the burglary the principal stabs the house owner, it will be presumed that the accomplice foresaw the use of the knife. In *Powell and English* Lord Hutton expanded this, explaining:

> if the weapon used by the primary party is different to, but as dangerous as, the weapon the secondary party contemplated he might use, the second party should not escape liability because of the difference in the weapon, for example, if he foresaw that the primary party might use a gun to kill and the latter used a knife to kill or *vice versa*.

On the facts of *Powell and English*, the accused knew that the principal had a wooden post, but the principal pulled out a knife (which the accused knew nothing about) and stabbed the victim. These were held to be fundamentally different kinds of weapon and so the accused could not be held to be an accomplice to the stabbing. It was fundamentally different in that a knife is a 'deadly weapon', whereas a post is not. Had the accused pulled out an iron bar and hit the victim, a jury might well have decided that the weapon was not of a different kind from that foreseen and so the accused would have been guilty as an accomplice to the assault caused by the bar. In *Daniel v Trinidad and Tobago* [2007] UKPC 39 the Privy Council held that as the members of the gang knew the principal had a gun they were guilty of murder under the doctrine of joint enterprise when the principal killed the victims by setting fire to the house. This was on the basis that both a gun and fire run a risk of death. In *Yemoh* [2009] EWCA Crim 930 the defendant knew the principal had a Stanley knife (which has a small blade), but the principal used a knife with a large blade. The Court of Appeal held those weapons were not fundamentally different. In *Bazda* [2009] EWCA Crim 2695 it was emphasised that when considering whether the weapon was fundamentally different the jury would consider the way in which the weapon was likely to be used and degree of injury the weapon was likely to cause. In *Greatrex* [1999] 1 Cr App R 126 the Court of Appeal stressed that the question whether the weapon used by the principal is fundamentally different from that foreseen by the alleged accomplice is one for the jury to decide.

The cases suggest that this is a presumption of fact. So a defendant can seek to introduce evidence to rebut the presumption. There are a number of ways that might be done: the accessory might claim to know the principal had a gun, but thought that the gun was unloaded; or that it was to be used only to frighten the victim (*Powell* of *Powell and English*); or did not foresee that the principal would encounter anyone while committing his crime (*Perman* [1996] 1 Cr App R 24) or did not foresee that the principal would use the weapon in the way he or she did. More recently the Court of Appeal in *Bazda* suggested that knowledge of the weapon was "very relevant" in deciding what the principal foresaw. That might suggest that we are not discussing, strictly speaking, a rule, but rather a point about evidence, namely that if the defendant knew the principal had a weapon, it will be hard for a defendant to persuade the jury not to foresee that he will use it.

17.5.6 Withdrawal from accessorial liability

If the defendant has assisted the principal or is embarking on a joint enterprise with the principal and decides he no longer wants to be a part of what is going on, is it possible for him to extract himself and be no longer liable as an accessory? The justification for enabling an accused to withdraw from an enterprise is fairly obvious. There needs to be an incentive to persuade people to withdraw from criminal enterprises, and anyway one who has withdrawn is certainly less to blame than one who has been consistently involved. If any member of the gang effectively withdraws from the criminal enterprise, he may escape liability as an accomplice for any crimes committed after his withdrawal. He will remain liable for any crimes committed before the withdrawal while he was a member of the enterprise (*Robinson* [2000] EWCA Crim 8).

The law is very strict about when an accomplice can withdraw from a planned criminal enterprise. It is not enough just to run away (*Becerra* (1975) 62 Cr App R 212); one must dissociate oneself from the crime in an unequivocal way (*Baker* [2000] Crim LR 700). A change of heart which is not accompanied by an expression of withdrawal will be insufficient (*Mitchell* [2008] EWCA Crim 2552). In Fletcher, the accused said to the principal 'don't do it' and 'don't be a fool'; these words were said to be equivocal and insufficient to end his association with the principal's actions. But the court stated that he could have withdrawn by attempting to prevent the principal from committing the crime. In *O'Flaherty* [2004] EWCA Crim 526 Mantell LJ stated in the context of murder:

> To disengage from an incident a person must do enough to demonstrate that he or she is withdrawing from the joint enterprise. This is ultimately a question of fact and degree for the jury. Account will be taken of inter alia the nature of the assistance and encouragement already given and how imminent the infliction of the fatal injury or injuries is, as well as the nature of the action said to constitute withdrawal.

Simply not turning up on the day planned for the crime after being involved in its planning is also insufficient (*Rook* [1993] 2 All ER 955). However, announcing two weeks before the crime is due to take place that you will have nothing more to do with the plan may be sufficient (*Whitefield* [1984] QB 318). In *Bryce* [2004] EWCA Crim 1231 it was suggested there needed to be a clear revocation of any previous assistance.

At one time it was thought that the law was less strict if the attack was a spontaneous one by a group of people, so that any one of them could withdraw by simply leaving. However, in *Robinson* it was emphasised that even in a spontaneous attack someone wanting to withdraw had to communicate their intent to dissociate themselves from the attack.

It is not always easy to tell whether a case involves a fresh new attack of which the accomplice is not part or a continuation of an attack for which an accomplice is liable. In *Mitchell* three people (A, B and D) attacked a victim and walked away leaving him prostrate. One of them (D) returned a few minutes later to give the victim a further beating. It was held that A and B were not accessories to the further beating. By returning, D had commenced a new attack to which A and B were not party. In *O'Flaherty*, however, a gang (including the appellants) attacked a young man. He managed to escape, but some of the gang pursued him and found him. They attacked him again, this time killing him. One appellant claimed that although he was responsible for the injuries suffered during the first attack he was not responsible for the killing as he was not a party to that attack. The Court of Appeal suggested that it was for the jury to consider whether the second attack was in reality a continuation of the first or a separate incident. However, it suggested the jury's main focus should be on whether the defendant had disengaged himself from the gang by the time the second attack took place by making an effective withdrawal.

17.6 Criticisms of the law

This *mens rea* requirement may seem rather harsh, especially where the *mens rea* requirement for the principal is only intention. For example, for a principal to be guilty of murder he must have intended to cause death or serious injury; but for the accomplice to be liable for assisting the crime of murder in the context of a joint enterprise he need only have foreseen that death or serious injury might occur (*Powell and English* [1997] 3 WLR 959). Lord Steyn in *Powell and English* sought to justify this position by three arguments: first, that the accessory who foresees that the principal may commit murder and nevertheless decides to join with him in a criminal enterprise can justly be convicted of murder. He noted that foresight is required both as to the act which causes death and the *mens rea* of the accomplice. This means that the *mens rea* for an accessory to murder is not the same as that required for the principal in a manslaughter case where foresight of death is required only for reckless manslaughter (see Section 10.4). Second, he argued:

> The criminal justice system exists to control crime. A prime function of that system must be to deal justly but effectively with those who join with others in criminal enterprises. Experience has shown that joint criminal enterprises only too readily escalate into the commission of greater offences. In order to deal with this important social problem the accessory principle is needed and cannot be abolished or relaxed.

Third, Lord Steyn in Powell of *Powell and English* relied on practical grounds: '[i]n the real world proof of an intention sufficient for murder would be well nigh impossible in the vast majority of joint enterprise cases', he argued. All these arguments carry force, but critics respond by arguing that convicting the accessory who foresees (but does not intend) that the principal will kill of manslaughter would better accord with principle and would perform the deterrence function to which Lord Steyn refers. The Court of Appeal in Concannon rejected an argument that the present law on accessories to murder infringed an appellant's rights under Article 6 of the European Convention on Human Rights. The Court of Appeal explained that Article 6 dealt with fairness of the trial, not the fairness of the law applied. While Parliament might take the view that the present law was unfair and needed reform, it was a matter for it, not for the court.

It must also be acknowledged that these cases raise very difficult issues for the jury. The key element of the *mens rea*, as we have seen, is what the defendant foresaw the principal might do. In cases of spontaneous violence that can be very difficult. The Court of Appeal in *Mendez* [2010] EWCA Crim 516 have acknowledged this:

> In a case of spontaneous or semi-spontaneous group violence, typically fuelled by alcohol, it is highly unlikely that the participants will have thought carefully about the exact level of violence and associated injury which they intend to cause or foresee may be caused. All that a jury can in most cases be expected to do is form a broad brush judgment about the sort of level of violence and associated risk of injury which they can safely conclude that the defendant must have intended or foreseen. They then have to consider as a matter of common sense whether P's unforeseen act (if such it was) was of a nature likely to be altogether more life-threatening than acts of the nature which D foresaw or intended. It is a question of degree, but juries are used to dealing with questions of degree. There are bound to be border line cases, but if the jury are left in real doubt they must acquit.

17.7 Interaction between accomplice liability and principal liability

If the principal is acquitted, can the accomplice still be found guilty? This depends on why the principal was acquitted. If the principal was acquitted because she had a special defence personal to her (for example, duress in *Bourne* (1952) 36 Cr App R 125, or infancy in *K and B* [1997] Cr App R 36) or because she lacked *mens rea* (*Cogan and Leak* [1976] QB 217) then the accomplice can still be convicted. However, if the principal was acquitted because the *actus reus* had not taken place then the accomplice cannot be convicted (*Thornton v Mitchell* [1940] 1 All ER 339). This can perhaps be made clearer by considering two recent driving offence cases. In *Millward* [1994] Crim LR 527, the principal was a driver employed by a company which had inadequately maintained the vehicle; the vehicle crashed but the driver (the principal) was acquitted of reckless driving as he could not reasonably have been aware of the dangerous condition of the vehicle; but the company was convicted of procuring reckless driving as it should have realised that the vehicle was faulty. By contrast, in *Loukes* [1996] Cr App R 444 the appellant ran a business and was charged with procuring the offence of causing death by dangerous driving (an offence created by the Road Traffic Act 1991 which replaced the offence of causing death by reckless driving). One of the appellant's employees, who had driven a van which had been inadequately maintained by the firm, was involved in a car accident in which a death resulted. It was held that because the driver had been acquitted on the ground that he had not been driving dangerously there was no *actus reus*. The case was distinguished from *Millward*, as there the *actus reus* was driving, and the principal was acquitted because he lacked *mens rea* (he was not reckless). By contrast, in *Loukes* the *actus reus* was dangerous driving (dangerousness does not involve a state of mind); there was no dangerous driving as the driver had taken all reasonable care, and so there was no *actus reus* and the defendant could not be said to have procured the offence.

17.8 Victims as accomplices

If an offence is designed to protect a particular group of people then the victim cannot be said to aid and abet the offence against herself. So, in *Tyrell* [1984] 1 QB 710, the court considered the offence of taking a girl away from her parents. A man did so and was convicted, but the girl was charged with aiding and abetting him, as it was said that she was willingly involved. The court held that as the offence was designed to protect young girls, it could not be used against them to charge them with aiding and abetting. She could not therefore be guilty as an accomplice. Similarly a child who is the victim of incest by her father cannot be convicted of being an accomplice to his crime (as stated in Whitehouse).

17.9 Assistance after an offence

According to s 4 Criminal Law Act 1967:

> Where a person has committed an arrestable offence, any other person who, knowing or believing him to be guilty of the offence or of some other arrestable offence, does without lawful authority or reasonable excuse any act with intent to impede his apprehension or prosecution shall be guilty of an offence.

The offence typically involves misdirecting police, or providing a get-away car. It seems that the offence cannot be committed by omission because the statute refers specifically to 'an act'. The *mens rea* requires the defendant to know or believe that someone was guilty of an arrestable offence. There is no need to show that the defendant knew which arrestable offence had been committed, but simply that an arrestable offence had been committed. The other aspect of the *mens rea* is an intention to impede the apprehension of the offender. There is no need to show that the defendant was aware of the offender's identity (*Brindley* [1971] 2 QB 300).

According to s 5(1) Criminal Law Act 1967:

> Where a person has committed an arrestable offence, any person who, knowing or believing that the offence or some other arrestable offence has been committed, and that he has information which might be of material assistance in securing the prosecution or conviction of an offender for it, accepts or agrees to accept for not disclosing that information any consideration, other than the making good of loss or injury caused by the offence, or the making of reasonable compensation for that loss or injury, shall be liable on conviction on indictment to imprisonment for not more than two years.

The *actus reus* of this offence requires that an arrestable offence be committed and that the defendant must accept consideration for not revealing the information. If the defendant requested the consideration then this would constitute the offence of blackmail and is a more serious offence (see Section 14.3). The *mens rea* is that the defendant knew or believed that the arrestable offence had been committed and intended to accept consideration (if it is more than reasonable consideration).

17.10 Serious Crimes Act 2007

The Serious Crimes Act 2007 creates a series of offences concerning the encouragement or assistance of an offence, either intending or believing that the offence will be committed. These are discussed in Section 18.2. Their significance is that, as we have seen in this chapter, if a defendant offers an act of assistance or encouragement but the principal does not commit the crime, then the defendant cannot be liable as an accessory. However, these offences mean that a defendant could be charged under the 2007 Act.

Hot Topic – Why do we have liability for accessories?

There is a range of ways in which a legal system could deal with those who help others to commit crimes. One of the difficulties with the English and Welsh law is that it has not clearly adopted an overarching approach to accessories which would provide the law with a clear conceptual basis. Here are some of the ways in which a legal system could deal with accessories.

1. *Derivative liability.* This theory has been well explained by Dressler: A is held accountable for the conduct of P because, by intentionally assisting him, he voluntarily identifies himself with the primary party. His intentional conduct, therefore, is equivalent to manifesting consent to liability under the civil law.

   This is the theory which seems best to explain the present law. The principal is seen as the wrongdoer, the accessory is a person who by his or her action has associated him- or herself with that crime. In the same way in which a person chooses to enter a contract and therefore to be bound by it, an accessory chooses to join in with the principal and is therefore liable for his or her crime. The criticisms of this approach can be seen in the following discussion on other approaches.

2. *Inchoate theory.* We could define being an accessory as an inchoate offence. It would be an offence to encourage or assist a crime. There would be no need to show that a crime took place, or if it did, the acts of the 'accessory' encouraged or assisted the principal. In other words, accessorial liability would look much more like the offence of incitement (see Chapter 18). This is the model found in the Serious Crimes Act 2007.

   The argument in favour of such approach is a peculiarity of the present law. The argument is well made by Spencer (1987):

   > If you commit the crime I knew you intended with my help to commit, I am likely to be an accessory, but if you do not, I may well commit no offence at all ... This is very strange. In either case, I have

done all that I have to do to incur criminal liability. It is no fault of mine – or to be accurate, it is not due to any lack of fault on my part – that the crime was never committed. If my behaviour was bad enough to punish where you actually made use of the help I gave you, it was surely bad enough to punish where I fully expected you to use it but you got caught before you had the chance.

Adopting the inchoate model of accessorial liability would mean that whether the principal went on to commit the crime would be irrelevant to the liability of an accessory. The key wrong of the offence would be the offering of assistance to someone who is believed to be going to commit a crime.

Opponents of the inchoate offence model might argue that if someone offers assistance in the commission of a crime but no crime takes place, there is insufficient harm to justify a conviction. Just as we do not punish a person for planning to commit an evil crime until he or she has gone beyond mere preparation and committed an attempt (see Section 18.4), so we should not punish a person who has offered help to someone who may be some time from committing an offence. In simple terms, there is not enough harm caused by an accessory if the principal does not commit a crime to justify a criminal conviction. This is a powerful objection to the inchoate model. However, supporters of the model would argue that the objection does not take sufficient account of the fact that the law is much stricter where people join together to commit crimes than where individuals act alone. Incitement and conspiracy are offences even where no objective harm results. In fact the line between incitement and where a person seeks to offer assistance is so fine that it is difficult to believe there is a fundamental difference between the two.

A second objection to the inchoate model is that it does not describe well the wrong committed. If Noel knew Myleene was planning to kill Kym, and so Noel gave Myleene a machine gun which she then used to kill Kym, what would be a better description of what Noel did: that he contributed and to an extent was responsible for Kym's killing or that he gave Myleene a gun believing she would use it to kill? The general public might suggest that the former rather than the latter (as the inchoate model would have it) better describes what was done. This objection is another variation on the argument about whether we should be responsible only for our acts or

whether we should also be responsible for the consequences of our acts (see Section 1.4.4).

3. *A causation analysis*. K. Smith (1991) has suggested that the law should ask whether the accessory caused, or was a cause of, the crime which the principal committed. In the example just discussed, Noel was a causal influence on the commission of the offence because his actions contributed to the way in which Kym died. This would require a widening of the rules of causation and a removal of the rule that the free, voluntary acts of a third party necessarily break the chain of causation.

Few commentators have been willing to follow K. Smith in this analysis, partly because if the *novus actus interveniens* doctrine is dispensed with something needs to replace it if the potential net of criminal liability is not to be spread enormously wide. It is far from clear what rule could replace it which did not then exempt many accessories.

4. *A specific statutory offence*. It would be possible to create a specific statutory offence of involvement in a crime. There is an example of this in English and Welsh law. Under s 2(1) Suicide Act 1961:

> A person who aids, abets, counsels or procures the suicide of another, or an attempt by another to commit a suicide, shall be liable on conviction to imprisonment for a term not exceeding 14 years.

Glazebrook (1996) suggests that a similar statutory offence could be created covering all forms of accessorial liability. If desired, the statute could set out clearly the meaning of the *actus reus* and the *mens rea* required. The benefit of this approach would be that there would be no need to have a special set of rules for 'accessorial liability'; there would be no need to distinguish between principals and accessories; and accessorial liability would not need to (although it could) depend on the commission of a crime by someone else. However, it may be that although it would mean helping in the commission of a crime, it would simply be the *actus reus* of a crime and many of the real problems of accessorial liability would remain. This proposal in the end turns out to be really an issue about whether we wish to define accessorial liability in a statute (perhaps as part of a code) or whether we wish it to be defined by the common law. It does not provide an overarching solution to the complexities involved in accessorial liability.

Summary

17.1 The law not only punishes those who commit the *actus reus* but also those who assist them. Punishing accomplices could be based on seeing them as having partly caused the commission of the crime, their liability deriving from the crime which the principal commits. Alternatively one could see an act of assistance as in itself harmful and appropriate for punishment, even if there is no actual crime committed.

17.2 The principal is the person who causes the *actus reus*. The one exception to this is where the *actus reus* is caused by a person who is an innocent agent. One can be an innocent agent if one lacks the capacity to commit the crime or has no *mens rea*. In such a case the person who causes the innocent agent to commit the *actus reus* will be regarded as the principal.

17.3 One can be an accomplice by being a party to joint enterprise with the principal or by aiding, abetting, counselling or procuring the principal. These words are to be given their ordinary meaning. If the person whom the accused attempted to assist does not go on to commit a crime then the accused cannot be guilty as an accomplice.

17.4 The *mens rea* of being an accomplice is intending to be party to a joint enterprise or aid, abet, counsel or procure the principal and foreseeing that the principal may go on to commit the crime he does. There is no need to show that the accomplice wanted the principal to go on and commit the crime.

17.5 An accomplice may withdraw from being an accomplice if she makes an unequivocal withdrawal. This may require some kind of action positively to try to stop the principal committing the crime.

17.6 The law on the *mens rea* for accessories is controversial. This is because an accessory can be liable with a lower *mens rea* than that required for a principal. This is justified in part by the policy of discouraging people from joining together to commit crimes.

17.7 If the principal is acquitted because she did not commit the *actus reus* then the accomplice cannot be convicted as an accomplice to that crime. However, if the principal is acquitted because of a lack of *mens rea* or because she has a special defence then the accomplice can still be convicted.

17.8 If the victim of the crime is of a class of people intended to be protected by the offence then she cannot be charged as an accessory to the crime committed against her.

17.9 It is an offence to impede the apprehension or prosecution of a person one believes to have committed an offence.

17.10 The Serious Crimes Act 2007 has created three new offences which make it a crime to do an act which is capable of assisting or encouraging the commission of the offence, with the intent or belief that the offence will be committed.

Further Reading

K. Smith (1991) provides a detailed, if controversial, analysis of the whole subject. Taylor considers innocent agency. The *mens rea* requirements are examined in Duff, Krebs, and J. Smith (1997). For reform proposals see Buxton, Glazebrook, the Law Commission, Spencer, Sullivan, and Wilson.

Buxton, 'Joint enterprise' [2009] Crim LR 233.
Duff, 'Can I Help You? Accessorial Liability and the Intention to Assist' (1990) 10 LS 165.
Glazebrook, 'Structuring the Criminal Code: Functional Approaches to Complicity, Incomplete Offences and General Offences', in Simester and Smith (eds), *Harm and Culpability* (Oxford University Press 1996).

Further Reading cont'd

Krebs, B. 'Joint Criminal Enterprise' (2010) MLR 73: 578.

Law Commission, *Inchoate Liability for Assisting and Encouraging Crime* (Law Commission 2006).

J. Smith, 'Criminal Liability of Accessories' (1997) 113 LQR 453.

K. Smith, *A Modern Treatise on the Law of Criminal Complicity* (Oxford University Press 1991).

K. Smith, 'Withdrawal in Complicity: A Restatement of Principles' [2001] Crim LR 769.

Spencer, 'Trying to Help Another Person Commit a Crime', in Smith (ed.), *Criminal Law: Essays in Honour of J.C. Smith* (1987, Butterworths 1987).

Sullivan, 'Participating in Crime: Law Com No. 305 – Joint Criminal Ventures' [2008] *Criminal Law Review* 19.

Taylor, 'Procuring, Causation, Innocent Agency and the Law Commission' [2008] Crim LR 32.

Wilson, 'A Rational Scheme of Liability for Participation in Crime' [2008] Crim LR 3.

Case Notes

▶ *R v A, B, C and D* [2010] EWCA Crim 1622. Court of Appeal

A gang of friends attacked the victim with fists. It was not clear which of them had inflicted the fatal blows, but they were all convicted of murder. The appellants claimed that the judge had failed to direct the jury adequately on the *mens rea*. The Court of Appeal allowed the appeal on the basis that the judge had failed to make it clear that an accomplice to murder could only be liable if he or she foresaw that the principal might do the act which caused the death, with the intention to kill or cause grievous bodily harm.

▶ *Bryce* [2004] EWCA Crim 1231. Court of Appeal

The appellant had driven the principal to a caravan close to where the intended victim lived. The next day the principal killed the victim. The Court of Appeal held that the *mens rea* for an accessory included intending to assist the principal and foreseeing as a real risk that the principal would commit the crime he did. However, in cases of joint enterprise the intent requirement did not need to be proved. In relation to the concepts of aiding, abetting, counselling and procuring there must be some kind of causal link between the accessory's act and the principal's crime. Applying this to the present case, the driving of the hitman to his caravan, although the day before the killing and not in a very

direct way connected to the killing, involved sufficient causal connection to the ultimate death to amount to aiding. The Court of Appeal upheld the conviction.

▶ *Calhaem* [1985] 2 All ER 266. Court of Appeal

The appellant was convicted of murder. She had hired another person (who pleaded guilty to murder) to kill the victim. The killer claimed at the appellant's trial that he had intended only to pretend to attempt to kill the victim, but when the victim screamed he had killed her. The appellant argued on appeal that there must be a causal connection between the counselling and the killing. The court dismissed the appeal, holding that there was no need for such a causal connection as long as the killing was within the authority or advice of the accessory. 'Counsel' should be given its ordinary meaning of 'advise' or 'solicit'.

▶ *Gnango* [2010] EWCA Crim 1691

Gnango and X started an exchange of gun fire at each other. X fired at Gnango and missed, killing a passer-by. X was convicted of murder, relying on the doctrine of transferred malice. G was convicted of murder on the basis of a joint enterprise. The joint enterprise was said to be that the parties were together engaging in an affray. However, the Court of Appeal held that there was no joint enterprise in this case. The parties had not acted together with a common purpose of committing an affray. Rarely would two people fighting each other be engaging in a common purpose because normally one person wanted to hurt the other, but not be hurt themselves. A common purpose would be found if the parties shared a purpose to shoot *and be shot at*, but that could not be said to be the case here.

▶ *Gillick v West Norfolk and Wisbech Area Health Authority* **[1986] AC 112. House of Lords**

The plaintiff brought an action against her local area health authority and the Department of Health and Social Security (DHSS) seeking a declaration that a memorandum of guidance issued by the DHSS to area health authorities on giving contraceptive advice and treatment to children under 16 was unlawful. The judge at first instance held that the advice was not unlawful, but the Court of Appeal held that it was, on the ground that a doctor could not treat a girl under 16 without the consent of her parents. The House of Lords allowed the appeal, holding that a girl under 16 could validly consent to contraceptive advice and treatment provided that she had sufficient understanding and intelligence to know what was involved. In exceptional cases, a doctor might be justified in prescribing contraception without the knowledge and consent of the girl's parents if: (i) he was satisfied that the girl, although under 16, understood his advice; (ii) she would not inform her parents; (iii) she was very likely to have sexual intercourse whether or not contraception was prescribed; (iv) her physical or mental health would suffer if she were not given contraceptive advice or treatment and (v) it was in her best interests to give her such advice or treatment without her parents' consent. It was also held that if the advice or treatment was given in a bona fide exercise of the doctor's clinical judgement then there would be no *mens rea* necessary for the offence of aiding and abetting unlawful sexual intercourse.

▶ *Maxwell* **[1978] 3 All ER 1140. House of Lords**

The appellant was convicted of planting a bomb at the Crosskeys Inn in Northern Ireland, contrary to s 3(a) Explosive Substances Act 1883. He was a member of the Ulster Volunteer Force, and had guided the bombers to the Inn in his car. He appealed against conviction on the ground that it was necessary to prove that he knew what offence was to be committed. His appeal was dismissed by the Court of Criminal Appeal in Northern Ireland and by the House of Lords. It was held that if the crime committed by the principal offender was one which was within the contemplation of the accessory, the accessory would be liable. In this case the appellant was a member of an organisation which regularly committed acts of violence with explosives and firearms, and must have known that bombing was an obvious possibility which he was intentionally assisting.

▶ *Millward* **[1994] Crim LR 527. Court of Appeal**

The appellant was convicted as an accomplice to the principal who was charged with causing death by reckless driving. The principal was a driver employed by the appellant to drive a tractor. The principal was said to be not guilty, as he was not reckless as to the dangerous state of the vehicle. However, the *actus reus* of the offence (causing death by driving) occurred and the accomplice had the *mens rea* (he should have been aware of the condition of the vehicle), and so the charge against the accomplice could be made out.

▶ *National Coal Board v Gamble* **[1959] 1 QB 11. Divisional Court**

The National Coal Board (NCB) was convicted of being an accessory to a contravention of the Motor Vehicles (Construction and Use) Regulations 1955. A weighbridge operator, an employee of the NCB, had allowed an overweight lorry to drive away, having issued the driver with the prescribed ticket. The NCB argued on appeal that knowledge of an illegal purpose was not sufficient for aiding and abetting; there must be a purpose of furthering the crime or encouraging the principal. The court held that there must be proof of an intent to aid. Supplying an article essential to the crime with knowledge of the use to which it is to be put is strong evidence of such an intention. However, there is no need to prove in addition a purpose or motive of encouraging the crime.

▶ *Rahman* [2008] UKHL 45. House of Lords

The deceased died following a fight between two gangs. The cause of the death was a stab wound. The appellant had been involved in the attack on the victim, but had not inflicted the fatal wound. He was convicted of murder on the basis of joint enterprise. He was aware that people had with them weapons including cricket bats and metal bars. The key question was whether or not the appellant had foreseen what the principal might do. The fact that the defendant had not foreseen that the principal would intend to kill or cause serious harm did not affect liability.

▶ *Powell and English* [1997] 3 WLR 959. House of Lords

The House of Lords heard two appeals. In one, Powell (the accused) and two friends called at the house of a drug dealer. A fight broke out and the drug dealer was shot dead. Powell stated that he had not killed the man and was unaware that either of the others had a gun. The prosecution argued that either he had fired the shot or he was an accomplice to the shooting. In the other appeal, English and Weedle had attacked a police officer with a wooden post. Weedle produced a knife and stabbed the police officer to death. English stated that he had not foreseen that Weedle would act in this way. Powell's conviction was upheld, with the House of Lords holding that a party to a joint enterprise could be convicted as an accomplice to murder if he foresaw that the principal might have intent to kill or cause grievous bodily harm. English's appeal was allowed, with the House of Lords holding that

if in a joint enterprise one party acted in a way not foreseen by the other party then the other could be found not guilty as an accomplice to their crime. If a party to a joint enterprise was not aware that another was armed with a deadly weapon, the use of the weapon would be outside the scope of the joint enterprise and the party would not be liable as an accomplice to the principal's use of the weapon. However, the party could be convicted if he or she was aware that the principal had a weapon of a similar level of dangerousness to the kind used by the principal. Applying this to the facts of the case, English knew that Weedle had a post but not a knife, and so English could not be convicted as an accomplice to Weedle's act of murder.

▶ *Uddin* [1999] QB 431. Court of Appeal

After an altercation between the occupants of two cars, a group of six people attacked the victim. Three were hitting the victim with what appeared to one witness to be the bottom end of a snooker cue, and three were kicking the defendant. During the attack, one person pulled out a knife and stabbed the victim to death. The appellant argued that the use of the knife was outside the scope of any joint enterprise and so he should not have been convicted of murder. The Court of Appeal allowed the appeal, setting out the detailed guidelines quoted in the body of this chapter. Applying them to the facts of the case, it could not be shown that the defendant was aware that the principal had a knife. The jury should have been asked whether the stabbing was so different from hitting the victim with the sticks or shod feet that the stabbing was outside the common purpose of the attack.

▶ *Woollin* [1999] 1 AC 82. House of Lords

See Chapter 5 Case notes.

Chapter 18

Inchoate offences

Key Terms

▶ Attempt – where the defendant does an act which is more than merely preparatory to the commission of an offence, with intent to commit the offence.
▶ Conspiracy – where two or more people agree to pursue a course of conduct which will necessarily involve the commission of a crime.

18.1 The inchoate offences

This chapter involves inchoate offences. But what are they? The word 'inchoate' indicates that these offences are in a sense incomplete. They are not concerned with the direct causing of harm to a victim, but with either encouraging or planning with others to commit crimes, or trying to commit the crime itself. Several justifications for their existence have been offered. One is to see inchoate offences as preventive measures: liability is imposed for acts which fall short of a complete offence, such as murder or theft, but which come close enough to threaten public order and the Queen's Peace. The criminal law intervenes to prevent the complete offence (usually termed the 'substantive offence') from being committed. This gives the state the justification for arresting and prosecuting an individual who is on the point of committing a crime. Another justification relies on the moral wrongfulness of the acts. It may be, for example, that someone's unsuccessful attempt to injure another fails only because of the quick response of the victim, in which case the attempt may be as morally blameworthy as a completed crime.

In each inchoate offence the mental element is crucial: it is the intention of the actor that the substantive offence be committed which makes her conduct potentially dangerous and justifies the intervention of the criminal law before any concrete harm has been done to another person or property. However, it is very important to remember that there is no liability for merely planning, alone, to commit an offence. There must be an *actus reus*, even for the inchoate offences, although, of course, this will differ from the *actus reus* of the substantive offence. In other words, merely having evil thoughts is not an offence.

If a plan to commit an offence is communicated to another person with a view to persuading the other to commit the substantive offence or assistance is offered to them then this amounts to the offence of encouraging or assisting an offence under the Serious Crimes Act 2007. If the other person agrees to commit the offence and a joint plan is formulated, this is a conspiracy. If the plan goes beyond the preparatory stage and one of the conspirators embarks on committing the substantive offence, but is prevented from completing it, this will be an attempt. An attempt may be committed by one person acting alone and need not be preceded by a conspiracy.

The essence of the inchoate offence is that the substantive offence is not committed; if it is, then it will be appropriate to charge the accused with that substantive offence, although the mode of participation may vary. A person committing the offence of encouraging or assisting an offence, who succeeds in getting the other person to commit an offence, becomes liable as an accessory (a counsellor and procurer). A conspirator may become either a principal offender or an accessory, depending on the part he plays in the commission of the substantive offence. A person who succeeds in an attempt to commit an offence becomes a principal offender. That said, it is not a bar to a conviction for an inchoate offence that the substantive offence has been committed. In practice, conspiracy is sometimes charged even where the substantive offence has been committed, especially where there are a number of defendants and the prosecution may be unsure of the role played by each one. As conspiracy is easier to prove than many substantive offences and its boundaries more uncertain, this use of conspiracy is controversial.

18.2 Serious Crimes Act 2007

The Serious Crimes Act 2007 has created a number of new inchoate offences and abolished the old offence of incitement (s 59). These arise where the defendant has offered an act of assistance or encouragement to someone to commit a crime. There is no need to show that as a result the person assisted or encouraged went on to commit an offence.

44 Intentionally encouraging or assisting an offence

(1) A person commits an offence if –
   (a) he does an act capable of encouraging or assisting the commission of an offence; and
   (b) he intends to encourage or assist its commission.
(2) But he is not to be taken to have intended to encourage or assist the commission of an offence merely because such encouragement or assistance was a foreseeable consequence of his act.

45 Encouraging or assisting an offence believing it will be committed

A person commits an offence if –

(a) he does an act capable of encouraging or assisting the commission of an offence; and
(b) he believes –
   (i) that the offence will be committed; and
   (ii) that his act will encourage or assist its commission.

46 Encouraging or assisting offences believing one or more will be committed

(1) A person commits an offence if –
   (a) he does an act capable of encouraging or assisting the commission of one or more of a number of offences; and
   (b) he believes –
      (i) that one or more of those offences will be committed (but has no belief as to which); and
      (ii) that his act will encourage or assist the commission of one or more of them.
(2) It is immaterial for the purposes of subsection (1)(b)(ii) whether the person has any belief as to which offence will be encouraged or assisted.
(3) If a person is charged with an offence under subsection (1) –
   (a) the indictment must specify the offences alleged to be the 'number of offences' mentioned in paragraph (a) of that subsection; but
   (b) nothing in paragraph (a) requires all the offences potentially comprised in that number to be specified.
(4) In relation to an offence under this section, reference in this Part to the offences specified in the indictment is to the offences specified by virtue of subsection (3)(a).

These offences create inchoate liability for assistance in or encouragement of an offence. They can be used even if the principal does not go on to commit an offence. Imagine Rohan gives Lucy a gun so that she can kill their enemy, but Lucy decides not to commit the offence and she throws the gun away. Rohan could not be liable under the common law of being an accomplice, but he could be guilty of an offence under s 44 or 45 of the Serious Crimes Act 2007. Indeed if Lucy does go on to commit murder, the prosecution could choose to prosecute Rohan either as an accomplice to murder or under the Serious Crimes Act 2007.

There are several things to notice about these new offences. First, as already emphasised, there is no need to show that the person encouraged or assisted in fact goes on to commit the offence. Second, the offences can be committed if the defendant intends to assist the commission of an offence (s 44) or he believes an offence will be committed (ss 45 and 46). The offences require intent or belief that the offences (with both the necessary *actus reus* and *mens rea*) will be committed. Foresight that the offence or offences may be committed will not be sufficient. Belief requires more than perceiving a risk that the offence will be committed; it requires a conviction that the offence will be. Third, it is enough for the purposes of s 44 that the defendant 'intended to encourage or assist the doing of an act which would amount to the commission of that offence' (s 47(2)). It does not need to be shown that the defendant intended to commit a crime. In other words, if Lisa helps Mario commit bigamy it does not need to be shown that Lisa knew that bigamy was a crime.

The *actus reus* of the offences is doing an act which is capable of assisting or encouraging another to commit an offence. Section 47(8) states that omissions are included within the scope of the offence. It also covers an attempt to do an act of assistance or encouragement (s 47(9)). So if Imogen tells Brian that Su is in the library with the intention that Brian will use this information to kill Su, the s 44 offence will be committed even if in fact Su is not in the library and so the information is of no assistance at all. It is enough that she was trying to do an act of assistance.

One issue on which the statute is not crystal clear is where the offence the defendant intends to assist or encourage is impossible. So what if Luke asked Dale to kill Nicole, but Nicole was already dead? It seems from a straightforward reading of s 44 that if Luke intended Dale to kill that would be sufficient, and the fact that it was impossible was irrelevant. It might be argued that his act of encouragement could not be an act 'capable of encouraging or assisting the commission of an offence', and so the offence cannot be proved in these circumstances. In response, however, s 47(8)(c) states that an attempt to do an act of assistance or encouragement is covered by the offence, and that would appear to indicate that in our example Luke would be guilty of an offence.

There is an important defence under s 50 of the Act where the defendant is acting reasonably in the circumstances as he believed them to be. When deciding whether or not it was reasonable for him or her to act the jury should consider:

1. the seriousness of the anticipated offence;
2. any purpose for which he claims to have been acting;
3. any authority by which he claims to have been acting.

A shopkeeper who sells a kitchen knife to a dodgy-looking person, aware that it could be used in committing a crime, may therefore have a defence. But it would be for the jury to decide whether it is reasonable for a shopkeeper to refuse to sell something on the basis that the individual looks suspicious.

Fourth, it should be noted that s 51 means that if an offence is designed to protect a category of people then they cannot be charged under these offences. This is relevant, for example, to sexual offences against children. A child could not be charged under s 44 for encouraging an adult to have sex with him or her.

For the offences under ss 45 and 46 a defendant will be taken to believe the offence will be committed even if the defendant believes that the proposed offence will take place only if certain conditions are met (s 49(6)). So Peter, who gives assistance to Jane whom he believes will steal a painting from an art gallery if there are no security guards around, will have committed the offence. This is so even if he believes it unlikely that the security guards will be absent. As long as he believes that if the conditions are right the offence will be committed, he can be convicted.

18.3 Conspiracy

A conspiracy is essentially an agreement to commit a criminal offence. Conspiracy is an offence triable only on indictment. A charge of conspiracy to commit a summary offence requires the consent of the Director of Public Prosecutions (s 4(1) Criminal Law Act 1977). The maximum term of imprisonment which may be imposed will depend on the maximum for the substantive offence involved (s 3 of the 1977 Act). The maximum term for conspiracy to defraud is 10 years' imprisonment (s 12 Criminal Justice Act 1987). Conspiracy was a creation of the common law and still exists, to a limited extent, as a common law offence. However, a new offence of statutory conspiracy was created by ss 1–5 Criminal Law Act 1977, and the vast majority of conspiracies are now prosecuted under s 1 of this Act. The small compass of the common law was retained, with the intention that it should be replaced with statutory offences once the topic was considered by the Law Commission. However, the reform has not yet taken place, and so the law is uncertain and complicated. In particular, the relationship between what is left of common law conspiracy and statutory conspiracy has proved difficult to apply in a rational and practical way.

18.3.1 Common law conspiracies

Only two categories of common law conspiracy survive:

1. *Conspiracy to corrupt public morals.* A conspiracy to engage in conduct which tends to corrupt public morals is a common law conspiracy, but only to the extent that such conduct would not amount to a criminal offence if committed by one person (s 5(3)). The offence is very narrow and is rarely prosecuted (*Knuller v DPP* [1973] AC 435). One of the few successful prosecutions concerned a group of people who joined together to produce a magazine ('Ladies Directory') which contained advertisements encouraging readers to engage in 'fornication and ... other disgusting and immoral acts and exhibitions' (in the words of Lord Tucker, *Shaw v DPP* [1962] AC 220). Corrupting public morals requires an agreement to perform acts which 'the jury might find to be destructive to the very fabric of society'.(*Shaw v DPP* and *Knuller v DPP*).
2. *Conspiracy to defraud.* The offence was defined by Viscount Dilhorne in *Scott v MPC** [1975] AC 819 as:

   > an agreement by two or more by dishonesty to deprive a person of something which is his or to which he is or would be or might be entitled [or] an agreement by two or more by dishonesty to injure some proprietary right of his.

It seems that there are two key requirements for a conspiracy to defraud:

(a) The conspiracy involves dishonesty (*Wai Yu-tsang* [1992] 1 AC 269).
(b) The conspiracy if carried out will cause some prejudice to the victims' property rights (*Moses and Arsbo* [1991] Crim LR 617).

It is not essential to demonstrate a deception, nor does it need to be shown that any victim has suffered a financial loss (*Moses and Arsbo*). It does not matter that the conspiracy to defraud is designed to persuade or encourage others to be dishonest rather than enable the conspirators themselves to carry out a dishonest scheme. A price-fixing agreement in itself is not sufficient to amount to a conspiracy to defraud, unless there is some aggravating feature such as fraud, misrepresentation, violence, intimidation or inducement of a breach of contract (*Norris v United States* [2008] UKHL 16; *GG Plc* [2008] UKHL 17). In reaching this conclusion the House of Lords emphasised that the law should be predictable. It had not previously been suggested that a price-fixing agreement would be a criminal offence and it would be unfair to extend the notion of conspiracy to defraud to make it so.

Conspiracy to defraud has been so widely defined that it covers agreements to commit many criminal offences, such as theft, robbery and obtaining property by deception, as well as agreements to do things which are not in themselves criminal (*Hollinshead** [1985] AC 975). Section 12 Criminal Justice Act 1987 makes it clear that, even in cases involving an agreement to commit an offence, the prosecution has a discretion to charge conspiracy to defraud. This puts into statutory effect the decision in the case of *Cooke** [1986] AC 909, and prevents a defendant from seeking to claim that he should not have been convicted of a conspiracy to defraud as he planned to commit an offence. Undoubtedly, conspiracy to defraud still has an active part to play in criminal prosecutions, and the Law Commission has proposed its retention (Law Commission Report No. 228).

18.3.2 Statutory conspiracies

Any conspiracy to commit a criminal offence must now be charged under s 1 of the 1977 Act. Section 1 Criminal Law Act 1977, as amended by s 5(1) Criminal Attempts Act 1981, provides:

(1) ... if a person agrees with any other person or persons that a course of conduct shall be pursued which, if the agreement is carried out in accordance with their intentions, either –
  (a) will necessarily amount to or involve the commission of any offence or offences by one or more of the parties to the agreement, or
  (b) would do so but for the existence of facts which render the commission of the offence or any of the offences impossible, he is guilty of conspiracy to commit the offence or offences in question.
(2) Where liability for any offence may be incurred without knowledge on the part of the person committing it of any particular fact or circumstance necessary for the commission of the offence, a person shall nevertheless not be guilty of conspiracy to commit that offence by virtue of subsection (1) above unless he and at least one other party to the agreement intend or know that that fact or circumstance shall or will exist at the time when the conduct constituting the offence is to take place.

The effect of this section is that a conspiracy to commit any criminal offence is a statutory conspiracy. It used to be thought that a conspiracy to outrage public decency was a common law conspiracy, but it has recently been stated that outraging public decency is an offence in its own right (*Gibson* [1990] 2 QB 619), and so a conspiracy to outrage public decency should now be charged as a statutory conspiracy.

Having looked at the difference between common law and statutory conspiracies, the elements of a conspiracy will now be discussed.

18.3.3 The *actus reus* of conspiracy

The *actus reus* of conspiracy is the agreement between two parties to engage on a course of conduct which necessarily involves an offence or one of the statutory conspiracies. This can be broken down into the following elements:

1. *An agreement.* The *actus reus* of conspiracy is, then, the agreement itself. There is no need for the parties to have taken any steps to carry out their agreement (*DPP v Nock* [1978] AC 979). The agreement can be express or implied. It is sufficient if an agreement in general terms is reached; there is no need for all the elements of the plan to be settled upon. It is not even necessary for all the parties to the conspiracy to have met with each other, or even communicated with all the other members (*Ardalan* [1972] Crim LR 370). So if A, B and C all agree with D to commit a crime, there can be a conspiracy even if A, B and C do not communicate with each other. However, the parties must, of course, agree to commit the same crime. In *Taylor* [2004] Crim LR 72 the Court of Appeal said that if one person agreed to import Class A drugs and the other Class B drugs this did not amount to conspiracy.
2. *Two parties.* There must be at least two parties to a conspiracy (though there may be many more), and the statute provides in s 2(2) that if the only other party to the agreement falls within one of three exempt categories, there can be no conspiracy. The exempt categories are:

   (a) The victim of the conspiracy. This is not defined in the statute and the courts are yet to define the term.
   (b) The spouse of the alleged conspirator. This exemption does not apply where the spouses conspire with a third party (*Chrastny* [1992] 1 All ER 189). So, if there are only two parties to the conspiracy, husband and wife, no offence is committed. However, if there are three parties to the conspiracy, husband, wife and a friend, then the offence is made out. The spousal exemption is controversial. It has been justified on the basis that husband and wife traditionally have been regarded as one for the purposes of the law, although there are few other examples in the law where this is reflected. It should be noted that this exemption does not apply to an unmarried cohabiting couple.
   (c) A person under the age of criminal responsibility (currently 10 years old).

The need for there to be at least two parties for there to be a conspiracy creates a problem where one party in a two-person conspiracy is acquitted (or all but one are acquitted in a larger conspiracy). Does this necessarily lead to the acquittal of the remaining party to the agreement? Not necessarily, because the answer will depend on the evidence in the particular case, and the reasons for the acquittal. The statute provides in s 5(8) that the acquittal of all the other parties to an agreement shall not be a ground for quashing the conviction of the remaining party 'unless under all the circumstances of the case his conviction is inconsistent with the acquittal of the other person or persons in question'. Such a conviction may be possible and consistent: for example, where one conspirator has confessed – his confession will be admissible evidence only against him, and the evidence against the alleged co-conspirators may be very weak; or a defendant may have a special defence. The jury may be sure that the defendant is guilty of conspiracy but unsure with whom he conspired: the alleged co-conspirators or persons unknown. It is for the judge to direct the jury whether all the accused must be convicted or acquitted together, or whether there is a material difference in the evidence against them so that a conviction of only one accused would be possible (*Longman and Cribben* [1981] Crim LR 38).

3. *The involvement of the parties in the agreement.* In statutory conspiracy, the agreement must involve the commission of an offence 'by one or more of the parties to the agreement'. So an agreement which involves the commission of an offence by a third party is not covered. If Bryony and Steven reach an agreement that Sam will commit an offence, this will not amount to a conspiracy until Sam joins in the agreement. This is narrower than the common law, where the conspiracy can involve a plan which involves the commission of the offence by a third party.

4. *The 'course of conduct' must be criminal.* The Criminal Law Act states that the 'course of conduct' agreed upon must amount to a substantive offence; this must include all the elements of the offence, including the consequences and circumstances. So it is insufficient in establishing a conspiracy to murder just to show that the conspirators agreed to put poison in the victim's egg nog; it needs also to be shown that they agreed that the victim should die as a result. If the allegation is one of a conspiracy to rape, it must be shown that the parties intended or believed that the victim would not consent. If only one of the parties to the conspiracy is aware of the relevant circumstances or intends the consequences then the offence of conspiracy has not been committed. It is not an offence to conspire to aid and abet (*Kenning* [2008] EWCA Crim 1534).

5. *The 'course of conduct' must necessarily involve an offence.* The statutory definition uses the word 'necessarily', but this must be treated with care. It does not mean that the conspirators must agree to commit the offence in every conceivable circumstance. Every conspiracy will be conditional to some extent; an agreement to rob a bank may include an express or implied reservation relating to the presence of police on the premises. In *Jackson* (1985), the Court of Appeal held that 'necessarily' does not mean inevitably; it can include planning for contingencies. In that case it was agreed that if W was convicted of burglary the others would shoot him in the leg in the hope that this would lead to a lower sentence. This was held to be a conspiracy. Indeed the court suggested that the parties to the conspiracy may believe that the plan is unlikely to succeed but can still be guilty of conspiracy. In a useful example, the court considered a scenario where two people agreed to drive from London to Edinburgh in a certain length of time. If it was possible to carry out that journey in the agreed time within the speed limits then there would be no conspiracy to break the speed limits, even if, given the severity of the traffic, it might be very unlikely that they could make the journey without breaking the speed limits. Whereas if they agreed to travel in a time mathematically possible only if the speed limits were exceeded, a conspiracy to break the speed limits could be shown. The clearest test (formulated by Donaldson LJ in *Reed* [1982] Crim LR 819) is to ask whether the plan would have 'failed' if the offence had not been committed: there is a conspiracy if carrying out the agreement according to the parties' hopes involves the commission of an offence.

18.3.4 The *mens rea* of the conspiracy

There are three elements to the *mens rea* of conspiracy.

1. The defendant must agree to pursue the course of conduct.
2. The wording of s 1(1) indicates that all the conspirators must intend the full offence to be committed: the course of conduct must involve the commission of an offence 'if the agreement is carried out in accordance with their intentions'. Lord Griffiths in *Yip Chiu-Cheung** [1995] 1 AC 111 explained:

   > The crime of conspiracy requires an agreement between two or more persons to commit an unlawful act with the intention of carrying it out. It is the intention to carry out the crime that constitutes the necessary *mens rea* for the offence.

   A conspiracy to commit criminal damage, for example, would require an intention to commit criminal damage (*Saik** [2006] UKHL 18). The *mens rea* is present even if the intent is conditional. So if the conspirators intend to commit burglary of a building if there are no security guards there, the *mens rea* will be present (*Saik*).
3. There must be intention or knowledge of the circumstances rendering the conduct criminal. Lord Nicholls in *Saik* explained that the prosecution had to show that the defendant had an 'intention or knowledge that a fact or circumstances necessary for the commission of the substantive offence will exist'. Take the offence of handling stolen goods. One of its ingredients is that the goods must have been stolen. That is a fact necessary for the commission of the offence. Notice that this requires proof of intent or belief, suspicion will not be enough. So a conspiracy to handle property which the conspirators think might be stolen would not be a criminal conspiracy. It would be if they believed it was stolen.

In *Anderson** [1986] AC 27, Lord Bridge made a further point. He said:

> Beyond the mere fact of agreement, the necessary *mens rea* of the crime is, in my opinion, established if, and only if, it is shown that the accused, when he entered into the agreement, intended to play some part in the agreed course of conduct in furtherance of the criminal purpose which the agreed course of conduct was intended to achieve. Nothing less will suffice; nothing more is required.

This seems to suggest that each conspirator must perform some kind of role in the plan. Professor Smith calls this a 'novel limitation' on the offence of conspiracy. Indeed a subsequent Court of Appeal decision, *Siracusa* (1990) 90 Cr App R 340, refused to apply Lord Bridge's dicta and instead held that if someone conspires with others to commit a crime but intends to play no role in actually carrying out the plan she can still be convicted of conspiracy. There is much to be said for the approach in *Siracusa* because it enables the mastermind of a criminal gang who is the dominant force in the gang, but does not intend to play an active role in performing the crime, to be convicted.

18.3.5 Impossible conspiracies

In looking at impossible conspiracies it is necessary to distinguish between statutory and common law conspiracies.

1. *Impossible common law conspiracies.* As a result of the decision of the House of Lords in *DPP v Nock*, an agreement to perform an act which is impossible may not amount to a statutory conspiracy. To decide whether impossibility is a defence to a statutory conspiracy you have to ask: why is it impossible? If it is impossible because what

the conspirators were trying to do was impossible then there is a defence. If it is impossible because the means the conspirators used were not adequate for them to do what they wanted to do then the impossibility does not provide a defence. The test for impossibility is to be judged at the time of the agreement. So, if the plan was possible at the time of the agreement but later became impossible, it still may amount to a conspiracy.

2. *Impossible statutory conspiracies*. This is dealt with by s 1(1)(b) Criminal Law Act, quoted above. For statutory conspiracies impossibility is not a defence. So it is an offence to conspire to kill someone who is already dead; or to conspire to handle goods believed to be stolen but which in fact are not.

18.3.6 Reform proposals

The Draft Criminal Code suggests a redefinition of conspiracy (Clause 48):

A person is guilty of conspiracy to commit an offence or offences if –

(a) he agrees with another or others that an act or acts shall be done which, if done, will involve the commission of the offence or offences by one or more of the parties to the agreement; and
(b) he and at least one other party to the agreement intend that the offence or offences shall be committed.

This, if enacted, would certainly clarify the present law. Law Commission Report 274 recommended the abolition of the offence of conspiracy to defraud.

18.4 Attempt

What are attempted crimes?

When criminal lawyers talk about attempted crimes they include within that phrase three different kinds of situation:

1. *A thwarted attempt*. This is where the defendant plans to commit the crime but, just before he is able do so, someone or something intervenes to prevent the defendant committing the crime. For example, the defendant is about to shoot the victim when a police officer knocks the gun out of the defendant's hands.
2. *A failed attempt*. Here the defendant does everything he plans to do but his plan is ineffective. For example the defendant shoots at the victim but is so far away that the bullet misses; or the victim jumps out of the way at the last minute.
3. *An impossible attempt*. Here what the defendant intends to do is in fact not possible. For example the defendant shoots at the victim, but the victim is in fact dead.

It should be noted that in attempted crimes, the intention of the defendant can play a crucial role. The same act could constitute attempted murder or be perfectly innocent, depending on the mental state of the defendant. Offering someone a cup of tea becomes attempted murder if you believe the tea to be poisoned and intend it to kill the recipient.

18.4.1 Why punish attempts?

Some of the most commonly cited reasons for punishing attempts are as follows:

1. *Subjectivism*. Subjectivists (see Section 1.4.4) focus on the moral wrong of the accused. The blameworthiness of an accused who attempts to commit an offence may be the

same as that of someone who completes the crime. For example, if Matthew shoots at Emma, but Emma at the last moment jumps out of the way, missing the bullet, some people would see Matthew as blameworthy as if he had succeeded in shooting her. It was no thanks to Matthew that his attempt did not succeed. Indeed a pure subjectivist would see no practical difference between an attempted crime and a complete one; in each, the defendant may have done all that she could to produce the desired result. What happened as a result of her actions was to some extent a matter of chance. Each should therefore receive the same sentence and be guilty of the same offence. Ashworth, while adopting a subjectivist stance, supports separate liability for attempts by referring to the popular understanding among the general public that there is a difference between an attempted crime and a successful crime. Ashworth (1987) argues that the labelling function of criminal law (see Section 1.5.1) requires that the law should reflect this commonly perceived difference, even if in moral terms there is no real distinction.

2. *Objectivism.* Objectivists (see Section 1.4) have tended to focus on the harm to the victim or the Queen's Peace which has been caused by the attempt. This would justify criminal liability for an attempt where the victim is terrified by the efforts of the defendant or where passers-by are terrified at witnessing the attempted crime. However, some attempts under this approach would not appear to create such a harm, as where, for example, the defendant puts what he thinks is poison into the victim's cup of tea, but in fact it is sugar. In such a case it would be difficult to locate a harm to the victim or the Queen's Peace.

3. *Duff.* Some commentators try to take a middle approach between the purely objective and purely subjective approaches. Duff (1997) has suggested that the law should consider attempts as attacks on interests protected by the law. This has the benefit of capturing both the subjective and objective elements of an attempt. It focuses on the intent of the accused as well as the threat to the victim's interests.

4. *Incapacitation.* Those who emphasise the importance of incapacitation in punishment (see Section 2.6) might argue that removing someone who has attempted to commit a crime from society protects law-abiding citizens from the danger of a person who has demonstrated that he is a danger to society. Such an approach typically places greater weight on protection of the public than 'minimalisation' of the criminal law (see Section 1.3).

5. *Police powers.* Some argue that the justification for attempts lies in permitting and encouraging the police to arrest someone who is about to commit an offence, rather than waiting until the offence has been committed.

Much more could be written about the theoretical issues surrounding attempts (see Further Reading at the end of this chapter). The problem for the analysis of the law is that the courts have not clearly articulated the principles which underlie the law, and so it is difficult to find a single approach which can explain the present law.

18.4.2 What crimes is it an offence to attempt to commit?

The law of attempts, like that of conspiracy, has been put into statutory form, and the Criminal Attempts Act 1981 abolishes the common law offence of attempt (s 6(1)). Attempting to commit a summary offence is not a crime; it is only an offence to attempt to commit an offence which is triable in England and Wales as an indictable offence (s 1(4)), although this includes offences which are triable either way. Some indictable offences cannot be attempted (s 1(4)): an attempt to conspire is not an offence. A criminal attempt is limited to an attempt to commit an offence as principal offender; an attempt to be an accessory is not an offence. This is one of the few remaining distinctions between the principal and the accessory. The exclusion of accessories extends to the separate offences of assisting offenders and withholding information about an arrestable offence, under ss 4(1) and 5(1) Criminal Law Act 1967 (see Section 17.10). The thinking behind these limitations is that attempting to be an accomplice is too far removed from the commission of a substantive offence and the criminal law would become too broad if such acts were to be included within liability for attempts. In some statutes there are particular offences created which are, in effect, attempt crimes. For example under s 61 Sexual Offences Act 2003, it is an offence for the defendant to administer a substance to the victim 'with the intention of stupefying or overpowering [him or her], so as to enable any person to engage in a sexual activity that involves [the victim]'.

Section 1(1) Criminal Attempts Act (which is quoted below) requires the defendant to have performed an act, and this, some commentators have suggested, indicates that there can be no attempts liability in relation to an omission. For example, if a husband seeing his wife dangerously ill leaves her and does not summon help hoping she will die, but fortunately a passer-by summons help and her life is saved, the husband cannot be convicted of attempted murder. Other commentators argue that this is reading too much into the word 'act' in s 1(1) and a person, such as the husband in the above example, deserves a conviction, based on the law's general approach to liability for omissions (see Section 3.3).

18.4.3 The *actus reus* of an attempt

What then needs to be proved in order to convict a person of a criminal attempt? The *actus reus* of an attempt marks the moment at which the non-criminal planning of an offence turns into a criminal attempt. It has proved elusive and difficult to define. Not only does the *actus reus* of every offence differ, but each offence can be committed in a variety of ways and circumstances (consider murder, for example).

The correct definition of the *actus reus* of attempts in theoretical terms depends upon what is regarded as the justification for punishing attempts. Those who focus on the moral blameworthiness of the defendant may just require an act which clearly indicates that the defendant intends to commit the crime. The *actus reus* is essentially playing an evidential role, revealing the defendant's *mens rea*. Those who focus on the harm caused in an attempt will require an act which produces that harm (harm to the victim or the Queen's Peace). Here the *actus reus* will play a crucial role in creating the justification for criminal liability.

As indicated above, the courts have refused to outline which justification for attempts liability explains the law, and so the courts' discussion of the law on the *actus reus* for an attempt is difficult to explain in a principled way. Before 1981, the leading decision was one of the House of Lords: *Haughton v Smith* [1975] AC 476. There, Lord Reid said that it must be left to common sense in each case to determine whether the accused has gone beyond mere preparation. The formulation chosen for the statutory offence, which represents the present law, is hardly more precise. Section 1(1) Criminal Attempts Act 1981 provides:

> If, with intent to commit an offence ... [which is triable in England and Wales as an indictable offence], a person does an act which is more than merely preparatory to the commission of the offence, he is guilty of attempting to commit the offence.

The basic distinction which was made at common law, and which the Criminal Attempts Act 1981 preserves, is between acts of mere preparation, which are not criminal, and acts of perpetration of the substantive offence (*Stonehouse* [1978] AC 55), which can amount to the *actus reus* of an attempted offence. Criminal liability arises at the point where the plan begins to turn into reality, and the accused embarks on the offence itself. The most useful test in the case law is that stated by the Court of Appeal in *Geddes** [1996] Crim LR 894:

> has [the defendant] done an act which shows that he has actually tried to commit the offence in question, or ... has [he] only got ready or put himself in a position or equipped himself to do so?

In *Moore v DPP* [2010] EWHC 1822 Tolson LJ supported this formulation:

> preparatory conduct by D which is sufficiently close to the final act to be properly regarded as part of the execution of D's plan can be an attempt. ... In other words, it covers the steps immediately preceding the final act necessary to effect D's plan and bring about the commission of the intended offence.

Although the courts have been reluctant to go into greater detail, they have been willing to state what the 'more than merely preparatory' test does not mean. They have rejected a test suggesting that an attempt is committed when the accused has performed the first of a series of acts which will culminate in the commission of the *actus reus*. The courts have also rejected a test suggesting that an attempt occurs only when the defendant has done the act which is the last act to be performed before the *actus reus* occurs (*Gullefer* [1987] Crim LR 195). So even if a number of acts have to be done before the *actus reus* occurs, the defendant can be convicted of an attempt. However, if the defendant has performed the last act he needs to do before the *actus reus*, it is very likely that this will be regarded as more than mere preparation. The Court of Appeal in Tosti has stressed the importance of the requirement that it has to be shown that the defendants were acting in a way which was *more* than merely preparatory. The defendants, who were found with some cutting equipment examining the lock on a barn, could claim that they were preparing to commit the crime but could not claim they were merely preparing for the crime. Their conviction was therefore upheld.

It is useful to consider the facts of four of the leading cases, which give a flavour of how the courts have interpreted the 'more than merely preparatory stage':

1. In *Jones* [1990] 3 All ER 886, a man hid in bushes beside the victim's car. When the victim got into the car the defendant ran up, got into the car, and pointed a gun at him. This was held to be sufficient for an attempt to murder. The court rejected the argument that the defendant could not be convicted of an attempt because he still had several acts to perform, namely the removing of the safety catch, putting his finger round the trigger and pulling it. The court added that while the defendant was waiting in the bushes he would be seen as acting in mere preparation; but by the time the accused was pointing the gun at the victim, the offence of attempt had been committed.
2. In *Kelly* (1992) 97 Cr App R 245, the defendant was charged with attempted rape. The defendant had dragged the victim behind a hedge and started to pull at her clothing. The Court of Appeal held this was more than mere preparation, even though a number of individual acts needed to take place before intercourse was to occur.

3. In *Campbell* (1991) 93 Cr App R 350, a man wearing a balaclava and carrying a replica gun was seen outside a post office. He approached the post office door several times but did not enter it. He was held not to be guilty of an attempted robbery. The court suggested that the mere preparation would have ended and the attempt begun once the accused had entered the post office.

4. In *Mason v DPP* [2009] EWHC 2198 the defendant who was drunk was robbed of his keys and car just as he was getting into the car. It was held he had not committed an attempt to 'drink drive' because he was not sufficiently close to driving the car. Had he started the engine he might have been guilty.

From these cases and similar ones it seems the courts are more willing to find the defendant has embarked on the crime (and so is guilty of an attempt) once he is in the presence of the victim. Further, once it is clear that the defendant is not likely to change his mind and has clearly decided to carry out the crime then the court again is more likely to decide that the threshold has been crossed. Where there is a realistic possibility that the defendant will change his mind and decide not to complete the offence, the courts will be more reluctant to convict. This seems the best explanation for the decision in *Campbell*.

It is for the judge to decide whether the acts alleged are capable of being more than mere preparation. If they are not, the judge must withdraw the case from the jury. If they are, it is for the jury to decide whether they think the acts are more than mere preparation. The judge may give the jury guidance as to the law's understanding of what more than mere preparation means.

18.4.4 The *mens rea* of an attempt

The *mens rea* of an attempt is an intention to commit the offence (s 1 Criminal Attempts Act 1981). For example, in order to be guilty of attempted murder it is necessary to show an intention to kill (*Mohan* [1976] QB 1). It would not be sufficient to show an intention to cause grievous bodily harm, even though such a state of mind would be sufficient for the crime of murder itself (*Fallon* [1994] Crim LR 519). Intention here has the same meaning as that discussed in Section 5.3. That intention is key to the *mens rea* for an attempt is readily understandable: to attempt to commit a crime is to try to do it – to act with the purpose of committing the crime – which is what intention is. This observation has led some commentators to argue that intention here should be restricted to where the defendant has a purpose to commit the crime and should not cover defendants who did not have that purpose but knew that the forbidden result was virtually certain to result from their actions. However, the Court of Appeal has stated that intention in the area of attempts is to have the same meaning as that generally applied in the common law, and so to include such an oblique intent (*Walker and Hayes* (1990) 90 Cr App R 226; *Perman* [1996] 1 Cr App R 24).

This straightforward intent test can be difficult to use in crimes which require an act to be performed in certain circumstances. Unfortunately the position is confused, and alternative tests have been proposed in the two leading cases before the Court of Appeal.

1. *The 'circumstances' test.* The Court of Appeal in *Khan* (1990) suggested that it was necessary to distinguish the defendant's acts from the circumstances in which he acts. Consider a crime where the *actus reus* involves proof that the defendant did an

act in certain circumstances. Where the crime requires the defendant to be reckless as to the circumstances, the *mens rea* of an attempt to commit such a crime only requires recklessness as to the circumstances. In other words, the defendant must intend to do his act but can be reckless as to the circumstances in which he acts if recklessness as to the circumstances is sufficient for the actual crime itself. The facts of *Khan* involved an attempted rape where the defendant tried (without success) to have sexual intercourse with a woman without her consent. The Court of Appeal, looking at the *actus reus* of rape, explained that the lack of consent was a circumstance whereas the sexual intercourse was an act. The *mens rea* for an attempted rape was therefore that the defendant intended to perform sexual intercourse being reckless as to whether or not the victim was consenting.

The Court of Appeal purported to apply the *Khan* test in *A-G's Ref (No 3 of 1992)** [1994] 1 WLR 409), but in a controversial way. The case involved a charge of attempting to cause criminal damage, thereby endangering the lives of others. It was held that it was sufficient if arson was intended, but that the defendant was reckless as to whether lives were endangered. The controversy surrounds whether it was correct to call the 'endangerment of lives' a circumstance. Is not the endangerment of lives better classified as a consequence of the defendant's actions, rather than a circumstance in which he acts? Some commentators have even suggested that, following *A-G's Ref (No 3 of 1992)*, recklessness as to either the circumstances in which the defendant acts or the consequences of his actions is sufficient for the attempted offence if it is enough for the substantive offence.

2. *The 'missing element' test.* The Court of Appeal in *A-G's Ref (No 3 of 1992)* proposed an alternative test to the *Khan* test, which it thought might be easier for juries to understand. This was to decide what is the 'missing element' in the attempt. The missing element is the thing which prevents the offence from being a successful crime. It is then necessary to show that the defendant intended to supply that missing element. For those elements which are not missing, it is sufficient that the defendant had the *mens rea* required for the completed offence. An example may make this clearer. Imagine a defendant, like *Khan*, who tried but failed to have sexual intercourse with a woman who did not consent, aware that she was not consenting. Here the 'missing element' is the lack of sexual intercourse. If the sexual intercourse had occurred the complete offence of rape would have been established. So, to be guilty of attempted rape the man must have intended to have sexual intercourse (*Khan*). Note that it is not necessary to show that he intended that the woman would not consent, because the lack of consent is not 'missing' in this case. It is enough if he had the relevant *mens rea* in relation to the victim's consent that is necessary for rape. Another example is when some football fans jumped up and down on a fence. Although they did not break it, they were reckless as to whether it would be damaged. They would be not guilty of an attempt to commit criminal damage, as the 'missing element' here was the damage to the property, and the defendants did not intend damage (*Millard and Vernon** [1987] Crim LR 393).

Faced with these two conflicting tests, a subsequent court may prefer the 'missing element test' as it avoids the difficulty in distinguishing circumstances from other elements of the offence. That said, the 'missing element test' is not without difficulties of its own (see Further reading at the end of this chapter).

Another issue over the *mens rea* which has caused fewer problems is 'conditional intent'. This is where the defendant has decided to perform a crime but has not yet decided on all the details of the crime. For example, the defendant rummages in a woman's handbag to see if there is anything worth stealing but is arrested by the police before he finds anything. What can it be said that the defendant has attempted to steal? The answer is to charge the defendant with attempting to steal from a handbag belonging to the victim, without specifying what is intended to be stolen. Similarly, if the defendant plants a bomb but has not decided who to kill by detonating it, a charge of simply attempting to kill persons unknown is likely to succeed. This issue was discussed in greater detail in Section 5.3.

18.4.5 Impossibility and attempts

A persistent problem in attempts has arisen in cases where the substantive offence cannot possibly be completed. Does proof of attempt depend on proof that the attempt could have proceeded to the commission of the full offence? Is it possible to convict a person of attempting to steal from a wallet or pocket which is empty? Or of attempting to handle stolen goods, when it can be shown that the goods in question were not stolen at the relevant time? The common law in this area was notoriously difficult, and a number of not very convincing distinctions were made between allegedly different types of 'impossibility'. This led to the statutory reform, which now governs attempts and statutory conspiracy. Section 1 Criminal Attempts Act 1981, after the basic definition of attempt in s 1(1) given above, provides:

> (2) A person may be guilty of attempting to commit an offence to which this section applies even though the facts are such that the commission of the offence is impossible.
> (3) In any case where –
>> (a) apart from this subsection a person's intention would not be regarded as having amounted to an intention to commit an offence; but
>> (b) if the facts of the case had been as he believed them to be, his intention would be so regarded, then, for the purposes of subsection (1) above, he shall be regarded as having had an intent to commit that offence.

The meaning of the section was thrown into confusion by a decision of the House of Lords (*Anderton v Ryan* [1985] Crim LR 560) which suggested that the section had not reversed the case of *Haughton v Smith*, which was the leading authority prior to the Criminal Attempts Act 1981. This was very surprising as the Act had clearly intended to change the law. This was recognised almost exactly a year later, in the case of *Shivpuri** [1987] AC 1, by the House of Lords itself. It is rare for the House of Lords to reverse one of its own decisions, and to do so within a year is extraordinary. However, Lord Bridge, who had given one of the judgments in *Anderton v Ryan*, admitted that the earlier decision could not be justified. He said that he could not find 'a clear and coherent principle' in *Anderton v Ryan* distinguishing cases of attempting the impossible which were criminal from those which were not. He argued that an attempt is an inchoate offence, and so by definition a substantive offence has not been committed. The reason for the failure of the attempt, whether inherent impossibility or an interruption by the police, should not affect the criminality of the attempt. The correct approach, giving effect to s 1(3) of the 1981 Act, was to concentrate on the intention of the accused. Lord Bridge said:

> What turns what would otherwise, from the point of view of the criminal law, be an innocent act into a crime is the intent of the actor to commit an offence.

The present law therefore simply asks whether, on the facts as the accused believed them to be, he would have committed a crime if he acted in line with his intentions. If so, the *actus reus* of an attempt is made out. Thus, it is an attempted murder to stab a pillow, believing it to be a person and attempted aiding and abetting suicide to assist if you believe you are helping someone to commit suicide, even though in fact they have no intent to commit suicide (*R v S*, 21 March 2005, Unreported, CA). No distinction is made between different types of factual mistake which render the commission of the intended offence impossible.

One final point needs to be made. In this section we have been examining cases where the accused intended to commit an offence (such as theft, handling stolen goods or murder) but failed to do so because of some mistake which made the commission of the offence impossible. He can now be convicted of attempted theft, or handling, or murder, as long as he had the necessary *mens rea*. If, however, the accused made a mistake, not of fact but as to the criminal law, so that he wrongly believed that what he intended to do was a crime, then he cannot be guilty of a criminal attempt (*Taafee* [1983] 2 All ER 625). For example, a person who commits adultery believing that it is a criminal offence has not committed an attempted crime. He cannot be guilty of attempting to commit the imaginary criminal offence of adultery. This principle is sometimes referred to as 'legal impossibility' because the mistake is one of criminal law, and a person cannot be convicted of attempting to commit a crime which is not known to the law.

18.4.6 Reform of the Law on Attempts

In a consultation paper, *Conspiracy and Attempts*, the Law Commission proposed that the Criminal Attempts Act 1981 should be abolished and replaced with two offences. The first would be an offence of criminal attempt, which would be limited to the defendant committing the last act needed before committing the intended offence. The second would be the offence of criminal preparation. This would involve acts of preparation which are part of the execution of a plan. It would need to be shown that the defendant intended to commit the offence. There is no sign at the moment that the Government intends to implement these proposals.

Hot Topic – **Are the new offences under the Serious Crimes Act 2007 too broad?**

There are clearly dangers in making a broad offence of assisting or encouraging people to commit crimes. If you were to search the World Wide Web you could find pages telling you how to make a gun, how to grow cannabis plants and how to make poisons. Indeed the ignorant criminal seeking advice would be able to find help to commit almost any crime. But would the provision of such information involve an offence? When does telling someone how to commit a crime cross the line from giving information to amounting to incitement? Even this book, which has occasionally mentioned potential loopholes in the law, could be used by a rogue hoping to commit a dastardly deed without any punishment.

There are two main protections offered by the offences in the Serious Crimes Act 2007 to those writing materials which could, in theory, help a criminal. The first is that the defendant is guilty only if he intends or believes that what he or she is doing will assist or encourage a person to commit the offence. So a writer of a detective story may realise there is a risk that her story line could assist a killer, but neither intend nor believe that what she is writing will do so. The second is that there is a defence if she is acting reasonably (s 50: see 18.2 above). But there the defendant must rely on the jury. If a detective story writer describes in detail how to poison someone in a way which is untraceable, it is not impossible that a jury will not accept it was reasonable to do so.

The case of Marlow is instructive. The case involved a defendant who wrote and published a book about a particular method of cultivation and production of cannabis. He advertised the book and about 500 copies were sold. On investigation by the police it was discovered that several people who had purchased copies of the book had followed its instructions and successfully grown cannabis. Marlow was charged with incitement to cultivate cannabis contrary to s 4(2) Misuse of Drugs Act 1971. The offence would now be charged under the Serious Crimes Act 2007. Three main arguments were put forward by the defence. First, it was said that the book was in fact a 'genuine contribution to the debate about the legalisation of cannabis' and so should not be regarded as incitement to commit a crime. Second, it was said that the book provided information which was freely available elsewhere. Third, it was suggested that the writing of the book was 'too remote' from the commission of any crime. The prosecution case was that the subject matter and nature of the book made it clear that the book was designed to encourage and enable readers to cultivate cannabis, and so constituted an offence. The Court of Appeal accepted the prosecution's argument. The simple fact was, as the defendant knew, that people would read the book and be encouraged to grow cannabis. The fact that they were going to commit the crime anyway provided no defence to incitement (Goldman), nor would the fact that the information was provided elsewhere get away from these conclusions.

What the court did not consider is whether this is consistent with Article 10 of the European Convention on Human Rights, which protects 'the right to freedom of expression'. From one perspective it clearly is; after all, Article 10(2) specifically states that restrictions on this right are permissible if they are 'prescribed by law and are necessary in a democratic society in the interests of ... the prevention of disorder or crime, for the protection of health or morals'. On the other hand, as mentioned above, there is a fine line to be drawn here. Imagine if Marlow had written an article discussing how cannabis was commonly cultivated, but then arguing that these were dangerous methods and that legalisation of cannabis would enable safer methods to be developed. Such an argument might be seen as a useful contribution to the legal response to cannabis. It should be recalled that people writing or producing documentaries about criminal activities cannot seek protection by making a clear statement that the activity was unlawful if the court interprets the overall effect of the publication as to encourage the readers or viewers to commit crimes.

Summary

18.1 There are three inchoate offences: encouraging or assisting the commission of an offence, conspiracy and attempt. They are committed before the substantive offence is completed, and should normally be charged only where the substantive offence is not completed.

18.2 The Serious Crimes Act 2007 has created new offences involving encouraging or assisting in the commission of an offence. There is no need to show that the person encouraged or assisted went on to commit the offence. However, it must be shown that the defendant believed or intended that the other person would go on to commit the offence.

18.3 There are a few areas where common law conspiracy is available, most notably conspiracy to defraud. However, most conspiracies are statutory conspiracies which involve an agreement between at least two persons to commit a criminal offence. A conspirator must know of any circumstance forming part of the *actus reus* of the substantive offence, and must intend the commission of the offence by one of the parties to the agreement.

18.4 It is a criminal offence to attempt to commit an offence which is triable on indictment. To be liable for an attempt, the accused must do an act which is more than merely preparatory to the commission of the substantive offence, and this means that she must have embarked on the *actus reus* of the substantive offence. She must intend to commit the 'missing elements' of the offence, including any consequences which form part of the *actus reus*. In cases of impossible attempts, a defendant can be convicted if, on the facts as he believed them to be, he was performing an act which was more than merely preparatory to the commission of an offence.

Further Reading

For a general discussion on inchoate crimes read Ashworth and also Glazebrook. The leading work on liability for attempts is Duff. Other works on attempts include Buxton, Clarkson, Horder, Rogers, and K. Smith. Impossible attempts are considered in Christie, Hogan, and Williams. Ormerod and Forston discuss the Serious Crimes Act.

Ashworth, 'Defining Criminal Offences without Harm', in Smith (ed.), *Criminal Law: Essays in Honour of J.C. Smith* (Butterworths 1987).

Buxton, 'Circumstances, Consequences and Attempted Rape' [1984] Crim LR 25.

Christie, 'The Relevance of Harm as the Criterion for the Punishment of Impossible Attempts' (2009) 73 J Crim L 153.

Clarkson, 'Attempt: The Conduct Requirement' (2009) 29 OJLS 25.

Duff, Criminal Attempts (Oxford University Press 1997).

Duff, 'Criminalizing Endangerment', in Duff and Green, *Defining Crimes* (Oxford University Press 2005).

Glazebrook, 'Should We Have a Law of Attempted Crime?' (1969) 85 LQR 27.

Hogan, 'The Criminal Attempts Act and Attempting the Impossible' [1984] Crim LR 584.

Horder, 'Varieties of Intention, Criminal Attempts and Endangerment' (1994) 14 LS 335.

Law Commission, *Conspiracy and Attempts* (Law Com CP No 183, 2007).

Law Commission, *Participation in Crime* (Law Com No 305, 2007).

Ormerod and Fortson, 'Serious Crime Act 2007: The Part 2 Offences' [2009] Crim LR 389.

Rogers, 'The Codification of Attempts and the Case for "preparation" '[2008] Crim LR 937.

J. Smith, 'Conspiracy to Defraud: The Law Commission's Working Paper No. 104' [1995] Crim LR 209.

K. Smith, 'Proximity at Attempt: Lord Lane's Midway Course' [1991] Crim LR 576.

Williams, 'The Lords and Impossible Attempts, or quis custodiet ipos custodes' (1986) 45 CLJ 33.

Case Notes

▶ *Anderson* [1986] AC 27. House of Lords

The appellant was convicted of conspiracy. He had agreed to supply diamond wire with a view to assisting the brother of a co-conspirator to escape from prison. He claimed that he had not intended to take any further part in the escape plan, and had not expected it to succeed. The Court of Appeal and the House of Lords dismissed his appeal. The House of Lords held that statutory conspiracy did not require the prosecution to prove an intention on the part of each conspirator that a criminal offence should be committed. Knowledge that the agreed course of conduct would necessarily involve the commission of an offence by one or more of the parties to the agreement, together with an intention to play some part in the agreed course of conduct, in furtherance of the criminal purpose, was enough.

▶ *A-G's Ref (No 3 of 1992)* [1994] 1 WLR 409. Court of Appeal

The defendants were acquitted on a charge of attempted arson, being reckless as to whether life would thereby be endangered. The defendants threw petrol bombs at a car, missing the car. The Court of Appeal was asked whether on such a charge it was necessary for the prosecution to show that the defendants intended to endanger life. The Court of Appeal said that recklessness was sufficient as the missing element (the element which was lacking from the commission of the substantive offence) was the damage to the car, and the defendants intended that. For those elements which were not missing it was sufficient for the defendants to have the *mens rea* required for the substantive offence.

▶ *Cooke* [1986] AC 909. House of Lords

The appellant was convicted of conspiracy to defraud. He was a member of the buffet car crew on a British Rail train who had taken their own food onto the train and sold it, keeping the proceeds. He argued on appeal that he should, following Ayres, have been charged with a statutory conspiracy under s 1(1) Criminal Law Act 1977, as the agreed course of conduct would involve the commission of an offence under s 25(1) Theft Act 1968 (going equipped to cheat). The Court of Appeal agreed with this submission and allowed the appeal, but the House of Lords restored the conviction. It was held that an agreed course of conduct might in part involve the commission of an offence, in which case s 1(1) could be used. However, it might also defraud the victim in such a way as not to involve the commission of an offence. In such a case, conspiracy to defraud could be charged in addition or in the alternative to the statutory conspiracy.

▶ *Geddes* [1996] Crim LR 894. Court of Appeal

The appellant was found in a boys' lavatory block at a school with a cider can, a knife, rope and masking tape. He had no right to be there. He was convicted of attempting to commit the offence of false imprisonment against a boy. The Court of Appeal overturned his conviction, arguing that the evidence had not shown that he had moved beyond the realm of preparation into the commission of the offence. It noted that he had not actually approached a potential victim and his conduct did not clearly reveal his intentions. He had got himself in a position where he could commit the offence, but he had not embarked on the crime proper.

▶ *Hollinshead* [1985] AC 975. House of Lords

The appellant was convicted of conspiracy to defraud. He had agreed to supply 'black boxes' to another man for sale to third parties. They would then be used to interfere with electricity meters and defraud electricity boards. The Court of Appeal allowed the appeal, but the House of Lords restored the conviction, holding that in the case of a conspiracy to defraud it was not essential for the act of defrauding to be carried out by a party to the agreement, as long as the parties to the agreement intended that dishonest use of the boxes (by a third party) should result from the sale.

▶ *Millard and Vernon* [1987] Crim LR 393. Court of Appeal

The appellants were convicted of attempting to damage property belonging to another. They had pushed against the wooden fence of a football stand. They denied any intention to damage the fence, and the trial judge directed the jury that recklessness was sufficient. The appeal was allowed on the ground that, although the substantive offence could be committed recklessly, recklessness as to a consequence was not sufficient on a charge of attempt. The court expressly left open the question whether recklessness with respect to a circumstance would be sufficient on a charge of attempting to commit a substantive offence, such as rape, where recklessness as to the circumstance was sufficient for the complete offence.

▶ *Saik* [2006] UKHL 18. House of Lords

Saik was convicted of the offence of conspiracy to launder money. He ran a currency exchange office in London and the prosecution's case was that he had converted sterling which was the proceeds of crime into foreign currency. His defence was that he suspected, but did not know, that the property had been the proceeds of crime. On appeal the key issue was whether mere suspicion that the property was the proceeds of crime was sufficient for a conviction for conspiracy. The House of Lords held that to be guilty of a conspiracy a defendant must intend to pursue a course of conduct which would necessarily involve the commission of the crime and intend or know any fact which was necessary for the commission of the crime. Here whether the money was the proceeds of crime was a necessary element of the crime. It had to be proved that he knew this, rather than merely suspected it. His appeal against his conviction was therefore allowed.

► *Scott v MPC* [1975] AC 819. **House of Lords**

The appellant was convicted of conspiracy to defraud. He had taken and made pirated copies of films in order to sell them on his own account. He argued on appeal that an element of deception or deceit was necessary in a conspiracy to defraud. His appeal was dismissed by the Court of Appeal and the House of Lords. It was held by Viscount Dilhorne in the House of Lords that although in very many fraud cases there would be deceit, this was not essential. The ordinary meaning of 'to defraud' was 'to deprive a person dishonestly of something which is his or of something to which he is or would or might but for the perpetration of the fraud be entitled'.

► *Shivpuri* [1987] AC 1. **House of Lords**

The appellant was convicted of attempting to be knowingly concerned in dealing with a prohibited drug. He was arrested with a suitcase which he said he knew contained prohibited drugs. In fact the case contained a non-prohibited vegetable substance. His appeal was dismissed by the Court of Appeal and by the House of Lords. It was held by Lord Bridge that an attempt is committed if the accused does an act which is more than merely preparatory to the commission of the offence which he intends to commit, even if the commission of that offence is in fact impossible. Any distinction between the different types of factual impossibility could not be reconciled with the wording of s 1(1), (2) and (3) Criminal Attempts Act 1981.

► *Yip Chiu-Cheung* [1995] 1 AC 111. **Privy Council**

The defendant was convicted of conspiracy to traffic in heroin. He was alleged to have conspired with Needham, an undercover drugs enforcement agent. The defendant argued before the Privy Council that he could not be convicted of a conspiracy as Needham did not have the necessary *mens rea* of a conspiracy and he could not form a conspiracy on his own. The Privy Council held that Needham (who was not charged) could have been convicted of a conspiracy as he intended the offence to be committed (in that he intended that the drugs be exported); he also intended that the defendant should be arrested after the trafficking. It was added that the *mens rea* for a conspiracy was an intention that the crime be carried out.

Index